POETRY

POETRY

AN INTRODUCTION

JEFFREY D.
Hoeper

Arkansas State University

JAMES H.
Pickering

University of Houston

Macmillan Publishing Company
New York

Editor: D. Anthony English
Production Supervisor: Katherine Evancie
Production Manager: Nick Sklitsis
Cover Designer: Patrice Fodero
Cover Photograph: D. Anthony English

This book was set in Baskerville by Arcata Graphics/Kingsport, and printed and bound by Halliday Lithograph. The cover was printed by Phoenix Color Corp.

Macmillan Publishing Company
866 Third Avenue, New York, New York 10022

Collier Macmillan Canada, Inc.

LIBRARY OF CONGRESS CATALOGING-IN-PUBLICATION DATA
Hoeper, Jeffrey D.
  Poetry: An introduction / Jeffrey D. Hoeper, James H. Pickering.
  p. cm.
  ISBN 0-02-395465-5
  1. English poetry—History and criticism. 2. American poetry—History and criticism. 3. American poetry. 4. English poetry. 5. Poetry. I. Pickering, James H.
II. Title.
PR502.P54 1990
808.1—dc20   89–38866
                  CIP

Printing: 1 2 3 4 5 6 7   Year: 0 1 2 3 4 5 6

Acknowledgments

The Antioch Review, Inc. PETER MEINKE, "Advice to My Son." Copyright © 1965 by The Antioch Review, Inc. First appeared in the *Antioch Review,* Vol. XXV No. 3 (Fall, 1965). Reprinted by permission of the Editors.
Atheneum Publishers, an imprint of Macmillan Publishing Company. DONALD FINKEL, "Hunting Song." Reprinted with permission of Atheneum Publishers, an imprint of Macmillan Publishing Company, from *Selected Shorter Poems* by Donald Finkel. Copyright © 1959, 1987 by Donald Finkel. W. S. MERWIN, "Leviathan" from *The First Four Books of Poetry* by W. S. Merwin. Copyright © 1955, 1956 by W. S. Merwin. Reprinted by permission of Atheneum Publishers, an imprint of Macmillan Publishers. "The Drunk in the Furnace" from *The First Four Books of Poems* by W. S. Merwin. Copyright © 1956, 1957, 1958, 1960 by W. S. Merwin. Reprinted by permission of Atheneum Publishers. MARK STRAND, "Keeping Things Whole" from *Reasons for Moving.* Copyright © 1964 by Mark Strand. Reprinted by permission of Atheneum Publishers.
BBC Radio and Drama. HENRY REED, "Naming of Parts" from *A Map of Verona* by Henry Reed. Copyright © by Henry Reed. Reprinted by permission of John Tydeman.
BMI Music Company. JIMMY BUFFETT, "Wastin' Away Again in Margaritaville" from *Changes in Latitudes, Changes in Attitudes* (1977).
Jack Butler. JACK BUTLER, "Attack of the Zombi Poets" from *The Kid Who Wanted to Be a Spaceman* (August House, 1984). Reprinted by permission of Jack Butler.

Columbia Records. BRUCE SPRINGSTEEN, "Glory Days" from *Born in the USA* (1984). Reprinted by permission.

Combine Music Corporation. KRIS KRISTOFFERSON, "Me and Bobby McGee" by Kris Kristofferson and Fred Foster. Copyright © 1969 Combine Music Corporation from *The Songs of Kris Kristofferson* by Kristofferson and Foster. Lyrics of "Me and Bobby McGee" by Kris Kristofferson. All rights controlled and administered by SBK Blackwood Music Inc. All rights reserved. International copyright secured. Used by permission.

Continental Total Media Project, Inc. LEONARD COHEN, "Suzanne," Copyright © 1966 by Project Seven Music, a division of Continental Total Media Project, Inc., 120 Charles Street, New York, N.Y., 10014, U.S.A. Used by permission.

Curtis Brown, Ltd. MAXINE KUMIN, "Together" from *The Nightmare Factory* published by Harper & Row, Publishers. Copyright © 1970 by Maxine Kumin. Reprinted by permission of Curtis Brown, Ltd.

The David Company. GWENDOLYN BROOKS, "We Real Cool," "The Chicago *Defender* Sends a Man to Little Rock," and "The Bean Eaters," all from *Blacks* published by The David Company, Chicago. Copyright 1987 by Gwendolyn Brooks Blakely. Reprinted by permission of Gwendolyn Brooks.

Doubleday & Company, Inc., a division of Bantam, Doubleday, Dell Publishing Group, Inc. THEODORE ROETHKE, "Dolor" and "Root Cellar" copyright 1943 by Modern Poetry Association, Inc.; "Elegy for Jane" copyright 1950 by Theodore Roethke; "I Knew a Woman" copyright 1954 by Theodore Roethke; and "The Waking" copyright 1953 by Theodore Roethke, all from *The Collected Poems of Theodore Roethke* by Theodore Roethke. Reprinted by permission of Doubleday & Company, Inc.

Dwarf Music. BOB DYLAN, "All Along the Watchtower." Copyright © 1968 by Dwarf Music. All rights reserved. International copyright secured. Reprinted by permission.

EMI Blackwood Music Inc. "Imagine" by John Lennon. © 1971 Lenono Music. All rights controlled and administered by EMI Blackwood Music Inc. All rights reserved. International copyright secured. Used by permission.

Faber & Faber Ltd., Publishers. PHILIP LARKIN, "Sunny Prestatyn" from *The Whitsun Weddings* by Philip Larkin. Reprinted by permission of Faber & Faber Ltd.

Farrar, Straus & Giroux, Inc. ELIZABETH BISHOP, "Sandpiper," "At the Fishhouses," and "The Armadillo," all from *The Complete Poems 1927–1979* by Elizabeth Bishop. Copyright © 1947, 1957, 1962 by Elizabeth Bishop. Copyright renewed © 1974 by Elizabeth Bishop; copyright © 1983 by Alice Helen Methfessel. Reprinted by permission of Farrar, Straus & Giroux, Inc. THOM GUNN, "Vox Humana" from *Selected Poems 1950–1975* by Thom Gunn. Copyright © 1958, 1979 by Thom Gunn. Reprinted by permission of Farrar, Straus & Giroux, Inc. "Black Jackets" from *Moly and My Sad Captains* by Thom Gunn. Copyright © 1972 by Thom Gunn. Reprinted by permission of Farrar, Straus & Giroux, Inc. RANDALL JARRELL, "The Death of the Ball Turret Gunner" and "Eighth Air Force" from *The Complete Poems* by Randall Jarrell. Copyright © 1945, 1947 by Randall Jarrell. Copyright renewed © 1969, 1972 by Mrs. Randall Jarrell. Reprinted by permission of Farrar, Straus & Giroux, Inc. ROBERT LOWELL, "For the Union Dead" and "The Mouth of the Hudson" from *For the Union Dead* by Robert Lowell. Copyright © 1960, 1964 by Robert Lowell. "Skunk Hour" from *Life Studies* by Robert Lowell. Copyright © 1958 by Robert Lowell. Copyright renewed © 1986 by Caroline Lowell and Sheridan Lowell. All reprinted by permission of Farrar, Straus & Giroux, Inc.

G. K. Hall & Co., Publishers. CLAUDE MCKAY, "The Harlem Dancer" from *Selected Poems of Claude McKay* by Claude McKay. Copyright © 1953 by Twayne Publishers, Inc., and reprinted by permission of Twayne Publishers, a division of G. K. Hall & Co., Boston.

Gnomon Press. "One Man's Moon" by Issa; translated by Sid Corman. Reprinted by permission.

Harcourt Brace Jovanovich, Inc. T. S. ELIOT, "The Love Song of J. Alfred Prufrock" and "Journey of the Magi" from *Collected Poems 1909–1962* by T. S. Eliot. Copyright 1936 by Harcourt Brace Jovanovich, Inc.; copyright © 1963, 1964 by T. S. Eliot. Reprinted by permission of the publisher. CARL SANDBURG, "Fog" and "Chicago" from *Chicago Poems* by Carl Sandburg. Copyright 1916 by Holt, Rinehart and Winston, Inc., and renewed 1944 by Carl Sandburg, reprinted by permission of Harcourt Brace Jovanovich, Inc. ALICE WALKER, "Women" from *Revolutionary Petunias & Other Poems,* copyright © 1970 by Alice Walker, reprinted by permission of Harcourt Brace Jovanovich, Inc. RICHARD WILBUR, "Museum Piece" and "A Simile for Her Smile" from *Ceremony and Other Poems* by Richard Wilbur, copyright 1950, and renewed 1978 by Richard Wilbur. Reprinted by permission of Harcourt Brace Jovanovich, Inc. "Sleepless at Crown Point," copyright © 1973 by Richard Wilbur and "The Star System" from "Flippancies" in *The Mind-Reader: New Poems by Richard Wilbur,* copyright © 1976 by Richard Wilbur. Reprinted by permission of Harcourt Brace Jovanovich, Inc.

1926 by Ezra Pound. Reprinted by permission of New Directions. STEVIE SMITH, "Not Waving but Drowning" and "Was He Married" from *Collected Poems of Stevie Smith*. Copyright © 1972 by Stevie Smith. Reprinted by permission of New Directions. DYLAN THOMAS, "The force that through the green fuse drives the flower," "Fern Hill," "In My Craft or Sullen Art," and "Do not go gentle into that good night" all from *Poems of Dylan Thomas*. Copyright 1939, 1946 by New Directions Publishing Corporation; 1945 by Trustees for the Copyrights of Dylan Thomas; 1952 by Dylan Thomas. Reprinted by permission of New Directions. WILLIAM CARLOS WILLIAMS, "Queen-Anne's Lace," "The Red Wheelbarrow," and "This Is Just to Say" from *Collected Poems, Vol. I 1909–1939* by William Carlos Williams. Copyright 1938 by New Directions Publishing Corporation. "The Dance" and "Landscape with the Fall of Icarus" from *Collected Poems Vol. II 1939–1962* by William Carlos Williams. Copyright 1944, 1962 by William Carlos Williams. All poems reprinted by permission of New Directions Publishing Corporation.

The New Yorker. MORRIS BISHOP, "E = mc²" from *The Best of Bishop: Light Verse from the New Yorker and Elsewhere* (Ithaca, N.Y.: Cornell University Press). Copyright © 1946, 1974 by Alison Kinsbury Bishop. This selection originally appeared in *The New Yorker*. Reprinted by permission of *The New Yorker*.

W. W. Norton & Company, Inc. A. R. AMMONS, "City Limits" from *Collected Poems, 1951–1971* by A. R. Ammons. Copyright © 1972 by A. R. Ammons. Reprinted by permission of W. W. Norton & Company, Inc. ADRIENNE RICH, "Storm Warnings" and "The Knight" from *Poems, Selected and New, 1950–1974* by Adrienne Rich. Copyright © 1975, 1973, 1971, 1969, 1966 by W. W. Norton & Company, Inc. Copyright © 1967, 1963, 1962, 1961, 1960, 1959, 1958, 1957, 1956, 1955, 1954, 1953, 1952, 1951 by Adrienne Rich. Reprinted by permission of W. W. Norton & Company, Inc.

Harold Ober Associates, Inc. LANGSTON HUGHES, "Theme for English B" and "Advice" from *Montage of a Dream Deferred* by Langston Hughes. Copyright 1951 by Langston Hughes. Copyright renewed 1979 by George Houston Bass. Reprinted by permission of Harold Ober Associates, Inc.

Oxford University Press, Inc. RICHARD EBERHART, "The Groundhog" from *Collected Poems 1930–1986* by Richard Eberhart. Reprinted by permission of Oxford University Press, Inc. ROBERT GRAVES, "The Naked and the Nude" from *Collected Poems 1975* by Robert Graves. Copyright © 1975 by Robert Graves. Reprinted by permission of Oxford University Press, Inc.

Linda Pastan. LINDA PASTAN, "Jump Cabling" from *Light Year '85* (Bits Press). Reprinted by permission of Linda Pastan.

Princeton University Press. PATTIANN ROGERS, "Portrait" from *Poetry* by Pattiann Rogers. Copyright © 1981 by Princeton University Press. Reprinted by permission of Pattiann Rogers. "Portrait" first appeared in *Poetry*.

Random House, Inc./Alfred A. Knopf, Inc. W. H. AUDEN, "Look Stranger" copyright 1937 and renewed 1965 by W. H. Auden. "Musée des Beaux Arts" and "The Unknown Citizen" copyright 1940 and renewed 1968 by W. H. Auden. All reprinted from *W. H. Auden: Collected Poems* edited by Edward Mendelson, by permission of Random House, Inc. EDWARD HIRSCH, "Fast Break" from *Wild Gratitude* by Edward Hirsch. Copyright © 1985 by Edward Hirsch. Reprinted by permission of Alfred A. Knopf, Inc. LANGSTON HUGHES, "The Negro Speaks of Rivers" and "Dream Variation" copyright 1926 by Alfred A. Knopf, Inc. and renewed 1954 by Langston Hughes. Reprinted by permission of Alfred A. Knopf, Inc. "Harlem" ("Dream Deferred") from *Selected Poems of Langston Hughes* by Langston Hughes. Copyright 1951 by Langston Hughes. Reprinted by permission of Alfred A. Knopf, Inc. ROBINSON JEFFERS, "Hurt Hawks" copyright 1928 and renewed 1956 by Robinson Jeffers. Reprinted from *The Selected Poetry of Robinson Jeffers* by permission of Random House, Inc. SYLVIA PLATH, "Medallion," copyright © 1962 by Sylvia Plath. Reprinted from *The Colossus and Other Poems* by Sylvia Plath by permission of Alfred A. Knopf, Inc. JOHN CROWE RANSOM, "Bells for John Whiteside's Daughter," "Winter Remembered," and "Piazza Piece" copyright 1924, 1927 by Alfred A. Knopf, Inc., and renewed 1952, 1955 by John Crowe Ransom. Reprinted from *Selected Poems* by John Crowe Ransom by permission of the publisher. KARL SHAPIRO, "Drug Store" and "Auto Wreck" © 1978 by Karl Shapiro. Reprinted from *Poems* by Karl Shapiro by permission of Random House, Inc. W. D. SNODGRASS, "April Inventory" copyright © 1957 by W. D. Snodgrass. Reprinted from *Heart's Needle* by W. D. Snodgrass by permission of Alfred A. Knopf, Inc. STEPHEN SPENDER, "Word" from *Collected Poems 1928–1953* by Stephen Spender. Copyright © 1955 by Stephen Spender. Reprinted by permission of Random House, Inc. WALLACE STEVENS, "Disillusionment of Ten O'Clock," "Peter Quince at the Clavier," "Anecdote of the Jar," and "The Emperor of Ice Cream" all copyright 1923 and renewed 1951 by Wallace Stevens. Reprinted from *The Collected Poems of Wallace Stevens* by permission of Alfred A. Knopf, Inc. BERT LESTON TAYLOR, "Upon Julia's Arctics" from *The So-Called Human Race* by Bert Leston Taylor. Reprinted by permission

PREFACE

One of our principal motives in writing this textbook and in selecting poems for inclusion has been to proselytize for poetry. We believe that Edgar Allan Poe was essentially correct in contending that "poetry is the rhythmical creation of beauty." To be sure, that beauty is sometimes frightening or awe-inspiring, as in William Blake's famous description of the "Tyger, tyger, burning bright / In the forests of the night." The beauty may even, paradoxically, be hideous or revolting, as when Anthony Hecht writes of a religious dissenter burned at the stake:

> Nor was he forsaken of courage, but the death was horrible,
> The sack of gunpowder failing to ignite.
> His legs were blistered sticks on which the black sap
> Bubbled and burst as he howled for the Kindly Light.

> —from "More Light! More Light" [1967]

There is, it seems, a beauty in fine poetry that transcends our outrage, a beauty that arises from the phenomenon of fine words finely arranged. But exactly why do we find such words beautiful? What devices do poets use to create their effects and to make us return over and over again to well-loved poems? Those questions—and the curiosity that creates such questions—are the basis of literary criticism. By providing a thorough and methodical introduction to the techniques used by poets, we hope to help you get more enjoyment from the poems you read. Moreover, we hope you will become a lifelong reader of poetry.

The heart of this text is to be found in its first 16 chapters. These chapters will take you from a brief overview of the process of reading and writing about poetry, through a gradual introduction to each of the major elements of a successful poem. We have tried to keep these chapters short enough so that each can be covered in one or two class periods. And in each chapter we have reprinted at least three poems that can be used to illustrate the importance of the particular poetic technique under consideration.

If the 16 chapters on the elements of poetry are the heart of the text, then it follows that the collection of poems in Chapter 17 is its soul. It is, indeed, the poems themselves that we most wish you to read and enjoy. Fortunately, our publisher has allowed us to put together a very ample anthology. The text includes over 380 poems, ranging from medieval to modern and from brief lyrics to lengthy verse tales. Because of its comprehensiveness, this anthology may be used in a variety of ways. Some instructors will pick out their favorite poems in Chapter 17 and assign groups of them to be studied in conjunction with the earlier chapters on the elements of poetry. Others may wish to give you a rapid introduction to the elements of poetry in the opening weeks of the course before moving on to a historical or thematic study of poetry. Still other instructors may decide to skip the opening chapters altogether, using the extensive alphabetical "Handbook" at the end of this book to introduce the various elements of poetry as seems warranted in the course of studying individual poems. And still others may wish to focus on a select number of individual poets; this text makes such an approach possible by including multiple selections by a large number of poets. Twenty major poets are represented by five or more poems each.

Our intention has been to make the text both flexible and comprehensive. If we have succeeded, it can only be because of the many helpful suggestions of our students and our colleagues in the study of literature. The book would not have been possible, however, without the advice, support, and friendship of Tony English and Katherine Evancie, the editors at Macmillan with whom we have worked most closely and most directly in bringing this collection of poems to the press.

JEFFREY D. HOEPER
Jonesboro, Arkansas
JAMES H. PICKERING
Houston, Texas

CONTENTS

Contents

INTRODUCTION

❋❋❋❋❋❋❋

Reading, Studying, and Writing About Literature

Our impulse to read literature is a universal one, answering a number of psychological needs that all of us, in certain moods and on certain occasions, share. Such needs, to be sure, vary greatly from individual to individual, for they are, in turn, the products of our separate tastes, experiences, and educations. They also vary *within* each of us; they shift and alter as we change and grow. Certain books that are "right" for us at one stage of life seem "wrong" or irrelevant later on. *The Wizard of Oz* and *Treasure Island* thrill us as children. While we may and do reread these classics in adulthood and find new pleasure in them, we are likely to find the quality of the experience quite different from the one remembered. Our reading tastes will also vary from one day to the next, depending on our current moods and intellectual and aesthetic needs. More than one professor of English, for example, has been known to teach Shakespeare or Melville by day, only to turn in the evening to the latest spy novel by John Le Carré. There is nothing particularly unusual in such a contrast for one may have many purposes in reading. Four of these purposes come at once to mind.

WHY WE READ

Reading for Escape

All of the works already mentioned—*The Wizard of Oz, Treasure Island*, the plays of William Shakespeare, and the novels and short stories of Herman Melville—offer exciting narratives that can be read uncritically simply because they allow us to escape the problems and responsibilities of our everyday lives and to participate, however briefly, in a world of experience that differs radically from our own. The average student is most likely to think of vicarious reading

1

in terms of the spy or detective story or the science fiction or historical novel—any kind of fiction that is read for the fun of it. **But many works of literature, classics as well as pulps, survive precisely because they succeed in temporarily detaching us from time and place and transporting us to some imaginary world that we otherwise would never know.** Although some people tend to regard such a motive as adolescent or even anti-intellectual, the fact remains that literature flourishes, in part at least, because of the escape it affords our imaginations.

Reading to Learn

Literature offers the reader "knowledge" in the form of information. Part of our interest in works as different as Joseph Conrad's "Heart of Darkness," Geoffrey Chaucer's "The Miller's Tale," or Anton Chekhov's *The Cherry Orchard* lies in the fact that in reading them we gain a good deal of information about colonial Africa, medieval England, or Czarist Russia—information that is all the more fascinating because it is part of the author's re-created world. Literature read in this way serves as a social document, giving us insight into the laws, customs, institutions, attitudes, and values of the time and place in which it was written or in which it is set.

When you think about it, there is scarcely a story, a poem, a play we read that doesn't offer us some new piece of information that broadens our knowledge of the world. Not all of this "knowledge" is particularly valuable; and much of it will be forgotten quickly. Some of it may, in fact, turn out to be misleading or even false—but history books, too, may be in error, and the errors in both sorts of literature at least teach us about the preconceptions of the times when such errors found their way into history and fiction.

Reading to Confront Experience

One of the most compelling aspects of literature is its relationship to human experience. **Reading is an act of engagement and participation. It is also, simultaneously, an act of clarification and discovery.** Literature allows us the chance to overcome, as perhaps no other medium can, the limitations of our own subjectivity and those limitations imposed by sex, age, social and economic condition, and the times in which we live. Literary characters offer us immediate access to a wide range of human experiences we otherwise might never know. As readers we observe these characters' public lives, while also becoming privy to their innermost thoughts, feelings, and motivations. So intimate is this access that psychologists have traditionally found imaginative literature a rich source for case studies to illustrate theories of personality and behavior.

The relationship between literature and experience, however, is highly reciprocal. Just as literature allows us to participate in the experiences of others, so too it has the power to alter our attitudes and expectations. To know why we identify with one character and not another may tell us about the kind of person we are or aspire to be. If we are sensitive and perceptive readers, we can learn from these encounters to enrich the quality and alter the direction of our lives, though the extent of such learning is impossible to predict and will vary from one reader to the next. One mark of a "great" work of literature is its ability to affect nearly every reader, and this affective power of fiction, drama, and poetry helps to explain the survival of those works we regard as "classics." Joseph Conrad's "Heart of Darkness," William Shakespeare's *Othello*, and the poems of Robert Frost, for example, survive as "classics" because they have offered generations of readers the opportunity to clarify and modify their views of life, and also because they shed light on the complexity and ambiguity of human existence.

Reading for Aesthetic Pleasure

We also read for the sheer aesthetic pleasure of observing good craftsmanship. And if, as the poet John Keats insisted, "A thing of beauty is a joy forever," then well-ordered and well-chosen words are certainly one form of immortality. Whatever its other uses, a poem, a play, or a novel is a self-contained work of art, with a describable structure and style. Sensitive and experienced readers will respond to unified stylistic effects, though they may not be initially conscious of exactly what they are responding to, or why. When that response is a positive one, we speak of our sense of pleasure or delight, in much the same way that we respond to a painting, a piece of sculpture, or a musical composition. If we push our inquiry further and try to analyze our response, we begin to move in the direction of literary criticism.

LITERARY CRITICISM

Contrary to rumor, literary criticism is not always an exercise in human ingenuity that professors of English engage in for its own sake. Neither is the word *criticism* to be confused with the kind of petty faultfinding we sometimes encounter in caustic book reviews. **Literary criticism is nothing more or less than an attempt to clarify, explain, and evaluate our experience with a given literary work.** It allows us to explain what we see in a literary work that others may have missed or seen less clearly. It allows us to raise and then answer, however tentatively, certain basic questions about an author's achievement and about the ways in which he or she achieved it. It also allows us to form some judgments about the relative merit or quality of the work as a whole. Literary criticism is a method of learning about literature, and the more we learn about how to approach a story, poem, or play, the greater our appreciation of a truly great work becomes, and greater still the sense of pleasure and enjoyment we can derive from it.

Literary criticism is the inevitable by-product of the reading process itself, for if we take that experience seriously, then criticism of some sort becomes inevitable. The only question is whether the judgments we form will be sensible ones. Literary criticism begins the moment we close our book and start to reflect on what we have just read. At that moment, to be sure, we have a choice. If we have been engaged in light reading, say in a detective story, where our interest and curiosity are satisfied once the solution to the crime is revealed and the criminal apprehended, we may simply put the book aside without a second thought and turn to weightier matters. Such an act, in itself, is a judgment. But if our reading has moved us intellectually or emotionally, we may find ourselves pausing to explore or explain our responses. If, in turn, we choose to organize and define those responses and to communicate them to someone else—to a parent, a roommate, or a close friend—we have in that moment become a literary critic.

The nature of literary criticism and the role of the critic have been simplified in this example for the sake of making a point; however, the illustration is a perfectly valid one. **Criticism is the act of reflecting on, organizing, and then articulating, usually on paper, our response to a given literary work.** Such an activity does not, however, take place in a vacuum. Like all organized fields of academic study, the study of literature rests on at least three key assumptions that critics and readers must be willing to accept. Literary criticism, first of all, presupposes that a piece of literature contains relationships and patterns of meaning that the reader-critic can discover and share. Without such prior agreement, of course, there can be no criticism, for by definition there would be nothing worthy of communication. Second, literary criticism presupposes the ability of the reader-turned-critic to translate his experience of the work into intellectual terms that can be communicated to and understood by others. Third, literary criticism presupposes that the critic's experience of the work, once organized and articulated, will be generally compatible with the experience of other readers. This is not to imply that critics and other readers will always see eye to eye, for of course they don't and never will. It *is* to say that **to be valid and valuable the critic's reading of a work must accord, at least in a general way, with what other intelligent readers over a reasonable period of time are willing to agree on or at least accept as plausible.**

To move from this general consideration of the function of literary criticism to the ways in which it can profitably be applied to the study of a given work of fiction, poetry, or drama is our task in the pages that follow. The approach we have chosen in this book is an *analytical* one that attempts to increase the understanding and appreciation of literature by introducing students to the typical devices, or *elements,* that comprise a story, a poem, or a play and to the way in which these elements relate to each other and to the work as a whole. Such an approach has much to recommend it to the student coming to the formal study of literature for the first time.

To begin with, **the analytical approach provides a critical vocabulary of such key terms as** *point of view, character, image, scene,* **and** *protagonist.* Such a set of generally agreed-upon definitions is essential if we are to discuss a work intelligently. Without the appropriate vocabulary we cannot organize our responses to a work or share them. A common vocabulary allows us to move our discussion from one literary work to another—it allows us to discuss *literature,* not just individual and isolated literary works. The theory and vocabulary of the elements of literature, along with their application to literary analysis, are neither remote nor arcane. They are the working tools of authors, critics, and intelligent readers. **Their great virtue is the common ground they provide for discussing, describing, studying, and ultimately appreciating a literary work.**

A second advantage of the analytical approach follows from the first. In order to identify and describe the various elements in a text and their interrelationship, we must ask and then attempt to answer certain basic questions about the text itself: What is the story's point of view and how does it influence our knowledge of the characters? What are the central images of the poem and how do they relate to one another? How do each of the play's scenes contribute to our understanding of the protagonist? Such questions and their answers help us not only to determine what the work says and means but also to form value judgments about how effectively (or ineffectively) the author has used his or her material.

The analytical method is just one of a number of approaches that may be taken in the study of literature. It is, however, the cornerstone of literary criticism. In emphasizing a literary work itself and the terminology useful in describing that work, the analytical method provides a framework for other critical approaches. Just as some buildings—ranging from log cabins to castles— make their structural supports the focus of attention, so too many critical essays emphasize the formal and structural elements of literature. Other buildings, however, conceal their framing timbers behind walls of stucco, stone, or wood. Similarly, other forms of criticism use the analysis of a literary work's elements as support to emphasize the relationships between the literary work and its author, its reader, or its place in history. Each of these critical approaches deserves attention. In the beginning, however, we must give priority to literary analysis; before we can profitably turn to the larger implications of a literary work, that work itself must be understood.

WRITING ABOUT LITERATURE

Most of the writing you will be asked to do in this course will require you to understand and analyze the ways in which individual works of literature convey their meaning to readers. For this reason, you must understand the elements of literature and be able to explain how they work together to make up the meaning of the entire literary work. Ordinarily, however, you will not need to be thoroughly grounded in literary history, the history of ideas, the author's biography, or any other form of specialized knowledge. An assignment focusing on the elements of literature requires only careful study of the work itself, sensitivity to the uses of language, and recognition of the ways in which language affects readers. Instructors tend to favor this form of assignment precisely *because* it demands so little specialized information of students and makes the text itself sufficient for the task at hand.

Explication

Essays focusing on the literary work alone generally fall into two categories: explication and analysis. An *explication* **(a term derived from a Latin word meaning** *unfolding***) is a detailed attempt to explain or unfold the entire meaning of a work.** Because explication is so detailed, it is normally limited to short poems or short prose passages that seem in some way central to the meaning of a story or play. Shakespeare's "Sonnet LXXIII" ("That time of year thou may'st in me behold") or one of Othello's soliloquies would make a fine topic for an explication. But the student who attempts to explicate *all* of the sonnets or *all* of *Othello* will end up writing a book, not an essay.

Typically, an explication begins with a brief paragraph identifying the poem or prose extract and explaining its place within the context of any larger work of which it is a part. You may also wish to identify the speaker, the situation, the setting, and the tone in this introductory paragraph. Remember, however, that the goal of the introduction is to present a general thesis isolating the key ideas that unify the poem or passage—and therefore unify the explication itself.

The body of the explication often unfolds through a line-by-line or idea-by-idea commentary on the entire piece. Because the reader cannot be assumed to have memorized the poem or passage, it should be quoted either in its entirety before the beginning of the explication or in coherent units (perhaps sentences or stanzas) as the explication itself takes them up. You are expected to identify and comment upon everything unusual or important in the lines under consideration. Remember that in general your reader will not have studied the passage with as much care as you have. **Your goal in an explication is to help the reader to see everything that you have discovered through patient and meticulous analysis.** Thus, the denotative meanings of any unfamiliar words must be explained; important connotations should be discussed; allusions, ambiguities, puns, paradoxes, and ironies should be identified and explained; images and image patterns should be considered; the various forms of figurative language (such as metaphor and simile) should be pointed out and their contribution to the development of the imagery and hence to the meaning of the poem should be analyzed; any symbols or allegorical systems of symbols should be discussed; and finally the contributions of rhythm and sound to the unfolding meaning of the poem should be examined. Each of these elements of poetry is defined and discussed in the introductory chapters on poetry.

At times, too, you may wish to consider elements most frequently associated with the study of fiction or drama (and therefore defined and discussed in those chapters). For example, an explication of Othello's meditations before he smothers Desdemona in act 5, scene 2, would certainly need to examine the contribution of the lines to the plot and to the characterization of Othello. Such an explication might also show how Othello's rhetorical flourishes and poetic diction contribute to Shakespeare's conception of his character. Of course, not all of the elements of literature will have an important role in any particular line of a poem or passage of prose, and therefore not all of them must be discussed in your explication. But each element should be considered during the process of study and evaluation that precedes writing.

The explication of a brief passage from a play, a short story, or a novel can often be used to provide important insights into the entire work. For example, the many comparisons in Othello's speech at the beginning of act 5, scene 2, may be taken as evidence of his fertile poetic imagination. He describes Desdemona's skin as whiter than snow and "smooth as monumental alabaster." He somewhat chillingly compares the murder he contemplates with quenching a light or plucking a rose. Like a poet, then, Othello tends to see things that he only imagines and to feel more passionately than ordinary men. From such insights, it is but a small step to the assertion that perhaps Othello's most pitiable human flaw is bound up in just this poetic tendency. Because he so easily makes imaginary events vivid and real (as he did, for example, in courting Desdemona with stories of his "battles, sieges, fortunes"), he is easily able to imagine all that Iago falsely tells him about Desdemona's wanton infidelity. In this way the explication of the poetic language in a very brief passage can serve as a microcosm, revealing insights about the character of Othello that help one to better understand the causes of his tragedy.

There is no rigid formula guiding the organization of an explication, though individual instructors may have preferences which you should attempt to find out in advance. The explication may unfold, as we have indicated, through a stanza-by-stanza (or sentence-by-sentence) analysis of everything that seems important. It may, however, also be organized in terms of the elements of literature themselves, with separate sections, for example, on poetic diction, figurative language, imagery, versification, and form. Keep in mind, however, that **the purpose of your explication is to explain fully to your reader what makes the passage meaningful, interesting, and effective.** An explication is not simply a piece of writing in which one demonstrates an understanding of literary terminology. Nor is it a mere paraphrase—or restatement—of the poem's literal meaning. Like any good essay, it should be organized in such a way that it develops a coherent thesis, and the number of words spent in the discussion of any particular element of the passage should be roughly proportional to the importance of that element in creating the meaning and in proving the essay's thesis. Typically, the essay's concluding paragraph redirects the reader's attention to that thesis in a final effort to show how the explication of the entire passage has led to a better understanding of its artistry and achievement.

An Explication of Shakespeare's 'Sonnet LXXIII'

That time of year thou may'st in me behold
When yellow leaves, or none, or few, do hang
Upon those boughs which shake against the cold,
Bare ruined choirs, where late the sweet birds sang.
5   In me thou seest the twilight of such day,
As after sunset fadeth in the west,
Which by and by black night doth take away,
Death's second self, that seals up all in rest.
In me thou seest the glowing of such fire,
10   That on the ashes of his youth doth lie,
As the death-bed whereon it must expire,
Consumed with that which it was nourished by.
This thou perceiv'st, which makes thy love more strong,
To love that well which thou must leave ere long.
[1609]

William Shakespeare's "Sonnet LXXIII" begins as a poignant meditation on approaching death. It was written when Shakespeare was somewhere between the ages of twenty-nine and forty-five and, hence, may reflect his own feelings at a time when he was (by Renaissance standards) decidedly middle-aged. However, it is not certain that the poem is in any way autobiographical. Indeed, it is not even certain that the poem is addressed to a woman. What is certain is that in "Sonnet LXXIII" the speaker's death grows more imminent in each quatrain, and simultaneously the warmth of his attachment to the one he loves (and must soom leave!) increases.

The first four lines create a metaphor comparing the speaker's age and the season of autumn. Because this metaphor extends beyond what is needed to identify the speaker's age, we immediately expect there to be correspondences between the autumn woods and the autumnal man. In looking more closely, we may note the unusual order of the words "yellow leaves, or none, or few." Clearly, this series does not simply describe the progressive dropping of the leaves. Shakespeare's word order and the repetition of the conjunction "or" suggest an observation followed by two clarifications. In the autumn of a man's years what begins to change color and fall out is hair, not leaves—a condition with which Shakespeare was quite familiar, judging from the famous Droeshout portrait of the balding poet. The hesitations and clarifications in the series "yellow leaves, or none, or few" give the image an immediacy, as if the speaker were seeing himself clearly for the first time in years: "I'm grey! And bald! Or nearly so!"

The similarities between the aging man and the autumnal tree continue in line 3 with the reference to "those boughs which shake against the cold, / Bare ruined choirs, where late the sweet birds sang." A tree denuded ("bare") of its leaves has the general appearance of a man, and its boughs, like thin, shivering arms, shake in the cold breezes. Furthermore, a leafless tree with its crisscrossing branches looks something like the open woodwork that frequently screens the choir in a cathedral, but in late fall the members of that choir, the songbirds, have departed. Perhaps, too, in late middle-age it may sometimes seem as if the sweet song of a man's youth—the high spirits and carnal desires—have taken flight like birds in winter.

The second quatrain moves us from the season of autumn to the hour of sunset. Just as late fall is the end of the year, so twilight is the end of the day. Just as the leaves that hang upon wintry trees linger after turning brown, so too the light that brightens the west lingers after the sun has set. This sense of lingering is well brought out by the poem's meter. Consider, for example, the scansion of lines 5 and 6:

> Ĭn mē/ thŏu sēest/ thĕ twī/līght ŏf/ sŭch dāy,
> Ăs āf/tĕr sūn/sĕt fā/dĕth ĭn/ thĕ wēst.

Unless we choose to stress the prepositions "of" and "in," the last half of each line is dominated by unaccented syllables so that the line lingers after its central idea has been expressed. This impression is augmented by the words "seest" and "fadeth"—in each of which the second syllable actually seems to fade away and be almost unpronounced. This correspondence between sound and sense also carries over into consonance and assonance. In each line vowel sounds are echoed or reflected in almost the same way that twilight is reflected from the clouds. In line 5 the long "e" of "me" is repeated in "seest," and a short "i" is repeated in the two syllables of the word "twilight." In line 6 the short "a" of "as" reoccurs in "after" and a sybillant "s" reoccurs in "sunset." In line 7 the explosive consonant "b" is repeated in the phrase "by and by black night." At the same time, a long "i" echoes as a result of its repetition in the two "by's" and in "night." "Doth" in line 7 alliterates with "death" in line 8, where we also have the alliteration of "second," "self," and "seals." Thus, the sounds in this quatrain linger on, just as the light it describes does.

The season of autumn, which was reduced to the hour of sunset in the second quatrain, is further reduced in the third to the final glowing moments of a fire. The speaker makes his bed on the ashes of a youth that presumably was full of romantic attachments. If this is his deathbed, it is so only because he is consumed by that love which also nourishes him. The lines are rich in paradoxical possibilities. Most literally, the speaker compares himself to a fire which is put out by rising ashes ("that which it was nourished by"). In this sense, the speaker is like those dissipated youths who are said to shorten their lives by "burning the candle at both ends." At one further remove, the speaker's deathbed is a bed of ashes, which in religious symbolism would suggest remorse. Taken together these two senses imply that the excesses of youth are catching up with the speaker, shortening his life, and driving him toward repentance.

In yet another sense, however, it is a deep bed of ashes that holds the fire overnight and makes possible its Phoenix-like rebirth the next morning. So far from repenting his past is this speaker that all of these reflections have only served to intensify his passion. The progression of imagery throughout the poem *does* emphasize the brevity of the life remaining to the speaker, but it also creates a warm, romantic setting. The bleak, wintery exterior has become a hearth at sunset. And now we note, if we have not earlier, that the speaker uses the intimate pronoun "thou" (with its passionate connotations) throughout the poem. As the final couplet shows, the speaker has used these reflections about imminent death as a rhetorical (and hopeful) argument urging his mistress to "lŏve/ thăt wĕll/ whĭch thŏu/ mŭst leave/ eře lŏng." The seven stresses in the line drive home the speaker's urgent desire that this *should* be true.

Thus, the entire poem is a rhetorical argument, and as an argument, the poem takes full advantage of the structure of a Shakespearean sonnet. Its three quatrains present three successive images of the brevity of an old man's life, but also three images of his lingering youthfulness—in the yellow leaves, the last daylight, and the glowing embers. If those three quatrains gradually close in on the poem's theme, the final couplet snaps it into clear focus. This is an old man's means of seduction, relying on pity and an engaging hopefulness that the dying embers can still brighten into the flame of love.

At the same time, however, the entire poem uses figurative language to suggest the outlines of a story, complete with time, place, situation, and anticipated consequences. On an autumn evening, a man settles down with his mistress before a warm hearth and bemoans his advancing years. After hearing such moving words, who can doubt that his mistress's sympathetic kisses will fan those fading embers into flame once more?

Analysis

Although explication requires the careful examination of *each* element in a short passage, literary *analysis* requires a very thorough study of *one* element in a long and complex work. For example, one might analyze the rural dialect used in Eugene O'Neill's *Desire Under the Elms*, the plot of Guy de Maupassant's "The Necklace," or the theme of Lord Tennyson's "Ulysses." A thorough explication of *Desire Under the Elms*, "The Necklace," or even

"Ulysses" would run to many pages, but analysis imposes limitations that make the topics more manageable.

The formation of a specific thesis is one means of imposing such limitations and is even more important in an analysis than it is in an explication. After all, most of us intuitively see the value of a thorough explication of an important passage. Such writing helps us to understand the work more fully and to appreciate its richness and complexity. Analysis is different. For example, the use of dialect in *Desire Under the Elms* may at first seem peripheral, unimportant, and somewhat annoying. Thus, an analysis of the dialect will seem belabored and boring unless the writer's thesis is immediately presented to the reader and is made interesting. The contention that O'Neill uses a regional dialect because of the play's setting in rural New England in 1850 is so obvious that it would even put to sleep an instructor well fortified with coffee. More promising is the thesis that the characters' limited ability to communicate (or even understand) their thoughts and feelings is a sign of their limited development as human beings and one cause of their tragic downfall.

Yet how is one to discover an interesting and original thesis? No general guidelines can guarantee success. However, you can often make your writing more intriguing by considering the relationships between the literary work and other subjects that interest you. If you are interested in Freudian psychology, for example, you may observe that in *Desire Under the Elms* Eben Cabot has all of the characteristics of the classical Oedipal fixation. He prays for his father's death and lusts after women old enough to be his mother. From here it is only a short step to formulating a stimulating thesis about the role of the Oedipal fixation in Eben's character. Similarly, a student with an interest in the Greek classics may choose to write an analysis of the uses of the Phaedra legend in the plot of the play. A student with an interest in religion may wish to examine the many Biblical allusions in order to show how Ephraim manipulates these allusions in creating a God that is as hard and lonely as he himself is. And a student with an interest in early American history may choose to examine the extent to which Ephraim Cabot's life and failings illustrate the influence of the Puritan heritage on the American character.

Be aware, however, that a literary analysis can rarely focus *entirely* on something so narrow as any of the topics listed in the preceding paragraph. Just as one cannot unravel a single thread from a tapestry without manipulating the entire fabric, so too **one cannot trace a single element through a work of literature without touching upon many of the other important elements.** An analysis of dialect in *Desire Under the Elms* would almost certainly examine (however briefly) the animal imagery, the Biblical allusions, and the connotations of the word "purty," since each of these is a prevalent feature in the speech of the characters. Similarly, the following character analysis of John the Carpenter in Goeffrey Chaucer's "The Miller's Tale" develops frequent comparisons between the Carpenter and the other major characters in the poem. Even more intriguingly, the essay raises speculations about the character of the Miller (who narrates the story), Chaucer (who wrote it), and the reader (who enjoys it). Each aspect of this penetrating analysis is nicely unified by the essay's thesis that an "examination of the Carpenter and his fate . . . leads to the discovery that the reader's sense of justice and fair play may be disturbingly similar to the values of the coarse, repulsive Miller."

Just Deserts:
An Analysis of the Carpenter in
Chaucer's "The Miller's Tale"

by
Deborah Chappel

Chaucer's bawdy, well-timed "Miller's Tale" leaves a sweet taste of
satisfaction in the mouth. Each of the four lively and human characters
seems to get exactly what he or she deserves, so that the reader, having
been caught up for an hour or so in the "and then?" excitement of good
narrative, closes the book with contentment. A closer examination of
the Carpenter and his fate, however, leads to the discovery that the
reader's sense of justice and fair play may be disturbingly similar to
the values of the coarse, repulsive Miller. What the reader is actually
applauding at the end of "The Miller's Tale" is the downfall of a character
who is meek, gentle, honest, loving, trusting, and moral.

The Carpenter stands in direct opposition to the other major characters
of the story. They are young, while he is old. In fact, he is so old that,
while Nicholas and Alisoun busy themselves with amorous play the whole
night long, and even Absolon roams the streets like any tomcat until
daybreak, poor John can't stay awake, not even in expectation of the
second flood. The lustful temperaments of Absolon, Alisoun, and Nicholas
seem natural to their ages, so that John's jealous guarding of his young
wife opposes the inevitable forces of nature.

The Carpenter's attitude toward love and marriage is vastly different
from the attitude of the other major characters. Love for Alisoun is
practicality and lust. There is no evidence in the story that she loves
John or Nicholas. Love for Nicholas and Absolon is conquest and physical
pleasure. Only the Carpenter is depicted as loving his wife "more than
his lyf." When Nicholas warns him of the second flood, this good man's
first fear is for his wife. John is loving, too, toward those in his charge.
When he fears that something is wrong with Nicholas, John sends his
knave to check on him, and even visits Nicholas in his chamber.

Also in opposition to the other major characters, the Carpenter is
fervently religious. When he hears his knave's report of Nicholas'
condition, the Carpenter blesses himself and calls on St. Frideswide for
help: "Men sholde nat knowe of Goddes privitee, / Ye, blessed be alwey
a lewed man, / That noght but oonly his bileve can!" When he visits
Nicholas in his room, John makes the sign of the cross on all four walls
and the threshold and says a prayer. When Nicholas tells the Carpenter
of the coming of a second flood and gives him instructions concerning
preparation, Nicholas knows how to give his story impetus. He makes
Biblical reference to Solomon, since Biblical references obviously carry
great weight with John.

Never is the Carpenter obviously dishonest or immoral. He is gentle
and considerate of his wife. When he hears Absolon wooing Alisoun in
the middle of the night, John is so trusting that he does nothing about it
except ask her if she hears it too. John is also so gullible that he believes
both Nicholas' prophecy and his instructions for their survival, being

perfectly willing to take the advice of a younger man. Not only does the poor Carpenter believe his young wife and lodger; they talk him into doing all of the work to prepare for the flood—and he never complains. When Nicholas sarcastically says, "Thou art so wys, it nedeth thee nat teche, / Go, save our lyf," poor John scurries to do his bidding.

The only actual criticism of John in the text of "The Miller's Tale" is that his wit was rough, and the reader can certainly perceive this to be the case. Not knowing of the wisdom of Cato, who "bad man sholde wedde his similitude," John was foolish enough to wed a lusty, attractive young girl. Having wed her, he was foolish enough to love her, and so was doomed to spend his life in the constant fear of being cuckolded. At no time does he exhibit the wit and understanding of any of the other major characters in the story. When Absolon is undone, he quickly conceives a plot for revenge. When Nicholas and Alisoun are on the brink of discovery and ruination, they turn the situation to their advantage by pretending that John is mad. Poor John, on the other hand, so precipitously cuts the rope on his boat at the first mention of water, that he doesn't even look to see if the supposed flood had indeed arrived. The Miller refers to John repeatedly as "this sely carpenter," and he seems to be always at the mercy of some powerful fear, from fear of being cuckolded to fear of drowning in the second flood.

In the end, then, the Carpenter's abiding flaw is great, overwhelming stupidity. This great fault is not compensated by his honesty, gentleness, love, and religious belief. We are made to feel that he deserves everything he gets—to be made the butt of Nicholas and Alisoun's jokes, to be cuckolded, and to have his wife and her lover convince his neighbors that he is mad. The Carpenter, the most virtuous character but the most stupid, suffers the worst fate of all: people laugh at him openly and he gets no revenge for his wrongs.

The reader can easily perceive why the Miller would be uncharitable toward the poor Carpenter, who is everything that he is not. The Miller is a rough, uneducated man, but a crafty one, as evidenced by his witty story. He is a thief, good at stealing grain—coarse and ugly, but, in his own way, a leader of his pack. The Miller is irreligious, tells filthy stories, drinks heavily, batters down doors with his head, and scoffs at fidelity in marriage. Nicholas, Alisoun, and even Absolon are scoundrels with whom the Miller can identify, since they are cunning, deceitful, and cynical about marriage and religion. The Carpenter, being a stupid and virtuous man, is a man to be made a fool of. "The Miller's Tale" makes a fool of the Carpenter with gusto.

There may be a lot of the Miller in Chaucer, too, for Chaucer seems to share the Miller's view of the characters in this tale. Chaucer apparently didn't prize deep religious feeling, particularly when this feeling manifested itself in superstition or self-righteousness; religious folk are the most wickedly satirized of the characters in *The Canterbury Tales*. Several of Chaucer's tales, most notably that of the Wife of Bath, reveal further cynical views toward love and marriage. A practical, logical man, Chaucer evidently thought an excess of affection to be a foolish thing, and suspect. Chaucer was human enough, too, to mock anyone who would let himself be made the butt of a joke. The characters Chaucer draws with flair are original rogues and rascals, such as Alisoun,

Nicholas, the Wife of Bath, and even Absolon. Chaucer seems to prefer these characters to the dull, virtuous ones like John the Carpenter. Perhaps Chaucer also felt that the Carpenter got exactly what he deserved.

To account for the Miller's satisfaction at the Carpenter's fate, and even to explore Chaucer's similarity to the Miller, doesn't end the story, however. There is still the matter of our response as readers. I laughed aloud as the Carpenter "got his" at the end of "The Miller's Tale." Perhaps there's more of the Miller in me than I would like to admit. Perhaps, too, part of the genius of Chaucer is his subtle appeal to that part of us that is like the Miller—coarse, bawdy, unloving, and irreligious.

As should be clear from the discussion and the accompanying examples, explication and analysis—each in its own way—forward the process of critical inquiry by providing an explicit occasion to explore, clarify, organize, and share our experience with a given literary work. Like all forms of writing, writing about literature involves the process of discovery, for as we write about what we have read, we almost inevitably enlarge our understanding and our appreciation in a way that is simply not possible with reading alone. The previous discussion has emphasized specific ways to approach the writing of an explication or analysis; the following general comments are included as broader guidelines to the writing process itself.

1

※※※※※※※

What Is Poetry?

What is poetry? One modern poet, perhaps a little vexed by this question, replied that poetry, unlike prose, is a form of writing in which few lines run to the edge of the page. Although this half-facetious response may have been intended to force the questioner to formulate his own definition of poetry, it also expresses how difficult it is to distinguish between poetry and prose on any grounds other than their appearance on the printed page. All imaginative literature—whether poetry, prose, or drama—is primarily concerned with human feelings and attitudes. This is why literature is one of the humanities. And nearly all great literature tries to recreate human experiences that involve the reader emotionally and intellectually. What then makes poetry unique and important? What *is* poetry?

Let us begin our study of poetry by considering a sentence in prose: "So much depends upon a red wheelbarrow, glazed with rain water, beside the white chickens." After a brief puzzled frown, few readers would give that sentence a second thought. It is certainly not a poem. Or is it? When the words are arranged somewhat differently on paper, they do take on the appearance of poetry:

THE RED WHEELBARROW

so much depends
upon

a red wheel
barrow

glazed with rain
water

15

beside the white
chickens.

In fact, this is a very well-known poem, written by William Carlos Williams and published in 1923.

Only two things have changed: we now know that the words were written by a well-known poet, and their arrangement on paper is different. Perhaps in principle we should not be influenced by our knowledge of the author's name. After all, a good poem should be able to stand on its own merits. In practice, however, we *do* look more closely at words—even apparently ordinary words—if we know that they were written by a famous poet. Hence Robert Frost once contended that "poetry is the kind of thing poets write."

If "The Red Wheelbarrow" *is* a poem, then its poetic nature must somehow grow out of the interplay between the meaning of the words and their arrangement on paper. It turns out, in fact, that this relationship between form and content is one of the key characteristics of poetry. But how does the arrangement of these words—their *form*, if you will—relate to meaning in this particular case? First, we might notice that Williams's rearrangement of the words creates an intriguing visual pun. The first line, "so much depends," stands out all alone on the page. The rest of the poem quite literally "depends" on that line, in the original sense of *hanging down* from it. Note, too, how the first two lines constitute a *stanza*, a group of lines separated by white space from the other stanzas in the poem. That first stanza does not itself contain any imagery. The content of the poem—however "much" that is—all "depends" upon the first stanza both visually, grammatically, and logically.

Once we begin thinking about form, we might go on to note that there is a pleasing pattern of repetition in the lines. There are four stanzas. In each stanza the first line contains three words while the second line contains only one. Furthermore, Williams continues to play with visual effects. By breaking up the word *wheelbarrow* in the second stanza, Williams arrests the eye. As soon as we form the picture of a "red wheel" in our minds in line 3, line 4 instructs us to transform it into a "red wheel / barrow." The same sort of thing happens as the rain in line 5 becomes rain water in line 6. Throughout the poem in fact, the first line of each stanza depends upon the second to expand, complement, or even alter the meaning. Thus the form of the poem helps to communicate its message that all things in life are interdependent.

Obviously, "The Red Wheelbarrow" is not a typical poem, but surely any adequate definition of poetry must allow its inclusion. Hence, we can reach one conclusion about part of the definition of poetry: **a poem is a composition that makes you think about words and their arrangement.**

Furthermore, if "The Red Wheelbarrow" is a poem, we can reach five other conclusions about what poetry is not.

1. **Poetry is not always rhymed.** "The Red Wheelbarrow" is unrhymed. Most of the great poetic passages in the plays of Shakespeare are unrhymed. Milton's *Paradise Lost* is unrhymed. So much of the poetry of the twentieth century is unrhymed that the return to traditional forms (including rhyme) by contemporary poets is seen as a surprising new trend.

2. **Poetry is not always metrical.** While we have noted a pattern in the structure of "The Red Wheelbarrow," the lines do not sustain any particular

rhythm. Despite Edgar Allan Poe's contention that "poetry is the rhythmical creation of beauty," formal rhythmic patterns, or meters, are no more necessary than rhyme in great poetry. A composition in meter and rhyme is entitled to be called verse, but not necessarily poetry. Nursery rhymes like "Jack and Jill" or "Twinkle, Twinkle Little Star" are not poetry; nor are the facile verses on greeting cards. Poetry is *often* metrical, but it need not always be.

3. **Poetry is not always concerned with beauty.** William Carlos Williams's lines on the red wheelbarrow may strike readers as funny, or pretentious, or simply matter-of-fact, but it is a rare reader who would cry out at the beauty of this description. Generally, the goal of a poet is to recreate human experience as vividly, powerfully, and originally as possible. Sometimes the poet seeks to make the words beautiful, as Edgar Allan Poe does in "Annabel Lee" (1850) or as John Keats does in his "Ode to a Nightingale" (1819). But often the subject of the poem itself is distinctly unbeautiful and the poem, in keeping with its subject, sounds harsh, grating, or downright ugly. How else could Wilfred Owen write about a mustard gas attack during World War I in "Dulce et Decorum Est" (1920)? How else could Jonathan Swift describe a grimy eighteenth-century street in "A Description of the Morning" (1709)?

4. **Poetry is not always high-toned and moral.** In "The Red Wheelbarrow" Williams makes what some may consider a pompous pronouncement about rain water and white chickens, but the moral significance of the lines—if indeed they have any—is certainly not apparent. Since great poetry always involves human perceptions and human experiences, there is perhaps always a moral and ethical dimension to poetry. Yet good poetry is rarely preachy. When Robert Browning, for example, describes a bizarre sexual strangulation in "Porphyria's Lover" (1836), or a cruel, tyrannical duke in "My Last Duchess" (1842), or a petty, spiteful monk in "Soliloquy of the Spanish Cloister" (1842), he lets the characters speak for themselves, and he lets the readers reach whatever moral conclusions they wish.

5. **Poetry is not always profound.** William Carlos Williams wrote only sixteen words in "The Red Wheelbarrow." Although most of us accept that poetry is more concentrated than ordinary speech, we expect too much if we expect great profundity from only sixteen words. Nevertheless, Williams does challenge us to think for ourselves about the significance of the wheelbarrow, the rain water, and the chickens. When we do so, we may well conclude with Thomas Dilworth that these three images "suggest the major components of agrarian life—which may, in turn, suggest all civilized life in its practical aspect. The wheelbarrow represents human labor and ingenuity; the chickens represent animals bred for human nourishment; and the rain represents the life-giving natural elements. The interrelationship of these components makes possible civilized life."[1] While some may object that Dilworth's analysis is fabricating symbols in order to make the poem seem more significant than it is, we are probably all willing to grant that Williams's poem is capable of stimulating us to think about the interdependence of life. If the poem itself is not profound, it may nonetheless cause us to think about life a bit more deeply.

So far our quest to define poetry leaves us in much the same predicament first described by the great eighteenth-century critic and lexicographer Samuel

[1] "Williams' 'The Red Wheelbarrow,' " *The Explicator*, 40 (Summer 1982): 40–41.

Johnson. When asked for a definition of poetry, he replied, "Why, sir, it is much easier to say what it is not. We all know what light is; but it is not easy to *tell* what it is." Two hundred years later we are not really much closer to an answer. Indeed, poets themselves have often struggled to define poetry without, perhaps, shedding much light—or at least without providing definitive answers. Nevertheless, here are a handful of poems about poetry (or the experience of reading it) that may help you develop a better feel for the meaning of the word.

Five Poems on Poetry

SOUND AND SENSE
(From *An Essay on Criticism,* part 2)

True ease in writing comes from art, not chance,
As those move easiest who have learned to dance.
'Tis not enough no harshness gives offence,

365 The sound must seem an echo to the sense.
Soft is the strain when Zephyr° gently blows,   *the west wind*
And the smooth stream in smoother numbers flows;
But when loud surges lash the sounding shore,
The hoarse, rough verse should like the torrent roar.

370 When Ajax² strives, some rock's vast weight to throw,
The line too labours, and the words move slow;
Not so, when swift Camilla³ scours the plain,
Flies o'er the unbending corn, and skims along the
    main
Hear how Timotheus'⁴ varied lays surprise,

375 And bid alternate passions fall and rise!
While, at each change, the son of Libyan Jove⁵
Now burns with glory, and then melts with love;
Now his fierce eyes with sparkling fury glow;
Now sighs steal out, and tears begin to flow:

380 Persians and Greeks like turns° of nature° found,   *changes / mood*
And the world's victor stood subdued by sound!
The power of music all our hearts allow,
And what Timotheus was, is Dryden now.

—Alexander Pope [1711]

❧ QUESTIONS ❧

1. How accurate is the analogy between writing good poetry and dancing well?

---

² A hero in the *Iliad* celebrated for his strength.   ³ A heroine in the *Aeneid*.
⁴ See "Alexander's Feast," p. 817.   ⁵ Alexander the Great.

2. What does Pope do to make the sound of his lines echo their sense in lines 366–373?

3. What is the effect of the brief references to Zephyr, Ajax, Camilla, Timotheus, Jove, and Dryden?

4. Do you agree that in good poetry "The sound must seem an echo to the sense"?

ON FIRST LOOKING INTO CHAPMAN'S HOMER

Much have I travell'd in the realms of gold,
And many goodly states and kingdoms seen:
Round many western islands have I been
Which bards in fealty to Apollo° hold.   *the god of poetry*
5   Oft of one wide expanse had I been told
That deep-browed Homer ruled as his demesne;°   *domain*
Yet did I never breathe its pure serene
Till I heard Chapman speak out loud and bold:
Then felt I like some watcher of the skies
10   When a new planet swims into his ken;
Or like stout Cortez[6] when with eagle eyes
He stared at the Pacific—and all his men
Looked at each other with a wild surmise—
Silent, upon a peak in Darien.

—John Keats [1816]

✄ QUESTIONS ✄

1. What does Keats mean by "the realms of gold"?

2. What is the effect of the brief references to Apollo, Homer, Chapman, and Cortez?

3. Examine the imagery in the poem. What are its ranges in the sweep of time and space?

4. What general situation does Keats describe in the first eight lines?

5. What new sensation does he describe in the last six lines? What has caused that new sensation?

6. How effective is the analogy with Cortez in describing the emotions you feel upon reading a poem that truly moves you? How effective is the analogy with an astronomer discovering a new planet?

7. Does it make a difference that this poem records an actual experience of Keats? When Keats was twenty-one, his former teacher Cowden Clarke showed him a copy of George Chapman's vigorous translations of Homer's

---

[6] Hernando Cortés (1485–1547) conquered the Aztecs in Mexico, but he did not discover the Pacific Ocean. Vasco Núñez de Balboa did that in 1513. Darien is in eastern Panama.

Iliad and *Odyssey*. Keats and Clarke stayed up all night in rapture reading and discussing the poems. After returning home at dawn, Keats immediately composed this famous sonnet and sent it to Clarke as an expression of thanks.

ARS POETICA

A poem should be palpable and mute
As a globed fruit,

Dumb
As old medallions to the thumb,

5   Silent as the sleeve-worn stone
Of casement ledges where the moss has grown—

A poem should be wordless
As the flight of birds.
         *
A poem should be motionless in time
10   As the moon climbs,

Leaving, as the moon releases
Twig by twig the night-entangled trees,

Leaving, as the moon behind the winter leaves,
Memory by memory the mind—

15   A poem should be motionless in time
As the moon climbs.
         *
A poem should be equal to:
Not true.

For all the history of grief
20   An empty doorway and a maple leaf.

For love
The leaning grasses and two lights above the sea—

A poem should not mean
But be.

         —Archibald MacLeish [1926]

❧ QUESTIONS ❧

1. This poem is divided into three parts, with the divisions indicated by an asterisk. What is the subject of each separate division? Can you put

into your own words the statement about poetry made in each of the three sections?

2.   This poem uses many comparisons (similes and metaphors). Which comparisons do you especially like? Are there any you think are inappropriate in defining the nature of poetry? Explain your views.

3.   To what extent does MacLeish's own poem live up to his definition of poetry?

WORD

The word bites like a fish.
Shall I throw it back free
  Arrowing to that sea
Where thoughts lash tail and fin?
  Or shall I pull it in
  To rhyme upon a dish?

—Stephen Spender [1949]

❧ QUESTIONS ❧

1.   In what sense does a good word, a poetic word, bite like a fish? Try to explain what you think Spender means.

2.   What does Spender seem to be saying about the differences between free verse and rhymed verse?

3.   Judging from this poem, what kind of verse does Spender himself prefer?

AMERICAN POETRY

Whatever it is, it must have
A stomach that can digest
Rubber, coal, uranium, moons, poems.

Like the shark, it contains a shoe.
It must swim for miles through the desert
Uttering cries that are almost human.

—Louis Simpson [1963]

❧ QUESTIONS ❧

1.   What is the effect of opening this poem on American poetry with the words "Whatever it is . . ."?

2.   What kind of stomach is capable of digesting "Rubber, coal, uranium, moons, poems"? Is there anything particularly American about that list of indigestibles?

3.   Do you think that poetry is anything like a shark? Explain your opinion.

4.   How can a shark (or a poem) "swim for miles through the desert"? Is this paradox appropriate in a description of poetry or the task of an American poet?

5.   Why are the cries of the poet (or the poem) "almost human"?

As the previous examples illustrate, poets throughout the ages have differed in their assumptions about the genre, and it is unrealistic to expect a single definition of poetry to serve equally well for all periods in literary history. If we stand outside the spectrum of history, we can see how one view dominates an age only to give way to another. So long as poetry remains a vital form of human expression, we can expect that its techniques and purposes will continue to change.

What *is* poetry? We ask again. Although we may be unable to answer this question for all time, we *can* summarize those elements in the definition of poetry that have remained nearly constant throughout the ages.

Poetry, like all literature, attempts to communicate an author's emotional and intellectual responses to his or her own existence and to the surrounding world. It is an expression of what is thought and felt, rather than what is known as fact. It depends on observation, just as science does, but poetry draws comparisons between phenomena that science might find distant and unrelated. When Keats wishes to share his emotions upon first reading Chapman's translation of Homer's poetry, he finds an apt metaphor in the conquistador's silent wonder at the vast Pacific Ocean. When MacLeish wishes to describe the unity and concreteness of poetry, he uses a vivid comparison: "A poem should be palpable and mute / As a globed fruit." Such comparisons require a bold leap of imagination in both the poet and the reader. When they are effective, they reproduce emotions in the reader similar to those actually experienced by the author. Thus, **poetry is fundamentally metaphoric and is capable of communicating in very few words thoughts and emotions of great complexity.**

Prose literature, of course, is capable of achieving everything suggested in the preceding paragraph. As a result of modern experiments with free verse and the increasing literary artistry of short story writers and novelists, the distinctions between poetry and prose are often slight and sometimes blurred. Hence, all of the techniques of poetry can, on occasion, be properly considered in the critical explication of fiction and drama. However, poetry ordinarily does differ from prose in several significant ways. First, **poetry provides a traditionally accepted format (in ballads, lyrics, odes, and sonnets) for the publication of short but independent pieces of narration, description, or reflection.** Second, **"poetic license" permits verse to depart on occasion from the standard rules of logic and grammar governing ordinary prose.** Third, **poetry tends to make more use than prose of symbolism, imagery, and figures of speech.** And finally, **poetry relies more heavily than prose on the sound and rhythm of speech and hence often employs both rhyme and meter.**

The formal patterns of meter and rhyme, which continue to dominate poetry despite modern experiments with free verse, place obvious restrictions on the poet's choice of words. The poet must write carefully and reflectively in order to find words that not only fulfill the demands of meter and rhyme, but also express the meaning in a manner that complements the imagery and tone of the rest of the poem. This careful use of language is the most significant difference between ordinary prose and poetry. The ordinary prose writer neatly builds an argument using words the way a mason builds a house using bricks; the poet is a craftsman who creates a fieldstone hearth—each stone or each word is turned over, examined, and often laid aside until it can be placed where its shape, weight, and color will contribute to the strength and beauty of the whole. **Prose, according to Samuel Taylor Coleridge, is "words in their best order," and poetry is "the best words in their best order."**

Very little of the poetry of any age comes up to the high standards set in the previous paragraph. Even great poets write relatively few great poems, and our disappointment in the inferior works of notable poets is often greater than it is in the secondary works of great novelists. This, too, points out a difference between prose and poetry. Mediocre prose is often enjoyable in much the same way that a walk in the city can be enjoyable even though it is not so fresh and invigorating as a hike through the wilderness. But if prose is like walking, then poetry is like riding. Either the rider *or* his mount will have control over the rhythm, the pace, and the direction of the journey. When the horse is in command—that is, when the meter and rhyme govern the poet—the ride will be uneven, misdirected, unintelligible, and sometimes fearsome. When the rider is in control—that is, when the poet fully controls the rhythm and sound—the gait will be swift, smooth, graceful, and elegant.

In the preceding paragraphs we have compared the poet with an artisan and an equestrian. Both comparisons convey something about the essential quality of poetry. Perhaps, however, they emphasize too strongly the skill of the poet and not strongly enough the skills that are necessary in an appreciative reader. Poetry shares with all other literary genres the fact that it is a form of communication between the author and the reader. It depends as much on the good will, intelligence, and experience of the latter as on the genius of the former. Robert Frost once said that writing free verse is like playing tennis with the net down. Regardless of whether we agree with Frost's implied criticism of free verse, his remark underscores the fact that poetry is a game played according to established rules between poet and form and also between poet and reader. In order to play the game, in order to understand poetry, one must first learn the rules.

2

✖✖✖✖✖✖✖✖✖

Denotation and Connotation

Words are the building blocks of poetry. By the time students enter college, they have heard at least 100 million words in school; spoken 30 million words in school and out; and read, in spite of television, some 10 million words. During the years of formal schooling, language is so ingrained in us that we cannot imagine an existence without words; our most private thoughts often take the form of an inner dialogue and even our dreams incorporate words. In short, we become so sophisticated in language, and at such an early age, that we seldom realize the complexity of the language we read, speak, and hear.

Our understanding of language, whether as listeners or as readers, depends almost entirely on two factors: our knowledge of the meaning of individual words and our recognition of various cues (syntax, punctuation, and structure in reading; syntax, emphasis, and vocal pauses in listening) which direct our attention to the relationships among the words.[1] When we read a poem, our first concern is with the meaning of individual words, but it soon becomes clear that meaning is largely determined by context and by the interrelationships of words in a sentence. Several of the elements of poetry, however, are occasionally independent of context: particularly denotation and connotation. **A word's** *denotation* **is its dictionary definition; its** *connotation* **is that set of associations and emotional overtones carried by the word.** Each word in a language is distinguished from every other word by its unique combination of denotations and connotations; there are no perfect synonyms. Poetry is the form of writing

[1] Literary critics have not sufficiently emphasized the fact that poetry gives—through rhythm, rhyme, and verse form—more cues about meaning than prose. This was even more obvious in the Middle Ages than it is now. Our elaborate gradations of punctuation are relatively recent inventions; medieval scribes used only the slash and the period. Consequently, medieval manuscripts are much easier to read in verse than in prose and, perhaps as a result, verse was often preferred for any composition of lasting value.

24

that takes greatest advantage of the personalities of words; it welcomes their eccentricities. **No word in great poetry can be moved or replaced without changing and perhaps harming the whole.** An understanding of the meaning of individual words, therefore, is essential in understanding poetry.

DENOTATION

"When I use a word," Humpty Dumpty said in rather a scornful tone, "it means just what I choose it to mean—neither more nor less."

"The question is," said Alice, "whether you *can* make words mean so many different things."

"The question is," said Humpty Dumpty, "which is to be Master—that's all."

Alice was too much puzzled to say anything, so after a minute Humpty Dumpty began again. "They've a temper, some of them—particularly verbs, they're the proudest—adjectives you can do anything with, but not verbs—however, *I* can manage the whole lot of them! Impenetrability! That's what *I* say!"

—From *Through the Looking Glass,* Lewis Carroll [1871]

As is often the case, Lewis Carroll's humor is far from absurd. In fact, the quotation points to an interesting paradox about words: **A word is only an accurate tool of communication if it conveys the same idea to both the speaker and the listener; yet the meanings of words continually change and, despite the existence of dictionaries, can only be said to mean what people *think* they mean.** New words are continually entering the language and old words dropping out or changing their implications. Furthermore, the same word can mean different things to different people or different things in different contexts. If, for example, we say of someone, "He's a bit red," we may mean that he is embarrassed, sunburned, or attracted to Communism, depending on the context. Similarly, if a man living in the fifteenth century introduced a woman as John Smith's "mistress," he would have been praising her as an honest wife of noble blood. Today, such an introduction might openly suggest her lack of a marriage license.

If we object to using words that carry the clutter of variant definitions based on history, location, and context . . . well, we can turn to *new* words, freshly minted to meet their creators' needs. Lewis Carroll was remarkably adept at coining such words. We are indebted to him for the *boojum* (which is now the name of a species of tree found in southern California), the *snark* (now used as the trade name of a small sailboat), and the Cheshire Cat's smile. To Joseph Heller, we owe the expression *Catch-22,* and to Harriet Beecher Stowe, we owe *Uncle Tom.* The military's fondness for acronyms has produced *radar* (radio detection and ranging) and *snafu* (situation normal all fouled up).[2] The list goes on.

The various meanings of the words we have been discussing so far are all *denotations*—that is, they are listed as definitions in nearly any good dictionary. Most of us, when asked the meaning of any particular word, reply with a single, rather loose, definition. But **we know that nearly every word has many**

---

[2] Not all acronyms are felicitous or dignified. Richard Nixon's ill-fated Committee to Re-elect the President was known as CREEP, the device used by NASA to blow up misguided ·missiles is called EGADS (Electronic Ground Automatic Destruct System), and the policy governing our nuclear defense strategy is known as MAD (Mutual Assured Destruction).

definitions and that its denotation in a particular instance will depend largely on the context. These multiple meanings make the whole issue of a word's denotation much more complex and much less clear-cut than it may seem at first. It is an indication of the complexity of this issue that the most authoritative dictionary in the language, *The Oxford English Dictionary* (1933), is 16,464 pages long. In it one finds, for example, more than eighteen pages (with three columns of print to the page) defining the verb *set,* which is capable of taking on 154 separate senses with nearly a thousand minor subdivisions of meaning.

The first task in understanding a poem, then, is to understand thoroughly each word in it. Often, the best clues to the meaning of an unfamiliar word are to be found within the poem itself. Suppose, for example, that one wishes to know the meaning of "heal-all" in the following sonnet by Robert Frost:

DESIGN

I found a dimpled spider, fat and white,
On a white heal-all, holding up a moth
Like a piece of rigid satin cloth—
Assorted characters of death and blight
5   Mixed ready to begin the morning right,
Like the ingredients of a witches' broth—
A snow-drop spider, a flower like a froth,
And dead wings carried like a paper kite.
What had that flower to do with being white,
10   The wayside blue and innocent heal-all?
What brought the kindred spider to that height,
Then steered the white moth thither in the night?
What but the design of darkness to appall?—
If design govern in a thing so small.
                                        —Robert Frost [1936]

A dictionary only tells us that a "heal-all" is either a panacea of some kind or one of a number of plants (*Rhodiola rosea, Valeriana officinalis, Prunella vulgaris,* and *Collinsonia canadensis*) that are thought to have medicinal value. Although accurate, this definition is no real help. If we don't know what a "heal-all" is in the first place, we certainly aren't going to know anything about a *Rhodiola rosea* or any of the other species listed. If we turn to a book on horticulture for help, we will learn where these plants grow, how large they get, how many stamens and pistils the flowers have, and so on. We may even find pictures of each of the four plants, but without referring to the poem we won't learn anything telling us which of the four Frost meant or what emotions he hoped to evoke in the reader through the name. In comparison, look at the information about the word contained in the poem itself. There we learn that a heal-all is a blue flower (lines nine and ten) of substantial height and size. It is large enough to support a fat spider and tall enough so that Frost is surprised to see the spider on it. We learn that it grows by the wayside and that it is innocent; if it doesn't heal everything, as its name suggests, it is not ordinarily poisonous either. But the particular heal-all in the poem is unusual and almost an object of horror. It is blighted and white, a deformed member of its species. Thus, Frost sees its frothlike flowers as a fitting element in a witches' brew— and a fitting element in a poem that raises the possibility of malevolent destiny.

In the course of the poem, Frost has defined what he means by a heal-all. He has told us about the flower and, more importantly, he has told us about himself and the destiny he thinks governs existence. We learn what the word *heal-all* means and also what it symbolizes for Frost. The risk involved in defining a word from its context is, of course, that we are often unable to differentiate between the general denotative meaning of the word and its special significance for the poet. For this reason it is wise to check any definitions derived from context with those given in the dictionary.

Any ample dictionary will answer most of the needs of the student-critic. Yet one should keep in mind that **the meaning of words changes with time,** and dictionaries of only one volume seldom trace historical change. As a result of the civil rights movement of the 1960s, for example, the verb *discriminate* has come to mean "to make a decision based on prejudice." In the *Oxford English Dictionary,* however, the history of the word reveals that prior to about 1880 the verb meant only "to distinguish, differentiate, or exercise discernment." According to these early meanings of the word, an intelligent person should always be discriminating; today, we hope to avoid discriminating. Such changes in language are so common that we can expect to find some archaism in virtually every poem written before the beginning of the eighteenth century.

CONNOTATION

As we have seen, denotation refers to the dictionary meaning of a word. Connotation, on the other hand, is determined by the ideas associated with or suggested by the word. **Denotation is the meaning a word gives *to* a sentence; connotation is the verbal coloring a word takes on *from* those sentences in which it is commonly used.** When a word like *discriminate* is uniformly employed in a narrow set of circumstances (in this case, involving some form of prejudice), its connotations may eventually be incorporated into the definition of the word itself. This is the principal process by which the definitions of words change. Thus, a word's connotations may be compared to the living, growing bark of a tree, and its denotations, like the rings in the tree's core, are the permanent record of its past growth. To change the simile slightly, the denotations of a word are visible, like a tree's branches and leaves; the connotations are the roots, which go deeply into the subsoil of our experience creating invisible ties between contexts and associations and drawing up nourishment for a continuing growth above ground.

Most of us manipulate the connotations of words every day. The person described scornfully as "my old man" during a "rap session" in the dormitory is apt to become "Dad" during the weekly "chat" on the phone about the high costs at college and finally to become "my father" during a formal "interview" with the financial aid officer. In each set of examples, the denotative meanings remain essentially unchanged—the father remains a father and the conversation remains a conversation—but the connotations change dramatically. As these examples demonstrate, **speakers and writers manipulate connotations in an almost instinctive effort to set a tone**—whether it be the laid back informality of the "rap session" or painful formality of an "interview."

Many words have multiple and even conflicting connotations. For example, in the sonnet by Frost on page 632 the spider, the moth, and the flower are all white. Most of the time we associate the adjective *white* with innocence, purity, and cleanliness. A young bride is customarily married in a white gown and angels are depicted wearing white robes. In other contexts, however, this color can also signify pallor, illness, blight, or even death. Frost is probably drawing on both sets of connotations in his poem. The white moth fluttering toward its destruction in the darkness is harmless and innocent; the white flower that attracts it is blighted and unusual; and the fat white spider is a ghastly object of poison and death. Frost expects us to react—perhaps even shudder—at this departure from the normal and expected. Indeed, Frost's own attitude changes. In the last six lines he moves from questioning to despair—("What had . . . ? What brought . . . ? What but . . . ?")—as his conviction grows that such an evil distortion of "whiteness" can only be brought about by "the design of darkness to appall." This evolution is summarized in that final word "appall," the original denotation of which is "to make pale" or even (considering the many uses of "white" in the poem) "to make white." Thus, Frost creates an ironic pun based on the denotation of "appall," but in this instance the burden of the word's meaning is carried by its connotation. In ordinary usage the word "appall" inevitably carries connotations of horror— so much so that "horrify" is usually listed as one of its definitions in modern dictionaries—and indeed Frost *is* horrified by this design of darkness and hopes through his poem to make us share his horror.

A word's connotations, like its denotations, may change over time. A humorous example of change in a word's connotations occurs in Samuel Taylor Coleridge's "Sonnet to the Reverend W. L. Bowles" (1796). Coleridge claims that the verses of Reverend Bowles were capable of soothing a tumultuous mind:

> As the great Spirit erst with plastic sweep
> Mov'd on the darkness of the unform'd deep.

Coleridge here uses *plastic* to mean having the superhuman "power of molding or shaping formless material"—a meaning of the word that the dictionary still lists. Most modern readers, however, think of cheap merchandise when they hear the word *plastic* and think of brooms when they hear the word *sweep*. Thus, because of these changes in connotation, we may mistakenly picture the Holy Spirit pushing a cheap plastic broom when we first read Coleridge's lines.

Poems for Further Study

THE NAKED AND THE NUDE

For me, the naked and the nude
(By lexicographers[3] construed
As synonyms that should express
The same deficiency of dress
5   Or shelter) stand as wide apart
As love from lies, or truth from art.

Lovers without reproach will gaze
On bodies naked and ablaze;
The Hippocratic[4] eye will see

---

[3] Those who make dictionaries.
[4] Hippocrates (c. 460–377 B.C.) was the Greek physician generally thought to have founded medical science.

10   In nakedness, anatomy;
     And naked shines the Goddess when
     She mounts her lion among men.

     The nude are bold, the nude are sly
     To hold each treasonable eye.
15   While draping by a showman's trick
     Their dishabille[5] in rhetoric,
     They grin a mock-religious grin
     Of scorn at those of naked skin.

     The naked, therefore, who compete
20   Against the nude may know defeat;
     Yet when they both together tread
     The briary pastures of the dead,
     By Gorgons[6] with long whips pursued,
     How naked go the sometime nude!

       —Robert Graves [1957]

❧ QUESTIONS ❧

1. Use a dictionary to check the denotations of the words *naked* and *nude*. Is Graves correct in calling them synonyms?

2. What does Graves mean when he says that for him "the naked and the nude . . . stand as wide apart / As love from lies, or truth from art." How far do you think that Graves wishes to carry his simile? Does Graves equate the nude with love or lies? Truth or art? (Look for the answers to these questions in stanzas two and three.)

3. What are the differences in connotations of the words *naked* and *nude*? How successfully does Graves develop the implications of these differing connotations?

4. What is the denotation of the word *dishabille* in the third stanza? What are its connotations? Why are both the denotation and connotation of the word useful to Graves?

5. What is a "mock-religious grin"? Why would the nude stare in that way at the naked? Why does Graves choose the word *grin* instead of *smile*?

6. Explain the meaning of the poem's final line.

CARGOES

Quinquireme of Nineveh from distant Ophir,
Rowing home to haven in sunny Palestine,

---

[5] State of being undressed.
[6] Hideous, terrifying women of Greek mythology—the mere sight of whom turns men to stone.

With a cargo of ivory,
And apes and peacocks,
5   Sandalwood, cedarwood, and sweet white wine.

Stately Spanish galleon coming from the Isthmus
Dipping through the Tropics by the palm-green shores,
With a cargo of diamonds,
Emeralds, amethysts,
10   Topazes, and cinnamon, and gold moidores.°   *Portuguese coins*

Dirty British coaster with a salt-caked smoke stack,
Burning through the Channel in the mad March days,
With a cargo of Tyne coal,
Road-rails, pig-lead,
15   Firewood, iron-ware, and cheap tin trays.

—John Masefield [1902]

✁ QUESTIONS ✁

1.   This poem is divided into three stanzas. What is the subject of each
stanza? What are the similarities between the stanzas? What are the differences—especially in the third stanza?

2.   Discuss the connotations of the names of the various cargo ships.
Discuss the connotations of the ports the ships service and of the cargo
in each ship.

3.   What thematic point about the British empire does Masefield make
through his manipulations of connotations?

3

※※※※※※※

Allusion

When the English peasants marched against London in their ill-fated revolt of 1381, it is said that they rallied their spirits by chanting this brief ditty:

> When Adam dalf°   *delved, farmed*
> And Eve span°   *spun (yarn)*
> Who was then the gentleman?

The peasants wanted to throw off their serfdom and assume the rights of free-born citizens. Their argument, at least in the chant, depended on a Biblical allusion: in Genesis, when God created mankind, he made Adam and Eve, not nobles and serfs—how then is serfdom justified?

A literary *allusion* **is a brief reference to a person, place, phrase, or event drawn from history or literature. Allusions are effective not because of the meaning of the words themselves but because of the associations or connotations that allusive words carry for the informed reader. The use of allusion allows poets to reinforce an argument by illustration, to compress complex ideas into brief phrases, and to suggest thoughts they may not wish to state directly.** In the case at hand, the peasants' allusive chant allowed them to request their freedom without putting it in the form of (a) rebellious demand and to support their position with the authority of the Bible.

Names, as in the example just cited, **are the most common forms of allusion** and the easiest to identify. As another example of names used allusively, let us look at a stanza from Lord Byron's *Don Juan:*

> When amatory poets sing their loves
>   In liquid lines mellifluously bland,
> And pair their rhymes as Venus yokes her doves,
>   They little think what mischief is in hand;

31

> The greater their success the worse it proves,
>   As Ovid's verse may give to understand;
> Even Petrarch's self, if judged with due severity,
>   Is the Platonic pimp of all posterity.
>   —From *Don Juan*, Lord Byron [1821]

Byron uses four allusions in eight lines. The first is almost self-explanatory: a poet's rhymes are paired in the same way as the doves that draw Venus's chariot through the heavens are yoked into pairs. The allusion is intended less to send the reader stumbling off to consult his copy of Ovid's *Metamorphoses* than to imitate the similes of conventional love poetry; it requires only that the reader remember that Venus is the goddess of love. Byron then goes on to argue that the more successful poets are in writing about love, the worse it is for public morality, "As Ovid's verse may give to understand." Although Byron only expects from his reader the general knowledge that Ovid is renowned as the most seductive of all love poets, he may also be alluding to the rumor that Ovid was banished from Rome because his verse had tempted the daughter of Emperor Caesar Augustus into having an illicit love affair. The reference to Petrarch in line seven assumes that the reader will know that this fourteenth-century Italian poet (who wrote 227 sonnets about his unrequited love for Laura living and another 90 about his love for Laura dead) has inspired many seductive sonnet cycles. A final allusion is contained in the incongruous expression "Platonic pimp." Byron's point here is that Petrarch's verse may well have been spiritual or Platonic in fact, but it was erotic and seductive in effect. The brief allusion to *Platonic love,* which denotes "spiritual love" to literate readers, serves to emphasize that allusion, like denotation and connotation, is one of the factors in determining the meaning of words.

   Allusion through literary name-dropping is generally less effective than allusion through quotation or imitation of an author's works. Historically important and well-stated words have an emotional impact that transcends their denotative meaning. **A literary allusion that is created through quotation draws on our reaction to the quoted work, the circumstances under which the work was written, and the whole range of our attitudes toward the author.** We respond with patriotism to the idealism of the *Declaration of Independence* ("We hold these truths to be self-evident . . ."); with mystical piety to the Gospel according to St. John ("In the beginning was the Word, and the Word was with God, and the Word was God"); and with a shiver to the opening of Edgar Allan Poe's "The Raven" ("Once upon a midnight dreary . . ."). When Keats wrote of "deep-browed Homer" (see p. 625), he was imitating Homer's penchant for such epithets as his often repeated "rosy-fingered Dawn." When Coleridge, in his sonnet to Reverend Bowles, compared the calming of his mind to the calming of waves after the great Spirit "Mov'd on the darkness of the unform'd deep," he was alluding to Genesis, Chapter 1, verse 2:

   And the earth was without form, and void; and darkness was upon the face of the deep. And the Spirit of God moved upon the face of the waters.

   Such examples of allusion all refer to *famous* people, events, or words, because **an allusion is only effective if it is understood and appreciated by the reader. But poets themselves often gain considerable notoriety as public figures, so that allusions to events in their personal lives come to be widely understood.** For instance, Byron alludes to events in his own life when he writes in the first canto of *Don Juan,*

'Tis pity learned virgins ever wed
  With persons of no sort of education.
Or gentlemen, who, though well born and bred,
  Grow tired of scientific conversation:
I don't choose to say much on this head.
  I'm a plain man, and in a single station,
But—Oh! ye lords of ladies intellectual,
Inform us truly, have they not hen-peck'd you all?
    —From *Don Juan,* Lord Byron [1819]

The irony in the stanza may elude us if we fail to recognize that Byron's wife Annabella had been a "learned virgin," that he often called her the "Princess of Parallelograms" and "a walking calculation," and that their separation proceedings provided scandal enough to delight gossips throughout England *and* Europe. Similarly, when Laurence Sterne, the eighteenth-century novelist and clergyman, was married, he wryly made reference to this event in his personal life by taking as his keynote for the following day's sermon this passage from Luke 5:5: "We have toiled all the night and taken nothing."

Poems for Further Study

THE GARDEN OF LOVE

I went to the Garden of Love,
And saw what I never had seen:
A Chapel was built in the midst,
Where I used to play on the green.°   *lawn*

5   And the gates of this Chapel were shut,
And "Thou shalt not" writ over the door;
So I turned to the Garden of Love
That so many sweet flowers bore;

And I saw it was filled with graves,
10   And tombstones where flowers should be;
And priests in black gowns were walking their rounds,
And binding with briars my joys and desires.

    —William Blake [1794]

❧ QUESTIONS ❧

1. The speaker in this poem describes the "Garden of Love" as he remembers it from his innocent youth and as it appears to him now. What was the garden like in the past? How has it changed? How does the speaker feel about these changes?

2. To what is Blake alluding when he says that "Thou shalt not" was written over the door of the chapel. (There are two fairly obvious possibilities. See if you can identify them both.)

3. Why does Blake capitalize the words *Garden* and *Love?* Is he merely creating a proper name (like the Rose Garden at the White House)? Or does he want us to concentrate on the garden? What other garden is associated with religion, love, the loss of innocence, and the unwelcome presence of death? How does the discovery of this allusion affect your interpretation of the poem?

4. Explain the allusion in the last line of the poem.

5. To what extent does this poem portray each individual's experiences in growing to maturity? To what extent does the poem synopsize the historical development of the Christian church? How do you think Blake feels about the organized church and the "mature" adult?

MYTH

Long afterward, Oedipus, old and blinded, walked the
roads.   He smelled a familiar smell.   It was
the Sphinx.   Oedipus said, "I want to ask one question.
Why didn't I recognize my mother?"   "You gave the
5   wrong answer," said the Sphinx.   "But that was what
made everything possible," said Oedipus.   "No," she said.
"When I asked, What walks on four legs in the morning,
two at noon, and three in the evening, you answered,
Man.   You didn't say anything about woman."
10 "When you say Man," said Oedipus, "you include women
too. Everyone knows that."   She said, "That's what
you think."

                                          —Muriel Rukeyser [1973]

✻ QUESTIONS ✻

1. To what is Rukeyser alluding when she begins her poem with the words "long afterward"? Long after what? (If you are not familiar with the story of Oedipus, read *King Oedipus* in the drama section of this anthology—or consult a standard encyclopedia.)

2. In what sense does "man" walk on four legs in the morning, two at noon, and three in the evening? What do morning, noon, and evening symbolize?

3. What is the point of Rukeyser's poem? (To what extent does Rukeyser link Oedipus's failure to include women in answering the Sphinx's riddle with his later failure to recognize his own mother?)

4

꙰꙰꙰꙰꙰

Repetition and Ambiguity

Thus far, we have been examining elements in the meaning of words that are nearly independent of their context in a poem. It is the poetic context, however, that now requires attention because context alone allows us to distinguish among the competing possibilities offered by a word's denotations and connotations. **A word will rarely mean exactly the same thing in two different contexts, even within the same poem.**

The *repetition* of a word or phrase in itself tends to change the emphasis and to make prominent what otherwise might be overlooked. This is Robert Frost's intention in repeating the last line in the final stanza of the following well-known poem:

STOPPING BY WOODS ON A SNOWY EVENING

Whose woods these are I think I know.
His house is in the village though;
He will not see me stopping here
To watch his woods fill up with snow.

5
My little horse must think it queer
To stop without a farmhouse near
Between the woods and frozen lake
The darkest evening of the year.

He gives his harness bells a shake
10
To ask if there is some mistake.
The only other sound's the sweep
Of easy wind and downy flake.

The woods are lovely, dark and deep,
But I have promises to keep,

15   And miles to go before I sleep,
             And miles to go before I sleep.
                         —Robert Frost [1923]

At first we are inclined to take the last line literally: the narrator must not
linger because his trip home is a long one, and presumably he is already late.
But, when repeated, the line attains an emphasis that makes this literal interpretation unsatisfactory. We may then ask ourselves a number of questions: What
"promises" might go unkept because of this sojourn in the woods? What have
the dark woods to do with "sleep?" And, finally, what kind of sleep is the
poet talking about? The literal interpretation of the lines seems too mundane
to accept the emphasis that Frost's repetition suggests, and we are tempted
to look for additional meaning. The "promises to keep" perhaps suggest the
whole burden of life's obligations, while the dark woods may be a bittersweet
symbol of escape from these responsibilities into fantasy, fairyland, or premature
death. And the final word "sleep," when repeated, assumes a greater finality
because we know that our final sleep is death itself. The simple repetition of
a line thus encourages us to change our interpretation of the entire poem,
affecting both its denotation and symbolism.

Frost achieves a different transformation of meaning by repeating the word
"white" in the first three lines of his sonnet "Design":

             I found a dimpled spider, fat and white,
             On a white heal-all, holding up a moth
             Like a white piece of rigid satin cloth—

By repeating the word "white" he focuses our attention on it. Nothing obliged
Frost to repeat himself; adjectives like *pallid, bleached, sallow, wan, hoary,* and
pale are roughly synonymous and could have introduced the variety in style
and imagery that ordinarily is desirable in a poem. But each of these alternatives
suggests a slightly different shade of white and each carries a slightly different
connotation. Only by repeating the *same* word can Frost make the point that
the colors are identical. The blighted flower has perfectly concealed the hideous
albino spider, and the single white flower in a field of blue has, presumably,
enticed the moth into the trap. The incident is remarkable because of its improb-
ability and suggests to the poet that this eerie nighttime rendezvous may have
been foreordained. The repetition of "white," a color associated with both
innocence and death, builds in the reader a foreboding of evil design, a bleak
and blighted destiny in which even the purest of colors can serve the purposes
of darkness.

**In stanzaic poetry and ballads, repetition is often introduced in the form
of a *refrain*, or chorus. The refrain generally occurs at the close of a stanza,
where it helps to establish meter, influence mood, or add emphasis.** A refrain
may be identical in each stanza or it may vary in subtle but important ways
during the course of the poem. An example of the effective use of a refrain
is found in Rudyard Kipling's "Recessional":

RECESSIONAL

             God of our fathers, known of old,
                 Lord of our far-flung battle-line,
             Beneath whose awful Hand we hold
                 Dominion over palm and pine—

5   Lord God of Hosts, be with us yet,
       Lest we forget—lest we forget!

       The tumult and the shouting dies;
           The captains and the kings depart:
       Still stands Thine ancient sacrifice,
10   An humble and a contrite heart.
       Lord God of Hosts, be with us yet,
       Lest we forget—lest we forget!

       Far-called, our navies melt away;
           On dune and headland sinks the fire:
15   Lo, all our pomp of yesterday
           Is one with Nineveh and Tyre![1]
       Judge of nations, spare us yet,
       Lest we forget—lest we forget!

       If, drunk with sight of power, we loose
20   Wild tongues that have not Thee in awe,
       Such boastings as the Gentiles[2] use,
           Or lesser breeds without the Law—
       Lord God of Hosts, be with us yet,
       Lest we forget—lest we forget!

25   For heathen heart that puts her trust
           In reeking tube and iron shard,
       All valiant dust that builds on dust,
           And guarding, calls not Thee to guard,
       For frantic boast and foolish word—
30   Thy mercy on Thy people, Lord!
                         —Rudyard Kipling [1897]

A recessional is a hymn sung at the end of a religious service to signal the stately withdrawal of the priest and choir. Kipling's "Recessional," however, was not intended as a contribution to Anglican church music. It was written at the end of the festivities commemorating Queen Victoria's Diamond Jubilee, in her sixtieth year on the throne of England, and it reflects Kipling's emotions as he contemplates the end of an era. In 1897 Great Britain still governed an extensive empire, but her colonial power had already been challenged by the Sepoy rebellion in India and the Boer War in South Africa. Kipling was born in India and had sympathy for the native population, even though he endorsed the ideals of English colonial government. As we will see, Kipling's poem expresses the complexity of his attitudes and, in doing so, draws on many of the literary devices we have discussed earlier. Behind the celebration of the Diamond Jubilee—behind even Kipling's expression of faith in God—we sense in the poem a prophetic lament for the decline of a once glorious empire.

Three of the poem's five stanzas contain an identical two-line refrain:

       Lord God of Hosts, be with us yet,
       Lest we forget—lest we forget!

[1] Nineveh and Tyre: Prosperous Old Testament cities destroyed by God because of their impiety.
[2] Gentiles: Any persons who are not Jewish. Here used to mean anyone who does not believe in the true faith as, for example, the inhabitants of Nineveh and Tyre.

The contribution of this refrain to the meaning of the poem depends in part on its literary allusions, in part on the meaning of the words themselves, and in part on repetition. The phrase "Lord God of Hosts" or "Lord of Hosts" occurs frequently in the Bible, especially in the passages describing the destruction of Nineveh by heathen hordes and God's subsequent warnings against impiety. The analogy with the British empire is obvious. Apart from these Biblical allusions, Kipling's two-line refrain combines both a prayer and a warning: a prayer for God's continuing presence in the hearts of Englishmen and an implicit warning about the consequences of neglecting Him. The repetition of "lest we forget" in the second line of the refrain makes this warning all the more solemn. Thus, the refrain and the repetition within it not only add an air of solemnity and piety to the mood of the poem, but also underscore the slight differences in the refrain of the third stanza and the radical differences in the last stanza. As it happens, these stanzas present us with important clues to the meaning of the poem, clues best discussed in the context of *ambiguity*.

   The use of a word or phrase in such a way as to give it two or more competing meanings is called *ambiguity*. In many instances, ambiguity is both a stylistic flaw and an annoyance because it creates confusion. In fact, the famous "Charge of the Light Brigade," immortalized in verse by Alfred Lord Tennyson, would never have taken place were it not for an ambiguity in Lord Raglan's orders to the commander in the field, Lord Lucan: "Lord Raglan wishes the cavalry to advance rapidly to the front, and try to prevent the enemy carrying away the guns." Unfortunately, as Tennyson pointed out, there were cannon to the right of them, cannon to the left of them, and cannon straight ahead. When the baffled Lord Lucan asked *which* guns were meant, the officer who had delivered the order frowned, pointed vaguely into the valley, and said sharply, "There, my Lord, is your enemy. There are your guns." With more courage than common sense, the Light Brigade charged the most distant guns—into the pages of history. As a result of ambiguity in the initial orders, of the 673 horsemen who entered the valley, only 195 returned.

   As was the case in Lord Raglan's order, **ambiguity is often a result of imprecise wording. Other forms of ambiguity involve a play on the dual meanings of a particular word or a particular syntactic structure.** As an example of the former, let us say that you are driving a friend home for the first time. As you approach an intersection, you ask, "Which way? Left?"

   "Right!" your companion replies.

   No exercise of logic can tell you whether the word *Right* here means "That is correct, turn left!" or "No! Turn right!" Only more information can clarify your friend's meaning.

   Most cases of ambiguity involve a similar play on the meanings of a particular word, but it is also possible to have syntactic ambiguity—that is, ambiguity caused by the ordering of words. For example, there is a story that when Pyrrhus, the king of Epirus, consulted the oracle at Delphi before going into battle, he was encouraged by the prophesy that "Pyrrhus the Romans shall conquer," which he interpreted as meaning that he, Pyrrhus, would prove victorious. The Romans, however, were also encouraged because the sentence seemed to them equivalent to "The Romans shall conquer Pyrrhus." The actual battle demonstrated that the ambiguity of the oracle was appropriate. Although Pyrrhus won the field, he did so at such a cost that he was recorded as saying, "Another such victory, and we are lost." This battle, by the way, gave rise to the phrase *Pyrrhic victory*, which in itself incorporates the paradox (a form of ambiguity) of a costly and thus undesirable victory.

As the preceding example illustrates, **ambiguity can be used by a careful writer to increase the subtlety, impact, and concision of an expression. It can conceal truths that are only superficially contradictory** (as in the oracle's prophesy), **display an honest ambivalence, expand poetic meaning, or create humor or shock.**

Ambivalence and expanded meaning are both revealed in Kipling's "Recessional." Here the ambiguity is not created by a single word with contradictory meanings, but rather by the dual interpretations that the poem as a whole invites. Each stanza is appropriate to the occasion of Victoria's Diamond Jubilee, at the end of which the captains and the kings depart, the naval vessels return to their normal duties, the celebratory bonfires die into embers, and the satisfied English masses boast of the national might. But at the same time each stanza can also be interpreted as a comment on the future of the empire, and it is precisely this prophetic element that makes the poem so memorable.

This duality of meaning is not forced on us until the third stanza. If by the lines, "Far-called, our navies melt away;/ On dune and headland sinks the fire," Kipling is referring to the dispersal of ships after the naval display on the Thames and to the fading of bonfires, then surely he is exaggerating when he says, "Lo, all our pomp of yesterday/ Is one with Nineveh and Tyre." The end of a celebration is scarcely like the annihilation of these two biblical cities and their civilizations. And surely his prayer, "Judge of Nations, spare us yet,/ Lest we forget—lest we forget!" is nonsensical because nothing about the close of the Jubilee directly suggests the fall of the British empire.

In order to make sense of the stanza we must interpret it *figuratively*, paying as much attention to connotation as to denotation. It is true that the bonfires of the Jubilee were set on England's "dune and headland," but these words are equally applicable to the extremities of the empire—Egypt, India, and Africa. In discussions of empires, a "fire" or conflagration may be used to describe a minor uprising, such as the Indian Mutiny of 1857, the first Boer War in 1881, or the British defeat at Khartoum in 1885. All of these well-publicized "fires" along the outskirts of the British empire occurred during the years preceding Victoria's Diamond Jubilee. Furthermore, in primitive regions, the campfire is the symbol of civilization, which staves off encroaching savagery. The sinking fire, when accompanied by allusions to the fall of Nineveh and Tyre, thus suggests unrest and upheaval along the fringes of the empire. The same suggestion is included in the preceding line, "Far-called, our navies melt away"—especially because melting (as with ice) is ordinarily an irreversible process. By implication, the strength of a navy that melts away is permanently diminished. Furthermore, "far-called" is not quite the same as "widely deployed." Kipling's term suggests that the navy has been called into action rather than merely reassigned to simple peace-keeping missions.

After Kipling has drawn our attention to his intentional ambiguity in this third stanza, we may turn with renewed interest to the earlier stanzas. If we pursue Kipling's allusions to Nineveh and Tyre by reading in the Bible Chapters 26–28 of Ezekiel and Chapters 1–3 of Nahum, we discover that Nineveh, like England, had "multiplied [her] merchants above the stars of heaven" and that her "crowned are as the locusts, and [her] captains as the great grasshoppers, which camp in the hedges in the cold day, but when the sun ariseth they flee away." Suddenly Kipling's simple statement that "the captains and the kings depart" takes on ominous connotations. No longer is this just a reference to their return to other duties after the Diamond Jubilee; now it has become a prophesy of their unreliability during future upheavals in the empire.

Similarly, the expression "Lord God of Hosts" becomes ambiguous as the poem progresses and as we begin to track down Kipling's Biblical allusions. In the first stanza it seems obvious that God is on England's side. He is, after all, "Lord of our far-flung battle-line." His "Hosts" are the hordes of British soldiers and loyal Indian sepoys who have long and successfully defended the empire. But again, after reading the Bible, we discover that the "Lord of Hosts" destroys Tyre by raising up in revolt "the terrible of nations." Like England, Tyre had been a great sea power but eventually had begun to boast, "I am a God, and I sit in the midst of the seas." These boasts, like those Kipling admonishes in the fourth and fifth stanzas, were made by men "drunk with sight of power" who put their trust in "reeking tube and iron shard" (guns and bullets) instead of in God. Their fate was to be swallowed up by the "lesser breeds without the law" and this is exactly what Kipling fears may happen to England. Thus, in commemorating Queen Victoria's Diamond Jubilee, Kipling has written what he fears may prove to be the empire's dirge. He is obviously ambivalent—torn between his pride in the "far-flung battle-line" and his shame in the "reeking tube and iron shard" that maintain it. This ambivalence laps at his consciousness like the waves of a rising tide through the repetitions of the word "lest," meaning "for fear that . . . for fear that!" Eventually his fears predominate and he bursts out with the concluding prayer:

> For frantic boast and foolish word—
> Thy mercy on thy people, Lord!

Poems for Further Study

DESERT PLACES

Snow falling and night falling fast, oh, fast
In a field I looked into going past,
And the ground almost covered smooth in snow,
But a few weeds and stubble showing last.

5 The woods around it have it—it is theirs.
All animals are smothered in their lairs.
I am too absent-spirited to count;
The loneliness includes me unawares.

And lonely as it is that loneliness
10 Will be more lonely ere it will be less—
A blanker whiteness of benighted[3] snow
With no expression, nothing to express.

They cannot scare me with their empty spaces
Between stars—on stars where no human race is.

[3] Overtaken by darkness or night.

15   I have it in me so much nearer home
            To scare myself with my own desert places.

                              —Robert Frost [1936]

❦ QUESTIONS ❦

1.   As in "Stopping by Woods on a Snowy Evening" (page 641), the solitary speaker pauses near nightfall to watch the woods fill up with snow. How is the speaker's situation and attitude different in "Desert Places"?

2.   Why is the field emphasized in this poem and why is the woods emphasized in the other?

3.   What difference does it make that the speaker is absolutely alone in this poem and accompanied by a horse in the other?

4.   In "Stopping by Woods on a Snowy Evening" Frost continually suggests interactions between the speaker and the owner of the land, between the speaker and his horse, and between the speaker and those to whom he has made promises. Are there any interactions in "Desert Places"? Indeed, are there any people, animals, or objects with which the speaker can interact?

5.   Why does Frost describe the animals as "smothered in their lairs" (l. 6)? Why does he not provide antecedents for any of the *it*'s in line 5— "The woods around it have it—it is theirs"? Why does he not provide an antecedent for *they* in line 13—"They cannot scare me with their empty spaces"?

6.   Lines 11–12 suggest that the snow will have "no expression, nothing to express." Would one expect snow to have something to express? Could the speaker now be describing his own loneliness?

7.   Where are the speaker's "own desert places"? What is he afraid of? How can he—indeed how does he—combat his fear?

8.   Frost uses repetition frequently in this poem—particularly in lines 1, 5, 8 through 10, and 12. Analyze the effects of the repetition in each of these instances.

BOTH SIDES NOW

            Bows and flows of angel hair,
            And ice cream castles in the air,
            And feather canyons ev'rywhere,
            I've looked at clouds that way.
5   But now they only block the sun,
            They rain and snow on ev'ryone.
            So many things I would have done.
            But clouds got in my way.
            I've looked at clouds from both sides now,
10   From up and down and still somehow

It's cloud illusions I recall;
I really don't know clouds
At all.

15 Moons and Junes and ferris wheels,
The dizzy dancing way you feel,
As ev'ry fairy tale comes real,
I've looked at love that way.
But now it's just another show,
You leave 'em laughing when you go.
20 And if you care, don't let them know,
Don't give yourself away.
I've looked at love from both sides now,
From give and take and still somehow
It's love's illusions I recall;
25 I really don't know love
At all.

Tears and fears and feeling proud,
To say "I love you" right out loud,
Dreams and schemes and circus crowds,
30 I've looked at life that way.
But now old friends are acting strange,
They shake their heads, they say I've changed.
But something's lost but something's gained,
In living ev'ry day.
35 I've looked at life from both sides now,
From win and lose and still somehow
It's life's illusions I recall;
I really don't know life
At all.

—Joni Mitchell [1967]

❧ QUESTIONS ❧

1. Mitchell's song is divided into three stanzas. What is the subject of each stanza? Consider the development from one stanza to another. What is implied about the changes in the speaker's age and point of view as the poem unfolds?

2. Consider the structure of each stanza. What three divisions of thought are repeated in each stanza? What do these sections within each stanza tell us about the growth and development of the speaker?

3. Each stanza includes a refrain, but the refrains are not all identical. What does the refrain contribute to the meaning of each stanza and how do the slight changes in the refrain help to develop Mitchell's theme? What major statement do you think she wishes to make about life and illusions?

5

✄✄✄✄✄

Puns and Paradoxes

THE PUN

An ambiguous statement that is intended to be humorous is called a *pun*. Puns almost invariably attain their effect by using one of the thousands of word pairs in English (called homonyms) that are identical in sound and spelling but differ in meaning. If, for example, a woman tells us she knows nothing of labor, she has either never borne children or never held down a job, depending on whether she is using *labor* to mean "the pains and efforts of childbirth" or "employment." **A pun that is risqué or sexually suggestive is called *double entendre*** (a French phrase meaning "to understand in two ways").

Shakespeare uses *double entendre* with exuberance in the final couplet of Sonnet CXLIII:

CXLIII

Lo, as a careful housewife runs to catch
One of her feathered creatures broke away,
Sets down her babe, and makes all swift dispatch
In pursuit of the thing she would have stay;
5   Whilst her neglected child holds her in chase,
Cries to catch her whose busy care is bent
To follow that which flies before her face,
Not prizing her poor infant's discontent:
So runn'st thou after that which flies from thee,
10   Whilst I thy babe chase thee afar behind;
But if thou catch thy hope, turn back to me,
And play the mother's part, kiss me, be kind;
So will I pray that thou mayst have thy "Will,"
If thou turn back and my loud crying still.
          —William Shakespeare [ca. 1600]

43

If we have read Shakespeare's other sonnets (particularly, numbers CXXXIII, CXXXIV, CXLII, and CXLIV), we know that this one is addressed to the famous "woman colour'd ill," with whom he is in love; we also know that she is in love with Shakespeare's friend, "a man right fair." The first twelve lines of the poem carefully prepare us for the concluding couplet. The dark lady is compared with a housewife who chases after a "feathered" creature (presumably a cock or hen, but possibly also a fashionable, "feathered" courtier),[1] while her "neglected child" (Shakespeare) chases after her. Thus, the phrase "have thy 'Will' " may mean:

> So I will pray that thou mayst recapture the hen
> If thou turn back and my loud crying still.

But the original phrase "have thy will," when applied to relations between the sexes, may also mean to "satisfy one's lust"; and finally, to "have thy 'Will' " may mean—rather shockingly—that "Will" Shakespeare is prepared to tolerate his mistress's sexual infidelities so long as she returns to him afterward. In effect, Shakespeare has created a *triple entendre!*

THE PARADOX

Just as a pun is a form of ambiguity that plays on words, a paradox plays on *ideas*. When Mark Twain wrote, for example, that soap and education are less sudden than a massacre but more deadly in the long run, he was using a paradox. He expected his readers to recognize that, although the analogy is literally untrue, it would pass for truth with anyone who has seen the anguish of a schoolboy forced to wash or sit still. The paradox turns on the difference between physical death and the "deadly fear" of soap or the "deadly boredom" of school, and it alludes to the death of imagination that sometimes results from the "civilizing" influence of soap and education. Thus, **a *paradox* is a statement that is true in some sense, even though at first it appears self-contradictory and absurd. When a paradox is expressed in only two words (living death, wise fool, etc.) it is called an *oxymoron*.**

Paradoxes are used in poetry for at least three reasons. First, they invariably startle the reader. They are unexpected and, initially, inexplicable. Next, paradoxes involve the reader in an effort at understanding. And finally, if that effort is successful, each paradox delights the reader with a personal sense of discovery. **Like allegory and metaphor, a paradox requires the reader to participate intellectually in the creation of literary meaning.** Without this active participation, a paradox is simply incomprehensible.

In the sonnet "Design" (p. 632) Frost builds toward a paradox by lulling us into complacency with his fluid and unanswerable rhetorical questions:

> What had that flower to do with being white,
> The wayside blue and innocent heal-all?
> What brought the kindred spider to that height,
> Then steered the white moth thither in the night?

---

[1] The phrase *"feathered creatures"* is, therefore, *ambiguous* and can serve as one more example of that rhetorical device.

Then, just as we are beginning to reassure ourselves that such incidents may be the result of pure happenstance, Frost startles us by suggesting a paradoxical solution:

> What but design of darkness to appall?—
> If design govern in a thing so small.

According to Frost, the appalling congruence of whites in the poem is the "design of darkness." At first, perhaps, our intellects rebel against the paradox that darkness controls these three white objects—it is, after all, a little nonsensical. But Frost's intention is to hint at the possibility that malevolence or evil lurks beneath the otherwise orderly surface of the natural world. By creating the paradox of a darkness that transforms the purest of whites into "assorted characters of death and blight," he makes us question our faith in the eventual triumph of good over evil.

In general, a paradox involves a contradiction between the physical or material meaning of words and their spiritual, emotional, or supernatural connotation, as in the case of Frost's poem. Such contradictory connotations also govern Mark Twain's lighthearted paradox, for soap and education are emotionally, but not physically, painful. Because paradoxes are capable of playing on the contrasts between earthly and spiritual truths, they are particularly common in religious revelations. In the ancient *Upanishads* of India (the chief theological documents of Hinduism), we learn, for instance, that "the gods love the obscure and hate the obvious." And the *Katha Upanishad* contains a number of paradoxes that raise questions about the interrelationship among mind, matter, and reality:

> If the slayer thinks he slays,
> If the slain thinks he is slain,
> Both these do not understand:
> He slays not, is not slain.
> —From the *Katha Upanishad*
> [700–600 B.C.]

Similarly, Taoism, a Chinese religion that dates back more than 2,000 years, teaches that

> One may know the world without going out of doors.
> One may see the Way of Heaven without looking through the windows.
> The further one goes, the less one knows.
> Therefore the sage knows without going about,
> Understands without seeing,
> And accomplishes without any action.
> —From *The Way of Lao-tzu* [600–200 B.C.]

Later, in the Gospel according to St. John, 11:25–6, we find Jesus saying,

> I am the resurrection, and the life: he that believeth in me, though he were dead, yet shall he live:
> And whosoever liveth and believeth in me shall never die.
> —From the *New Testament* [first century A.D.]

In each case the paradox is initially disconcerting, or at least difficult to understand; however, each ultimately extends to us the principal consolation of religion: the faith in an existence that is more permanent and more attractive than the nasty, brutish, and short life sometimes said to be allotted to ordinary man.

Pure paradoxes, involving wholly contradictory ideas, are relatively uncommon in poetry. However, *incongruity,* a similar rhetorical device, is plentiful. **A word, a phrase, or an idea is said to be incongruous when it is out of keeping, inconsistent, or inappropriate in its particular surroundings.** As was the case with ambiguity, incongruity is sometimes a stylistic flaw—a sign of sloppy thinking or imprecise writing—but when used carefully, it can subtly change the meaning of the surrounding words. When Byron wrote about amatory poets who "sing their loves/ In liquid lines mellifluously bland," he relied on the incongruity of the word "bland" to indicate his satiric disapproval of most love poetry. Byron knew very well that bland writing, like bland food, is usually dull or tasteless—the very opposite of the spicy passion one would expect to find in love poetry. This startling word choice hits us like a slap in the face when we have been expecting a gentle goodnight kiss and effectively conveys Byron's distaste for conventional love poetry.

Poems for Further Study

"WHOSO LIST TO HUNT, I KNOW WHERE IS AN HIND"[2]

Whoso list° to hunt, I know where is an hind!   *wishes*
But as for me, helas!° I may no more!   *alas*
The vain travail° hath wearied me so sore,   *labor*
I am of them that furthest come behind!
5   Yet may I, by no means, my wearied mind
    Draw from the deer! but as she fleeth afore,
    Fainting I follow. I leave off therefore,
Since in a net I seek to hold the wind!
Who list her hunt, I put him out of doubt,
10   As well as I, may spend his time in vain!
    And graven with diamonds, in letters plain,
There is written, her fair neck round about,
    'Noli me tangere![3] *for CÆSAR's I am;*
And wild for to hold, though I seem tame.'

—Sir Thomas Wyatt [posthumous, 1557]

---

[2] Adapted from Petrarch, *Rime,* sonnet 190.
[3] "Touch me not!" Wyatt's sonnet is thought to refer to the situation of Anne Boleyn (1507–1536) in whom Wyatt took an interest both before and after her liaison with Henry VIII (1491–1547).

❦ QUESTIONS ❦

1.   What is the literal situation described in the poem? What has the speaker been hunting? Why is he wearied? What advice does he give to the reader?

2.   How does Wyatt's pun involving the word *deer* give to the poem a second—and more scandalous—meaning? How do the various elements in the poem (the hunt, the hind, the vain travail, the diamond necklace, the reference to Caesar, and the final warning) all fit this second reading?

3.   How do the connotations of the hunt serve to characterize both the speaker and the woman he pursues?

4.   What do you make of the paradox of seeking to hold the wind in a net? How well does that paradox describe the situation of a man on the verge of abandoning his pursuit of a fleet-footed deer? How well does it fit the situation of one who is despairing of success in an illicit love affair with a married woman?

THE MAN HE KILLED

"Had he and I but met
By some old ancient inn,
We should have sat us down to wet
Right many a nipperkin![4]

5
"But ranged as infantry,
And staring face to face,
I shot at him as he at me,
And killed him in his place.

"I shot him dead because—
10
Because he was my foe,
Just so: my foe of course he was;
That's clear enough; although

"He thought he'd 'list, perhaps,
Off-hand like—just as I—
15
Was out of work—had sold his traps—
No other reason why.

"Yes; quaint and curious war is!
You shoot a fellow down
You'd treat if met where any bar is,
20
Or help to half-a-crown."

—Thomas Hardy [1909]

[4] Half-pint of beer or ale.

❧ QUESTIONS ❧

1.   What paradox about warfare is at the heart of this poem? Does Hardy explain and resolve the paradox or simply bring it to your attention?

2.   How does the repetition in the third stanza affect the poem's tone?

3.   The speaker in this poem is a common soldier. What were his motives for enlisting? What is his attitude toward "the enemy"?

4.   Why does Hardy avoid any mention of the reasons for the warfare? Do you think he is being fair or merely manipulating the reader? Explain your position.

Irony

The term *irony* **refers to a contrast or discrepancy between appearance and reality.** This discrepancy can take on a number of different forms.

In *dramatic irony* **the state of affairs known to the audience (or reader) is the reverse of what its participants suppose it to be.** This is the form of irony used in *King Oedipus*. When the action of the play begins, Oedipus believes that, by fleeing his homeland as a youth, he has evaded the prophesy that he will murder his father and marry his mother. The audience knows, however, that he has already committed these crimes. (The audience's knowledge derives in part from the fact that Sophocles was writing about a widely known Theban legend and in part from the prophecies made by the oracle Tiresias early in the play.) Thus, the tragic impact of *King Oedipus* depends largely on our fascination with the plight of a man who is unaware of his own past, unable to avoid his own destiny, and driven remorselessly toward his fate by his very efforts to avoid it.

In *situational irony* **a set of circumstances turns out to be the reverse of what is appropriate or expected.** Richard Cory, the "hero" of Edwin Arlington Robinson's poem, is widely envied and admired because of his wealth, his charm, and his apparently agreeable life. Everything about him leads the "people on the pavement"—and the reader as well—to assume that he must be happy. He is "a gentleman from sole to crown," "clean favored," "quietly arrayed," and "richer than a king." In a world polarized between rich and poor, beautiful and plain, dignified and common, "them" and "us," Richard Cory seems without question to be "one of them," until the last lines of the poem show us otherwise:

RICHARD CORY

Whenever Richard Cory went down town,
We people on the pavement looked at him:

He was a gentleman from sole to crown,
Clean favored, and imperially slim.

5   And he was always quietly arrayed,
And he was always human when he talked;
But still he fluttered pulses when he said;
"Good-morning," and he glittered when he walked.

And he was rich—yes, richer than a king—
10   And admirably schooled in every grace:
In fine, we thought that he was everything
To make us wish that we were in his place.

So on we worked, and waited for the light,
And went without the meat, and cursed the bread;
15   And Richard Cory, one calm summer night,
Went home and put a bullet through his head.
                    —Edwin Arlington Robinson [1897]

Henry David Thoreau once wrote that "the mass of men lead lives of quiet desperation." Ironically, Richard Cory's suicide suggests that he was, after all, "one of us."

The most common form of irony, *verbal irony,* **involves a contrast between what is literally said and what is actually meant.** Lord Byron wittily uses this figure of speech to satirize religious hypocrisy in explaining that a serious illness has made him pious—presumably because of the usual fear of dying unrepentant:

The first attack at once proved the Divinity
    (But that I never doubted, nor the Devil);
The next, the Virgin's mystical virginity;
    The third, the usual Origin of Evil;
The fourth at once established the whole Trinity
    On so uncontrovertible a level
That I devoutly wished the three were four,
On purpose to believe so much the more.
                    —From *Don Juan,* Lord Byron [1823]

Verbal irony always requires the reader to detect the discrepancy between the denotative meaning of the words and the author's intention in using them—in this case, between Byron's *claim* that he wished the three persons of the Trinity were four and his *purpose* in satirizing death-bed piety. Thus, verbal irony is the riskiest of all poetic devices because there is always the possibility that the author's intentions will go unrecognized. In 1702, for example, Daniel Defoe, who was himself a Puritan "dissenter," anonymously wrote an essay called "The Shortest Way with the Dissenters," in which he tried to satirize the excessive zeal of his Anglican opponents by ironically contending that Puritan ministers should be hanged and all members of their congregations banished. To his surprise, no one perceived the irony: the Anglican establishment fully endorsed his proposals. Public unrest followed, the government intervened, and Defoe was fined, pilloried, and imprisoned—all because his irony was so badly misunderstood.

Jonathan Swift, Defoe's contemporary, escaped a similar misunderstanding by making his ironic exaggerations so extreme that no one could miss the point and take them seriously. In 1729, when he wanted to draw the attention of the Anglican government to the plight of starving Catholic children, he published *A Modest Proposal for Preventing the Children of Poor People in Ireland from Being a Burden to Their Parents or Country, and for Making Them Beneficial to the Public.* In this pamphlet he suggested that they be fattened, slaughtered, and sold as a delicacy like veal:

A child will make two dishes at an entertainment for friends; and when the family dines alone, the fore or hind quarter will make a reasonable dish, and seasoned with a little pepper or salt will be very good boiled on the fourth day, especially in winter.

—From *A Modest Proposal,* Jonathan Swift [1729]

In using such overstatement to ridicule the government's disregard of the sufferings of the Irish Catholics, Swift hoped to force a change in British policy. Just as a surgeon's blade cuts so that it may cure, Swift's language is corrosive so that it may be corrective. **Writing** such as this, **which holds up persons, ideas, or things to varying degrees of ridicule or contempt in order to bring about some desirable change, is known as** *satire.*

Swift, Defoe, and Byron all sought to underscore and identify their ironies through exaggeration or *overstatement* (sometimes called *hyperbole*). Each hoped that the reader would perceive the exaggeration and therefore interpret the text as meaning the opposite of what it appeared to say. Swift really recommended Christian charity, not infanticide; Defoe really endorsed Christian tolerance, not narrow bigotry; and Byron really advocated Deism or agnosticism, not hypocritical piety.

The other principal means by which poets signal irony is *understatement*—as when J. Alfred Prufrock, the protagonist of T. S. Eliot's famous poem, sadly reflects in a moment of self-disparagement that he has "measured out [his] life with coffee spoons." Just as overstatement is too emphatic, too exuberant, or too harsh, an understatement is too mild or too reserved. In both cases the reader's attention is arrested and his sensitivity to potential irony heightened because the poet's words are literally unbelievable.

Understated irony is often sarcastic. Unlike satire, *sarcasm* **(from the Greek word** *sarkazein* **meaning "to tear flesh") is intended to hurt, not heal.** Prufrock's bitter reflections about his life are often sarcastic. For a more modern and clearer example of sarcasm, consider Sir Winston Churchill's characterization of his political rival, Clement Atlee (Prime Minister of England, 1949–1951): "a very modest man—and with reason." Sarcasm, however, is not always so understated. Oscar Wilde, the nineteenth-century English novelist and dramatist, for example, was obviously exaggerating when he sarcastically claimed that "there are two ways of disliking poetry: one way is to dislike it, the other is to read Pope."

Although we have suggested that both overstatement and understatement often signal irony, it is wise to remember that they are not invariably ironic. Overstatement is especially susceptible to use and abuse in everyday speech by those who hope to be vivacious and enthusiastic. It is the linguistic equivalent of a facile smile. Thus, we sometimes exclaim, "How time flies!" when we mean, "it's getting late"; or, when we meet someone for the first time, we may say, "I'm delighted to meet you!" when we mean only, "Hello." Sometimes poets also overstate the truth as a means of showing enthusiasm; but, they, of course, find fresh and original ways of revitalizing tired hyperbolic formulas. Andrew Marvell expresses the idea of time flying by writing in "To His Coy Mistress" (1681),

> But ever at my back I hear
> Time's winged chariot hurrying near.

And Dr. Faustus, in Christopher Marlowe's play of that name (1589), greets Helen of Troy, not with a lame "pleased to meet you," but with a rhetorical question that combines metonymy and overstatement in an expression of sheer rapture:

> Was this the face that launched a thousand ships,
> And burnt the topless towers of Ilium?

Indeed, it may be that exuberance and a delight in words are the fundamental qualities of poetry. Poetry, it has been said, is what is lost in translation. The poet's use of ambiguity, irony, puns, and paradoxes depends almost entirely on the fact that certain words have multiple meanings. A skilled poet is almost by definition sensitive to the specific denotations and connotations of each word at his or her command. A poet knows that any change in word choice is a change in poetic meaning; that any attempt to translate, paraphrase, or summarize a poem is also an attempt to rewrite it—an act that inevitably damages its essence. Even the gentlest touch can be destructive. One cannot, even in admiration, stretch out the wings of the monarch butterfly without brushing the gold from their tips.

But if, in criticism as in entomology, we murder to dissect, what we murder through literary criticism is imperishable. After we have learned all we can from dissection, we have only to turn away from the battered specimen on the critic's pages—we have only to turn back to the poem itself—in order to find our monarch butterfly both alive and made more beautiful by understanding.

Poems for Further Study

OZYMANDIAS[1]

> I met a traveller from an antique land
> Who said: "Two vast and trunkless legs of stone
> Stand in the desert. Near them, on the sand,
> Half sunk, a shattered visage lies, whose frown,
> And wrinkled lip, and sneer of cold command,
> Tell that its sculptor well those passions read
> Which yet survive, stamped on these lifeless things,
> The hand that mocked them and the heart that fed.[2]
> And on the pedestal these words appear—

5

[1] The Greek name for Ramses II, a king of Egypt in the thirteenth century B.C.
[2] "Hand" and "heart" are the direct objects of the verb "survive." The sneering passions shown in the sculpture have outlived the hand of the artist and the heart of Ozymandias.

10   'My name is Ozymandias, king of kings:
Look on my works, ye mighty, and despair!'
Nothing beside remains. Round the decay
Of that colossal wreck, boundless and bare
The lone and level sands stretch far away."

—Percy Bysshe Shelley [1818]

❧ QUESTIONS ❧

1. What can you tell about the personality of Ozymandias from the expression on his sculpted face and from the size of the sculpture? What can you tell about the sculptor?

2. What forms of irony are used in this poem? What conclusion about the durability of human achievements do you think Shelley wishes us to reach?

3. What attitude toward kings is implicitly conveyed in this poem? (If possible, do some background reading about Shelley himself and the times in which he lived.)

4. Consider the structure of the poem. What is the main subject of the first eight lines? How is that subject slightly changed and developed in the last six lines?

"IS MY TEAM PLOWING"

"Is my team ploughing,
    That I was used to drive
And hear the harness jingle
    When I was man alive?"

5   Ay, the horses trample,
    The harness jingles now;
No change though you lie under
    The land you used to plough.

"Is football playing
10   Along the river shore,
With lads to chase the leather,
    Now I stand up no more?"

Ay, the ball is flying,
    The lads play heart and soul;
15   The goal stands up, the keeper
Stands up to keep the goal.

"Is my girl happy,
    That I thought hard to leave,

And has she tired of weeping
20   As she lies down at eve?"

Ay, she lies down lightly,
   She lies not down to weep:
Your girl is well contented.
   Be still, my lad, and sleep.

25   "Is my friend hearty,
   Now I am thin and pine,
And has he found to sleep in
   A better bed than mine?"

Yes, lad, I lie easy,
30   I lie as lads would choose;
I cheer a dead man's sweetheart,
   Never ask me whose.

          —A. E. Housman [1896]

———————— ❀ QUESTIONS ❀ ————————

1. What do you know about each of the two speakers in this poem?

2. What reassurance does the first speaker seem to desire and receive?

3. Discuss the use of ambiguity and *double entendre* in the living friend's responses during the second half of the poem. How are these responses ironic?

4. In answer to each of the dead man's questions about changes in the world, the living friend says in essence, "Everything remains as it was before you died; nothing has changed." Is he telling the truth?

5. Housman is often seen as a cynical poet. How and where does his cynicism show up in this poem?

7

Imagery

Words that call upon our senses are referred to as *images*. Images may appeal to any of our five senses and may be expressed in a single word, a phrase, a sentence, or even several sentences. Poets use imagery, for example, to paint a verbal picture of a calm mountain lake, to capture a fleeting birdsong, or to recall the odor of dead fish, the taste of champagne, or the feel of a wool sweater on bare skin. Notice how William Shakespeare uses imagery to capture the essence of spring and winter in the following poems from *Love's Labour's Lost* (1594):

[SPRING]

When daisies pied,° and violets blue,   *many-colored*
   And lady-smocks all silver white,
And cuckoo-buds, of yellow hue,
   Do paint the meadows with delight,
5   The cuckoo then on ev'ry tree
Mocks married men, for thus sings he;
           Cuckoo!
Cuckoo! cuckoo!—O word of fear,
Unpleasing to a married ear!

10   When shepherds pipe on oaten straws,°   *reed pipes*
   And merry larks are ploughmen's clocks,
When turtles tread° and rooks and daws,   *turtledoves mate*
   And maidens bleach their summer smocks;
The cuckoo then on every tree
15   Mocks married men, for thus sings he;

Cuckoo!
Cuckoo! Cuckoo!—O word of fear,
Unpleasing to a married ear!

—William Shakespeare [1594]

❧ QUESTIONS ❧

1. What is the predominant mood in the first four lines of each stanza? Where does the delight in spring seem to lead one and why is spring a season to be feared by married men?

2. Paraphrase line 4. Why is Shakespeare's highly figurative language more effective than an explicit, literal statement about the many-colored meadows?

3. What note of discord enters the poem in lines 5–9? How does this unexpected shift in the poem's direction reflect the poet's awareness both of the natural changes caused by spring and of the emotional changes that spring encourages? What connotations are suggested by the cuckoo's cry? Does this incongruity in the various ideas connoted by spring make the poem better or worse? Why?

4. Examine the poem's imagery. How much does the combination of visual and aural imagery contribute to its effectiveness? How much is added by the range of images (springtime flowers, birds, and people)?

5. What conventions of pastoral poetry play a part in the second stanza? Is the cuckoo's "word of fear" a part of the pastoral tradition or does it add a note of realism?

6. Why does Shakespeare break his metrical pattern in lines 7 and 16?

[WINTER]

When icicles hang by the wall,
  And Dick the shepherd blows his nail,
And Tom bears logs into the hall,
  And milk comes frozen home in pail;
5   When blood is nipt, and ways be foul,
  Then nightly sings the staring owl,
          Tu-whoo!
Tu-whit! tu-whoo! a merry note,
While greasy Joan doth keel° the pot.   *stir*

10   When all aloud the wind doth blow,
  And coughing drowns the parson's saw,°   *proverb*
And birds sit brooding in the snow,
  And Marian's nose looks red and raw;
When roasted crabs° hiss in the bowl,   *crabapples*
15   Then nightly sings the staring owl,

Tu-whoo!
Tu-whit! tu-whoo! a merry note,
While greasy Joan doth keel the pot.

—William Shakespeare [1594]

❧ QUESTIONS ❧

1. Compare this poem with "Spring." What similarities do you find in meter, rhyme scheme, and organization?

2. Why does Shakespeare use specific names—Dick, Tom, Joan, and Marian—in this poem, while he did not in "Spring"? What emotions and activities does Shakespeare wish you to see as being nearly universal in the spring? Are there any emotions or activities that he wishes you to believe are equally widespread in the winter?

3. Is the owl's cry really "a merry note"? What are the connotations of the owl's hooting? Why does Shakespeare use irony here?

4. Compare the imagery in "Winter" and "Spring." Which poem evokes a wider range of senses?

As Shakespeare's poems suggest, everything we know about the seasons of the year (not to mention the seasons in our lives and the phenomena of nature) is a result of what we have seen, heard, smelled, tasted, touched, and felt internally. Our senses provide the link between our minds and external reality. Sensations alone create for us the familiar world of men and women, mountains and valleys, lakes and rivers, physical pleasure and physical pain. So, too, with poetry. Poems without imagery are like a people without vision or hearing. Both exist in darkness and in silence, struggling for understanding in a world of inexpressible abstractions.

One of the achievements of mankind, of course, is the development of languages and systems of thought that allow us to intellectualize our experiences. When we read a poem we are actually declaring ourselves independent of the sensations of the moment. We call forth from our memories various sensual experiences or images. We rearrange those memories in the patterns suggested by the poet—patterns that often do not correspond with any of our actual experiences. In so doing, we participate in vicarious experiences. Images, therefore, are the windows through which we see (or imagine) how other men and women live, and love, and die. They enable us to make discoveries about ourselves, about others, and about the world in which we live.

To some extent, all words create images. The most abstract terms, as well as the most precise verbal pictures, require us to find meaning *in the words* by recollecting, however vaguely, experiences of our own in which we have read, heard, or used those words. Words such as *dragonfly, hollow,* and *heft* summon up fairly specific sensual responses based on sight, sound, and muscular exertion. We see mentally the bulbous eyes, the quivering wings, and the slim, hovering body of the dragonfly. We hear mentally the "hollow" sound of a voice in an empty room. We feel mentally a muscular play in the forearm and shoulder at the "heft" of a nine-iron, a favorite tennis racquet, or a crammed suitcase.

But if we replace these imagistic words with scientific or generic terms—if, that is, *dragonfly* becomes *insect, hollow* becomes *void,* and *heft* becomes *specific gravity*—suddenly our mental images are deflated, like limp balloons, because the new terms are mere abstractions divorced from physical sensation.

A good poet always searches for an exact image—an image with its own spicy taste, aroma, and appearance—in preference to the trite and overly general words or combinations of words served up like a tasteless pasta in sentimental verse. The difference between concrete, original imagery and imprecise, over-worked banality can be illustrated by comparing the first stanza of George Meredith's *Modern Love* with three stanzas on the same subject (the discovery of infidelity) in "Lady Byron's Reply to Lord Byron's 'Fare Thee Well' ":

> By this he knew she wept with waking eyes:
> That, at his hand's light quiver by her head,
> The strange low sobs that shook their common bed,
> Were called into her with a sharp surprise,
> And strangled mute, like little gaping snakes,
> Dreadfully venomous to him. She lay
> Stone-still, and the long darkness flowed away
> With muffled pulses. Then, as midnight makes
> Her giant heart of Memory and Tears
> Drink the pale drug of silence, and so beat
> Sleep's heavy measure, they from head to feet
> Were moveless, looking through their dead black years,
> By vain regret scrawled over the blank wall.
> Like sculptured effigies, they might be seen
> Upon their marriage-tomb, the sword between;
> Each wishing for the sword that severs all.
>   —From *Modern Love,* George Meredith [1862]

> Yes, farewell, farewell forever,
>   Thou thyself hast fix'd our doom,
> Bade hope's sweetest blossoms wither,
>   Never more for me to bloom.
>
>   .   .   .
>
> Wrapt in dreams of joy abiding
>   On thy breast my head hath lain,
> In thy love and truth confiding,
>   Bliss I cannot know again.
>
> When thy heart by me "glanc'd over"
>   First displayed the guilty stain,
> Would these eyes had closed forever,
>   Ne'er to weep thy crimes again.
>   —From "Lady Byron's Reply,"
>   Anonymous

Both poets describe their feelings of betrayal, but "Lady Byron's" hack work is entirely devoid of real action and imagery. It is made up of sentimental commonplaces whose only virtue is that we can understand them without bother-ing to think. Each line from "Yes, farewell, farewell forever" to "Ne'er to weep thy crimes again" deserves, and most likely gets, nothing more than an exasperated groan from readers who recognize that this "poet" has nothing new to say, nothing original to describe, no actions to represent, no knowledge of the world, and no understanding of poetic style beyond that which allows her to pull at the "throbbing heart-strings" of the most sentimental and imperceptive readers.

In contrast, Meredith's poetry is packed with specific sensory experiences. It is true that throughout the stanza the unhappy marriage partners lie almost motionless. But Meredith allows us to see the wife as she weeps with "waking eyes," to watch her reaction at "his hand's light quiver by her head," to hear and feel "the strange low sobs that shook their common bed," and perhaps even to taste the bitterness of "the pale drug of silence." Furthermore, a series of vivid phrases builds a sense of muscular tension: the wife's sobs were *"strangled mute"*; she *"lay stone still";* together they looked back on "dead black years,/ By vain regret *scrawled* over the blank wall."

Few poets find ways to call into play as many different senses as Meredith has in this stanza. Only the sense of smell is missing; and, as if to make up for the deficiency, Meredith manages to work an image of smell into his second stanza, where the wife's beauty sickens the husband, "as at breath of poison flowers." No doubt this exhaustive catalogue of sensory imagery is intentional. Meredith's purpose is to show that the subtle change in the relationship between the former lovers has uprooted their lives and left them unable to engage in any human experience without seeing it anew and finding in it signs of their own emotional distress.

Thus, Meredith makes a thematic point by showing that every sensation the couple feels is altered by their present unhappiness. The use of poetic imagery does far more than simply add vigor to his writing; and what is true of Meredith's poem is true of poetry in general. **Poets often choose their imagery according to some *principle of selection* and develop it with some meaningful pattern in mind.** In Meredith's case, the principle of selection is an attempt to convey the fact that all of the husband's senses have been altered by the discovery of his wife's infidelity. A second principle of selection is at work in Meredith's preoccupation throughout the poem with images of death. The first stanza alone makes reference to snakes, venoms, pale drugs, dead black years, sculptured effigies, and marriage tombs. At no point in the stanza does Meredith *tell* us that he is describing the death of love; however, his images allow us to determine that this must be his theme—that the wife's slight stiffening at her husband's touch is a sign of marital *rigor mortis*.

We should also be aware of the *pattern of development* in the imagery of the stanza. Initially, the focus is on the woman's waking eyes and the quivering hand beside her head. Then Meredith expands our vision to take in the bed, the surrounding darkness, and finally midnight's "giant heart of Memory and Tears." The effect is like that achieved by "zooming out" while filming a movie. It puts the marriage partners at the center of a universe that resonates "with muffled pulses" to their sufferings. Having established this broad perspective, Meredith uses imagery that closes in again—first to the memories scrawled across the blank walls and then to the marriage-tomb and the imaginary sword between the man and wife. This cyclical pattern in the development of the imagery is one of several devices Meredith uses to make each stanza a self-contained and satisfying "sonnet."[3] It contributes to our impression that *Modern*

---

[3] The stanza is not technically a sonnet because it is formed entirely of quatrains and contains sixteen lines to the sonnet's fourteen. Nevertheless, critics from Swinburne to Trevelyan have recognized the independence of each stanza by using the term *sonnet*.

Love is an autobiographical series of journal entries chronicling the failure of an actual marriage. This poetic illusion, derived in large part from the pattern in the development of Meredith's imagery, makes *Modern Love* seem contemporary and realistic to each new generation of readers. It is one of the major stylistic features of the poem.

On rare occasions the principle of selection or pattern of development in imagery is more than simply a stylistic feature. It may provide a key to the entire poem or even to the poet's entire personality. In the poetry of Percy Bysshe Shelley, for example, we find repeated images involving sunsets, the wind and waves, moonlight, fountains, veiled women, and shadows. The very fact that Shelley returns so frequently to the same images suggests that he is giving voice to a philosophical preoccupation—namely, that the reality of life lies beneath its surface features and that everything we think to be real is in fact the product of unseen forces. As a result, Shelley's images are often indirect: the colors of the sunset proceed from the unseen sun; the waves are driven by the unseen wind, and the wind itself is caused by unknown forces; moonlight is reflected indirectly from the sun; fountains pulse as a result of unseen pressures; veils conceal feminine beauty; and shadows are indirect images. In each image there is a veil of some kind that conceals the true source of beauty, for Shelley was a strong believer in Platonic idealism.[4] Here, for example, is a brief poem by Shelley that reveals his typical concern for the reality that transcends appearances:

TO——

Music, when soft voices die,
Vibrates in the memory;
Odors, when sweet violets sicken,
Live within the sense they quicken.

5   Rose leaves, when the rose is dead,
Are heaped for the belovèd's bed;
And so thy thoughts, when thou art gone,
Love itself shall slumber on.

—Percy Bysshe Shelley
[posthumous, 1824]

❧ QUESTIONS ❧

1. Examine the imagery in the poem. What different senses does Shelley call into play?

2. What are the similarities between the various images in the poem?

3. What thematic statements about beauty, love, departure, and death grow out of the poem?

---

[4] In Plato's allegory of the cave in *The Republic,* human beings are chained in such a way that they see only shadows cast on the wall of the cave and hear voices echoing from that wall. Naturally, they mistake the shadows and echoes for reality.

4. Examine the syntactic ambiguity in the final two lines. Does Shelley mean that the memories of the beloved will become the bed of love? Does he mean that Love itself will continue to dream about ("slumber on") the loved one ("thy thoughts")? Could he mean both at once?

We have seen that images make writing tangible, and we have seen that the manipulation of imagery is implicit in creative thought. In general, the more exact and evocative the imagery in a poem, the more interested and entertained the reader will remain. Imagery is as indispensable to an exciting poem as action and emotion are to an exciting life. Furthermore, **the poet's choice and arrangement of images may provide important clues to thematic and artistic purposes in philosophical poetry.** Shelley's belief in the Platonic ideal of intellectual beauty was abstract in the extreme, and it was a continual challenge to his poetic capabilities to find a way to write about the themes that interested him without allowing his poetry to degenerate into images that the reader would be unable to comprehend intellectually or emotionally.

Even themes less abstract than Shelley's are necessarily difficult to express imagistically. Although Meredith examines the effect on the human spirit of disappointments in love, he finds no direct way to tell us that this is his theme. To cope with the difficulty of discussing abstract ideas in imagistic language, poets normally turn to poetic comparisons, the subject of our next chapter.

8

Comparisons

In one poem Margaret Atwood refers to a landcrab as a "mouth on stilts." In another Sylvia Plath listens to her new-born child's "moth-breath." Elsewhere John Updike describes an ex-basketball player named Flick Webb whose "hands were like wild birds." In Sonnet 129 Shakespeare describes lust as "a swallowed bait,/ On purpose laid to make the taker mad." And in Sonnet 116 he describes love as "an ever-fixed mark,/ That looks on tempests, and is never shaken." Each of these examples involves the use of a poetic comparison. **Poetic comparisons may take a variety of forms:** *simile, metaphor, conceit, synecdoche, metonymy,* **and** *juxtaposition.* Each form of comparison, however, serves the same basic set of purposes. **Poets generally use comparisons to express abstract ideas in imagistic language,** thereby stimulating the reader's imagination, providing additional information, and opening up endless opportunities for entertainment and persuasion. Consider, for example, the following poem in which the speaker tries to seduce a young woman by comparing the consequences of their lovemaking with those of an insignificant flea-bite.

THE FLEA

Mark but this flea, and mark in this,
How little that, which thou deny'st me, is;
Me it sucked first, and now sucks thee,
And in this flea our two bloods mingled be;
5   Confess it. This cannot be said
A sin, or shame, or loss of maidenhead,
Yet this enjoys, before it woo,

And pampered swells with one blood made of two,
And this, alas! is more than we would do.[1]

10 Oh stay, three lives in one flea spare,
Where we almost, nay more than married are.
This flea is you and I, and this
Our marriage bed and marriage temple is;
Though parents grudge, and you, we are met,
15 And cloistered in these living walls of jet.
Though use° make you apt° to kill me,   *custom / inclined*
Let not to that, self-murder added be,
And sacrilege, three sins in killing three.

Cruel and sudden, hast thou since
20 Purpled thy nail in blood of innocence?
Wherein could this flea guilty be,
Except in that drop, which it sucked from thee?
Yet thou triumph'st, and say'st that thou
Find'st not thyself nor me the weaker now;
25 'Tis true; then learn how false fears be:
Just so much honor, when thou yield'st to me,
Will waste, as this flea's death took life from thee.

—John Donne [1633]

———————————— ❧ QUESTIONS ❧ ————————————

1. What similarities between the flea-bite and lovemaking does the speaker develop in the first stanza?

2. What is the young woman about to do in the second stanza? How are the speaker's arguments that she should spare the flea related to his efforts to seduce her?

3. What has the woman done by the beginning of the third stanza? Why has she done so? How does the speaker turn her action into one more argument that she should give herself to him?

4. How convincing do you find the speaker's arguments? How ingenious are they? What do you think would be their effect upon the woman— that is, what do you think will be the consequences of this attempt at seduction? Why?

———————————————————————————————

In developing this analogy at such length, Donne is creating an **extended comparison.** He uses the flea as one argument to illustrate that the physical relationship he desires is not in itself a significant event: a very similar union has already taken place within the flea without "sin, nor shame, nor loss of maidenhead." Thus, in "The Flea," as in shopping or voting, a comparison

———

[1] I.e., and this swelling (suggesting pregnancy) is more than we would wish to do.

identifies and illustrates some of the issues involved in making a decision.

As we have noted, poetic comparisons may take a variety of forms. This variety is well represented by the five comparisons in the first two stanzas of John Donne's "Valediction: Forbidding Mourning" (1633):

> As virtuous men pass mildly away,
> And whisper to their souls, to go,
> Whilst some of their sad friends do say,
> The breath goes now, and some say, no:
>
> So let us melt, and make no noise,
> No tear-floods, nor sigh-tempests move,
> 'Twere profanation of our joys
> To tell the laity our love.

The first of the comparisons runs through four and one-half lines and says, in essence, "Let us be just as calm in separating as virtuous men are in dying." **Comparisons** such as this, **which formally develop a similarity between two things using** *as, as when, like, than,* **or other equivalent constructions, are known as** *similes* **(similes assert similarity). However, when a poet asserts that two terms are identical instead of merely similar he creates a** *metaphor.* In Donne's lines here, the hyphenated terms ("tear-floods" and "sigh-tempests"), although exaggerations, are good examples of metaphors; the speaker in the poem condemns those separating lovers who shed tears in a flood and sigh like a windy tempest. Most metaphors are expressed somewhat more fully than Donne's, using a form of the verb "to be," as in Shakespeare's assertion that "All the world's a stage."

Both similes and metaphors are common in everyday speech. We say somebody is "sharp as a tack" or "as slow as molasses"; a brand-new car may be either a "lemon" or a "peach." Such similes and metaphors may once have been original and exciting, but they have become overused. Indeed, a shiny new comparison, like the latest model from Detroit, may emerge from the factory with a built-in obsolescence. Even though the comparison may originally have been a very good one, constant repetition may eventually cause us to react with insensitivity, indifference, or even hostility. The better the metaphor is, the more miles are put on it and the more rapidly it is worn out. Good poets, like all good writers, know this and as a result seek constantly to manufacture new analogies.

All similes and metaphors contain two parts, or terms. The *principal* or *primary term* is the one that conveys the literal statement made in the poem. In Donne's metaphors of "tear-floods" and "sigh-tempests," the literal statement concerns tears and sighs—hence, these are his principal terms. The *secondary term* in a metaphor is used figuratively to add color, connotations, and specificity to the more abstract primary term. Thus, Donne's "floods" and "tempests" are his secondary terms. Some literary critics call the primary term in a metaphor its *tenor* and the secondary term its *vehicle.*

An analogy in which one or both of these terms is implied but not stated may properly be called a metaphor, but we prefer the term *implied comparison* as being clearer and more accurate. When, for example, Donne writes, " 'Twere profanation of our joys/ To tell the laity our love," he is using one form of implied comparison. What he means is that their love is holy and spiritual like a secret religious ceremony, but only the primary term of the simile ("our love") is actually expressed. The idea that this love is analogous to a religious rite is implicit in the use of the words "profanation" and "laity," but this similarity is left unstated.

On rare occasions, both terms in a comparison may be implied, as in Donne's phrase, "So let us melt." Here he is comparing the separation of spiritual lovers with the gentle natural process that transforms ice to water; however, he relies on the reader to reconstruct mentally this comparison from the single clue he provides in the verb "melt."

While metaphors, similes, and implied comparisons are useful to poets primarily because they offer a mechanism for stating abstract truths through specific images, they also contribute intellectual stimulation, emotional connotations, and conciseness. In the two stanzas just examined, Donne has been struggling to put into words his conception of the relationship between himself and his lover and of how their separation can best reveal the depth of their love. Donne wisely avoids any generalized statement of his intentions, choosing instead to express himself entirely through images of a dying man, of melting, of floods and tempests, and of clergy and laity. In addition to making his writing vivid and concrete, these images are intellectually stimulating, imaginative, and even a little audacious. The gist of Donne's argument is that true love is not wholly physical. It is capable of going through a change in state from physical to spiritual (as the soul does in death), or from fixed to formless (as hard ice becomes fluid water). By confronting, in the beginning, the exaggerated fear that separation foreshadows death, Donne is able to transform that fear into a religious consolation in which the secret joys of the lovers become sacramental experiences. In one bold and inherently sacrilegious sentence, Donne manages to tie together an awe-inspiring image of human mortality, a fundamental law of physics, the stormy forces of nature, and the powerful attraction of love. All of this imagery is permeated with emotional overtones (sorrow, resignation, fear, piety) that might have been lost in any direct statement about spiritual love, self-restraint, and patience. Finally, Donne's comparisons allow him to express all of this in only fifty-five words. Comparisons, in short, give to poetry both density and conciseness. They link the human senses with human psychology without acknowledging the stages in logic and analysis that underlie this union.

Several other forms of implied comparison may occasionally be encountered in poetry. **In *synecdoche*, a part of something is used to suggest the *whole* thing.** George Meredith includes synecdoche when he uses the phrase "she wept with waking eyes" (p. 664). Obviously the woman is awake—not just her "waking eyes." **In *metonymy* (meaning "change of name"), something associated with an object or idea replaces what is actually meant.** Shakespeare uses metonymy when he writes that "the poet's pen/ . . . gives to airy nothing/ A local habitation and a name," since the poet, and not his pen, is clearly responsible for imaginative creation. Both synecdoche and metonymy are frequently found in slang. A "redneck" is a working man whose neck has been toughened by years in the wind and sun; an "old hand" means an experienced workman; and the "heavy" in a movie is a villain whose enormous size and aggressive behavior have become conventional.

One final form of implied comparison is created through juxtaposition. **In *juxtaposition*, two items are merely placed side by side. The author makes no overt comparison between these items and draws no inferences.** The reader is free to make of them what he or she will. An interesting example of juxtaposition occurs in Henry Reed's post-World War II poem entitled

"Lessons of the War: Naming of Parts." Each of the five stanzas in the poem
describes a stage in the military exercise of breaking down and naming the
parts of an army rifle; and then, in juxtaposition to this, Reed "names" some
of the parts of springtime.

NAMING OF PARTS

Today we have naming of parts. Yesterday,
We had daily cleaning. And tomorrow morning,
We shall have what to do after firing. But today,
Today we have naming of parts. Japonica
5   Glistens like coral in all of the neighboring gardens,
          And today we have naming of parts.

This is the lower sling swivel. And this
Is the upper sling swivel, whose use you will see,
when you are given your slings. And this is the piling swivel,
10 Which in your case you have not got. The branches
Hold in the gardens their silent, eloquent gestures,
          Which in our case we have not got.

This is the safety-catch, which is always released
With an easy flick of the thumb. And please do not let me
15 See anyone using his finger. You can do it quite easy
If you have any strength in your thumb. The blossoms
Are fragile and motionless, never letting anyone see
          Any of them using their finger.

And this you can see is the bolt. The purpose of this
20 Is to open the breech, as you see. We can slide it
Rapidly backwards and forwards: we call this
Easing the spring. And rapidly backwards and forwards
The early bees are assaulting and fumbling the flowers:
          They call it easing the Spring.

25 They call it easing the Spring: it is perfectly easy
If you have any strength in your thumb: like the bolt,
And the breech, and the cocking-piece, and the point of balance,
Which in our case we have not got; and the almond-blossom
Silent in all of the gardens and the bees going backwards and
          forwards,
30   For today we have naming of parts.
                                        —Henry Reed [1947]

The first stanza is representative of the technique followed throughout the
poem. The first four sentences of the stanza are mechanical, denotative, and
dull, whereas the first clause in the next sentence ("Japonica/ Glistens like
coral in all of the neighboring gardens") is naturalistic, figurative, imagistic,
and appreciative. We see the author's mind at play just as it had been at
rather dull work in the preceding lines. We see him transform himself from
a military automaton to a sensually aware human being. We see him in an
act of mental rebellion against a numbing, mechanical, and inhumane routine.
At the same time that his hands and arms go through the rituals of slaughter,
his eyes and intellect follow the processes of natural rebirth. From a strictly
logical point of view, the two parts of Reed's stanza are incompatible, but he
unites them by his repetition of the final phrase, "today we have naming of

parts." And in that repetition Reed is implicitly asserting his ability to metamorphose his army experiences in a triumph of human feeling over inhumane behavior.

Juxtaposition is rarely used with as great a dramatic effect as in "Naming of Parts," but it is frequently important in creating the impression of fate or inevitability. When Edwin Arlington Robinson wrote that "Richard Cory, one calm summer night,/ Went home and put a bullet through his head," he was juxtaposing the calm, warm weather and the cold, irrational act of suicide in order to prod us into pondering possible reasons for Richard Cory's death. And when Robert Frost found "a dimpled spider, fat and white,/ On a white heal-all, holding up a moth," the juxtaposition of those symbols of death, blight, and innocence became ominous and profound.

Poems for Further Study

MORNING SONG

Love set you going like a fat gold watch.
The midwife slapped your footsoles, and your bald cry
Took its place among the elements.

Our voices echo, magnifying your arrival. New statue.
5   In a drafty museum, your nakedness
Shadows our safety. We stand round blankly as walls.

I'm no more your mother
Than the cloud that distils a mirror to reflect its own slow
Effacement at the wind's hand.

10   All night your moth-breath
Flickers among the flat pink roses. I wake to listen:
A far sea moves in my ear.

One cry, and I stumble from bed, cow-heavy and floral
In my Victorian nightgown.
15   Your mouth opens clean as a cat's. The window square

Whitens and swallows its dull stars. And now you try
Your handful of notes;
The clear vowels rise like balloons.

—Sylvia Plath [1961]

❦ QUESTIONS ❦

1. Who is Plath addressing in this poem? In what sense is it a "Morning Song"?

2. What similes and metaphors can you find in this poem? What emotions of a new mother do these comparisons help Plath to express?

3.   What do you think of Plath's reactions to motherhood? Do you find her reactions expected or unexpected? Are they believable? Are they uniformly commendable? Are they honest?

LANDCRAB

A lie, that we come from water.
The truth is we were born
from stones, dragons, the sea's
teeth, as you testify,
5   with your crust and jagged scissors.

Hermit, hard socket
for a timid eye,
you're a soft gut scuttling
sideways, a blue skull,
10   round bone on the prowl,
Wolf of treeroots and gravelly holes,
a mouth on stilts,
the husk of a small demon.

Attack, voracious
15   eating, and flight:
it's a sound routine
for staying alive on edges,
Then there's the tide, and that dance
you do for the moon
20   on wet sand, claws raised
to fend off your mate,
your coupling a quick
dry clatter of rocks.
For mammals
25   with their lobes and bulbs,
scruples and warm milk,
you've nothing but contempt.

Here you are, a frozen scowl
targeted in flashlight,
30   then gone: a piece of what
we are, not all,
my stunted child, my momentary
face in the mirror,
my tiny nightmare.

—Margaret Atwood [1981]

❧ QUESTIONS ❧

1.   Why does Atwood contend that we were "born from stones, dragons, the sea's / teeth"? What does such a contention imply about human beings?

2. Examine the similes and metaphors used in describing the landcrab. What emotional responses do those comparisons evoke?

3. What characteristics are necessary for "staying alive on edges"? How are these characteristics reflected in the landcrab's lovemaking and its attitude toward mammals?

4. Why does Atwood conclude her poem with a series of implied comparisons that show her kinship (and ours) with the landcrab?

9

❦❦❦❦❦❦

Personification, Apostrophe, and Animism

The portrayal of an idea, object, or animal as having human traits is called
personification. Storms and ships, for example, have traditionally been personified by being given human names. **Personification constitutes a form of implied comparison and allows the poet to describe with energy and vitality what might otherwise have remained inanimate or lackluster.** Notice how Edward FitzGerald's personification of an earthen wine bowl enlivens the following lines and makes his message about enjoying life clearer and more forceful:

> Then to this earthen Bowl did I adjourn
> My Lip the secret Well of Life to learn:
>   And Lip to Lip it murmur'd—"While you live
> Drink! for once dead you never shall return."

> —From *The Rubáiyát of Omar Khayyám,*
> Edward Fitzgerald [1859]

❧ QUESTIONS ❧

1. Explain the pun (involving the word *lip*) in line 3. How does it contribute to the personification?

2. Consider the connotations of an "earthen" bowl—especially in the context of a discussion of death.

3. The advice, "While you live / Drink!" is in one sense quite straightforward, but in another sense it is profoundly ambiguous. Drink what? What are the possibilities? (In answering this question, you may wish to read additional selections from the *Rubáiyát,* printed elsewhere in this anthology. See the *Index* for page numbers.)

Apostrophe, a limited form of personification, occurs when a poet or one of his characters addresses a speech to someone absent or something nonhuman. Although apostrophe is often ineffective in poetry, Geoffrey Chaucer uses it throughout his humorous "Complaint to His Empty Purse" (1399), which begins:

> To you, my purse, and to non other wight° *person*
> Complayne I, for ye be my lady dere!

and Shakespeare uses apostrophe during King Lear's ragings on the heath:

> Blow, winds, and crack your cheeks! Rage! Blow!
> You cataracts and hurricanoes, spout
> Till you have drench'd our steeples, drown'd the cocks!° *weathervanes*
> You sulph'rous and thought-executing fires,
> Vaunt-couriers° of oak-cleaving thunderbolts, *fore-runners*
> Singe my white head! And thou, all-shaking thunder,
> Strike flat the thick rotundity o' th' world!
> Crack nature's mold, all germens° spill at once *germs, seeds*
> That makes ingrateful man!
> —From *King Lear,* William Shakespeare [1605]

However, Chaucer's address to his purse is but a playful piece of foolishness and Lear's address to the storm is but a symptom of his madness. In neither case does the poet expect us to see any utility in talking to wallet and wind. If apostrophe were *always* used ironically, as in both of these examples, or comically, as in Robert Burns' poems "To a Mouse" and "To a Louse," then inept poets would undoubtedly have developed some other means of debasing the English language. As things are, however, too many second-rate poems are packed with silly and sentimental apostrophes to Truth, Beauty, Love, and a host of other capitalized abstractions. Weak poets, having worked themselves or their characters up to a stage of violent emotions, often degenerate into what John Ruskin called the "pathetic fallacy" of facile and unimaginative personification. The trite and insipid tribute of Anna Laetitia Barbauld to "Life" is a typical example of the worst form of apostrophe:

> Life! We've been long together,
> Through pleasant and through cloudy weather;
> 'Tis hard to part when friends are dear—
> Perhaps 'twill cost a sigh, a tear.
> —From "Life," Anna Laetitia Barbauld [1811]

Excessive personification or apostrophe is not the only way to ruin a poem, but it may be the most reliable.

A poet may also describe an idea or inanimate object as though it were living, without attributing human traits to it. Before the development of the motion picture, this device could be called animation, but because that term is now best confined to cartoons, **we will use the term *animism* for poetic comparisons that give life to inanimate objects.** Carl Sandburg employs animism to good effect in his brief poem "Fog":

FOG

> The fog comes
> on little cat feet

It sits looking
over harbor and city
5   on silent haunches
and then moves on.
—Carl Sandburg [1916]

Similarly, Robert Burns uses an animistic simile when he compares the high spirits of love with the appearance of a newly sprung rose:

O, my luve is like a red red rose
That's newly sprung in June
O, my luve is like the melodie
That's sweetly played in tune.
—From "A Red, Red Rose,"
Robert Burns [1796]

Of course, Burns is also comparing the woman he loves (as well as the emotion of love) with a red rose—young, fresh, fragrant, and beautiful. All depends on whether "my luve" is taken as meaning "my feeling when in love" or "my loved one." In the former, a feeling or idea is animated by comparison with the rose; in the latter, the appearance and personality of the maiden are described. Because both interpretations are compatible, this pleasant ambiguity is best left unresolved; however, we should at least mention that the second reading suggests yet another form of comparison. This technique of speaking about a person in terms that are more applicable to a plant, animal, or machine is just the opposite of personification, and yet, oddly, it has no commonly accepted name other than simile or metaphor. T. S. Eliot used this form of comparison in "The Love Song of J. Alfred Prufrock" (1917) to add to the narrator's scorn for his own insignificance:

I should have been a pair of ragged claws
Scuttling across the floors of silent seas.

Theodore Roethke, in his "Elegy to Jane," described the "sidelong pickerel smile" of one of his former students, whom he also compared to a wren, a sparrow, and a skittery pigeon. And early blues musicians, whose roots were in the soil of the Mississippi Delta, compared themselves to a variety of country creatures in such songs as "The Bull Frog Blues" (Willie Harris), "The Crawling Kingsnake Blues" (John Lee Hooker), and "The Milk Cow's Calf Blues" (Robert Johnson) in describing their passions and sorrows.

Poems for Further Study

"APPARENTLY WITH NO SURPRISE"

Apparently with no surprise
To any happy Flower
The Frost beheads it at its play—
In accidental power—
5   The blonde Assassin passes on—

The Sun proceeds unmoved
To measure off another Day
For an Approving God.

—Emily Dickinson
[posthumous, 1890]

─────────────── ❧ QUESTIONS ❧ ───────────────

1.   To what extent are the Flower and the Frost personified in this poem? What words are applied to them that are more typically used in discussions of human beings? How accurate is the poem as a literal description of the effect of frost on flowers?

2.   What attitude toward God is expressed in this poem? How much design does Dickinson see in the forces of nature?

EX-BASKETBALL PLAYER

Pearl Avenue runs past the high-school lot,
Bends with the trolley tracks, and stops, cut off
Before it has a chance to go two blocks,
At Colonel McComsky Plaza. Berth's Garage
5   Is on the corner facing west, and there,
Most days, you'll find Flick Webb, who helps Berth out.

Flick stands tall among the idiot pumps—
Five on a side, the old bubble-head style,
Their rubber elbows hanging loose and low.
10   One's nostrils are two S's, and his eyes
An E and O. And one is squat, without
A head at all—more of a football type.

Once Flick played for the high-school team, the Wizards.
He was good: in fact, the best. In '46
15   He bucketed three hundred ninety points,
A county record still. The ball loved Flick.
I saw him rack up thirty-eight or forty
In one home game. His hands were like wild birds.

He never learned a trade, he just sells gas,
20   Checks oil, and changes flats. Once in a while,
As a gag, he dribbles an inner tube,
But most of us remember anyway.
His hands are fine and nervous on the lug wrench.
It makes no difference to the lug wrench, though.

25   Off work, he hangs around Mae's luncheonette.
Grease-gray and kind of coiled, he plays pinball,

Smokes those thin cigars, nurses lemon phosphates.
Flick seldom says a word to Mae, just nods
Beyond her face toward bright applauding tiers
30 Of Necco Wafers, Nibs, and Juju Beads.

—John Updike [1957]

� QUESTIONS �

1. Where does Flick Webb work? On what kind of street? Doing what kind of job?

2. How and why does Updike personify the gasoline pumps at Berth's Garage?

3. How does Flick put to use the skills he learned as a basketball player? Describe the "crowd" that now observes and applauds his prowess.

4. How fulfilling is Flick's life after high school? What comment about high school athletics is implicit in this poem?

10

❧❧❧❧❧❧

Symbol and Allegory

As we noted in our discussion of fiction, **a *symbol* is something that stands for something else, and an *allegory* is a narrative that uses a system of implied comparisons—often including symbols—to develop two or more simultaneous levels of meaning.** Both devices occur naturally in literature to expand the suggestiveness and significance of literature.

Normally, a *symbol* is an image that has an overt literal function in a poem, but it also evokes a range of additional meanings. Like the physical universe, a symbol is finite but unbounded: finite in the sense that the symbol itself is specific and imagistic, but unbounded in the sense that the limits on the possible interpretations of the symbol are often difficult to define. For example, in Robert Frost's well-known poem, "The Road Not Taken," the road itself is vividly described. As readers, we easily imagine the yellow wood, the branching, grassy paths, the "leaves no step had trodden black," and the minor dilemma of the speaker as he pauses before making his choice. Thus far, the road is simply a road and the poem very pleasantly describes a woodland walk early in the morning. However, Frost puts greater emphasis on this choice of paths than the simple incident itself would seem to merit. If this choice really only involves two roads in a yellow wood, why should the speaker "be telling this with a sigh/ Somewhere ages and ages hence"? Surely no ordinary choice between woodland paths is so memorable and so important. And why should he repeat the fact that the roads fork and that he chose the "one less travelled by"? And finally, how could such a choice really make "all the difference"? Clearly, the poem has started out as a description of a simple incident, but somewhere along the way that incident has become a symbol of the more significant decisions in life that all of us are inevitably called upon to make. To be sure, the exact nature of those decisions remains unclear. We cannot say with absolute certainty that it is a poem about the choice of a career, for it could just as easily refer to any choice between two attractive options—the

75

choice between two hobbies, the choice between two weekend dates, the choice between two churches, or any number of other possibilities. All we can say with certainty is that the poem is about the choice between two roads in a yellow wood, but that it is *also* about other choices in life that may be taken casually and seem unimportant at the time, while ultimately making "all the difference."

As in the case of this poem by Frost, **a symbol is an image that expands in meaning through the friction of emphasis until it inflames the imagination. A symbol remains what it is as an image, but it also takes on new and tenuous meanings that cast a flickering, magical glow over the work as a whole.**

A symbol may be *private* **(its meaning known only to one person),** *original* **(its meaning defined by its context in a particular work), or** *traditional* **(its meaning defined by our common culture and heritage).** At its most complex, a symbol may be all three as, for example, in "The Whale," a poem that occurs in the ninth chapter of Herman Melville's *Moby Dick:*

THE WHALE

The ribs and terrors in the whale,
   Arched over me a dismal gloom,
While all God's sun-lit waves rolled by,
   And left me deepening down to doom.

5   I saw the opening maw° of hell,   *jaws*
     With endless pains and sorrows there;
     Which none but they that feel can tell—
       Oh, I was plunging to despair.

     In black distress, I called my God,
10   When I could scarce believe him mine,
     He bowed his ear to my complaints—
       No more the whale did me confine.

     With speed he flew to my relief,
     As on a radiant dolphin borne;
15   Awful, yet bright, as lightning shone
       The face of my Deliverer God.

     My song for ever shall record
     That terrible, that joyful hour;
     I give the glory to my God,
20   His all the mercy and the power.
           —Herman Melville [1851]

Here, and throughout *Moby Dick,* the whale is a private symbol, in the sense that it emerges from Melville's own whaling experiences. Melville once wrote, "If, at my death my executors (or more properly, my creditors) find any precious manuscripts in my desk, then I prospectively ascribe all the honor and glory to whaling; for a whale-ship was my Yale and Harvard." But actual experience with whales may have been responsible for only part of the private symbolism in the poem. The battle with the whale may also have served as a metaphor for confrontation with Melville's own despair and may also reflect the "dismal gloom" of his failure to make a living as a bank clerk, a teacher, a surveyor, a seaman, and finally an author. When he completed *Moby Dick,* Melville was in debt to his publisher and to his friends, and he saw little hope of attaining solvency.

No one, of course, can truly gauge the extent to which a poem symbolizes an author's personal turmoil, but there can be no doubt that the whale in *Moby Dick* is an original, powerful, and fully developed symbol within the novel. Even in this brief poem it is clear that the whale is an object of horror, a force of evil, and an embodiment of the darkest spiritual despair. These symbolic associations arise out of the poem itself and require of the reader only a sensitivity to the meaning of words.

The poem, however, also suggests the traditional *parable* **(an instructive moral story)** of Jonah, who was thrown to the whale because of a lack of faith in God, confined to the whale's belly in black distress, and finally resurrected after calling upon God for assistance. In this sense, the whale is an ***archetype* (a basic and repeated element of plot, character, or theme)** that symbolizes separation from God and even death; its symbolic associations are traditional— that is, common to all readers who share the Judeo-Christian heritage.

Symbols are not, however, always this complex. In one sense, symbolism is the most common of all linguistic devices. After all, a word is nothing but a sound that symbolizes a particular image or concept. No word has meaning unless our human ability to symbolize makes it so. There is no necessary connection, for example, between the word *dog* and the familiar four-legged animal we associate with that word; after all, people of other nations have developed the same symbolic associations with other sounds: *chien* in French, *Hund* in German, *canis* in Latin, and so on.

Even **literary symbols are often quite simple.** Winter, for example, often is a symbol of old age, spring of youth, summer of maturity, and autumn of decline. Similarly, a lamb may be a symbol of innocence, a lion of courage, a fire of vitality, and a rock of firmness. In each case, an implied comparison is drawn between a vivid image and an abstract quality.

The one-to-one correspondences set up by these symbols are akin to those established in simple *allegories* like the medieval morality play, *Everyman*. The hero, Everyman, is accompanied on his journey to the grave by characters whose actions and even names symbolize his Good-Deeds, Five Wits, Strength, Discretion, Beauty, and Knowledge. *Everyman* is known as an allegory because its simple symbols are systematically used to emphasize the moral point that only our good deeds are of lasting value both in life and after death. **An *allegory* is a type of narrative that attempts to reinforce its thesis by making its characters (and sometimes its events and setting as well) represent specific abstract ideas. The systems of symbols used in allegories often tend toward didacticism and overt moral instruction.** Such blatancy is a major reason why allegory is no longer a popular literary mode.

It is incorrect, however, to say that allegory no longer has a place in literature. Just as symbolism is a universal element of language, allegory is a universal element of fictional narration. Any literary (as opposed to journalistic) presentation of characters or events invariably prompts the reader to inquire, "What does it mean? What is the author's point?" And such questions represent the first step toward uncovering an allegorical purpose. Graham Hough, an important contemporary scholar, has developed a useful example of the process:

We read some report of, say, treachery, sexual misadventure, and violence in the newspapers, and it is there only to record the fact that such events took place. We read of the same sequence of events in a novel or a short story, and we can hardly escape the feeling that it is there to say something to us about human passions and motives in general. From there it is only a step to seeing the characters as types of Treachery, Violence and Lust. . . .[1]

If the actions of fictional characters are highly idiosyncratic and suggest no universal traits of humanity, we will probably be reluctant to identify them as allegorical "types"; but if the thematic element in the story is strong—that is, if the story seems to be making a general comment about humanity—it must to some extent suggest allegorical possibilities.

The problem facing the student of literature is not, then, whether a given story, poem, or play includes symbolism and allegory, but whether these nearly universal elements of literature are so important in the specific work that they need to be isolated, discussed, and evaluated. We can best resolve this problem by asking ourselves two questions. First, does the author put unusual emphasis on a particular image or series of images? Second, does the poem or story fail to make literal sense *unless* we interpret the images symbolically or allegorically? An affirmative answer to either or both questions should make us suspect that the author may be using images as symbols— perhaps, but not necessarily, in an allegory.

Discussions of symbolic or allegorical meanings in literature should always be pursued with caution. Because all words are in some sense symbolic and because every theme is in some sense allegorical, inexperienced critics (and even some experienced ones) are too easily tempted to "read things into" the works they study. Even at its best, symbol hunting is an attempt at mind reading. We can all easily identify the images an author uses, but we often get into trouble when we begin to speculate about what the author intended in choosing them. Unless we can find strong evidence in the poem to support our symbolic interpretations, there is a very high probability that the only mind we are reading is our own. When authors think their symbols are important, we can be quite confident that the authors will hint at their meaning in one or more places. When no authorial interpretation (or even acknowledgment) of the symbols can be found, the wise critic will think carefully before insisting on a symbolic interpretation. Like Hawthorne's Ethan Brand, who looked throughout the world for the Unpardonable Sin—before finding it in himself—we may find that the symbolic meanings we seek in the works of others exist only in the smithy of our own souls.

Poems for Further Study

"WHAT IS OUR LIFE? A PLAY OF PASSION"

> What is our life? A play of passion,
> Our mirth the music of division;
> Our mothers' wombs the tiring-houses° be   *dressing rooms*
> Where we are dressed for this short comedy;

[1] *An Essay on Criticism* (London: Duckworth, 1966), 121.

Heaven the judicious, sharp spectator is
That sits and marks still who doth act amiss;
Our graves that hide us from the searching sun
Are like drawn curtains when the play is done:
Thus march we, playing, to our latest° rest,   *last*
Only we die in earnest, that's no jest.

—Sir Walter Raleigh [1612]

❦ QUESTIONS ❦

1. A "play of passion" (now usually called a passion play) was a medieval or renaissance drama presenting the stages in the suffering and death of Jesus Christ. What allegorical relationships between such a play and human life are presented in this poem?

2. How long does the music last in the divisions between acts in a play? How much of human life is given over to mirth?

3. What does Raleigh mean when he speaks of life as "this short comedy"? Is he being ironic? Bitter? Cynical?

4. How does Raleigh portray God and man's relationship with God?

5. What is the effect of the final couplet upon the interpretation of the whole poem?

CROSSING THE BAR

Sunset and evening star,
     And one clear call for me!
And may there be no moaning of the bar,[2]
     When I put out to sea,

5   But such a tide as moving seems asleep,
     Too full for sound and foam,
When that which drew from out the boundless deep
     Turns again home.

Twilight and evening bell,
10   And after that the dark!
And may there be no sadness of farewell,
     When I embark;

For tho' from out our bourne° of Time and Place   *limits*
     The flood may bear me far,

[2] The sound of surf washing over a very shallow sand bar at the mouth of a river.

15   I hope to see my Pilot face to face
When I have crossed the bar.

—Alfred, Lord Tennyson [1889]

❧ QUESTIONS ❧

1. This poem is usually given an allegorical interpretation. In the first stanza, what are the allegorical referents of the "sunset," the "one clear call," the "moaning of the bar," and the putting out to sea?

2. In stanza two, why does the speaker wish to be carried on a tide that "moving seems asleep" and is too deep for "sound and foam"? And what is the force that "drew from out the boundless deep"?

3. How is the first line of the third stanza different from the first line of stanza one? What does "the dark" represent? And in what sense does the speaker embark?

4. Why does the speaker refer to escaping "our bourne of Time and Place" in stanza four? Who is meant by the Pilot?

5. How well does the title "Crossing the Bar" summarize the poem both as a statement on dying and on setting sail?

THE ROAD NOT TAKEN

Two roads diverged in a yellow wood,
And sorry I could not travel both
And be one traveler, long I stood
And looked down one as far as I could
5   To where it bent in the undergrowth;

Then took the other, as just as fair,
And having perhaps the better claim,
Because it was grassy and wanted wear;
Though as for that the passing there
10   Had worn them really about the same,

And both that morning equally lay
In leaves no step had trodden black.
Oh, I kept the first for another day!
Yet knowing how way leads on to way,
15   I doubted if I should ever come back.

I shall be telling this with a sigh
Somewhere ages and ages hence:
Two roads diverged in a wood, and I—
I took the one less traveled by,
20   And that has made all the difference.

—Robert Frost [1916]

❧ QUESTIONS ❧

1. How does Frost prod us into reading this poem symbolically? Specifically, how does the last stanza change the significance of this simple incident?

2. Can you speculate about the decisions in Frost's life (or anyone else's) which could have been made in this light-hearted way and yet could have "made all the difference"?

3. Laurence Perrine sees the poem as "an expression of regret that one's ability to explore different life possibilities is so sharply limited. It comes from a man who loves life and thirsts after more of it." What details in the poem support such an interpretation?

11

❧❧❧❧❧❧❧

The Plain Sense of Poetry

As I. A. Richards noted more than half a century ago in his seminal book *Practical Criticism* (1929), the chief problem faced by the student of poetry is "the difficulty of making out [the poem's] plain sense." In the preceding pages we have identified some of the sources of this difficulty by demonstrating that poets often use unfamiliar denotations, connotations, or allusions and may change the meaning of words through repetition, ambiguity, puns, paradoxes, and irony. Furthermore, poetic comparisons, although often vivid and delightful, may also be suggestive, symbolic, or ambiguous. Finally, poetry is, as a general rule, much more densely packed with meaning than prose. The author of a sonnet has, after all, only fourteen lines in which to make a point—a restriction that requires either making a very minor point or making every word count. A sonnetlike density is traditionally expected in poetry, even when the actual length of the poem is not limited by any formal strictures. In spite of these difficulties, the simple prose meaning of most poetry can be determined by using common sense and our accumulated knowledge of how poetry works.

As you study the poems in this text, you should sketch out mentally (or better yet record in your notebook) provisional responses to each of the seven steps in seeking the plain sense of poetry:

1. List Denotations and Connotations. As we have already shown, many words have multiple meanings, and poets often intentionally play on this multiplicity. We need to be cautious, of course, about assuming that an author is always—or even generally—toying with multiple denotations. In poetry, as in prose, an author normally intends to make a clear and forceful point, and ambiguity, by its very nature, must always interfere with the clarity of a statement. But even if the poet avoids ambiguity, he or she is almost certainly cognizant of the connotations of each word and may use them to modify the

82

meaning. Thus, in studying a poem for the first time, the reader should look up in the dictionary any difficult or unfamiliar words and jot down their definitions and connotations. Let us see how we can apply this first recommendation to the analysis of the following well-known lyric:

UPON JULIA'S CLOTHES

Whenas in silks my Julia goes
Then, then (methinks) how sweetly flows
That liquefaction of her clothes.

Next, when I cast mine eyes and see
That brave vibration each way free;
O how that glittering taketh me!
                    —Robert Herrick [1648]

Like most poetry written in an age and in circumstances quite different from our own, these six lines present several problems in denotation. After more than three hundred years, we have naturally changed some of the ways in which we use words, and Herrick's vocabulary, although not archaic, is uncommon and distinctive. To be on the safe side, we might look up a half-dozen words with the following results:

> *whenas:* whenever
> *goes:* moves about, leaves
> *methinks:* it seems to me
> *liquefaction:* fluidity
> *cast:* turn, direct, throw
> *brave:* courageous, showy, colorful

In moving from denotation to connotation and commentary, we find more to interest a literary critic:

silks: Silken clothing is thin, expensive, lustrous, and sensuous. Although Herrick is presumably referring to a silken dress, "silks" may also connote silk stockings or a silk nightgown. Thus, the connotations of the word are luxuriant and slightly sensual.

my Julia: The use of the possessive adjective "my" suggests that Julia may be Herrick's possession, his mistress—both confirming and compounding the sensuous connotations of "silks."

goes: This is a curious word choice. Clearly, when Julia "goes," she is walking. Perhaps Herrick thought that walking was too common an activity and perhaps, too, he was trying to be precise, for a woman in a long, full skirt may seem to glide about—or "go"—without seeming to walk at all. Possibly Herrick wanted to suggest that Julia was leaving, "going away." If so, "whenas" reminds us that this is something that she does frequently, and we may be tempted to assume that Herrick is describing her as she leaves after a lovers' tryst. In addition, the choice of "goes" was in part dictated by Herrick's need for a word to rhyme with "flows" and "clothes."

liquefaction: Here sound connotations come into play. The word itself is equivalent to "liquid action," but it rolls off the tongue more smoothly and thus is most appropriate.

cast mine eyes: The phrase is vigorous and active. Because Herrick had been watching Julia in the first three lines, these words must mean something more than that he simply continued to look at her. If indeed Julia had been leaving in the first sentence, then in "casting" his eyes, Herrick is probably turning his head to watch her receding figure. The phrase shows Herrick's strong attraction to Julia.

brave: We have already had something to say about the denotations of the adjective "brave." Undoubtedly, Herrick is using the archaic definitions, "showy" or "colorful"; however, those were secondary definitions even in Herrick's day, and therefore the connotations of "boldness" and "courage" cannot be escaped.

vibration: In the twentieth century we are apt to associate this word with very rapid oscillations—especially with the vibrations of automobiles, trains, and planes moving at high speed. In the seventeenth century, however, the word was most often used to describe the slow swing of a pendulum. In this poem, therefore, "that brave vibration each way free" suggests the gentle side-to-side swishing of a woman's skirts. And, in fact, the bravado and freedom of these oscillations may indicate that Julia's swaying motion is a trifle wanton.

2.   **Analyze the Syntax.**   If the meaning of a particular sentence is unclear, analyze its syntax by identifying the subject, the verb, the object, and the function of the major clauses. We have just as much right to expect syntactic clarity in verse as in prose, and no poet who habitually disregards the rules of English grammar can earn the respect of literate readers unless his or her verse has remarkable compensatory elements. Of course, good poets sometimes, by design, use syntax ambiguously to suggest competing interpretations (remember the Delphic oracle's "Pyrrhus the Romans shall conquer"?); however, this possibility merely underscores the need to understand fully the syntactic relationships among words.

Herrick's brief poem "Upon Julia's Clothes" is constructed of two parallel sentences. Each consists of a subordinate clause followed by an exclamation. Because the two sentences are similar in so many respects, the slight differences between them are all the more pronounced. The first sentence is introspective ("methinks") and intransitive ("how sweetly flows/ That liquefaction of her clothes"). In contrast, the second sentence is active ("I cast mine eyes") and transitive ("O how that glittering taketh me"). In the first sentence, Herrick is a reflective observer; in the second, he is acting and being acted upon. The two sentences combine to suggest that he is prey to a passion that intensifies as he watches the rustling of his mistress's clothing. Even in the choice of his syntactic subjects, we find him moving from water ("liquefaction") to fire ("glittering") and thus from tranquility to excitement.

3.   **Identify the Figures of Speech.**   By definition, figurative language is not meant to be taken literally. Poetic language differs from ordinary language to point the way toward meaningful emotional truths. When Herrick exclaims, "Then, then (methinks) how sweetly flows/ That liquefaction of her clothes," he certainly does not mean that Julia's dress dribbles down into a soggy pool at her feet—although that is the image we may get if we try to interpret his lines literally. Actually, Herrick is drawing an implied comparison between

the soft, shiny movements of Julia's silken dress and the gentle, rippling flow of a stream.

This is the only figure of speech used in Herrick's brief poem, and we should not ordinarily expect to find more in such short poetic passages. Figurative language is like champagne: the first glass or two raises the spirits, but too much of it befuddles and bewilders the brain. Whenever an author *does* use numerous figures of speech, it becomes absolutely essential to identify the various types being used (whether allusion, ambiguity, irony, paradox, pun, or one of the various forms of comparison), and it is often useful as well to recast those figures, at least temporarily, into language that is not poetic. Allusions, ironies, paradoxes, and puns should be explained; metaphors and implied comparisons should be rewritten as similes; and symbols should be identified. To do so without greatly distorting the poem, we must be sensitive to the connotations of words and to the uses of ambiguity.

4. **Paraphrase the Poem.** The purpose of a paraphrase is to help us understand the prose sense of a poem by changing the poetic language of difficult passages into language that we can easily comprehend. This process is the most direct means of making sure that we understand what a poem says— quite apart from how well it is said.

Having enumerated denotations and connotations, analyzed syntax, and identified figures of speech, it should not be difficult to write down a full prose statement of the poem's content. Thus, "Upon Julia's Clothes" might be paraphrased as follows:

Whenever my Julia walks in silks, then (it seems to me) that the sounds made by the movement of her clothing are as lovely as the rippling of a stream. Next, when I look at the colorful swaying of her skirts, O how their glittering attracts me!

Any paraphrase, as long as it is reasonable, helps us to check our understanding of a poem's literal meaning by expressing it in slightly different words. The process itself, however, is fraught with risks. We may be tempted to substitute our own prose statement for the poem itself, which may obscure our appreciation of the poem's style and feeling. Or, we may persuade ourselves that the poem means exactly what we say it means and nothing else—a conclusion that glosses over the questionable decisions about denotation and connotation that must be made in attempting to paraphrase any poem. For example, by changing only a few words in our paraphrase of "Upon Julia's Clothes" we can begin to interpret the poem more sensuously:

Whenever my mistress Julia comes toward me dressed in silks, then (it seems to me) that her clothes flow about her body as smoothly and beautifully as water in a stream. Next, when I turn my eyes and see the saucy and free swing in her walk as she passes, O how the sparkle of her skirts enamours me!

It would be difficult to determine a rational reason for preferring one of these paraphrases over the other. The first moves from the *sound* of Julia's dress to the *sight* of it, whereas the second implies that Herrick watches Julia as she walks by—admiring her figure from front and rear. The first paraphrase is a little too staid; the second a little too steamy. The poem itself contains something of both; it manages to be suggestive without the slightest trace of immorality. This elusiveness is, of course, exactly what makes poetry more interesting than common prose. Stripping the nuances from a poem is like skimming the cream from milk: it takes away the richness and taste. In each case, what remains is thin, watery, and almost denatured. The language of poetry is *not* static or technical or purely denotative; it is rich and complex, and no paraphrase can fully do it justice. Yet, the risks of leaving the poem's prose meaning unstated are even greater, for then the ambiguities of poetic diction may entice the reader into believing that his or her own preoccupations and fantasies are somehow mirrored in each line. If anything, the temptation to read something into the poem that its actual content will not justify implies a greater disrespect for the written word than the opposite risk of relying too heavily on the paraphrase. The latter may be nothing more than a shadow of the true poetic substance, but the former is too often the product of an overstimulated imagination, having little relationship to the poem.

5. **Visualize and Summarize the Imagery and Actions.** The preceding steps have all been analytical. They require us to look up definitions, to examine verbal structures, to reword sentences: to act, to think, and to write. In doing so, however, we have omitted what is certainly the most important process of all: to enjoy. When we relax and allow the poet's imagery to carry us into the world of imagination, we are most in harmony with the true poetic impulse. But more than that, visualizing the events in the poem and attempting to recreate imaginatively everything that the poet describes can often be indispensable to careful critical judgment. Careless writers sometimes juxtapose incongruous and even ludicrous images because they themselves fail to see clearly what they ask their readers to envision: for example, "In the game of life it's sink or swim, and you need to hang in there by your toenails, swinging for the bleachers whenever opportunity knocks." The use of such incongruous comparisons is called *mixed metaphor.*

Once we have tried to visualize everything that the poet describes for us, we will find it easier to summarize the action and circumstances in the poem. In so doing, we will generally wish to identify the speaker (who may or may not be the poet), the setting, and the circumstances. A summary of "Upon Julia's Clothes" will not add much to our understanding of the poem because the poem itself is so short and uncomplicated. However, Frost's sonnet "Design," which is only slightly longer, can snap into focus if we first visualize it and then summarize our vision in something like the following manner:

The poet, on a morning walk along a roadside, sees a white moth within the grasp of a white spider perched on a white and blighted wildflower. This strange and incongruous combination leads him to reflect about the role of fate in the events of the world.

A line-by-line paraphrase of "Design" might isolate and clarify problems in the interpretation of specific words and phrases, but it would also equal or exceed the length of the original fourteen-line poem. A simple three-line summary, such as the one proposed here, has an advantage: it allows us to think of the poem as a totality—to get a single image of it—and that image, if well formed, can serve as a starting point for further explanation, analysis, and understanding.

6. **Evaluate the Poem's Tone.** The tone of a poem is created by the author's overall attitude toward the subject or audience. It helps to determine the choice of words and rhetorical devices. Thus, when we wish to evaluate a poem's tone, we do so by examining the emotional effects of its words, images, and

figures of speech (particularly overstatement, understatement, irony, paradox, and ambiguity). In any collection of poetry, we will find some poems in which the tone is obvious; others in which it is complex; and still others in which it changes as the poet develops his or her thoughts.

In many cases, the author's tone is unmistakable. "Upon Julia's Clothes," for example, clearly reflects Herrick's passionate preoccupation with Julia. His attitude is expressed directly by his exclamations, "how sweetly flows/ That liquefaction of her clothes" and "O how that glittering taketh me!" And it is expressed indirectly by the fact that the poet's excitement is stimulated so easily. We recognize that he must indeed be deeply in love if so small a thing as the rustle of Julia's skirts drives him to such poetic expression. Herrick's tone, then, is enraptured, loving, and excited.

The analysis of tone becomes more difficult when the author uses irony, paradox, or ambiguity because conflicting meanings and, hence, conflicting attitudes toward the subject are implied by those devices. When, for example, Byron writes that a serious illness made him so devoutly religious that he wished the three persons of the Trinity were four "On purpose to believe so much the more," we will wholly misunderstand his tone and meaning unless we recognize that he is being ironic. The literal sense of the words is at odds with their real intention, and Byron's tone is sceptical, instead of pious, and playful, instead of serious.

The determination of tone becomes even more complex when, as in the case of Frost's "Design," the poet's attitude seems to change as he reflects more and more deeply on the significance of the events he describes. The first eight lines of Frost's poem are largely descriptive. The tone is observing, meticulous, and perhaps a little eerie. We see the flower, the moth, and the spider close up, as if through a magnifying glass; and the preoccupation with death and blight, along with the analogy to a witches' broth, is chilling. The next six lines present three rhetorical questions and a final conditional clause. Here Frost begins to inquire into the meaning of what he has just described. The first two questions merely underscore the unusual combination of events that brought together the blighted flower, the albino spider, and the innocent white moth. Frost's tone is inquisitive and concerned, but still fairly neutral and objective. In the last question, however, the tone suddenly becomes fearful. What else, Frost asks, can this incident be "but the design of darkness to appall?" Then Frost moves in a direction that at first appears reassuring when he doubts, almost as an afterthought, "If design govern in a thing so small." Yet the line also opens up the unsettling possibility that there is no design at all and the world is governed by chance. If there is any reassurance in these thoughts, that reassurance ought to be thoroughly undermined by the fearful realization that the scene *has* seemed fated. The designs of darkness *have* seemed to operate—even at the insignificant level of the moth, the spider, and the innocent heal-all! This sobering and somewhat horrifying possibility ultimately summarizes the direction toward which the poem—both in tone and in meaning—has been moving all along.

7.   Identify the Theme.   A literary *theme*, as we use the term in this text, is the central idea or insight that unifies and controls the total work. It is the main point an author wishes to make about his subject. As such, identifying a poem's theme involves two steps: finding the poem's subject and formulating the poet's main statement about that subject.

It is easy to determine the subject of most poems: often it is named or suggested by the title, and, of course, it is the focus of the whole poem. Herrick's title, "Upon Julia's Clothes," clearly names his subject—although we might add that the only significance of the clothes is that Julia is wearing them. At heart, the poem is an expression of Herrick's love for Julia. And this more general statement of the subject carries us far toward understanding the poem's theme, which—broadly stated—is that everything associated with the woman one loves becomes as beautiful and enchanting as she is.

The title of Frost's sonnet, "Design," reflects both the poem's subject and its theme. The subject is the possibility of design in the convergence of the white flower, the white moth, and the white spider. The theme—as nearly as one can state what Frost leaves only as a question—is that perhaps the designs of darkness control even the trivial and insignificant events in nature.

Stating a poem's theme in one sentence can be useful in summarizing its purpose and importance, but it also can be a coarse and misleading approach to poetry. If Herrick or Frost had wished to develop only those themes that we have assigned to their poems, then they could easily have stated their purposes more directly. In the case of Herrick's poem, we have probably looked too hard for the significance of his simple imagistic description. Herrick himself probably realized that a poem of six lines cannot state abstract truths without sounding pompous and grandiose. A brief description may suggest those truths, but it ought not insist on them. The scope of Herrick's poem is wisely confined to the movement of Julia's clothes; it does not actually describe her clothing nor does it describe her person, for these subjects, presumably, would require a much more lavish treatment. The poem does not mention Herrick's love for Julia, nor does it assert Julia's beauty—everything, therefore, that we have said about the poem's theme is deduced without any direct support from a text that is imagistic rather than judgmental or argumentative.

The attempt to determine the plain sense of a poem by following the seven steps outlined in this chapter will give you a much clearer understanding of the literal meaning of the poem and of the issues in it that are worthy of explication and analysis. However, a written explication or analysis will not necessarily include each of those seven steps as an explicit portion of the essay. Moreover, a formal explication will normally go on to examine the matters of versification and form discussed in the next two chapters. You should use the seven steps outlined and the section on 'Questions to Ask About Poetry' (pp. 755–756) to discover the ideas that you may wish to include in an essay. For advice on how to write your explication or analysis, see the section on 'Writing About Literature' (pp. 5–27).

Poems for Further Study

DELIGHT IN DISORDER

A sweet disorder in the dress
Kindles in clothes a wantonness:

A lawn° about the shoulders thrown   *fine linen shawl*
Into a fine distraction:
5   An erring lace, which here and there
Enthrals the crimson stomacher.[1]
A cuff neglectful, and thereby
Ribbands° to flow confusedly: *Ribbons*
A winning wave, deserving note,
10   In the tempestuous petticoat:
A careless shoe-string, in whose tie
I see a wild civility:
Do more bewitch me than when art
Is too precise in every part.

—Robert Herrick [1648]

❧ QUESTIONS ❧

1.   What is Herrick's principle of selection in choosing the imagery?

2.   What words in the poem give some indication of the speaker's response to the woman and his assumptions about her personality?

3.   How is the poem's imagery organized? Is there a pattern of development?

4.   Consider the poem's rhyme scheme and rhythm. Is Herrick's own verse "too precise in every part," or does it, like the lady's "sweet disorder in the dress," demonstrate "a wide civility"?

ANTHEM FOR DOOMED YOUTH

What passing-bells for these who die as cattle?
   Only the monstrous anger of the guns.
   Only the stuttering rifles' rapid rattle
Can patter out their hasty orisons°   *prayers*
5   No mockeries for them from prayers or bells,
   Nor any voice of mourning save the choirs,—
The shrill, demented choirs of wailing shells;
   And bugles calling for them from sad shires.

What candles may be held to speed them all?
10   Not in the hands of boys, but in their eyes
Shall shine the holy glimmers of good-byes.
   The pallor of girls' brows shall be their pall;
Their flowers the tenderness of silent minds,
And each slow dusk a drawing-down of blinds.

—Wilfred Owen [posthumous, 1920]

[1] A separate piece of cloth held in place by laces and covering a woman's bosom.

❧ QUESTIONS ❧

1.   What is an anthem? Does this poem meet the definition of an anthem?

2.   Who are the doomed youths in the poem? (Consider the date of publication in answering this question.)

3.   According to Owen, what passing bells, prayers, choirs, candles, pall, and flowers are accorded to the youths he is describing?

4.   How would you describe the speaker's tone and his attitude toward warfare?

5.   Is Owen successful in making the sound of this poem echo its sense? Explain your answer.

NOT WAVING BUT DROWNING

Nobody heard him, the dead man,
But still he lay moaning:
I was much further out than you thought
And not waving but drowning.

5   Poor chap, he always loved larking
And now he's dead
It must have been too cold for him his heart gave way,
They said.

Oh, no no no, it was too cold always
10   (Still the dead one lay moaning)
I was much too far out all my life
And not waving but drowning.

—Stevie Smith [1957]

❧ QUESTIONS ❧

1.   How many speakers are there in this poem? Do you think that the words are actually spoken—or are they the words that would have been or should have been spoken?

2.   If the drowned man lies "moaning" (line 2), how can he be "dead" (line 1)?

3.   Why did no one attempt to rescue the drowning man? Why does no one hear his moaning? How do the people on the beach misunderstand the dead man's personality and motives?

4.   In what sense did the dead man's heart give way?

5.   What is the effect of the repetition in the poem? What symbolic or allegorical interpretation of the events does it encourage?

12

❧❧❧❧❧❧❧

Rhythm and Meter

If you hold a conch shell to your ear, you will seem to hear within it the rhythmic rush and retreat of the sea surf. Although children find deep fascination and mystery in this audible reminder of the ocean, science explains away that magic meter as an echo of the blood throbbing in the listener's own inner ear. But in this case, as indeed in many others, the scientific explanation does less to erase our wonder than to transpose it and intellectualize it. The rhythm of the conch—the crashing of the sea—is also in the beat of our blood, the core of our very being. We are, it seems, rhythm-making creatures. When we listen to the monotone ticking of a wristwatch, we hear it as a rhythmic tic-tock. The rattle of a moving train is heard as a rhythmic clickety-clack. We hear the drumming of a horse's hooves as clip-clop. We make something rhythmic out of even the most dull and invariable experiences.

This affection for rhythm has never been fully explained, but it is probably the result of the natural rhythms of human life. In addition to the systolic and diastolic beat of the heart, there are similar rhythms in our breathing, in our movements as bipeds, and in a great variety of our habitual activities. Generations of farmers, pressing one ear to a cow's churning and drum-tight belly, have rhythmically squeezed her milk into a pail. Generations of farm men have raised and dropped a hoe or slung and recoiled a scythe. Generations of farm women have rhythmically kneaded dough or scrubbed at a washboard. Generations of children have grown up loving chants, nursery rhymes, and jingles.

It should come as no surprise then that both prose and poetry are rhythmic. According to the nineteenth-century French poet Charles Baudelaire, "rhythm and rhyme answer in man to the immortal needs of monotony, symmetry, and surprise." Furthermore, **strong emotions tend to find memorable expression through strong rhythms.** This is obviously true of music, dance, and poetry; but it can also be true of prose. Julius Caesar's pride in conquering

Gaul shone through the rhythms of his message to the Roman senate, "Veni, vidi, vici!" ("*I came, I saw, I conquered!*") Patrick Henry's belief in the cause of American independence was passionately expressed through the strong, rhythmical patterns in his speech to the Virginia Convention on March 23, 1775:

The gentlemen may cry, Peace, Peace! but there is no peace. The war is actually begun! The next gale that sweeps from the north shall bring to our ears the clash of resounding arms! . . . Is life so dear or peace so sweet as to be purchased at the price of chains and slavery? Forbid it, Almighty God. I know not what course others may take, but as for me, give me liberty or give me death!

Abraham Lincoln's firm belief in the need for reconciliation following the Civil War was beautifully embodied in the cadence of his second inaugural address of 1865:

With malice toward none, with charity for all, with firmness in the right as God gives us to see the right, let us bind up the Nation's wounds.

As we have just seen, poets have no monopoly on rhythm; it is also true that the correct use of meter does not make a poet, any more than the correct use of grammar makes a novelist or the correct use of chewing tobacco makes a baseball player. As Ralph Waldo Emerson observed in 1844, **"it is not meters, but a meter-making argument that makes a poem—a thought so passionate and alive that like the spirit of a plant or an animal it has an architecture of its own and adorns nature with a new thing."** Just as our hearts beat vigorously at moments of violent emotion, so, too, our words begin to beat more forcefully while we express those emotions—and the rhythms of poetic words often re-create in a careful reader the same sense of breathless excitement that possessed the poet.

Although we respond as readily to the rhythms of prose as poetry, the fact remains that most poetry (and little prose) is cast into formal metrical patterns. Perhaps the reason for this, as we have already suggested, is that the metrical patterns of verse help to create a more direct relationship to natural human rhythms than is possible in prose. When the alternating accents of iambic verse are read aloud, they almost inevitably match the 72 beats per minute of our pulse. Moreover, when we speak aloud, our words are naturally grouped in response to our breathing. After giving voice to eight or ten syllables, most speakers must pause for another breath. English verse makes the speaker's breathing easier by being written in lines of roughly equal length. The two most common measures in our language, tetrameter and pentameter, normally contain eight and ten syllables, respectively. Lines longer than pentameter are uncommon because they can be difficult to recite. Shorter lines, like trimeter which has six syllables, by encouraging rapid breathing, give the illusion of haste or excitement. Thus, verse itself is both a response to human physiology and an influence on it. **Like a natural force, verse sets up a pattern of expectations that we recognize intuitively and to which we respond both physically and emotionally.** The study of metrics allows us to name and to analyze the prevailing rhythms of most poems.

Meter **is basically a system for helping the reader reproduce the rhythm intended by the author.** The word *meter* comes from the Greek "metron," meaning "measure." These words, *meter* and *measure*, are used interchangeably in describing poetic rhythms. The units with which we measure verse are the syllable, the foot, the line, and sometimes the stanza and the canto. **A *syllable*, which is the smallest unit in metrics, is any word or part of a word produced in speech by a single pulse of breath.** It is a simple link in the chain of sounds. Between sixty and eighty percent of the words in English poetry are monosyllables—words like *root, tree, leaf, fruit, man, child, boy, girl, a, an,* and *the*. The remaining words are polysyllabic and are divided by dictionaries into their individual links of sound: *re-main-ing, pol-y-syl-lab-ic, di-vi-ded,* etc. **The basic rhythmic unit in verse is called a *foot* and is composed of an established number of stressed (emphasized) and unstressed syllables. An established number of feet makes up a *line* and an established number of lines often makes up a *stanza*. The number of lines or stanzas in a *canto* (a unit or section of a long poem) is rarely fixed in advance.**

SCANSION

The process by which we discover the dominant rhythm in a poem is called *scansion*. The basic steps in scanning a poem are quite simple and entail (1) finding the number of syllables in a typical line, (2) marking the stressed or accented syllables in each line and (3) identifying the prevailing foot and the number of feet per line. It should be noted that the entire process focuses on the number of syllables and stresses in a given line of poetry. For this reason, English verse is said to be written in syllabic-stress meters.

Now let us go through each step in the scansion process for a representative poem, "On First Looking into Chapman's Homer" by John Keats:

ON FIRST LOOKING INTO CHAPMAN'S HOMER

1 Much have I travell'd in the realms of gold
2 And many goodly states and kingdoms seen,
3 Round many western islands have I been
4 Which bards in fealty to Apollo hold.
5 Oft of one wide expanse had I been told
6 That deep-browed Homer ruled as his demesne:
7 Yet did I never breathe its pure serene
8 Till I heard Chapman speak out loud and bold.
9 Then felt I like some watcher of the skies
10 When a new planet swims into his ken;
11 Or like stout Cortez when with eagle eyes
12 He stared at the Pacific—and all his men
13 Look'd at each other with a wild surmise—
14 Silent upon a peak in Darien.

—John Keats [1816]

1. **Find the number of syllables in a typical line.** Inspection of the poem shows that the typical line contains ten syllables, but lines 4, 6, 12, and 14 present minor problems in syllabification. The word "fealty" in line 4 is usually divided into three syllables, "fe/al/ty," but because this would give the line a total of eleven, we may feel more comfortable eliding "fe/al" into one syllable which sounds like the word *feel*. There are, in fact, an unusual number of words in our language that are divided differently on different occasions: for example, *unusual* (un-use-yul, un-use-u-al), *our* (are, ow-er), *different* (diff-er-

ent, diff-rent), *occasions* (o-cay-zhuns, o-cay-zhi-ens). Moreover, the syllabification of certain words has changed over the centuries—notably in the pronunciation of the *ed* forms of verbs: *bathed* was once *bath-ed, in-spired* was once *in-spi-red, changed* was once *chang-ed,* and even now *aged* may be pronounced *age-ed.* Archaic forms are, of course, common in medieval verse, but they are sometimes deliberately used in more contemporary poetry where the unanticipated accents are generally marked *(changéd).* Keats, however, so often required his readers to pronounce the final *ed* of verbs that in the first line of "On First Looking into Chapman's Homer," he used the contraction "travell'd" to show that the end of the verb was *not* to be sounded.

Alternate pronunciations and archaisms are only two of the problems of syllabification. Many of us are unfamiliar with the pronunciation of some words used in poetry. In line 6, for example, the word *demesne* appears to have three syllables, but we learn from the dictionary that it may be pronounced to rhyme with *serene,* in line 7:

> *de·mesne* (di-mān′,-ēn′), n . . . . 3.any territory or domain.

Thus, line 6, like most of the others, contains the expected ten syllables. In line 14 we might again turn to a dictionary to reassure ourselves that "Darien" does indeed have the three syllables (Da/ri/en) required by the meter.

No reading of line 12, however, can produce any fewer than eleven syllables, and therefore we are forced to describe that one line as slightly irregular. **The expectation of a predictable number of syllables in a line is *only* an expectation. Slight variations are normal and even desirable when they serve some rhythmic function.** But in order to discuss a poem's rhythm, we must learn to identify the pattern of stressed and unstressed syllables.

2. Mark the stressed or accented syllables in each line. The problem of determining where the stresses fall in poetry is more complex than counting the syllables, but with a good ear and the guidance of a few simple rules, most readers can produce satisfactory results.

The first rule is that **a poem's meter should not change the normal pronunciation of a polysyllabic word.** In all words of two syllables or more, the accentuation is marked in most dictionaries.[1] Thus, in lines 3 and 4, for example, we can immediately mark several stressed syllables. The dictionary tells us that the accent falls on the middle syllable of "A·pól·lo" and on the first syllables of "mán·y," "wés·tern," "ís·lands," and "feál·ty." If we place a straight line over the accented syllables, the preliminary scansion of the lines looks like this:

> Round mány wéstern íslands have I been
>
> Which bards in feálty to Apóllo hold.

The second rule is that **monosyllabic words have no inherent stress; they take on stresses to fit the metrical pattern of the poem and the rhetorical rhythm of a particular sentence.** In other words, monosyllables may be either

---

[1] One should note, however, that not all dictionaries mark the secondary accents in polysyllabic words, and sometimes the same word can be pronounced in different ways. E.g., *infínitive* and *ínfinitìve.*

stressed or unstressed. In general, however, the emphasis should fall where it would in a normal prose reading of the lines. **Usually, the stresses will fall on the most important words—especially nouns and verbs.** Less important words, like articles, prepositions and conjunctions, are rarely stressed. In addition, in normal English prose, stressed and unstressed syllables tend to alternate. When we read Keats's lines aloud we find that weak, but still noticeable, stresses fall on "have" and "been," while more pronounced emphasis is placed on "bards" and "hold." If we now mark each of these as an accented syllable and mark the remaining unaccented syllables with a cup (ˇ), we will have produced a complete metrical picture of the lines:

> Round many western islands have I been
> Which bards in fealty to Apollo hold.

3. Identify the prevailing foot and the number of feet per line. Having scanned the lines, we now need only name the specific meter being used. **In the syllabic-stress system there are only five commonly used feet: iambic, anapestic, trochaic, dactylic, and spondaic.**

TABLE OF METRICAL FEET

Name	*Example*
Dactyl	"Much have I
Trochee	travell'd
Anapest	in the realms
Iamb	of gold."
Spondee	John Keats.

Of these, the iamb is by far the most popular and versatile. It is the principal foot used in such narrative and dramatic verse as Chaucer's *Canterbury Tales,* Shakespeare's plays, Milton's *Paradise Lost,* Wordsworth's *Prelude,* Byron's *Don Juan,* and most other substantial poems written in English. The iambic foot is equally popular in lyric verse and ballads and is required in sonnets. It is, therefore, used in Keats's sonnet, "On First Looking into Chapman's Homer," and the two lines that we have just scanned can be shown to have five iambic feet to the line:

> Round man/y wes/tern is/lands have/ I been
> Which bards/ in feal/ty to/ Apol/lo hold.

We use a vertical slash (/) to mark the divisions between the feet. These divisions are helpful in counting the feet, but they do not signal pauses in speech; they may fall either between words or between the syllables of a word.

In critical analysis we generally replace the wordy and awkward phrase "five feet to the line" with the term **pentameter.** The technical term for each of the possible lines in English poetry is provided in the following list:

> ***monometer:*** one foot per line
> ***dimeter:*** two feet per line
> ***trimeter:*** three feet per line
> ***tetrameter:*** four feet per line
> ***pentameter:*** five feet per line
> ***hexameter:*** six feet per line
> ***heptameter:*** seven feet per line
> ***octameter:*** eight feet per line

Of these, pentameter and tetrameter are the most commonly used.

Once chosen, the dominant metrical foot normally remains fixed throughout a given poem. Thus, for example, iambic rhythm prevails in Donne's "A Valediction: Forbidding Mourning" (p. 798), whereas trochaic rhythm prevails in Blake's "The Tyger" (p. 832) and anapestic rhythm dominates Poe's "Annabel Lee" (p. 715). **Although the principal metrical foot almost invariably remains unchanged throughout a poem, the length of the lines often varies according to a pre-established pattern.** "A Valediction: Forbidding Mourning" and "The Tyger" are tetrameter throughout, but in "Annabel Lee" tetrameter alternates with trimeter.

Thus, in choosing iambic pentameter for "Chapman's Homer," Keats commits himself to creating the possibility of a scansion that includes five metrical feet in each line, and he has to work within the expectation that each line will follow an iambic rhythm. We use the words *possibility* and *expectation* because the metrical pattern of a poem is not intended to be a straitjacket that restricts all movement and permits scant room to breathe. Rather, the pattern should be cut like a well-tailored dress that complements both the shape and the movement of the human form it adorns. Deviations from the expected metrical pattern create surprise, emphasis, and often delight.

Anapestic, dactylic, trochaic, and spondaic feet are all used more frequently to provide variety in iambic verse than to set the rhythm of an entire poem. As the examples in our Table of Metrical Feet show, each of these (except the spondee) is used in the first line of Keats's sonnet:

> *dactyl   trochee   anapest   iamb*
> Much have Ĭ/ travĕll'd/ĭn thĕ realms/ ŏf gold . . .

Keats's first line is, therefore, highly irregular, and two questions now confront us: What purposes are served by variations from an established meter? And how do different rhythms affect our emotional response to poetry?

A partial answer to the first question was proposed by Samuel Johnson when he wrote, in his "Life of Dryden" (1781), that "the essence of verse is regularity and its ornament is variety." This implies that **a poem should be regular enough to establish a pattern and varied enough to banish monotony.** It is a corollary to the familiar rule endorsing moderation in all things, and in recent years it has become almost commonplace to condemn poets whose meters are too regular.

There is, however, little value in a more detailed attempt to state a general principle about regularity and variety in meter. Such esthetic judgments can only be made within the context of a particular poem's meaning. What *can* be said, however, is that **rhythm and any deviations from rhythm should contribute to the overall effect sought in the poem. "What is wanted is neither**

a dead mechanical beat nor a jumble of patternless incoherence, but the rich expressiveness of a verse that is alive with the tension of living speech."[2]

"The tension of living speech" is an apt expression for the effect of metrical variation in "On First Looking into Chapman's Homer." If we look again at its first line, we see that, although it has ten syllables and can conceivably be read as iambic pentameter,

Much HĀVE/ Ĭ TRĀ/veĬl'd ĪN/ the RĒALMS/ ŏf GŌLD,

such a reading distorts the rhythms of living speech. But if we read the line naturally,

MŪCH hăve Ĭ/ TRĀveĬl'd/ ĭn the RĒALMS/ ŏf GŌLD,

we find neither a metrical pattern—indeed, each foot is different—nor the five feet we expect in pentameter. Clearly, Keats is creating a tension between living speech and our expectations of a sonnet. The line has fewer accents and more unstressed syllables than we expect; and because unstressed syllables roll rapidly from the tongue, the pace of the line is more rapid than in standard iambic pentameter. This can be stated as a general principle of metrics: **unaccented syllables in anapests and dactyls accelerate the pace; heavily accented syllables in spondees slow the pace.**

Furthermore, Keats has arranged the unstressed syllables so that nearly all of them pour forth in two rolling clusters. Thus, the poem begins with a sense of surprise and breathless excitement. As we continue reading, we learn that this tone is exactly right for the story Keats has to tell. Reading Chapman's translation of Homer was a new and exciting experience for Keats. It showed him that poetry could unexpectedly "speak out loud and bold"; it did not need to be a syrupy concoction of unvaried sweetness. The rhythm in the first line of the sonnet helps to capture and communicate Keats's emotions.

One line in a sonnet is, of course, insufficient to set the tone for the rest of the poem, but the rhythm of this first line is repeated again and again. The dactyl-trochee combination, which helps to make these first syllables forceful and rugged, occurs at the beginning of lines 5, 7, 9, 13, and 14:

1 Múch hăve Ĭ/ trávell'd/ . . .

5 Ōft ŏf one/ wīde ĕx/panse . . .

7 Yēt dĭd Ĭ/ nĕver/ . . .

9 Thēn fĕlt Ĭ/ līke sŏme/ . . .

13 Look'd ăt eăch/ other/ . . .

14 Sīlĕnt ŭp/on ă/ . . .

The tension between regular iambic pentameter and Keats's startling irregularity is especially noticeable in the final verses, both because these lines occur at the poem's climax and because two irregular patterns occur in immediate succession. Keats achieves a perfect blending of sound and sense when he says of Cortez:

[2] Cleanth Brooks and Robert Penn Warren, *Understanding Poetry*, 4th ed. (New York: Holt, Rinehart, and Winston, 1976), 503.

₁₂ He stared/ at the Pa/cific//—and all/ his men

₁₃ Look'd at each/ other// with a wild/ surmise—

₁₄ Silent// upon/ a peak/ in Da/rien.

In describing the metrical effects in this combination of lines, we will find it useful to define three more terms: *end-stopped verse, enjambment,* and the *caesura.* **An *end-stopped* line,** like line 13 in Keats's sonnet, **is simply one that concludes with a pause.** A strongly end-stopped verse ends with some mark of punctuation—a comma, semicolon, colon, dash, question mark, exclamation point, or period. The punctuation tells the reader to pause for breath and emphasis. Although a lightly end-stopped verse may have no formal punctuation, it must still mark a pause between phrases or clauses. Lines one, three, five, seven, and eleven are all lightly end-stopped. ***Enjambment* (or "striding over"),** as in line 12 of Keats's sonnet, **is the running on of one line into the next without a grammatical pause.** End-stopping tends to reinforce the metrical structure of a poem, whereas enjambment tends to minimize the difference between the sound of verse and that of prose. **A *caesura* (marked with a double slash, //) is a pause that occurs near the middle of most verses.** This pause may be indicated by punctuation, as in line 12; or it may fall between phrases, as in line 13. If a line has an even number of feet, the caesura tends to bisect it, as in line 13. One advantage of iambic pentameter is that its five accents can never be divided evenly. This ensures a certain amount of variety in even the most regular pentameters and opens up the possibility of a caesural pause as late as the fourth foot or as early as the first (line 14).

How do end-stopping, enjambment, and the caesural pause contribute to the impact of Keats's poem? It is quite apparent that a dramatic pause is signaled by the dash at the end of line 13. The effect of this pause is to emphasize the "wild surmise" and to encourage us to determine *what* is surmised. These men have discovered an entirely new ocean and are briefly struck dumb with wonder. They pause, just as Keats's punctuation forces us to pause. The content of these lines is in absolute harmony with their end-stopped rhythm.

The contribution of the enjambment from line 12 to 13 is also important, but it is atypical of the general effect of that device. If we examine Keats's poem as a whole, we find that exactly half of the lines are run-on or very lightly end-stopped. Thus, the poem has the typographical appearance of verse, but because strongly end-stopped lines are avoided, it has a fluid movement resembling that of melodious prose. In this respect, Keats's style is unusually mature for a poet who had not yet reached the age of legal majority. Most other great poets from Chaucer and Shakespeare to Byron and Wordsworth passed through a period of strong end-stopping before evolving at last to a more flexible style. But the enjambment at line 12 is grammatical only. In prose we do not ordinarily pause between a subject and verb. We use but one breath to say, "and all his men looked at each other." But when these words are put into a sonnet and scanned as on this page, a substantial pause before "Look'd" is almost obligatory for several reasons. In the first place most readers of poetry inevitably pause slightly at the end of a line of verse— even when such a pause is not syntactic. The end-line pause is one of our expectations in verse. Furthermore, in this particular case, the last syllable of line 12 ("men") is accented, as is the first syllable of line 13 ("Look'd"). As we mentioned before, strong accents in juxtaposition always slow the pace of poetry, here augmenting the natural end-line pause. And finally, it makes dramatic sense to pause before "Look'd." The pause helps to create suspense and emphasis. It informs us that this is a penetrating look, a look of rapture and astonishment. Hence, the grammatical enjambment between lines 12 and 13 is offset by a combination of poetic effects, and once again we have "verse that is alive with the tension of living speech."

The caesural pauses in lines 12 and 13 merit no special analysis—the one in line 12 is plainly grammatical and the one in line 13 falls at the exact midpoint of the line and between two prepositional phrases, each of which independently modifies the verb. We might, however, be tempted to omit the caesura we placed after the first foot in line 14,

$$\bar{\text{S}}\text{i}\breve{\text{l}}\text{ent}// \breve{\text{u}}\text{pon}/ \bar{\text{a}} \text{ peak}/ \text{in Da}/\text{ri}\bar{\text{e}}\text{n}.$$

It certainly could not be placed later in the line because it would then either divide words within a prepositional phrase or separate two phrases closely linked both in logic and in grammar. And in placing a caesura after "Silent," we disrupt the rhythm of the dactyl-trochee combination that has characterized the poem. But if we wish to protect that rhythm, we must omit the caesura altogether and scan the line in a way that produces an unusual monosyllabic foot:

$$\bar{\text{S}}\text{ilent } \breve{\text{u}}\text{p}/\text{on } \bar{\text{a}}/ \text{ peak}/ \text{in Da}/\text{ri}\bar{\text{e}}\text{n}.^3$$

Of the two options, the former is clearly preferable. It is closer to regular iambic pentameter; it includes the expected caesura at a grammatically acceptable place; and, most importantly, it helps the sound of the poem to echo its sense. A momentary silence *should* follow the word—as if in recognition of its meaning.

In summary, the goal of a metrical analysis is to clarify how the rhythm of language contributes to its poetic meaning. In order to assist in this process, the full scansion of a poem or passage should identify the underlying metrical pattern; analyze the important deviations from that pattern; and consider the effects of end-stopping, enjambment, and placement of the caesura. An analysis of rhythmic effects that is not based on scansion is likely to be imprecise and unintelligible; however, scansion that does not include analysis and interpretation is mechanical and meaningless.

Poems for Further Study

MY HEART LEAPS UP

My heart leaps up when I behold
  A rainbow in the sky:
So was it when my life began;
So is it now I am a man;

---

[3] Note that the placement of the caesura marks the only audible difference in the two possibilities in scansion. It makes no difference in the rhythm whether the feet are scanned as a trochee and four iambs or as a dactyl, a trochee, a monosyllable, and two iambs. Both scansions should be read in precisely the same manner.

5   So be it when I shall grow old,
           Or let me die!
       The Child is father of the Man;
       And I could wish my days to be
       Bound each to each by natural piety.

                            —William Wordsworth [1807]

———————————— ❧ QUESTIONS ❧ ————————————

1. How does the personification in line 1 help Wordsworth to communicate his emotional response to the rainbow?

2. What connotations—both biblical and otherwise—are associated with the rainbow?

3. How does the parallelism of lines 3–6 ("So was it . . . So is it . . . So be it . . .") increase the forcefulness of the entreaty? Why does Wordsworth wish to emphasize his enduring pleasure in natural beauty?

4. What truth is there in the paradox of line 7? What does Wordsworth mean by this paradox?

5. Scan the poem. What is the dominant rhythm? What meter prevails? What is the rhetorical effect of the shortened lines (lines 2 and 6)? Why does Wordsworth include an extra foot in the last line?

LA BELLE DAME SANS MERCI[4]

       "O what can ail thee, knight-at-arms,
           Alone and palely loitering?
       The sedge° is withered from the lake,   *coarse, clumped grass*
           And no birds sing.

5   "O what can ail thee, knight-at-arms,
           So haggard and so woe-begone?
       The squirrel's granary is full,
           And the harvest's done.

       "I see a lily on thy brow
10   With anguish moist and fever dew;
       And on thy cheek a fading rose
           Fast withereth too."

       "I met a lady in the meads,°   *meadows*
           Full beautiful—a faery's child,
15   Her hair was long, her foot was light,
           And her eyes were wild.

[4] The title, which means "The Beautiful Lady Without Mercy," is borrowed from a medieval French poem by Alain Chartier.

"I made a garland for her head,
   And bracelets too, and fragrant zone;°   *girdle (belt)*
She looked at me as she did love,
20   And made sweet moan.

"I set her on my pacing steed
   And nothing else saw all day long,
For sideways would she lean, and sing
      A faery's song.

25   "She found me roots of relish sweet,
   And honey wild and manna[5] dew,
And sure in language strange she said,
      'I love thee true!'

"She took me to her elfin grot,
30   And there she wept and sighed full sore;
And there I shut her wild, wild eyes
      With kisses four.

"And there she lullèd me asleep,
   And there I dreamed—Ah! woe betide!
35 The latest dream I ever dreamed
      On the cold hill's side.

"I saw pale kings and princes too,
   Pale warriors, death-pale were they all;
Who cried—'La belle dame sans merci
40   Hath thee in thrall!'

"I saw their starved lips in the gloam°   *twilight*
   With horrid warning gapèd wide,
And I awoke and found me here
      On the cold hill's side.

45   "And this is why I sojourn here
   Alone and palely loitering,
Though the sedge is withered from the lake,
      And no birds sing."

              —John Keats [1820]

❦ QUESTIONS ❦

1. How many speakers are in the poem and what are their situations?

2. What evidence suggests that the knight-at-arms is dying? What is the cause of his suffering?

[5] Miraculous and sustaining. See the Bible, Exodus 16:14–36.

3.   What does the setting contribute to the effect of the poem?

4.   Is the "lady in the meads" just "a faery's child," or is she a demon-lover who enchants men and then leaves them to die of love-longing? What details in lines 13–33 make her seem especially enchanting?

5.   Does the knight's dream in lines 37–44 do him any good? Why does the knight lose his lady? Why does the knight remain where the lady left him?

6.   Scan the poem. What is the dominant rhythm and what meters are used? How does the short, heavily accented line that ends each stanza contribute to the mood of the poem?

"I TASTE A LIQUOR NEVER BREWED"

I taste a liquor never brewed—
From Tankards scooped in Pearl—
Not all the Vats upon the Rhine
Yield such an Alcohol!

5   Inebriate of Air—am I—
And Debauchee of Dew—
Reeling—thro endless summer days—
From inns of Molten Blue—

When "Landlords" turn the drunken Bee
10   Out of the Foxglove's door—
When Butterflies—renounce their "drams"—
I shall but drink the more!

Till Seraphs° swing their snowy Hats—   *angels*
And Saints—to windows run—
15   To see the little Tippler
Leaning against the—Sun—

—Emily Dickinson [1861]

❦ QUESTIONS ❦

1.   What conceit dominates the poem and serves as its controlling metaphor? How do the various images in the poem—the "Inebriate of Air," the "Debauchee of Dew," the "inns of Molten Blue," and so on—contribute to the development of the conceit?

2.   How does the speaker characterize herself? What is her condition? What is her tone?

3.   Consider Dickinson's punctuation. Does it contribute to the creation of tone and meaning—or does it merely interfere with clarity?

4. Scan the poem. What is the dominant rhythm? What is the meter? Dickinson's speaker is a somewhat reeling "Inebriate of Air." Does she ever manipulate the rhythm to make the sound of the poem stagger along with its speaker?

13

❦❦❦❦❦

Rhythm and Meter
Part 2

Although the iambic pentameter of Keats's sonnet on "Chapman's Homer" is the most common of English meters, it is by no means the only possible rhythm. Nor is the syllabic-stress system the only possible approach to writing and scanning verse. Before closing our discussion of rhythm and meter, let us briefly survey the variety of poetic meters, the limitations of syllabic-stress scansion, and the other possible systems of scanning English verse.

VARIETY OF METERS. While trochees, anapests, and dactyls are most frequently used to provide variety within an iambic rhythm, each can also establish the underlying meter of a poem, and each creates a very different rhythmic effect. The rhythm of a poem does not, of course, dictate its tone. Rhythm is at best a contributing factor that can be used by able poets to complement the mood created through the denotations and connotations of words. There are, however, differences among the four basic meters of English poetry, and these differences can easily be heard, even though their effects cannot be perfectly described.

The *trochee* (travell'd) is the mirror image of the iamb and is perhaps even more common than the iamb in everyday speech. The plurals of many monosyllabic words become trochaic (*fishes, houses, axes,* etc.) and a great many two-syllable words are natural trochees (*poet, water, able,* etc.).

Trochaic and iambic meters do not differ greatly in their effects. In fact, trochaic pentameter can be described as iambic pentameter with a defective first foot and an extra syllable at the end.

$$\text{trochaic} \quad \bar{}\ |\ \smile\ \bar{}\ |\ \smile\ \bar{}\ |\ \smile\ \bar{}\ |\ \smile\ \smile$$
$$\text{iambic} \quad \smile\ \smile\ |\ \smile\ \bar{}\ |\ \smile\ \bar{}\ |\ \smile\ \bar{}\ |\ \smile\ \smile$$

Because the first syllable in a trochaic line is accented, poems in this meter often sound assertive and vigorous. But the use of trochees makes end rhyme difficult because rhyme words are usually stressed. Thus, some poems that start out with a trochaic rhythm end up iambic, as in the catalectic (meaning "incomplete") trochaic tetrameter of John Donne's "Song":

SONG

Go, and catch a falling star,
   Get with child a mandrake root,[1]
Tell me where all past years are,
   Or who cleft the Devil's foot.
5   Teach me to hear mermaids singing,
Or to keep off envy's stinging,
     And find,
     What wind
Serves to advance an honest mind.

10   If thou be'st born to strange sights,
   Things invisible to see,
Ride ten thousand days and nights,
   Till age snow white hairs on thee.
Thou, when thou return'st, wilt tell me
15   All strange wonders, that befell thee,
     And swear,
     No where
Lives a woman true and fair.

If thou find'st one, let me know,
20   Such a pilgrimage were sweet;
Yet do not, I would not go,
   Though at next door we might meet.
Though she were true when you met her,
And last, till you write your letter,
25   Yet she
     Will be
False, ere I come, to two or three.

—John Donne [posthumous, 1633]

❧ QUESTIONS ❧

1. To whom is the poem addressed? What is the speaker's tone? What is his opinion about the constancy of women?

2. Donne lists seven impossibilities in his first nine lines. What eighth impossibility does he have in mind throughout this stanza?

---

[1] The root of the mandrake resembles a human torso and legs.

3.   Where and with what effect does Donne use overstatement in this poem?

4.   Scan the poem. Where does Donne manipulate the rhythm to create rhetorical effects? How do the two short lines (monometers) in each stanza affect the rhythm of the poem? What is the advantage of slowing up the movement of the poem before the final line in each stanza? Where is this advantage most obvious and most effective?

Incantations are often trochaic, possibly because the strong accents that begin each trochaic line complement a chanting rhythm:

> Double/, double// toil and/ trouble;
> Fire/ burn and// cauldron/ bubble.

> —From *Macbeth*,
>   William Shakespeare [ca. 1607]

Very probably, this hint of the supernatural in trochaic rhythms guided Edgar Allan Poe in choosing the meter for "The Raven" (1845):

> Once up/on a/ midnight/ dreary,// while I/ pondered/ weak and/ weary,
> Over/ many a/ quaint and/ curious// volume/ of for/gotten/ lore—

A *dactyl* (Much have I) is a trochee with an extra unstressed syllable. Because unstressed syllables are pronounced easily, poems in dactylic meter move with a rapid, waltzing beat (dum-dee-dee, dum-dee-dee). The dactylic dimeter of Ralph Hodgson's "Eve" provides a good example of the lyrical but unsettling possibilities in the rhythm:

EVE

> Eve, with her basket, was
> Deep in the bells and grass,
> Wading in bells and grass
> Up to her knees,
5
> Picking a dish of sweet
> Berries and plums to eat,
> Down in the bells and grass
> Under the trees.

> Mute as a mouse in a
10
> Corner the cobra lay,
> Curled round a bough of the
> Cinnamon tall. . . .
> Now to get even and
> Humble proud Heaven and
15
> Now was the moment or
> Never at all.

"Eva!" Each syllable
Light as a flower fell,
"Eva!" he whispered the
20   Wondering maid,
Soft as a bubble sung
Out of a linnet's° lung,   *a small songbird*
Soft and most silverly
"Eva!" he said.

25   Picture that orchard sprite,
Eve, with her body white,
Supple and smooth to her
Slim finger tips,
Wondering, listening,
30   Listening, wondering,
Eve with a berry
Half-way to her lips.

Oh had our simple Eve
Seen through the make-believe!
35   Had she but known the
Pretender he was!
Out of the boughs he came,
Whispering still her name,
Tumbling in twenty rings
40   Into the grass.

Here was the strangest pair
In the world anywhere,
Eve in the bells and grass
Kneeling, and he
45   Telling his story low. . . .
Singing birds saw them go
Down the dark path to
The Blasphemous Tree.

Oh what a clatter when
50   Titmouse° and Jenny Wren   *a chickadee*
Saw him successful and
Taking his leave!
How the birds rated him,
How they all hated him!
55   How they all pitied
Poor motherless Eve!

Picture her crying
Outside in the lane,
Eve, with no dish of sweet
60   Berries and plums to eat,
Haunting the gate of the
Orchard in vain. . . .

Picture the lewd delight
Under the hill tonight—
65   "Eva!" the toast goes round,
"Eva!" again.

—Ralph Hodgson [1913]

——————— ❧ QUESTIONS ❧ ———————

1. Compare the story of Eve in this poem with the account in Genesis. What details does Hodgson add to the story? What is the effect of those details in creating setting, mood, motive, and character?

2. Examine the last stanza of the poem very carefully. How has the setting changed both in time and in space? Why does Hodgson change the setting?

3. Scan the poem (or at least several stanzas). What are the effects of the rhythm and meter? How do they contribute to the poem?

The dactyl is a rapid meter. Examine how Alfred Tennyson takes advantage of the strength and speed of dactyls to imitate the drumming of galloping horses in his famous "Charge of the Light Brigade":

Half a league,/ half a league
    Half a league/ onward,
All in the/ Valley of/ Death
    Rode the six/ hundred
"Forward the/ Light Brigade!
Charge for the/ guns!" he said:
Into the/ Valley of/ Death
    Rode the six/ hundred.

—From "The Charge of the Light Brigade,"
Alfred, Lord Tennyson [1854]

And Longfellow also uses the unfamiliar sound of the dactylic line to accentuate the primitive, pagan mood at the beginning of "Evangeline" (1847):

This is the/ forest prim/eval.// The/ murmuring/ pines and the/ hemlocks/ . . .
Stand like/ Druids of/ old.

The *anapest* (in the realms), like the dactyl, is a rapid meter, but in proceeding from unstressed syllables to stressed ones, it also parallels the iamb. Hence, it has none of the strangeness of the dactyl or trochee. It works well in rapidly paced poems:

The Assyr/ian came/ down// like the wolf/ on the fold,
And his co/horts were gleam/ing in pur/ple and gold;

And the sheen/ of their spears// was like stars/ on the sea,
When the Blue/ wave rolls night/ly on deep/ Galilee.

—From "The Destruction of Sennacherib,"
Lord Byron [1815]

And it also pleases in very mellifluous ones:

ANNABEL LEE

It was many and many a year ago.
    In a kingdom by the sea
That a maiden there lived whom you may know
    By the name of Annabel Lee;—
5   And this maiden she lived with no other thought
    Than to love and be loved by me.

She was a child and *I* was a child,
    In this kingdom by the sea,
But we loved with a love that was more than love—
10   I and my Annabel Lee—
With a love that the wingèd seraphs° of Heaven   *angels*
    Coveted her and me.

And this was the reason that, long ago,
    In this kingdom by the sea,
15   A wind blew out of a cloud by night
    Chilling my Annabel Lee;
So that her highborn kinsmen came
    And bore her away from me,
To shut her up in a sepulchre
20   In this kingdom by the sea.

The angels, not half so happy in Heaven,
    Went envying her and me:—
Yes! that was the reason (as all men know,
    In this kingdom by the sea)
25   That the wind came out of the cloud, chilling
    And killing my Annabel Lee.

But our love it was stronger by far than the love
    Of those who were older than we—
    Of many far wiser than we—
30   And neither the angels in Heaven above
    Nor the demons down under the sea,
Can ever dissever my soul from the soul
    Of the beautiful Annabel Lee:—

For the moon never beams without bringing me dreams
35   Of the beautiful Annabel Lee;

And the stars never rise but I see the bright eyes
 Of the beautiful Annabel Lee;
And so, all the night-tide, I lie down by the side
Of my darling, my darling, my life and my bride,
40   In her sepulchre there by the sea—
      In her tomb by the side of the sea.

—Edgar Allan Poe [posthumous, 1850]

❧ QUESTIONS ❧

1.   What was the speaker's relationship with Annabel Lee? What claims does the speaker make about their love?

2.   Throughout the poem, Poe frequently repeats the phrase "kingdom by the sea." What is the effect of that repetition? What, if anything, does the sea come to symbolize? What does the sky symbolize? What does the land symbolize?

3.   What does the speaker mean when he says that "we loved with a love that was more than love"? Why does he emphasize that "*She* was a child and *I* was a child"?

4.   How does the speaker explain the cause of Annabel Lee's death?

5.   How does the speaker console himself in the final stanza?

6.   Scan the poem. How do the rhythm and meter contribute to the mood of the poem?

Someone once argued that a long poem in anapests, like a long ride on a roller coaster, is apt to cause nausea, but there can be little doubt that this rolling meter is exquisitely suited to many brief pieces.

The *spondee* (John Keats) is never the dominant meter in a whole poem, but one or two spondees will tend to dominate a line. This is well illustrated in Alexander Pope's lines on the role of sound and rhythm in poetry:

True ease in writing comes from art, not chance,
As those move easiest who have learned to dance.
'Tis not enough no harshness gives offense,
The sound must seem an echo to the sense:
Soft is the strain when Zephyr gently blows,
And the smooth stream in smoother numbers flows;
But when/ loud sur/ges lash// the sound/ing shore,
The hoarse,/ rough verse// should like/ the tor/rent roar;
When A/jax strives// some rock's/ vast weight/ to throw,
The line/ too/ labors,/ and the words/ move slow.
—From "An Essay on Criticism," Alexander Pope [1711]

There is at least one spondee in each of the last four lines, and each time a spondee occurs three stressed syllables line up in front of us like hard blocks of granite that our voices must surmount. **Stressed syllables require more**

effort from the speaker and they take longer to pronounce than unstressed syllables. As a result, spondees always slow down the pace of a poem. They can be especially useful when an author wishes to express anger or violence, as in King Lear's line:

> Blow, winds,/ and crack/ your cheeks!// Rage! Blow!

In addition to the four principal rhythms (iambic, trochaic, anapestic, and dactylic) and that of the slow spondee, there are a great many feet with unpronounceable Greek names that pop up occasionally to vary the dominant rhythm of a poem: *pyrrhic* (˘ ˘), *bacchius* (˘ ⁻ ⁻), *antibacchius* (⁻ ⁻ ˘), *amphimacer* (⁻ ˘ ⁻), *amphibrach* (˘ ⁻ ˘), and so on. Although there is no need to remember these names, their existence demonstrates that, within the framework of a dominant rhythm, a poet may proceed almost as he or she pleases. The poet has what is called the "poetic license" to take liberties with meter, syntax, and even diction, *providing* the result is a more forceful, unified, and distinctive poem.

THE LIMITATIONS OF SYLLABIC STRESS SCANSION. **The rules of scansion are loose, and nearly every line of verse can be marked in a number of ways.** We have, for example, scanned King Lear's line as two spondees and two iambs:

> Blow, winds,/ and crack/ your cheeks!// Rage! Blow!

But because the line occurs in a passage that is predominantly iambic pentameter, we might choose to give it the required five feet by marking with a caret (ˆ) the pauses that would naturally fall after the two exclamation points:

> Blow, winds,/ and crack/ your cheeks!// Rage!ˆ Blow!ˆ

Similarly, we have scanned the first line of "On First Looking into Chapman's Homer" as a dactyl, trochee, anapest, and iamb.

> Much have I/ travell'd// in the realms/ of gold.

It could also be a trochee, iamb, pyrrhic, and two iambs:

> Much have/ I tra/vell'd in/ the realms/ of gold.

Such changes in scansion are cosmetic only and indicate no significant difference in the way each line *should be* read.

There is, however, considerable room for actual changes in the way a line *can* be read. Different readers rarely use stresses and pauses in precisely the same places, as anyone can testify after hearing one of Hamlet's soliloquies spoken by actors so different as Laurence Olivier, Richard Burton, and Richard Chamberlain. Sometimes we do not agree on the syllables that should be stressed or on the relative amount of stress on each. **Scansion is,** after all, **a system of simplifying and visually presenting the complex rhythm in a line. It is not an exact science.** Even if a precise system were possible, it would be too complicated to be useful in pointing out the simple, recurring rhythms of poetry. There must be a certain amount of flexibility in the scansion of any poem.

Although we must accept the limitations of our system and recognize that there will rarely be only one "right" way of scanning a poem, we must also recognize that this loosely constructed system is of considerable usefulness to both poets and readers. Because syllabic-stress meters are common in English poetry and their scansion is well understood, poets can confidently expect that readers will pick up most of the clues to rhythm that the meter conveys and therefore will read the lines with an emphasis closely approximating what was intended. Conversely, readers can easily determine a poem's underlying meter and then decide how they wish to read each line. The decisions made should be based, where possible, on the poem's content, its prose emphases, and its basic meter. The commonly accepted terminology of scansion allows us to explain more easily the decisions about the rhythm that we have made and how these decisions reflect and reinforce the meaning of the poem. Finally, the prevalence of syllabic-stress meters allows great poets to create a tension between the rhythm of ordinary speech and the heartbeat of the poetic line. The discovery of new possibilities in poetic rhythm in a poem like "Chapman's Homer" is one of the pleasures of travel in the realms of gold.

ALTERNATE SYSTEMS OF SCANSION. The syllabic stress system of metrics slowly came to dominate English poetry between the twelfth and sixteenth centuries because it proved better suited to the evolving English language than any of the competing systems: *accentual-alliterative meters, purely syllabic meters, quantitative meters,* and *free verse.* Nonetheless, each of these has left its mark on English poetry.

Alliterative, accentual, **or** *strong-stress* **verse was the metrical system native to our Anglo-Saxon forebears.** An impressive amount of alliterative poetry survived the Middle Ages, but only two medieval poems in this meter are encountered frequently enough to deserve mention here. *Beowulf,* the earliest surviving poem in a European language, was composed about A.D. 725; it describes the epic adventures of Beowulf in defeating the male monster Grendel and then Grendel's dam before Beowulf himself succumbs to a fire-breathing dragon. The poem is written in Old English, which is so different from modern English that it must be learned just like a foreign language. **Each line in standard alliterative tetrameter has a variable number of unaccented syllables and four strong stresses, three of which are usually emphasized by alliteration. The line is bisected by a caesural pause.**

The same alliterative meter is used in the Middle English Arthurian romance, *Sir Gawain and the Green Knight.* The following lines, which describe Gawain's sufferings during his winter quest for the Green Knight, provide an example of the original appearance of the meter. Note where the accents are in the following lines:

> For werre wrathed hym not so much,// that wynter was wors,
>
> When the colde cler water// from the clouds schadde,
>
> And fries er hit falle mygth// to the fale erthe.
>
> Ner slayn wyth the slete// he sleped in his yrnes
>
> Mo nyghtes then innoghe// in naked rokkes,

Ther as claterande fro the crest// the colde borne rennes,
And henged heghe// over his hede in hard ysse-ikkles.[2]

—From *Sir Gawain and the Green Knight,* anonymous [ca. 1375]

Of the poems considered in this text, "Eve" (p. 712) is perhaps classifiable as strong-stress dimeter rather than as dactylic dimeter. Each line has only two strong stresses, while the number of unstressed syllables varies from two to four. "Fog," by Carl Sandburg (p. 677), is also best classified as strong-stress dimeter. Each line has two major stresses that are surrounded, in no particular pattern, by weakly stressed or unstressed syllables. In addition, Gerard Manley Hopkins adopted a strong-stress system, which he called *sprung rhythm* and used in most of his poems; and W. S. Merwin in "Leviathan" (p. 998) directly imitated Old English verse forms. In general, the strong-stress system requires alliteration if it is to sound poetic, and the required alliteration is too limiting and too repetitive to appeal to most modern poets. When strong-stress verse is used without alliteration, as in Sandburg's "Fog," it has the appearance and sound of free verse. Here is a good example of an alliterative strong-stress poem that directly imitates the patterns of Old and Middle English verse:

ANGLOSAXON STREET

Dawndrizzle ended   dampness streams from
blotching brick and   blank plasterwaste
Faded housepatterns   hoary and finicky
unfold stuttering   stick like a phonograph

5   Here is a ghetto   gotten for goyim°   *non-Jews*
O with care denuded   of nigger and kike
No coonsmell rankles   reeks only cellarrot
attar° of carexhaust   catcorpse and cookinggrease   *fragrance*
Imperial hearts   heave in this haven

10   Cracks across windows   are welded with slogans
There'll Always Be An England   enhances geraniums
and V's for a Victory   vanquish the housefly

Ho! with climbing sun   march the bleached beldames
festooned with shopping bags   farded° flatarched   *made-up*
15 bigthewed Saxonwives   stepping over buttrivers
waddling back wienerladen   to suckle smallfry

Hoy! with sunslope   shrieking over hydrants
flood from learninghall   the lean fingerlings
Nordic nobblecheeked   not all clean of nose
20 leaping Commandowise   into leprous lanes

---

[2] Translation: For fighting troubled him not so much, that winter was worse,/ When the cold clear water from the clouds fell,/ And froze ere it might fall to the faded earth./ Near slain with sleet he slept in his irons (armor)/ More nights than enough in naked rocks,/ There where clattering from the crest the cold stream ran,/ And hung high over his head in hard icicles.

What! after whistleblow!   spewed from wheelboat
after daylong doughtiness   dire handplay
in sewertrench or sandpit   come Saxonthegns[3]
Junebrown Jutekings   jawslack for meat

25   Sit after supper   on smeared doorsteps
not humbly swearing   hatedeeds on Huns
profiteers politicians   pacifists Jews

Then by twobit magic   to muse in movie
unlock picturehoard   or lope to alehall
30   soaking bleakly   in beer skittleless[4]
Home again to hotbox   and humid husbandhood
in slumbertrough adding   sleepily to Angelkin

Alongside in lanenooks   carling° and leman°   *peasant girl / lover*
caterwaul and clip   careless of Saxonry
35   with moonglow and haste   and a higher heartbeat

Slumbers now slumtrack   unstinks cooling
waiting brief for milkmaid   mornstar and worldrise

—Earle Birney [1942]

─────────── ❦ QUESTIONS ❦ ───────────

1.   The first three stanzas give an overview of the Anglosaxon street—
perhaps at dawn. In what nation and in what time period is the poem
set?

2.   Is this a racist poem? If not, why does Birney use offensive racial
epithets in the second stanza?

3.   What organizational pattern dominates the poem from the fourth
stanza on? What different residents of the street come into prominence
at different times of the day? How kindly does Birney treat these residents?

4.   Why do you think that Birney imitates Old and Middle English alliterative verse in writing the poem? Mark off the stresses and the alliterating
syllables in a few lines of the poem. What is the effect of using this rather
archaic and primitive verse form?

─────────────────────────────────────

**Purely *syllabic meters*, which are based solely on the number of syllables
per line, represent another alternative to the syllabic-stress system.** Some
modern languages, notably French, make little use of stress in speech. Each

[3] Among the early Anglo-Saxons *thegns* or *thanes* were freemen who held land in return for military
service. In the context of this poem, however, "Saxonthegns" (and "Jutekings") appear to be
ironic descriptions of ordinary Englishmen—many of whom have Saxon or Jutish ancestry.
[4] Skittles is a form of bowling, and the expression "all beer and skittles" is commonly used to
mean *pure pleasure and enjoyment*. Apparently, there is little real enjoyment in the lives of those
besotted by "beer skittleless."

syllable is given roughly the same weight. As a result, French poetry is based almost entirely on syllable count.

After the French-speaking Normans conquered the Saxons at Hastings in 1066, our modern English language began to emerge as a hybrid between Old English and Old French; at the same time, modern syllabic-stress meters began to emerge, as the alliterative tradition of Old English poetry met with the syllabic tradition of French verse.

In the absence of other musical devices (rhyme, alliteration, etc.), *syllabic verse* **is often indistinguishable from prose,** as we see in the following poem:

VOX HUMANA[5]

Being without quality
I appear to you at first
as an unkempt smudge, a blur,
an indefinite haze, mere-
5   ly pricking the eyes, almost
nothing. Yet you perceive me.

I have been always most close
when you had least resistance,
falling asleep, or in bars;
10   during the unscheduled hours,
though strangely without substance,
I hang, there and ominous.

Aha, sooner or later
you will have to name me, and,
15   as you name, I shall focus,
I shall become more precise.
O Master (for you command
in naming me, you prefer)!

I was, for Alexander,[6]
20   the certain victory; I
was hemlock for Socrates;[7]
and, in the dry night, Brutus
waking before Philippi
stopped me, crying out, "Caesar!"[8]

25   Or if you call me the blur
that in fact I am, you shall

---

[5] The human voice.

[6] Alexander the Great (356–323 B.C.) helped through his conquests to spread Greek culture through Egypt and the East.

[7] The Greek philosopher Socrates (c. 470–399 B.C.) engaged in his most important and influential dialogues as a result of his trial, imprisonment, and condemnation for impiety and corrupting the youth of Athens.

[8] In Shakespeare's play, Brutus, who had earlier helped to murder Caesar, sees Caesar's ghost on the night before his defeat at Philippi.

                    yourself remain blurred, hanging
                    like smoke indoors. For you bring,
                    to what you define now, all
30   there is, ever, of future.

                                              —Thom Gunn [1957]

————————————— ❧ QUESTIONS ❧ —————————————

1.   What is the subject of this poem? In other words, what is that concept
or feeling or thing "without quality" that Gunn sets out to describe?

2.   Explain the apparent paradox that this concept without quality has
been "always most close / when you had least resistance"?

3.   Why does naming this concept bring it into focus?

4.   What is the effect of the allusions in the fourth stanza? What are the
similarities between Alexander's "certain victory," Socrates's hemlock, and
Brutus's vision of Caesar?

5.   What structure does this poem have, and how does Gunn's choice of
pure syllabic meter contribute to the poem's theme?

―――

Although Gunn's lines can be defended because their formlessness is in
harmony with the poem's theme, they are still open to the criticism that anyone
with the mental capacity to count on his fingers can write as poetically as
this. Under the circumstances, it is no surprise that few English poems are
written in purely syllabic verse.

A third alternative to syllabic-stress verse is made possible by the differences
in the amount of time it takes to pronounce various syllables. The word *truths*,
for example, takes longer to say than *lies*—even though each is monosyllabic.
Quantitative meter is based on the length (in units of time) of various syllables,
instead of on the relative degree of their stress.

Greek and Latin poetry was based on quantitative metrics, and therefore
the few English poems in quantitative verse have usually been written by poets
who were heavily influenced by the classics. During the late sixteenth century,
at the height of the English revival of Greek and Latin learning, such poets
as Spenser and Sidney experimented briefly with quantity in verse before concluding that most English syllables take up about the same amount of time in
pronunciation and that few readers are able to perceive the slight differences
that do exist.

It is, however, possible to demonstrate some quantitative differences in English pronunciation. The first line of the following couplet reads much more
rapidly than the second, even though both have an identical number of syllables:

                    By slight syllables we show
                    Those truths whose worth you now know.

But there is a great difference between this theoretical possibility and its application in fluent poetry. The most that can be said is that quantitative factors

sometimes play a secondary role in the impact of normal syllabic-stress verse. When, for example, Alexander Pope wrote about the effects of sound in poetry, he skillfully used lengthy vowel sounds (ow, oar, ough, ur) to slow down the movement of his lines:

> But when loud surges lash the sounding shore.
>
> The hoarse, rough verse should like the torrent roar.

Free verse, the final alternative to syllabic-stress meter, is not a meter at all. In free verse, the poet does not attempt to produce a formal pattern of metrical feet, quantitative feet, or syllable count, but instead allows the poem to develop "freely" in any manner that contributes to the overall rhythm and effect of the words. The only real distinctions between free verse and the rhythmical prose of Thomas Paine or Abraham Lincoln are that (1) free verse uses variable line length as a unit in rhythm, (2) free verse may use rhyme more frequently than would be acceptable in prose, and (3) free verse is less restrained than prose by the rules of logic and grammar. Free verse is sometimes also said to be written in **open form, meaning that the poet's choice of form is unconstricted by the fixed patterns of rhythm and rhyme.**

In Elizabeth Bishop's free verse poem "Sandpiper," for example, the number of syllables per line ranges from 6 to 13, the number of stresses ranges from three to six, and the metrical pattern remains irregular throughout the poem:

SANDPIPER

The roaring alongside he takes for granted,
and that every so often the world is bound to shake.
He runs, he runs to the south, finical, awkward,
in a state of controlled panic, a student of Blake.

The beach hisses like fat. On his left, a sheet
of interrupting water comes and goes
and glazes over his dark and brittle feet.
He runs, he runs straight through it, watching his toes.

—Watching, rather, the spaces of sand between them,
where (no detail too small) the Atlantic drains
rapidly backwards and downwards. As he runs,
he stares at the dragging grains.

The world is a mist. And then the world is
minute and vast and clear. The tide
is higher or lower. He couldn't tell you which.
His beak is focussed; he is preoccupied,

looking for something, something, something.
Poor bird, he is obsessed!
The millions of grains are black, white, tan, and gray,
mixed with quartz grains, rose and amethyst.
                              —Elizabeth Bishop [1947]

It would be inaccurate, however, to say that Bishop's free verse lacks form. The poem is broken up into four-line units, or stanzas, in which the second line always rhymes with the fourth. Thus, the poem has the visual appearance and sound of verse, while its rhythm remains as hectic and irregular as the darting motion of the sandpiper itself. The poem begins with two flowing and forceful lines describing the surf; then it continues with brief, erratic, and repetitious phrases that help to characterize the bird's mindless panic: "He runs, he runs . . . watching . . . watching . . . he runs, he stares . . . focussed . . . preoccupied,/ looking for something, something, something./ Poor bird, he is obsessed!"

The central portion of the poem is a descriptive tour de force, but it shows only the bleak and monotonous aspects of the sandpiper's existence. In the final lines, however, the point of view shifts. After being told *about* a bird "looking for something, something, something," we now see *with* him that the millions of grains of sand that slip through his toes are "black, white, tan, and gray,/ mixed with quartz grains, rose and amethyst." The existence that had seemed so futile and repetitious a moment earlier is now varied, and even beautiful. The endless patterns of sliding sand, like those in a child's kaleidoscope, offer their own delightful rewards. And suddenly, too, the poem achieves an unexpected unity. We may at first have chuckled at Bishop's description of the sandpiper as "finical, awkward,/ in a state of controlled panic, a student of Blake." The implied comparison makes fun of the often fanatical followers of the famous Romantic poet, William Blake, whose preoccupation with his own visionary experiences was so great that his wife once complained, "I have very little of Mr. Blake's company. He is always in Paradise." But by the end of the poem we learn to view the sandpiper and all "students of Blake" more sympathetically. Certainly they see something the rest of us do not; and perhaps in their preoccupation they see many things more closely, more clearly, and more perceptively than we. (It was Blake himself, after all, who remarked that one could see the world in a grain of sand.)

Free verse is no longer experimental or even new. Although it is an established and popular alternative to syllabic-stress meters, it does not appear that free verse will ever entirely supplant conventional metrics, for there are many advantages to meter. In the first place, poets use meter because it is traditional. It allies them with Chaucer, Shakespeare, Milton, Wordsworth, Byron, Tennyson, Frost, and scores of other distinguished literary men and women. A poem that breaks with this long tradition risks an unsympathetic response from an audience that is accustomed to meter in poetry. Second, the use of meter demonstrates that the author took at least some care in writing, and this implies that he or she considered the content of the poem important. Few authors are likely to bother versifying ideas they think are trivial. (It is true, of course, that prose and free verse may be every bit as carefully crafted as metrical poetry, but the latter signals its importance through its form.) Third, a regular rhythm is inherently musical. It lays down a beat that appeals to us not only in poetry, but also in the sonatas of Beethoven and the songs of The Beach Boys. Fourth, regular rhythms arise out of strong emotions and enhance them in an auditor. They seem to be tied in with the rhythms of our human body. And fifth, meter creates an opportunity for interaction between the sound and sense of language. The tension between the expected and the actual rhythm of a particular line makes it easier for a poet to establish a tone—to speed up the rhythm where the illusion of speed, excitement, or fluidity is wanted, and to slow it down where the content demands emphasis and sobriety.

Meter, then, is useful, but it cannot make an otherwise weak poem strong.

Meter is only one of many ingredients in verse, although it is a catalytic ingredient, as Coleridge noted in comparing it to yeast, "worthless or disagreeable by itself, but giving vivacity and spirit to the liquor with which it is proportionally combined." Dame Edith Sitwell may have been even closer to the truth, however, when she argued that rhythm is "to the world of sound, what light is to the world of sight." It is, finally, the rhythm of a poem, and not its meter, that should be the focus of commentary.

14

Rhyme and Other Manipulations of Sound

Two words *rhyme* when they end with the same sound. In *perfect rhyme,* the final vowel and any succeeding consonant sounds are identical, and the preceding consonant sounds are different. Although words in perfect rhyme may be similar in spelling, they need not be. Thus, *ripe* and *tripe* rhyme to the eye and to the ear, but *rhyme* and *sublime* or *enough* and *snuff* rely entirely on aural similarity.

Rhyme is the most unnatural, the most noticeable, the most controversial, and possibly the most common of all poetic devices. Almost as soon as critics began to examine the elements of poetry, they also began to bicker about the merits of rhyme. Milton, for example, claimed, in 1668, that rhyme is "the invention of a barbarous age" and appeals only to "vulgar readers," to which Edward Young added the observation, a century later (1759), that rhyme, "in epic poetry is a sore disease, in the tragic absolute death. . . . but our lesser poetry stands in need of a toleration for it; it raises that, but sinks the great, as spangles adorn children, but expose men." Interestingly enough, it is harder to find defenders of rhyme, although John Dryden, writing in 1664, felt that the device has so many advantages "that it were lost time to name them," and in 1702, Edward Bysshe called rhyme "the chief ornament of versification in any of the modern languages." On the whole, rhyme's detractors seem to make a more vigorous and impassioned argument; yet the great majority of all anthologized poetry in every period (including our own) is rhymed. Evidently, rhyme adds something to poetry. The question is, what?

Rhyme contributes to the effect of poetry in at least six ways:

1. **Rhyme rings an audible end to each line.** This is important because the rhythm of iambic verse is so similar to that of prose that without the aid of rhyme the sense of hearing poetry can easily be lost. Rhyme helps us to recognize aurally where one line ends and the next begins and thus reinforces the rhythmic pattern of the poem.

2.   **Rhyme makes words memorable.**   Of course, it cannot in itself make words *worthy* of being remembered; the content of the poem must do that. But rhyme has always been used to make things *easier* to remember. Wandering medieval minstrels, whose livelihood depended on their ability to delight a crowd with the lengthy adventures of Sir Gawain or King Arthur, used a tale's rhyming pattern as a prod to memory in the same way that we still use rhyming chants in daily life ("Thirty days hath September").

3.   **Rhyme is pleasing because it is inherently musical.**   Verse appeals to small children long before they understand the full meaning of the words they chant, and rhyme is almost always used in popular songs.

4.   **Rhyme can be used to affect the pace and tone of poetry, as well.**   In the following stanza from "The Rime of the Ancient Mariner," for example, Coleridge uses the first four rhyme words ("prow," "blow," "shadow," and "foe") at the eighth, sixteenth, twenty-first, and twenty-fourth syllables to enhance the illusion of a chasing (and gaining!) storm:

> With sloping masts and dipping prow,
> As who pursued with yell and blow
> Still treads the shadow of his foe,
> And forward bends his head,
> The ship drove fast, loud roared the blast,
> And southward aye we fled.
> —From "The Rime of the Ancient Mariner,"
>   Samuel Taylor Coleridge [1798]

5.   **Well-managed rhymes are a sign of skill.**   Much of the fun in reading a poem like Byron's *Don Juan* is to observe how the poet wriggles out of the tight spots created by words that seem impossible to rhyme. When, for example, he ends the first line of the following quatrain with "annuities," we may think him trapped, only to watch him scamper gleefully through the rhyme without the slightest apparent strain:

> 'Tis said that persons living on annuities
>   Are longer lived than others,—God knows why,
> Unless to plague the grantors,—yet so true it is,
>   That some, I really think, do never die.
>   —From *Don Juan,* Lord Byron [1819]

Conversely, poorly managed rhymes are a sign of clumsiness, as Pope made clear in "An Essay on Criticism":

> Where'er you find 'the cooling western breeze,'
> In the next line it 'whispers through the trees';
> If crystal streams 'with pleasing murmurs creep,'
> The reader's threatened (not in vain) with 'sleep.'
>   —From "An Essay on Criticism,"
>   Alexander Pope [1711]

6.   **Because worn rhymes are so tiring and because interesting ones are difficult to find, a good rhyme facilitates witticism.**   Rhyme used in comic or satiric poetry tends to sharpen a well-honed phrase, as, for example, in the "Epitaph Intended for his Wife," attributed to John Dryden:

Here lies my wife: here let her lie!
Now she's at rest, and so am I.

and in Hilaire Belloc's sardonic "Lines for a Christmas Card":

May all my enemies go to Hell.
Noel, Noel, Noel, Noel.

One has only to rewrite these lines without rhyme (substituting *dwell* for Dryden's "lie" and *Amen* for Belloc's "Noel") to recognize that, with the change of words, the humor is lost.

In summary, rhyme in poetry is like salt in cooking. It adds almost nothing to nutrition, but it appeals to our taste. A poem that is unseasoned by rhyme may be as dull as a saltless diet, whereas too much rhyme, like too much salt, may spoil the dish.

Rhyme ordinarily falls on an accented syllable at the end of a line, in which case it is called *masculine end rhyme*. In *feminine (or double) rhyme*, the final two syllables in a line rhyme, and the final syllable is unaccented. In *triple rhyme*, three syllables rhyme. Both double and triple rhyme are generally used to create a comic effect. In the following stanza, lines one, three, and five are masculine end rhymes, lines four and six are feminine end rhymes, and lines seven and eight are triple rhymes.

'Tis pity learned virgins ever wed
  With persons of no sort of education,
Or gentlemen, who, though well born and bred,
  Grow tired of scientific conversation:
I don't choose to say much on this head,
  I'm a plain man, and in a simple station,
But—Oh! ye lords of ladies intellectual,
Inform us truly have they not hen-peck'd you all?
        —From *Don Juan,* Lord Byron [1819]

Not all rhymes fall at the end of a line. *Internal rhyme* occurs within a line of poetry. Often the word preceding the caesura rhymes with the last word in the line, as in Poe's "The Raven":

Once upon a midnight *dreary,* while I pondered weak and *weary*

But internal rhyme may occur anywhere within a line or even between lines:

And the silken, sad, *uncertain* rustling of each purple *curtain*
  Thrilled me—*filled* me with fantastic terrors never felt before
So that now, to still the *beating* of my heart I stood *repeating*
  " 'Tis some visiter *entreating* entrance at my chamber door."
        —From "The Raven," Edgar Allan Poe [1845]

In *imperfect rhyme* the sound of two words is similar but it is not as close as is required in *true* or *perfect rhyme*. In the lines just quoted, "silken" and "uncertain" are imperfect rhymes, as are "filled," "felt," and "still." Ogden Nash combines imperfect rhyme with an ingenious play on words in the following anecdote on a happy marriage:

I believe a little incompatibility is
the spice of life, particularly if he has
income and she is pattable.

Imperfectly rhymed words generally contain identical vowels or identical consonants, but not both. Imperfect rhyme is also referred to as approximate rhyme, or as half-rhyme, near rhyme, oblique rhyme, off-rhyme, or slant rhyme.

False rhyme **pairs the sounds of accented with unaccented syllables.** In the lines we quoted from "The Rime of the Ancient Mariner," "shadow" is a false internal rhyme with "his foe:"

With sloping masts and dipping prow,
As who pursued with yell and blow
Still treads the *shadow* of *his foe* . . .

And at the same time, "prow" and "blow" are known as *visual rhymes.* These words—and such others as "rough-bough" and "love-prove"—rhyme to the eye, but not to the ear. Their spellings are similar, but their pronunciations are different.

Finally, *repetition* is occasionally used as an alternative to true rhyme. It provides the recurrence of sound expected in rhyme, but not the difference in meaning and initial consonants that makes rhyme delightful.

Modern poets have, on the whole, set themselves apart from much traditional poetry by replacing true rhymes with one or more of the alternatives, and so retaining some sense of music without rhyme's characteristic chime. Let us examine how W. H. Auden uses rhyme in describing the surf-washed shore of an island:

LOOK, STRANGER

Look, stranger, at this island now
The leaping light for your delight discovers,
Stand stable here
And silent be,
5   That through the channels of the ear
May wander like a river
The swaying sound of the sea.

Here at the small field's ending pause
Where the chalk wall falls to the foam, and its tall ledges
10   Oppose the pluck
And knock of the tide,
And the shingle scrambles after the suck-
ing surf, and the gull lodges
A moment on its sheer side.

15   Far off like floating seeds the ships
Diverge on urgent voluntary errands;
And the full view
Indeed may enter
And move in memory as now these clouds do,
20   That pass the harbor mirror
And all the summer through the water saunter.
—W. H. Auden [1936]

Although the words are musical, the poem is not arranged in any of the easily recognizable patterns of verse. The meter is loosely based on the strong-stress system, and the rhyme scheme is unconventional. The first line in each stanza is unrhymed. The second and sixth lines are imperfect rhymes. The third line rhymes perfectly with the fifth, as does the fourth line with the seventh. **We can simplify our description of the rhyme scheme in "Look, Stranger" (or any other poem) by representing each new rhyme sound by a different letter of the alphabet, with capital letters reserved for perfect rhymes and lower-case letters for imperfect, false, or visual rhymes, and by representing unrhymed lines with an X.** Thus, each of Auden's stanzas rhymes according to the scheme XaBCBaC. Identifying the *rhyme scheme* in this way is an important stage in cataloguing the manipulations of rhythm and rhyme within a specific poem. Although some critics prefer to ignore the various forms of partial rhyme, the system we have outlined allows us to indicate the subtle presence of imperfect, false, and visual rhymes without unduly complicating our representation of the total rhyme pattern. The rhyme schemes of most poems, of course, can be fully described using only the capital letters and the X for unrhymed lines.

Schematizing the rhyme in this way leads us to two important observations about the effect of Auden's verse. First, although six out of these seven lines rhyme, each of the first four lines ends with a different and unrelated sound. (In the first stanza the actual words are "now," "discovers," "here," and "be.") This means that each stanza is more than half complete before Auden begins to give it the sound of rhyming verse. Second, Auden never establishes a strong and repeated interval between rhymes. In most poetry, the rhymes recur predictably—every ten syllables in Pope's iambic pentameter couplets (p. 850), every twelve syllables in the anapestic tetrameter couplets of Byron's "The Destruction of Sennacherib" (p. 850), and so on. Almost immediately, we subconsciously pick up the rhyme pattern and begin to *expect* rhymes at the proper intervals. Auden makes it difficult for us to have any such expectations because he varies the interval between his rhymes. "Here" (line 3) is separated by twelve syllables from its rhyming partner "ear" (line 5), while "be" (line 4) is separated by twenty-two syllables from "sea" (line 7) and "discovers" (line 2) is separated by twenty-three syllables from its approximate rhyme with "river" (line 6). Although the second and third stanzas follow the same rhyme scheme, the number of syllables separating the rhyme words may vary because lines of strong-stress meter often differ in number of syllables. "Look, Stranger" is in fact rhyme-dense (for example, it has a total of six rhyming words in the forty-nine syllables of the first stanza, whereas a comparable number of rhymes in Pope's iambic pentameter would require sixty syllables). But we scarcely even perceive the rhyme in reading Auden's verse, whereas it is unmistakable in Pope's.

By declining to use a conventional, repetitive rhyme scheme, Auden willingly risks alienating those readers who feel his writing is "just not poetry" in order to capture that subtle sense of beauty and harmony that is the poem's theme. Auden is, indeed, attempting to describe the chalk cliffs, the surf-driven pebbles (or shingle), the perched gull, the urgent ships, and the drifting clouds, but he is even more interested in the process by which he and presumably all of us take such scenes of natural beauty to heart until "the full view/ Indeed may enter/ And move in memory as now these clouds do." Auden, no doubt, knows that a poet cannot hope to match the visual representation of the seaside in a photograph, a painter's landscape, or a film. But he knows as well that these visual media are not as effective as words in conveying the effects of rhythmic and natural movement on a human observer. Thus, his description of the setting is filled with activity: the "leaping light," "the pluck and knock of the tide," the "sucking surf," and even the memory of the whole scene that, like the drifting clouds, will "all the summer through the water saunter." And yet the actions he describes are not the purposeful and goal-oriented actions of hectic human life; they are sedate, rhythmic, and inherent in nature. Even the ships, which Auden knows "diverge on urgent voluntary errands," appear to him from the cliffs "like floating seeds."

What Auden wants, then, is not the methodical chime of repeated rhyme and not the businesslike stolidity of prose, but a more natural harmony that "through the channels of the ear/ May wander like a river" recreating "the swaying sound of the sea." Auden's idiosyncratic use of rhyme is but one of the musical devices that help him to do so. **The similarity of vowel or consonant sounds, which we call *imperfect rhyme* when it occurs at the ends of lines, may also occur within lines where it is known more specifically as *alliteration, assonance*, or *consonance*.**

Alliteration **is the repetition in two or more nearby words of initial consonant sounds** ("Where the chalk wall *f*alls to the *f*oam," line 9). *Assonance* **is the repetition in two or more nearby words of similar vowel sounds** ("ch*a*lk w*a*ll f*a*lls"). **And *consonance* is the repetition in two or more nearby words of similar consonant sounds preceded by different accented vowels** ("cha*lk*," "plu*ck*," "kno*ck*"). Each of these devices is melodious—although less so than rhyme itself. For this reason, each is particularly appropriate in developing Auden's description of a natural and harmonious setting. Virtually every line reverberates with the subtle music of one or more of these three devices, and in some lines several musical effects are interwoven. Take, for example, the second stanza. The *aw* sound in "small" is repeated in "pause," and then in the next line this assonance is compounded by consonance and internal rhyme in the series "chalk wall falls." The *f* of "falls" alliterates with "foam," and the *all* sound is picked up again in "tall." In the third line, the *p*'s of "oppose" are reiterated in "pluck." (This hybrid of consonance and alliteration is one of many musical effects in verse with no formal name.) The fourth line has consonance ("pluck/ knock"); the fifth has alliteration and assonance, which carry over into the sixth ("*s*hingle *s*crambles after the *s*uck-/ ing *s*urf" and "*s*ucking *s*urf and the *g*ull"); and the seventh line combines alliteration ("*s*heer *s*ide") with the repetition of the *m* sounds in "*mom*ent." This high concentration of musical effects is repeated in both of the other stanzas.

As if all this were not enough, Auden also uses the emotional overtones of the various vowels and consonants to further heighten the beauty of his description. **In general, those vowels that are produced through pursed and rounded lips tend to be soothing and *euphonious***—although sometimes somber. We say "Oooh," "Ahh," and "Oh" in spontaneous expressions of pleasure and surprise. Conversely, those vowels that are produced with widely stretched lips tend to convey excitement, astonishment, or fright. Scared women "SHRIEEEK" and unhappy children "whine" and "wail." Such **grating and unpleasant sounds are said to be *cacophonous*.** Consonants, too, tend to divide into euphonious and cacophonous groups. Among the former we should list the liquid sounds of *r* and *l*, the nasal sounds of *m* and *n*, and such gentle sounds as *f*, *v*, *th*, and *sh*. Auden uses these soft consonants in "Look, Stranger" when he is describing the static appearance of the ships,

> Far off like floating seeds the ships,
>
> Diverge on urgent voluntary errands;

He also uses them to reinforce the idea that the very harmony of the scene makes it memorable:

> And the full view
>
> Indeed may enter
>
> And move in memory as now these clouds do.

Other consonants, called explosives—*p, b, d, k, t,* and hard *g*—create harsh, cacophonous effects. Auden uses these in his second stanza to describe the crash of the surf against the shore:

> . . . its tall ledges
>
> Oppose the pluck
>
> And knock of the tide,
>
> And the shingle scrambles after the suck-
>
> ing surf and the gull lodges
>
> A moment on its sheer side.

In fact, in "Look, Stranger" the meaning of the words may be less important than their rhythm and sound. To be sure, Auden describes the setting clearly, but it is a scene that, in one form or another, has been experienced by all. We are impressed not so much by what Auden has to say, as by the way he says it.

In our analysis of Auden's poem perhaps we have emphasized too heavily the emotional overtones implicit in verbal sounds. If we examine any significant number of successful poems, we will find examples of harsh sounds used to create beauty or smooth sounds used with force and vigor. Few poets have ever been more conscious of the effects of sound than Pope in his lines on sound and sense in poetry (p. 624). It is indeed easy to applaud the liquid consonants (*f, r, n, m, th*) and melodious vowels ("soft," "blows," "smooth") in his couplet on the sound of smooth verse:

> Soft is the strain when Zephyr gently blows,
> And the smooth stream in smoother numbers flows.

In the next couplet, the sibilants (*s, sh*) and guttural vowels ("hoarse, rough verse") help to complement the stormy theme:

> But when loud surges lash the sounding shore
> The hoarse, rough verse should like the torrent roar.

And in the third couplet, a series of awkward consonantal combinations ("Ajax *str*ives some ro*ck's vast w*eight") helps to slow the pace of the labored lines:

> When Ajax strives some rock's vast weight to throw,
> The line too labors, and the verse moves slow.

Yet Pope's lines also show us the dangers of generalization about the emotional effects of vowel and consonant sounds. The "hoarse, rough verse" in the second couplet is packed with liquid and nasal consonants, "whe*n l*oud su*r*ges *la*sh the sou*n*ding *sh*ore," and the same is true in the third couplet where *"the l*i*n*e too *l*abo*r*s, a*n*d *th*e *ve*rse *mo*ves s*l*ow." In these lines the liquid sounds have little moderating effect on the prevailing harshness of the verse. Obviously, **the meaning of words can be more important than their sound in determining emotional connotations.** Softness of vowels and consonants cannot make "foulness" fair or "murder" musical. **With the exception of a few truly *onomatopoetic* words—for example, words like *moo, hiss,* and *clang,* whose sounds suggest their meanings—it is doubtful that the sounds of individual words often echo their senses.** When "loud surges lash the sounding shore" in Pope's verse, the words *sound* harsh and forceful because of their denotations. And although the *l* and *s*-alliteration may in fact be pleasing to the ear, it does less to create a liquid beauty than to increase our sense of harshness by emphasizing the important words.

In the final analysis, the manipulations of sound that we have examined in this section are characteristic of all good writing. Authors base their word choice in large part on what "sounds" best. Theoretically, then, every piece of prose or poetry could be examined for the effect of sound on sense, but the problem is that our techniques of analysis are coarse and many of the decisions that authors make are complex, delicate, and even subconscious. We are like chemists struggling to determine a molecular weight using a physician's scale. In such circumstances one must concentrate on the macroscopic, cumulative effect of many microscopic interactions, for it is out of such interactions that the sounds of poetry are created.

Poems for Further Study

JABBERWOCKY[1]

'T was brillig, and the slithy toves
    Did gyre and gimble in the wabe;
All mimsy were the borogoves,
    And the mome raths outgrabe.

5
"Beware the Jabberwock, my son!
    The jaws that bite, the claws that catch!
Beware the Jubjub bird, and shun
    The frumious Bandersnatch!"

He took his vorpal sword in hand:
10
    Long time the manxome foe he sought—
So rested he by the Tumtum tree,
    And stood awhile in thought.

And as in uffish thought he stood,
    The Jabberwock, with eyes of flame,

---

[1] From *Through the Looking Glass.* In Chapter 6 Humpty Dumpty attempts to explain the poem.

15 Came whiffling through the tulgey wood,
   And burbled as it came!

One, two! One, two! And through and through
   The vorpal blade went snicker-snack!
He left it dead, and with its head
20   He went galumphing back.

"And hast thou slain the Jabberwock?
   Come to my arms, my beamish boy!
O frabjous day! Callooh! Callay!"
   He chortled in his joy.

25 'T was brillig, and the slithy toves
   Did gyre and gimble in the wabe;
All mimsy were the borogoves,
   And the mome raths outgrabe.

—Lewis Carroll [1872]

❧ QUESTIONS ❧

1. This poem is filled with newly created words, but it is nonetheless possible to summarize the story told in it. Do so.

2. Make up your own brief definitions of the following words: *brillig, slithy, toves, gyre, gimble, wabe, mimsy, borogoves, mome, raths, outgrabe, Jabberwock, Jubjub bird, frumious, Bandersnatch, vorpal, manxome, Tumtum tree, uffish, wiffling, tulgey, galumphing, frabjous.*

3. Explain some of the effects of alliteration, consonance, and assonance in the poem. How do those sound devices help you to determine the meaning of the fabricated words?

WINTER REMEMBERED

Two evils, monstrous either one apart,
Possessed me, and were long and loath at going:
A cry of Absence, Absence, in the heart,
And in the wood the furious winter blowing.

5 Think not, when fire was bright upon my bricks,
And past the tight boards hardly a wind could enter,
I glowed like them, the simple burning sticks,
Far from my cause, my proper heat and center.

Better to walk forth in the frozen air
10 And wash my wound in the snows; that would be healing;

Because my heart would throb less painful there,
Being caked with cold, and past the smart of feeling.

And where I walked, the murderous winter blast
Would have this body bowed, these eyeballs streaming,
15 And though I think this heart's blood froze not fast
It ran too small to spare one drop for dreaming.

Dear love, these fingers that had known your touch,
And tied our separate forces first together,
Were ten poor idiot fingers not worth much,
20 Ten frozen parsnips hanging in the weather.

—John Crowe Ransom [1924]

❧ QUESTIONS ❧

1. What are the two evils that possessed the speaker? Does the speaker choose the word "Possessed" with a full awareness of its connotations in demonology?

2. What does the speaker mean when he says he remained cold, "Far from my cause, my proper heat and center" (line 8)?

3. Why does he prefer being out in the cold (lines 9–16)?

4. Describe the poem's rhyme scheme. What makes it unusual? Does the poem's rhyme scheme complement its predominantly melancholy mood?

5. What is the predominant rhythm of the poem? What are the effects of the deviations from the prevalent rhythm in lines 15 and 19?

6. The poem develops an extended comparison linking the effects of separation and of winter. How well does the last stanza bring both sides of the comparison to a climax? What do you make of the final image of "Ten frozen parsnips hanging in the weather"?

7. How effectively does Ransom use alliteration, assonance, and consonance in the poem? Explain your answer by citing examples.

DULCE ET DECORUM EST

Bent double, like old beggars under sacks,
Knock-kneed, coughing like hags, we cursed through sludge,
Till on the haunting flares we turned our backs,
And towards our distant rest began to trudge.
5 Men marched asleep. Many had lost their boots,
But limped on, blood-shod. All went lame, all blind;
Drunk with fatigue; deaf even to the hoots
Of gas-shells dropping softly behind.

Gas, Gas! Quick boys!—An ecstasy of fumbling,
10   Fitting the clumsy helmets just in time,
But someone still was yelling out and stumbling
And floundering like a man in fire or lime.—
Dim through the misty panes and thick green light,
As under a green sea, I saw him drowning.

15   In all my dreams before my helpless sight
He plunges at me, guttering, choking, drowning.

If in some smothering dreams, you too could pace
Behind the wagon that we flung him in,
And watch the white eyes writhing in his face,
20   His hanging face, like a devil's sick of sin;
If you could hear, at every jolt, the blood
Come gargling from the froth-corrupted lungs,
Bitter as the cud
Of vile, incurable sores on innocent tongues,—
25   My friend, you would not tell with such high zest
To children ardent for some desperate glory,
The old Lie: Dulce et decorum est
Pro patria mori.[2]

—Wilfred Owen [posthumous, 1920]

❧ QUESTIONS ❧

1. What can you tell about the speaker from this poem? What effects have the events described in the poem had upon him? What is his attitude toward war and toward the supposed glory of dying for one's country?

2. Owen uses many comparisons in the poem. Pinpoint as many of these comparisons as you can and discuss their effects.

3. Owen makes frequent use of alliteration, assonance, and consonance. Identify and analyze what you consider to be the most effective instances of these sound devices.

4. Analyze the metrics in the poem. What is the dominant rhythm? What is the prevailing meter? Where does Owen manipulate the rhythm particularly effectively?

[2] A line by the Roman poet Horace (65–8 B.C.) meaning, "It is sweet and fitting to die for your country."

15

❧❧❧❧❧❧❧❧

Structure and Form
in Poetry

Nearly all writing combines the narrative, dramatic, descriptive, and expository modes of expression. We rarely find any of these in a pure form in literature because an author's goal of creating interest and variety ordinarily requires that the modes be mixed. For the purpose of illustration, however, we can compose examples of how the same situation might be treated in each of the four modes:

Narrative: The boys crossed the street and entered the store.
Dramatic: "Look! There's a candy store."
"Let's cross over and buy some taffy."
Descriptive: On one side of the street stood the two boys, jingling the coins in their pockets; on the other side were the large-paned windows of the store front, advertising in antique letters: DAN'S OLD-FASHIONED CANDIES.
Expository: The boys wanted to cross the street to buy some candy.

A narrative approach concentrates on action. In its pure form, it uses only nouns and transitive verbs, but such writing usually lacks appeal to the senses and to the intellect. As a result, narration does not necessarily predominate in narrative poetry; rather, the impulse to tell a story remains uppermost in the narrative poet's mind as he or she interweaves narration, description, dialogue, and explanation.

The principal forms of narrative poetry are the *epic*, which tells the book-length adventures of the founders of a nation or a culture (for example, *The Iliad, Paradise Lost*); **the *romance*, which often resembles the epic in length and adventurousness but puts greater emphasis on love and supernatural events** (*The Odyssey*, Tennyson's *Idylls of the King*); **the *poetic tale* or short story in verse** (Chaucer's *Miller's Tale*, Burns' *Tam o' Shanter*); **and the *ballad*, a short narrative song** (see p. 742). The structure of narrative poetry closely resembles that of fiction: it proceeds from an exposition of the setting, circumstances, and characters, through a period of complication (rising action), to a crisis and subsequent resolution.

The dramatic approach focuses on dialogue. Action and setting are conveyed through the spoken comments of the characters rather than through direct authorial description. Because poetry makes use of the aural qualities of language, most plays written before the twentieth century were composed in verse. Verse is, however, an artificial form of speech, and therefore twentieth-century realistic drama has mainly been written in prose, although the continuing popularity of musicals serves to remind us that poetic effects do appeal to theatrical audiences.

The *dramatic monologue,* **which is the chief format for dramatic poetry, is a fairly long speech by a fictional narrator that is usually addressed to a second, silent character.** During such monologues as Robert Browning's "My Last Duchess" or Tennyson's "Ulysses," the narrator reveals both his character and his motives at some crucial moment in his life. Because a monologue is basically reflective, the structure of a dramatic monologue rarely follows that of the conventional short story. It is likely to be digressive, argumentative, and analytic rather than strictly narrative.

A poem that is primarily descriptive or expository is called a *lyric.* Lyric poems range widely in subject, theme, and scope of treatment, but they are alike in their preoccupation with ideas, emotions, and the poet's state of mind. Although a narrative element is sometimes present, the lyric poet never concentrates on the story.

Many of the poems in this anthology are lyrics, and by briefly examining a few of them, we can only begin to suggest the dozens of possible structures for lyric verse. A description may, for example, move from nearby objects to far-off ones, as in the second and third stanzas of Auden's "Look, Stranger" (p. 729). Or description may be followed by inquiry and analysis, as in Frost's "Design" (p. 632). Frequently a specific incident leads up to a more general conclusion, as when Shakespeare (see p. 649) describes the emotions of an infant crawling after its mother as a symbol of his own passion for his mistress. The presentation may be chronological, like Herrick's in "Upon Julia's Clothes" (p. 689); may increase in emotional intensity, like Kipling's "Recessional" (p. 642); or may be analogical, like Donne's "A Valediction: Forbidding Mourning" (p. 798). In addition, descriptions can conceivably be organized according to the various senses or emotions evoked, and an argument can use comparison and contrast, order of importance, or parallelism to give structure to the whole. No exhaustive list of organizational structures is either possible or desirable.

In each of its formats—narrative, dramatic, and lyric—poetry varies more in length and content than either fiction or drama. Hence, the only useful generalizations about poetic structure are the broad ones that every element in a well-structured poem should have an identifiable function, and that the poem itself should build to a unified effect or series of effects.

STANDARD VERSE FORMS

In prose fiction, form is almost entirely subservient to meaning, but in poetry the verse form provides guidelines to the development of ideas. Verse is, as we argued earlier, a game played between the poet and the form. As in other games, the rules are essentially arbitrary. Why must a baseball cross the plate to be called a strike? What practical purpose is served by hitting a tennis ball over a mesh net and into a rectangular court? Why cannot a pawn move backward or a bishop sideways? Why must a sonnet have just 14 lines? The answer in each case is that the rules of the game help to provide a structure within which we can act and a standard against which we can measure our skills and the skills of others. A poet is challenged by the verse form to write as well as possible within certain restrictions. These restrictions do make the writing more difficult, but they also add to the achievement; and by forcing the poet to experiment with different means of expressing thoughts, they often help better to define what the poet really wants to say and how it can best be said.

Blank Verse

As we have seen, verse can be either rhymed or unrhymed. **Unrhymed iambic pentameter is called** *blank verse.* English blank verse was first written in 1557 by Henry Howard, the Earl of Surrey, in his translation of Virgil's *Aeneid*. It was then adapted to use in drama by Sackville and Norton in *Gorboduc* (1565); however, not until Marlowe and Shakespeare took up the line in the 1580s did its strength, sonority, and variety become evident, as illustrated in Shakespeare's famous characterization of Julius Caesar:

> Why, man he doth bestride the narrow world
> Like a colossus, and we petty men
> Walk under his huge legs and peep about
> To find ourselves dishonorable graves
> —From *Julius Caesar,*
> William Shakespeare [ca. 1600]

In 1664 Milton extended the uses of blank verse to the epic in his *Paradise Lost*. Although little blank verse was written in the eighteenth century, it has been used extensively since.

Stanzaic Verse

Although blank verse is normally organized, like prose, into paragraphs of variable length, rhymed verse is usually cast into units called stanzas. Often, the meter, rhyme scheme, and number of lines are identical in each stanza of a given poem (as in Donne's "The Flea," p. 668). Occasionally, particularly in odes, the structure may vary from stanza to stanza, but no poem really deserves to be called stanzaic unless it regularly uses rhyme or a refrain. Individual stanzas must contain at least two lines and rarely exceed nine.

A *couplet,* **formed of a single pair of rhymed lines, is the smallest possible stanzaic unit. When many of the couplets in a poem express a complete thought in two rhetorically balanced lines** (as in Pope's lines on sound and sense, p. 624), **the poet is said to use the** *closed couplet.* The mere use of closed couplets does not, however, constitute a stanzaic structure. Pope's couplets are not visually separate from one another, nor are they always syntactically separate. Individual sentences frequently carry over into a third or fourth line. These run-on verses limit the utility of the couplet as an element of logical structure, and as a result Pope uses paragraphs instead of stanzas as his organizational units.

A few poems, however, are cast into stanzaic couplets. One of the most impressive is Gwendolyn Brooks's short study of young, inner city pool players:

WE REAL COOL

The Pool Players
Seven at the Golden Shovel

We real cool. We
Left school. We

Lurk late. We
Strike straight. We

Sing sin. We
Thin gin. We

Jazz June. We
Die soon.
                —Gwendolyn Brooks [1960]

Brooks's use of couplets, the simplest of all stanzaic structures, is only one of the ways in which she demonstrates the simplistic thinking of her speakers. Each word in the poem is a monosyllable, and each sentence but three words long. Although the speakers—apparently chanting in unison—may demonstrate how "cool" they are through their use of alliteration, assonance, consonance, and rhyme, they also demonstrate how uneducated they are through their limited vocabularies and their dialectical English. They are fully characterized by their short words, short sentences, short stanzas, short list of achievements, and short lives. In this case at least, the couplet is the perfect choice of stanza for the poem's purpose and content.

If couplets have rarely been used as independent stanzas, they have nevertheless been popular as complete poems. Most two-line poems are epigrams. **An epigram is a concentrated witticism that can be written in either verse or prose—although the couplet is the dominant choice. Whatever its form, an epigram must be short, sharp, and swift—as startling as a wasp and as quick to sting.** Both Belloc's "Lines for a Christmas Card" and Dryden's "Epitaph on His Wife" (p. 728) are epigrammatic. For a third example of an epigram, consider Coleridge's definition of the form:

What is an epigram? A dwarfish whole;
Its body brevity, and wit its soul.

Many epigrams are buried within longer poems. All of Pope's poems are packed with this form of wit (for example, the first two lines on sound and sense, p. 624); and the final couplets in many of the stanzas in Byron's *Don Juan* are epigrammatic (see pp. 638 and 639), as are the concluding couplets of many of Shakespeare's sonnets.

A three-line stanza is called a *tercet*. A *triplet* is a tercet in which all three

lines rhyme together. Herrick's "Upon Julia's Clothes" (p. 689) is an example of a poem using this stanza. *Terza rima,* **a form of three-line stanza popularized by the thirteenth-century Italian poet Dante, establishes an interlocking rhyme scheme in the following pattern: ABA BCB CDC, etc. The closing stanza is either a quatrain or a couplet.** Of the comparatively few famous English poems written in *terza rima,* perhaps the best known is Shelley's "Ode to the West Wind" (p. 858).

A unit of four lines, a *quatrain,* **is the most common stanzaic form in English poetry. Although many different rhyme schemes have been used in quatrains, the most often used is** *crossed rhyme,* **in which the first line rhymes with the third and the second with the fourth, ABAB.** Usually the first and third lines are tetrameter, the second and fourth trimeter. This is the pattern of Donne's "Valediction: Forbidding Mourning" (p. 798), Wordsworth's "She Dwelt Among the Untrodden Ways" (p. 844) and Poe's "Annabel Lee" (p. 715).

An iambic pentameter quatrain in which the first two lines rhyme with the last (AAXA) is known as a *rubais* **because it was popularized in the** *Rubáiyát of Omar Khayyám* **(1859) by Edward FitzGerald.** The stanza is particularly useful in epigrams because it is similar to a closed couplet, although it develops its point in four lines instead of just two. The first two lines in the quatrain are metrically identical to a closed couplet, but the next two lines, instead of developing a separate idea, extend and complement the first two. Thus, the entire quatrain is like a single couplet in which each line has twenty syllables and the first line contains an internal rhyme:

> *Couplet 1* ——Come, fill the Cup, and in the fire of Spring
> Your Winter-garment of Repentance fling:
> The Bird of Time has but a little way
> *Couplet 2* ------- To flutter—and the Bird is on the Wing.
> —From *The Rubáiyát of Omar Khayyám,*
> Edward FitzGerald (1859)

In short, the *rubais* combines the unity and wit of a couplet with the freedom and scope of a quatrain.

Other quatrains use rhyme schemes based on a single rhyme (AAAA), a pair of couplets (AABB), or an "envelope" (ABBA), but the most important quatrain of all is the stanza used in traditional folk ballads—a stanza composed of alternating lines of iambic tetrameter and iambic trimeter rhyming (XAXA).

A *ballad* **is a short narrative poem telling of a single dramatic incident. The** *traditional ballad* **is part of our oral heritage, and one basic story may evolve into dozens of variant forms as it is recited or sung at different times to different audiences.** "Bonny Barbara Allan" is certainly one of the most widely known and frequently altered of all ballads. It has gone through so many different versions over the years that one critic has observed wryly, "Barbara Allan's ninety-two progeny are something of a record achievement, certainly for a lady who, according to the ballad, scorned her lover. One is thankful that she did not encourage him!"[1] The version we reprint is the one sung so beautifully by Joan Baez on her *Ballad Book, Volume 2* (Vanguard, VMS-73115):

---

[1] Arthur Kyle Davis, Jr., *Traditional Ballads of Virginia.* (Cambridge, Mass.: Harvard UP, 1929) 302.

BONNY BARBARA ALLAN

Twas in the merry month of May
   When green buds all were swellin'
Sweet William on his death bed lay
   For the love of Barbary Allan.

He sent his servant to the town
   To the place where she was dwellin'
Saying, "You must come to my master dear
   If your name be Barbary Allan."

So slowly, slowly she got up,
   And slowly she drew nigh him,
And the only word to him did say,
   "Young man I think you're dying."

He turned his face unto the wall,
   And death was in him wellin',
"Goodbye, goodbye, to my friends all.
   Be good to Barbary Allan."

When he was dead and laid in grave,
   She heard the death bells knellin',
And every stroke to her did say,
   "Hard-hearted Barbary Allan."

"Oh mother, oh mother, go dig my grave.
   Make it both long and narrow.
Sweet William died of love for me,
   And I will die of sorrow.

"And father, oh father, go dig my grave.
   Make it both long and narrow.
Sweet William died on yesterday,
   And I will die tomorrow."

Barbary Allen was buried in the old churchyard.
   Sweet William was buried beside her.
Out of Sweet William's heart there grew a rose;
   Out of Barbary Allan's a briar.

They grew and grew in the old churchyard
   Till they could grow no higher.
At the end they formed a true lovers' knot,
   And the rose grew round the briar.

                 —Anonymous

Because traditional ballads (also referred to as *folk* or *popular ballads*) were composed for an oral presentation before an audience, they tell simple, direct stories using dialogue, repetition, and refrains in an effort to capture the interest and attention of an audience that may, after all, be hearing the story for the first time. Ballads tend to be objective, abrupt, and concise. The first few lines catch our interest with a question or a tense situation. Thereafter, the characters spring to life, acting and speaking with relatively

little external commentary by the author. Some ballads use the refrain for the purpose of advancing or commenting on the narrative. The themes of ballads are those of continuing popular interest: unhappy love, feats of war or bravado, shipwrecks, murder, and domestic quarrels.

After the end of the Middle Ages and after the development of the printing press, concern for originality in composition naturally increased, and the circulation and communal creation of folk ballads declined. The ballad stanza has, however, remained popular, particularly in the former slave states of the South, where Negro spirituals and blues evolved with the same format and vitality as in the traditional ballad. Furthermore, professional poets and songwriters ranging from Rudyard Kipling *(Barrack-Room Ballads)* to Bob Dylan ("The Ballad of the Thin Man," etc.) have composed delightful literary ballads that prove both the adaptability and the continuing popularity of the form.

Stanzas of five lines, or *quintets*, are infrequently found in English poetry and none of the many possible rhyme schemes has emerged as particularly prevalent. It says something about the unpopularity of this stanza that two of the best-known of the poems that employ it are such slight lyrics as Robert Herrick's "The Night-Piece, to Julia" (rhyming AABBA) and Edmund Waller's "Go, Lovely Rose" (rhyming ABABB). The two poems together total only forty lines.

A six line stanza is called a *sestet*. The most common pattern for sestets is the one Shakespeare always used for the last six lines (or sestet) in his sonnets. It is composed of a crossed rhyme quatrain followed by a couplet (ABABCC), all in iambic pentameter. Shakespeare first used this sestet in his innovative and popular erotic tale, *Venus and Adonis* (1593), in which his handling of the stanza is light, humorous, and witty; he normally describes the action in the quatrain and cleverly summarizes it or introduces a new and incongruous image in the succeeding, epigrammatic couplet. In the following lines Venus has just seen Adonis and courted him with breathless, burning phrases:

> With this she seizeth on his sweating palm,
> The precedent of pith and livelihood,
> And, trembling in her passion, calls it balm,
> Earth's sovereign salve to do a goddess good.
> > Being so enrag'd, desire doth lend her force
> > Courageously to pluck him from his horse.
>
> Over one arm the lusty courser's rein,
> Under the other was the tender boy,
> Who blush'd and pouted in a dull disdain,
> With leaden appetite, unapt to toy;
> > She red and hot as coals of glowing fire,
> > He red for shame, but frosty in desire.
> > > —From *Venus and Adonis*,
> > > William Shakespeare [1593]

Here, the concluding couplets emphasize the comic reversal of roles in the poem: Venus manfully plucks Adonis from his horse in the first stanza, and in the second she is flushed with dissolute passion while Adonis blushes in virginal shame.

The *septet*, or seven-line stanza, is normally cast into the pattern known as *rhyme royal* because it was used in the only long poem written by an

English-speaking king, *The King's Quhair* **by James I of Scotland (ca. 1425).** The rhyme scheme differs from that of the Shakespearean sestet by the addition of another B-rhyme at the end of the quatrain (ABABBCC); the line remains iambic pentameter.

Rhyme royal was first used in English poetry by Chaucer, who felt that the stanza was appropriate for the themes of "The Prioress's Tale," *Troilus and Criseyde,* and other serious poems. When Shakespeare came to write the "graver labour" that he had promised in the dedication to *Venus and Adonis,* he chose to use rhyme royal, and the result was the tragic and melodramatic *Rape of Lucrece* (1594). There is, however, nothing necessarily serious about poems written in this stanza. If anything, its closely packed rhymes and paired couplets may be most appropriate in witty verse, as in W. H. Auden's rambling and comic "Letter to Lord Byron."

The most important *octet* **or eight-line stanza is** *ottava rima,* **which is like a stretched Shakespearean sestet: eight lines of iambic pentameter rhyming (ABABABCC).** Lord Byron stamped this stanza with the witty, satiric, and exuberant characteristics of his own personality by using it in his epic comedy, *Don Juan* (p. 850).

One of the most intricate stanzaic patterns is the nine-line *Spenserian stanza.* **First used in 1590 by Edmund Spenser in** *The Faerie Queene* (p. 782), **this stanza is made up of eight lines of iambic pentameter rhyming ABABBCBC and a final C-rhyme of iambic hexameter (called an Alexandrine).** The stanza has often been praised for its majesty and effectiveness in poems with serious themes. To a large extent, this praise is only a recognition that Spenser made majestic and effective use of the stanza in *The Faerie Queene.* Because the stanza inevitably recalls Spenser's poem, later poets have generally used it to create a Spenserian sense of romance, morality, and heroism. So, too, *ottava rima* connotes Byron's witty hedonism, and the Shakespearean sestet connotes the light eroticism of *Venus and Adonis.* The impact of each form on the tone and mood of poetry is often less a product of the stanza itself, than of one unforgettable use of the stanza. Unlike most other stanzas, however, the Spenserian is capable of great variety. Depending on how the poet breaks up his or her thoughts, the stanza can either produce the sound of two couplets (ABA <u>BB</u> CB <u>CC</u>), of a modified *terza rima* (<u>ABA</u> BB <u>CBC</u> C), or of many variations of couplets, tercets, quatrains, and quintets. Spenser frequently molds his stanza into two clear quatrains and a final stark Alexandrine, as in the following description of a knight who has lost his honor and his chastity in a luxurious "Bower of Bliss":

> His warlike armes, the idle instruments
> Of sleeping praise, were hong upon a tree,
> And his brave shield, full of old moniments,
> Was fowly ra'st, that none the signes might see;
> Ne for them, ne for honour cared hee,
> Ne ought, that did to his advancement tend,
> But in lewd loves, and wastefull luxuree,
> His dayes, his goods, his bodie he did spend:
> O horrible enchantment, that him so did blend.
> —From *The Faerie Queene,* Book II, Canto XII,
> Edmund Spenser (1590)

By avoiding a monotonous pattern, poets using Spenserian stanzas can vary the effect of their rhymes in much the same way that musicians create variations of a melody. This variety of sound patterns may explain why the Spenserian is the only complex stanza that has been repeatedly used in long poems. In addition to *The Faerie Queene*, it is the stanza of Robert Burns's *Cotter's Saturday Night*, Shelley's *Adonais*, Keats's *Eve of St. Agnes*, and Byron's *Childe Harold*.

The Spenserian is the longest of the well-known stanzas, and it includes in itself many of the lyrical possibilities of shorter stanzas. As such it reconfirms a number of general observations about the nature and function of stanzaic verse itself. **First, stanzaic verse gives the poet an opportunity to impose something akin to the order and structure of prose (for stanzas have many of the virtues of paragraphs) without unduly restricting or sacrificing internally the peculiar expressiveness of poetry. Second, the type of stanza the poet chooses is important. Certain stanzaic patterns inevitably carry with them traditional associations which neither poet nor reader can ignore. The heroic couplet, for example, is unavoidably associated with Pope's satiric wit, in much the same way that ottava rima calls to mind Byron's risqué and exuberant humor. Finally, the less dense the rhymes in a particular stanza, the more frequently it is used in developing serious plots and themes; conversely, the more dense the rhyme, the less serious the subject matter and the greater the probability of a witty, satiric, or comic treatment.**

Not all stanzaic poems are constructed out of regular and repeating structural units. *Odes* **are particularly likely to be idiosyncratic, with each stanza differing from others in the same poem both in rhyme scheme and in length of line. This freedom is limited only by a common understanding that an ode must be a long lyric poem that is serious and dignified in subject, tone, and style.** It strives to create a mood of meditative sublimity. Some of the more notable free-form odes in English include Wordsworth's "Intimations of Immortality," Coleridge's "Dejection," and Allen Tate's "Ode to the Confederate Dead."

Historically, odes were not always as free in form as they usually are today. In ancient Greece they were strictly organized choral songs that sometimes were written to signal the division between scenes in a play and at other times to celebrate an event or individual. These *Pindaric odes,* **named after the Greek poet Pindar (518–438 B.C.), develop through sequences of three different stanzas:** *strophe, antistrophe,* **and** *epode.* **The metrical pattern of each strophe remains the same throughout the ode, as does the pattern of each antistrophe and epode.** Originally, the strophe was sung and danced by one half of the chorus, after which antistrophe was performed by the other half of the chorus using the same steps of the strophe in reverse. The epode was then performed by the combined chorus. Regular Pindaric odes are quite uncommon in English, the best known being Thomas Gray's "The Bard" and "The Progress of Poetry."

Horatian odes, **patterned after those of the Roman poet Horace (65–8 B.C.), retain one stanzaic structure throughout—that is, they are regular stanzaic poems dealing with lofty, lyrical subjects.** Some of the better-known Horatian odes are Keats's "Ode on a Nightingale" (p. 860), "To Autumn" (p. 864), "Ode on a Grecian Urn" (p. 863), and "Ode on Melancholy" (p. 865).

Fixed Poetic Forms

The stanzaic patterns we have described are only one way in which poets attempt to create a recognizable tune analogous to a song-writer's melody. The other way is to use one of the fixed poetic forms—the haiku, sonnet, ballade, villanelle, rondeau, sestina, limerick, and so on. Of these, the haiku, the limerick, and the sonnet have achieved a significant place in English poetry; however, all are alike in two respects: all are brief, and all create their moods through the combined effects of a fixed verse pattern and the traditional connotations associated with that pattern. The haiku, for example, is generally associated with brief suggestive images, the limerick with light humor, and the sonnet with love.

A *haiku* **is a form of poetry that originated in Japan during the thirteenth century. It consists of three lines of five, seven, and five syllables, respectively.** Because of the brevity of the form there is little room for anything more than the presentation of a single concentrated image or emotion. Thus, haiku poems, like these examples by Moritake and Basho, tend to be allusive and suggestive:

THE FALLING FLOWER

What I thought to be
Flowers soaring to their boughs
Were bright butterflies.
            —Moritake [1452–1540]

LIGHTNING IN THE SKY

Lightning in the sky!
In the deeper dark is heard
A night-heron's cry.
            —Matsuo Basho [1644–1694]

The influence of the Japanese haiku on the twentieth-century Imagist movement has been profound and is reflected in such familiar anthology pieces as Ezra Pound's "In a Station of the Metro" and William Carlos Williams' "The Red Wheelbarrow."

A *limerick* **is a form of light verse. Its five lines rhyme AABBA. The A-rhymed lines are in anapestic trimeter; the others are in dimeter.** Surprisingly, many serious authors have tried their hand at this little form—among them Edward Lear (who wrote over two hundred limericks), Robert Louis Stevenson, Rudyard Kipling, and Oliver Wendell Holmes. The following pun attributed to Holmes on the name "Henry Ward Beecher" helps to create one of the best of the printable limericks:

The Reverend Henry Ward Beecher
Called a hen a most elegant creature.
  The hen, pleased with that,
  Laid an egg in his hat.
And thus did the hen reward Beecher.
            —Anonymous

More typical, is the slightly off-color humor of the following:

I sat next the Duchess at tea.
It was just as I feared it would be.
  Her rumblings abdominal
  Were simply abominable,
And everyone thought it was me!
            —Anonymous

In comparison with the haiku and the limerick, the *sonnet* is a more distinguished and inspiring form. Indeed, poets often become so enamored of the "little song" (the literal meaning of *sonnet*) that some have written nothing else and a few—including William Wordsworth and Dante Gabriel Rossetti—have composed rapturous sonnets on sonnetry.

Technically, **a sonnet is a lyric poem of fourteen iambic pentameter lines, usually following one of two established models: the Italian form or the English form. The *Italian sonnet* (or *Petrarchan sonnet*, named after the Italian Renaissance poet Petrarch) consists of an eight-line octave, rhyming AB-BAABBA, followed by a six-line sestet, rhyming variously CDECDE, CDCDCD, etc. Normally, the octave presents a situation or issue, and the sestet explores or resolves it.** Both "On First Looking into Chapman's Homer" (p. 625) and "Design" (p. 632) are Petrarchan sonnets. Keats's octave relates what he had heard about Homer before reading his poetry, while the sestet examines Keats's emotions after discovering the beauties of Homer through Chapman's translation. Frost uses his octave to describe the three objects he encounters on his morning walk; his sestet raises questions about their origin and meaning.

The *English sonnet* (or *Shakespearean sonnet*) consists of three quatrains and a concluding couplet, rhyming ABAB CDCD EFEF GG. A variant of the English sonnet, the *Spenserian sonnet*, links its quatrains by employing the rhyme scheme ABAB BCBC CDCD EE. Although the English sonnet may describe an issue and its resolution using the same octave-sestet structure as in the Italian form, the three quatrains of the Shakespearean sonnet often present three successive images, actions, or arguments, which are then summed up in a final, epigrammatic couplet. A typical Shakespearean sonnet (number CXLIII) is quoted on page 649. Note that in this case the sonnet does take the form of an octave, presenting a hypothesis ("as a careful housewife"), and a sestet, presenting a conclusion ("So runn'st thou"). But the sonnet also breaks into three quatrains and a couplet. The first quatrain describes a housewife in pursuit of a stray cock or hen; the second tells how her neglected child chases after her; and the third explains that Shakespeare is in a situation like that of the child, whereas his mistress (who is presumably running after another man) is like the housewife. Finally, the concluding couplet summarizes and resolves the situation with a pun on William Shakespeare's first name:

> So I will pray that thou mayst have thy "Will,"
> If thou turn back and my loud crying still.

The sonnet became popular in England during the sixteenth century largely because of translations and imitations of Petrarch's passionate cycle of sonnets addressed to his mistress Laura. Similar sonnet sequences were written by Sir Philip Sidney (*Astrophel and Stella*, 1580), Samuel Daniel (*Delia*, 1592), Michael Drayton (*Idea*, 1593), Edmund Spenser (*Amoretti* and *Epithalamion*, 1595), and William Shakespeare (*Sonnets*, 1609). This deluge of amorous sonnets helped to establish the belief that the sonnet itself must always deal with love—a presumption that is still widespread. As early as 1631, Milton challenged this popular notion by writing sonnets of personal reflection, moral criticism, and political comment. The sonnets by Shakespeare, Keats, and Frost, quoted earlier in this text, demonstrate that Milton was correct and that the sonnet can be used in themes ranging from Shakespeare's barnyard humor to Keats's pleasure in reading to Frost's brooding about "the design of darkness to appall." It is this adaptability that makes the sonnet so much more important in literary history than other fixed forms, such as the haiku and the limerick.

VISUAL FORMS

All verse makes some appeal to the eye. We see where the lines begin and end, and from that information we can often tell something about the poetic emphasis and meaning. For some poets, however, this limited visual element is not enough. William Blake, for example, printed his poems himself so that he would be sure that both the calligraphy and the marginal illustrations would contribute to the overall effect. Thus, when we read the poems from his *Songs of Innocence* (1789) and *Songs of Experience* (1794), we must at the very least remember that the words only convey part of his intention. Few other poets have shared Blake's broad interests in both literature and graphic art, but many have experimented with three methods of expanding poetic meaning through visual form.

Typographical Analogies

Throughout history writers have underscored the content of their work by manipulating the way that words appear on the page. Capital letters convey urgency and loudness: STOP! HELP! COME HERE! Lower-case letters, particularly in names, suggest humility or timidity (but paradoxically also attract attention): *e.e. cummings, archie and mehitabel,* and so on. Additional letters or spaces in a line can suggest stuttering (*c-c-cold*), reverberation (*shockkk*), delay (*s l o w l y*), and distance (*l o n g*). Conversely, deleted letters or spaces indicate speed (*quickasawink*) and compactness (*huddld*). Misspellings, like *X-mass* and *Amerikkka,* make a visual statement by reminding us respectively of the cross borne by Christ and of the role played by the Ku Klux Klan during certain periods of American history. Furthermore, certain typesetting techniques allow the appearance of words to mirror their meanings: over, under, cramped, or tailing. e. e. cummings popularized the use of typographical analogies in modern poetry (see "Buffalo Bill's," p. 943). Although these devices sometimes become contrived and gimmicky, other contemporary poets such as Allen Ginsberg and Howard Nemerov have occasionally introduced tricks of typography into their poems.

Picture Poems

By careful word choice and clever typesetting, poets can sometimes create a visual image of the object or idea they are describing. Although picture poems have never been numerous, they are by no means new. One finds them in ancient Greek literature, as well as in the recent movement toward *concretism* (the concern with a poem's visual appearance rather than with its words). In most cases, visual poems tend to be lighthearted, as in Lewis Carroll's *Alice in Wonderland,* where the tale the Mouse tells Alice takes the form of a long, serpentine "tail" that wanders down half a page. The ingenious seventeenth-century poet George Herbert proved, however, that visual effects are not always frivolous. He formed his religious meditation on the altar of the human heart into the shape of an altar in the following poem:

THE ALTAR

A   broken   A<small>LTAR</small>,   Lord,   thy   servant   rears,
Made   of   a   heart,   and   cemented   with   tears:
   Whose   parts   are   as   thy   hand   did   frame;
   No   workman's   tool   hath   touched   the   same.
        A   H<small>EART</small>   alone
        Is   such   a   stone,
        As   nothing   but
        Thy   power   doth   cut.
        Wherefore   each   part
        Of   my   hard   heart
        Meets   in   this   frame,
        To   praise   thy   Name:
   That,   if   I   chance   to   hold   my   peace,
   These   stones   to   praise   thee   may   not   cease.
O   let   thy   blessed   S<small>ACRIFICE</small>   be   mine,
And   sanctify   this   A<small>LTAR</small>   to   be   thine.
              —George Herbert [1633]

Acrostics

An *acrostic* is a poem in which certain letters (ordinarily the first in each line) spell out a word when read from top to bottom or bottom to top. The best-known acrostics in English literature are those by John Davies in praise of Queen Elizabeth I. Every poem in his volume of *Hymns of Astraea* (1599) spells out the words *Elisabetha Regina*—Elizabeth, the Queen.

TO THE SPRING

E   arth now is green and heaven is blue,
L   ively spring which makes all new,
I   olly spring, doth enter;
S   weet young sun-beams do subdue
A   ngry, aged winter.
B   lasts are mild and seas are calm,
E   very meadow flows with balm,
T   he earth wears all her riches;
H   armonious birds sing such a psalm
A   s ear and heart bewitches.

R   eserve, sweet spring, this nymph of ours
E   ternal garlands of thy flowers;
G   reen garlands never wasting;
I   n her shall last our fair spring
N   ow and forever flourishing
A   s long as heaven is lasting.
              —John Davies [1599]

All of these visual effects may occasionally play a useful role in good poetry, but they are more often signs of weakness—superficial and relatively easy techniques used by poets who are content to be ingenious. In the final analysis, the words of poetry and the energy, intellect, and feeling communicated by those words are of far more importance to truly great writing than even the most meticulous adherence to the external requirements of verse form.

Poems for Further Study

DREAM VARIATIONS

To fling my arms wide
In some place of the sun,
To whirl and to dance
Till the white day is done.
5   Then rest at cool evening
Beneath a tall tree
While night comes on gently,
        Dark like me—
That is my dream!

10   To fling my arms wide
In the face of the sun,
Dance! Whirl! Whirl!
Till the quick day is done.
Rest at pale evening . . .
15   A tall, slim tree . . .
Night coming tenderly
        Black like me.

—Langston Hughes [1924]

❧ QUESTIONS ❧

1. Compare the two stanzas in this poem. How are the two dream variations alike? What are the differences? (Pay particular attention to changes
in the connotations of words.)

2. What rhythm and meter are used in the poem? How does Hughes
manipulate the rhythm to create mood and meaning?

3. Is this poem merely about dancing or does each stanza present a
somewhat different symbolic presentation of racial relations? How does
Hughes encourage us to read the poem symbolically?

"THEY FLEE FROM ME,
THAT SOMETIME DID ME SEEK"[2]

They flee from me, that sometime did me seek,
    With naked foot, stalking in my chamber.

---

[2] The first published version of this poem in Richard Tottel's miscellany, *Songs and Sonnets* (1557),
imposes the title "The Lover Showeth How He Is Forsaken of Such as He Sometimes Enjoyed."
No title is supplied in the authoritative *Egerton Ms. 2711.*

I have seen them gentle, tame, and meek;
That now are wild, and do not remember
5   That sometime they put themselves in danger
     To take bread at my hand: and now they range,
     Busily seeking, with a continual change.

Thanked be fortune! it hath been otherwise
Twenty times better! But once, in special,
10   In thin array, after a pleasant guise,
     When her loose gown from her shoulders did fall,
     And she me caught in her arms long and small,
      Therewithal sweetly did me kiss;
     And softly said, "Dear heart! how like you this?"

15   It was no dream! I lay broad waking!
     But all is turned, thorough my gentleness,
Into a strange fashion of forsaking;
     And I have leave to go, of her goodèness!
     And she also, to use newfangleness!
20   But since that I so kindèly am served,
    I would fain know what she hath deserved?

              —Sir Thomas Wyatt [posthumous, 1557]

❦ QUESTIONS ❦

1.   What comparison dominates the first stanza? What words in this stanza are appropriate in describing women? What change has taken place in those who once sought the speaker's chamber?

2.   The second stanza examines one instance when "it hath been otherwise." How do Wyatt's details in this stanza move from general to specific and contribute to the vividness and intensity of the scene he recalls? How does the double pun in the words "dear heart" contribute to the pattern of the poem's imagery?

3.   The third stanza restates the situation of the forsaken speaker. What has been the reward for his "gentleness"? Does the speaker really believe he has been treated "kindèly"? The word "kindely" may mean "according to kind" or "according to nature" in addition to "nicely." Do you think that Wyatt intended the word "kindely" to create an ironic pun? What is the speaker's attitude toward the woman who formerly sought his company?

4.   What stanzaic form does Wyatt use? What is the relationship between Wyatt's use of stanzas and the organization and development of his ideas?

"SINCE THERE'S NO HELP,
COME LET US KISS AND PART"

Since there's no help, come let us kiss and part;
Nay, I have done, you get no more of me;

And I am glad, yea, glad with all my heart,
That thus so cleanly I myself can free.
5   Shake hands for ever, cancel all our vows,
And when we meet at any time again,
Be it not seen in either of our brows
That we one jot of former love retain.
Now at the last gasp of love's latest breath,
10 When, his pulse failing, passion speechless lies,
When faith is kneeling by his bed of death,
And innocence is closing up his eyes,
    —Now if thou wouldst, when all have given him over,
    From death to life thou might'st him yet recover.

—Michael Drayton [1619]

❧ QUESTIONS ❧

1. What situation is described in this poem and what dramatic interactions may be presumed to occur between the speaking and non-speaking participants in the drama?

2. Why does Drayton personify love, passion, faith, and innocence in lines 6–14? What is the relationship between these personifications and the two separating lovers?

3. Can you deduce the reason(s) why the speaker insists upon breaking up with the woman? What must she do if their love is not to expire?

4. How does Drayton use the structure of sonnet in developing this episode?

THE WAKING

I wake to sleep, and take my waking slow.
I feel my fate in what I cannot fear.
I learn by going where I have to go.

We think by feeling. What is there to know?
5   I hear my being dance from ear to ear.
I wake to sleep, and take my waking slow.

Of those so close beside me, which are you?
God bless the Ground! I shall walk softly there,
And learn by going where I have to go.

10 Light takes the Tree; but who can tell us how?
The lowly worm climbs up a winding stair;
I wake to sleep, and take my waking slow.

Great Nature has another thing to do
To you and me; so take the lively air,
15   And, lovely, learn by going where to go.

This shaking keeps me steady. I should know.
What falls away is always. And is near.
I wake to sleep, and take my waking slow.
I learn by going where I have to go.

—Theodore Roethke [1953]

———————————— ❧ QUESTIONS ❧ ————————————

1. What is the subject of Roethke's poem and how is his attitude toward that subject revealed in the poem's first stanza?

2. What is Roethke's attitude toward thinking and feeling in stanza 2? How are thought and feeling related to waking and sleeping?

3. Stanzas 3 to 5 develop insights on life, death, and nature. How are the insights relevant to the poem's concern with waking and sleeping?

4. How does the poem's form (see villanelle in the *Handbook*) add to its effectiveness?

EASTER WINGS

Lord, who createdst man in wealth and store,°   *plenty*
Though foolishly he lost the same,
Decaying more and more
Till he became
5   Most poor:
With thee
O let me rise
As larks, harmoniously,
And sing this day thy victories:
10   Then shall the fall further the flight in me.

My tender age in sorrow did begin:
And still with sicknesses and shame
Thou didst so punish sin,
That I became
15   Most thin.
With thee
Let me combine,
And feel this day thy victory;
For, if I imp[3] my wing on thine,
20   Affliction shall advance the flight in me.

—George Herbert [1633]

[3] A term from falconry meaning to graft feathers into a wing to restore the ability to fly.

❧ QUESTIONS ❧

1.   This is a picture poem. What does the shape of each stanza depict?

2.   How does the shape of each stanza both complement and reveal Herbert's ideas?

3.   What religious insights does Herbert develop? Why is the title "Easter Wings" appropriate to both the poem's form and content?

16

❧❧❧❧❧❧❧

Questions to Ask
About Poetry

In the preceding pages we have discussed the formal elements of poetry. What follows is a set of questions that will draw upon your accumulated knowledge. These questions should clarify your response and help you to begin the interpretation of a poem that you are studying for the first time.

Before listing the questions, we should, however, add a few words of caution. First, poems differ greatly in their emphases. Not all of the questions that follow will be equally applicable to the analysis of every poem; therefore, you need to follow to some extent your intuition in order to understand what makes a particular poem vital and appealing. Second, although analysis of an author's success in manipulating the elements of poetry can add to an appreciation and understanding of any poem, you should not assume that poems that *require* extensive explication to be understood are necessarily better than those that do not. Explication is one means—and generally the most important means—of coming to understand why an author has written what he or she has. Some poems require much explication and some little. But great poetry should be a pleasure to read, not a punishment. We can expect this pleasure to grow as analysis and mature reflection increase our understanding, but the enjoyment of poetry is, and should remain, visceral as well as intellectual.

QUESTIONS TO ASK AND ANSWER

First, read the poem carefully (aloud at least once), making sure that you understand the *denotative meaning* of each word. (Be sure to use both your dictionary and the editor's notes, if any.)

1. Who is the speaker? What kind of person does he or she seem to be? To whom is he speaking and what are his point of view and his relation to

the subject? What is the general mood or *tone* of the poem? Is it consistent throughout, or is there a shift?

2. What is the situation or occasion of the poem? What is the setting in time and space?

3. Does the poet manipulate the meanings of words using any of the following devices: *connotation, allusion, repetition, ambiguity, punning, paradox, irony?* How does the use of these devices add to the resonance and significance of the denotative meaning?

4. Examine the poem's *imagery.* Are any images repeated or otherwise emphasized? Does the imagery in the poem develop according to a logical pattern? Can you determine why the poet uses the images that he or she does?

5. What forms of poetic comparison (*metaphor, simile,* etc.) are used and what do they add to the poem's imagery and meaning?

6. Does the poem make use of *symbol* or *allegory?*

7. *Paraphrase* and *summarize* the poem. What is the poem's *theme,* argument, or central idea and how is it developed? (Be alert to repeated images, the stanzaic pattern, rhetorical devices, etc.)

8. What are the *meter* and *rhyme scheme* of the poem? What other significant repetitions of sounds (*alliteration, assonance, consonance*) occur in the poem? How do they contribute to the effect of the poem? What is the form of the poem (*sonnet, ode, lyric, dramatic monologue,* etc.)? Are the meter, rhyme scheme, and form appropriate?

9. *Criticize* and *evaluate.* How well do you think the poet has achieved a total integration of the materials? What is *your* reaction to the poem? Do you like the poem? If so, why? If not, why not?

17

✤✤✤✤✤✤

Poems

✹ EARLY POPULAR SONGS AND BALLADS[1] ✹

"SUMER IS ICUMEN IN"[2]

Sumer is icumen in!
Lhude sing, cuccu!
Groweth sed and bloweth med,
And springth the wood nu.
5   Sing, cuccu!

Awe bleteth after lomb,
Lhouth after clave cu.

[1] The six anonymous poems that follow (two lyrics and four ballads) originated in England during the Middle Ages and, in a variety of versions, became part of our oral heritage in poetry. In each case we have selected the version of the poem that seems to us to have the greatest poetic value.
[2] This famous song from a monk's commonplace book of the mid-thirteenth century is a good example (using our modern alphabet) of the early English language. It may be translated as follows: "Summer is a-coming in! / Loudly sing, cuckoo! / Groweth seed and flowereth mead, / And springeth the wood now. / Sing, cuckoo! / Ewe bleateth after lamb, / Loweth after calf cow. / Bullock starteth, buck farteth. / Merry sing, cuckoo! / Cuckoo! cuckoo! / Well singest thou, cuckoo! / Nor cease thou never now. / REFRAIN / Sing cuckoo, now! Sing cuckoo! / [*One repeats this as many times as necessary, pausing at the end.*] / Sing cuckoo now! Sing cuckoo! / [*Another says this, pausing in the middle and not at the end, but immediately repeating the beginning.*]

Bulluc sterteth, bucke verteth.
Murie sing, cuccu!
10   Cuccu! cuccu!
Wel singes thu, cuccu.
Ne swik thu naver nu.

REFRAIN
Sing cuccu! Sing cuccu!
[*Hoc repetit unus quociens opus est, faciens pausacionem in fine.*]
15   Sing cuccu nu! Sing cuccu!
[*Hoc dicit alius, pausans in medio et no in fine, set immediate repetens principium.*]

"O WESTERN WIND"

O western° wind, when wilt thou blow   *I.e., spring*
That the small rain down can rain?
Christ, that my love were in my arms
And I in my bed again!

LORD RANDAL

"O where hae ye been, Lord Randal, my son?
O where hae ye been, my handsome young man?"
"I hae been to the wild wood; mother, make my bed soon,
For I'm weary wi' hunting, and fain wald lie down."

5   "Where gat ye your dinner, Lord Randal, my son?
Where gat ye your dinner, my handsome young man?"
"I dined wi' my true-love; mother, make my bed soon,
For I'm weary wi' hunting, and fain wald lie down."

"What gat ye to your dinner, Lord Randal, my son?
10   What gat ye to your dinner, my handsome young man?"
"I gat eels boiled in broo;° mother, make my bed soon,   *broth*
For I'm weary wi' hunting, and fain wald lie down."

"What became of your bloodhounds, Lord Randal, my son?
What became of your bloodhounds, my handsome young man?"
15   "O they swelled and they died; mother, make my bed soon,
For I'm weary wi' hunting, and fain wald lie down."

"O I fear ye are poisoned, Lord Randal, my son!
O I fear ye are poisoned, my handsome young man!"
"O yes! I am poisoned; mother, make my bed soon,
20   For I'm sick at the heart, and I fain wald lie down."

GET UP AND BAR THE DOOR

It fell about the Martinmas time,°   *Nov. 11*
And a gay time it was then,

When our good wife got puddings to make,
  And she's boiled them in the pan.

5   The wind sae cauld° blew south and north,   *So cold*
      And blew into the floor;
    Quoth our goodman to our goodwife,
      "Gae° out and bar the door."   *Go*

    "My hand is in my hussyfskap,°   *housework*
10   Goodman, as ye may see;
    An° it shoud nae be barred this hundred year,   *If*
      It's no be° barred for° me."   *not going to be / by*

    They made a paction° tween them twa,°   *pact / two*
      They made it firm and sure,
15 That the first word whaeer° shoud speak,   *whoever*
      Shoud rise and bar the door.

    Then by there came two gentlemen,
      At twelve o'clock at night,
    And they could neither see house nor hall,
20   Nor coal nor candle-light.

    "Now whether is this a rich man's house,
      Or whether is it a poor?"
    But neer a word wad ane° o them speak,   *either*
      For barring of the door.

25 And first they ate the white puddings,
      And then they ate the black;
    Tho muckle° thought the goodwife to hersel,   *much*
      Yet neer a word she spake.

    Then said the one unto the other,
30   "Here, man, tak ye my knife;
    Do ye tak aff the auld man's beard,
      And I'll kiss the goodwife."

    "But there 's nae water in the house,
      And what shall we do than?"
35 "What ails ye at the pudding-broo,°   *broth of the pudding*
      That boils into the pan?"

    O up then started our goodman,
      An angry man was he:
    "Will ye kiss my wife before my een,
40   And scad° me wi pudding-bree?"   *scald*

    Then up and started our goodwife,
      Gied three skips on the floor:
    "Goodman, you've spoken the foremost word,
      Get up and bar the door."

SIR PATRICK SPENS

The king sits in Dumferling town,
   Drinking the blude-reid° wine: *blood-red*
"O whar will I get guid° sailor,   *good*
   To sail this ship of mine?"

5   Up and spak an eldern° knicht,   *elderly*
   Sat at the king's richt knee:
"Sir Patrick Spens is the best sailor
   That sails upon the sea."

The king has written a braid° letter   *broad*
10   And signed it wi' his hand,
And sent it to Sir Patrick Spens,
   Was walking on the sand.

The first line that Sir Patrick read,
   A loud lauch° lauched he;   *laugh*
15   The next line that Sir Patrick read,
   The tear blinded his ee.°   *eye*

"O wha° is this has done this deed,   *who*
   This ill deed done to me,
To send me out this time o' the year,
20   To sail upon the sea?

"Mak haste, mak haste, my mirry men all,
   Our guid ship sails the morn."
"O say na° sae,° my master dear,   *not / so*
   For I fear a deadly storm.

25   Late, late yestre'en I saw the new moon
   Wi' the auld moon in her arm,
And I fear, I fear, my dear master,
   That we will come to harm."

O our Scots nobles were richt° laith°   *right / loath*
30   To weet° their cork-heeled shoon,°   *wet / shoes*
Bot lang° or° a' the play were played   *long / ere*
   Their hats they swam aboon.°   *above*

O lang, lang may their ladies sit,
   Wi' their fans into their hand,
35   Or ere they see Sir Patrick Spens
   Come sailing to the land.

O lang, lang may the ladies stand
   Wi' their gold kems° in their hair,   *combs*
Waiting for their ain° dear lords,   *own*
40   For they'll see them na mair.

Half o'er,° half o'er to Aberdour   *over*
  It's fifty fadom° deep,   *fathoms*
And there lies guid Sir Patrick Spens
  Wi' the Scots lords at his feet.

THE THREE RAVENS

There were three ravens sat on a tree,
  Down a down, hay down, hay down
There were three ravens sat on a tree,
  With a down
5   There were three ravens sat on a tree,
They were as black as they might be.
  With a down derry, derry, derry, down, down.[1]

The one of them said to his mate,
"Where shall we our breakfast take?"

10 "Down in yonder green field,
There lies a knight slain under his shield.

"His hounds they lie down at his feet,
So well they can their master keep.

"His hawks they fly so eagerly,
15 There's no fowl dare him come nigh."

Down there comes a fallow° doe,   *brownish-yellow*
As great with young as she might go.

She lift up his bloody head
And kissed his wounds that were so red.

20 She got him up upon her back
And carried him to earthen lake.°   *grave*

She buried him before the prime;°   *break of day*
She was dead herself ere even-song time.°   *dusk*

God send every gentleman
25 Such hawks, such hounds, and such a leman.°   *lover*

---

[1] In each subsequent stanza of the poem the pattern of lines is the same as in this one, with lines 2, 4 and 6 serving as unchanging refrains.

MEDIEVAL POETRY ❧

Geoffrey Chaucer   1342?–1400

THE CANTERBURY TALES

FROM *"General Prologue"*

Whan that Aprille with his shoures sote°   *sweet*
The droghte of Marche hath perced to the rote,
And bathed every veyne in swich licour,
Of which vertu° engendered is the flour;°   *power / flower*
5 Whan Zephirus° eek° with his swete breeth   *the west wind / also*
Inspired hath in every holt° and heeth°   *woods / heath*
The tendre croppes, and the yonge sonne
Hath in the Ram his halfe cours y-ronne,[1]
And smale fowles maken melodye,
10 That slepen al the night with open yë;°   *eye*
(So priketh° hem nature in hir corages):°   *pricks / hearts*
Than longen folk to goon on pilgrimages
(And palmers° for to seken straunge strondes)°   *pilgrims / lands*
To ferne halwes, couthe in sondry londes;[2]
15 And specially, from every shires ende
Of Engelond, to Caunterbury[3] they wende,°   *go*
The holy blisful martir for to seke,
That hem hath holpen,° whan that they were   *helped*
      seke.°   *sick*
   Bifel° that, in that seson on a day,   *It happened*
20 In Southwerk at the Tabard[4] as I lay
Redy to wenden° on my pilgrimage   *go*
To Caunterbury with ful devout corage,
At night was come in-to that hostelrye°   *inn*
Wel nyne and twenty in a companye,
25 Of sondry folk, by aventure° y-falle   *chance*
In felawshipe, and pilgrims were they alle,
That toward Caunterbury wolden° ryde;   *wished to*
The chambres and the stables weren wyde,
And wel we weren esed atte beste.[5]
30 And shortly, whan the sonne was to reste,
So hadde I spoken with hem everichon,°   *every one*

---

[1] The sun is young because it is only half-way through the Ram, or Aries (March 21 to April 20), the first sign in the medieval zodiac.
[2] I.e., to foreign shrines well-known in sundry lands.
[3] Canterbury, a cathedral city in England, where St. Thomas à Becket became a martyr ("the holy blisful martir," line 17) in 1170.
[4] The Tabard, an inn in Southwark, then a suburb of London.
[5] I.e., accommodated in the best manner.

That I was of hir felawshipe anon,° *at once*
And made forward° erly for to ryse, *a pact*
To take our wey, ther as I yow devyse.° *describe*
35 But natheles, whyl I have tyme and space,
Er that I ferther in this tale pace,
Me thinketh it acordaunt° to resoun, *according*
To telle yow al the condicioun
Of ech of hem, so as it semed me,
40 And whiche they weren, and of what degree;° *status*
And eek in what array° that they were inne: *clothing*

MILLER

545 The Miller was a stout carl,° for the nones *churl*
Ful big he was of braun, and eek of bones;
That proved° wel, for over-al ther° he cam, *was proven / wherever*
At wrastling he wolde have alwey the ram.[1]
He was short-sholdred, brood,° a thikke *broad*
 knarre,° *head*
550 Ther nas no dore that he nolde° heve of harre,° *could not / off hinge*
Or breke it, at a renning,° with his heed. *running*
His berd° as any sowe or fox was reed, *beard*
And ther-to brood, as though it were a spade.
Up-on the cop° right of his nose he hade *top*
555 A werte,° and ther-on stood a tuft of heres,° *wart / hairs*
Reed as the bristles of a sowes eres;° *ears*
His nose-thirles° blake° were and wyde. *nostrils / black*
A swerd and bokeler° bar° he by his syde; *shield / bore*
His mouth as greet was as a greet forneys.° *furnace*
560 He was a janglere° and a goliardeys,° *loudmouth / lewd joker*
And that was most of sinne and harlotryes.° *ribaldry*
Wel coude he stelen corn, and tollen thryes;[2]
And yet he hadde a thombe of gold,[3] pardee.° *by God*
A whyt cote° and a blew hood wered° he. *coat / wore*
565 A baggepype wel coude he blowe and sowne,
And ther-with-al he broghte us out of towne.

REEVE

The Reve° was a sclendre colerik man, *overseer*
His berd was shave as ny° as ever he can. *close*
His heer was by his eres round y-shorn.
590 His top was dokked° lyk a preest biforn. *cut short, tonsured*
Ful longe were his legges, and ful lene,
Y-lyk° a staf, ther was no calf y-sene.° *like / visible*
Wel coude he kepe° a gerner° and a binne,° *guard / granary / chest*

[1] The ram, first prize in medieval wrestling matches.
[2] I.e., take thrice his proper fee for grinding corn.
[3] Proverbially, "an honest miller has a thumb of gold."

Ther was noon auditour coude on him winne.°   *get the better of him*
595   Wel wiste° he, by the droghte, and by the reyn,   *knew*
The yelding of his seed, and of his greyn.
His lordes sheep, his neet,° his dayerye,   *cattle*
His swyn, his hors, his stoor,° and his pultyre,   *stock*
Was hoolly in this reves governing,
600   And by his covenaunt° yaf° the rekening,   *agreement / gave*
Sin that his lord was twenty yeer of age;
Ther coude no man bringe him in arrerage.°   *arrears*
Ther nas baillif, ne herde,° ne other hyne.°   *herdsman / farmhand*
That he ne knew his sleighte and his covyne,°   *deceit*
605   They were adrad° of him, as of the deeth.°   *afraid / the plague*
His woning° was ful fair up-on an heeth,   *dwelling*
With grene treës shadwed was his place.
He coude bettre than his lord purchace.
Ful riche he was astored prively,°   *stocked secretly*
610   His lord wel coude he plesen subtilly,
To yeve° and lene° him of his owne good,°   *give / lend / goods*
And have a thank, and yet a cote and hood.
In youthe he lerned hadde a good mister;°   *occupation*
He was a wel good wrighte,° a carpenter.   *workman*
615   This reve sat up-on a full good stot,°   *horse*
That was al pomely° grey, and highte° Scot.   *dappled / named*
A long surcote° of pers° up-on he hade,   *overcoat / blue*
And by his syde he bar a rusty blade.
Of Northfolk was this reve, of which I telle,
620   Bisyde a toun men clepen Baldeswelle.
Tukked[1] he was, as is a frere, aboute,
And ever he rood the hindreste of our route.

THE MILLER'S PROLOGUE

Here folwen the wordes bitween the Host and the Millere.

Whan that the Knight had thus his tale y-told,
3110   In al the route° nas ther yong ne old   *company*
That he ne seyde it was a noble storie,
And worthy for to drawn to memorie;
And namely the gentils° everichoon.   *well bred folks*
Our Hoste lough and swoor, "so moot° I goon,°   *might / go (walk)*
3115   This gooth aright; unbokeled is the male;°   *pack*
Lat see now who shal telle another tale:
For trewely, the game is wel bigonne.
Now telleth ye, sir Monk, if that ye conne,°   *can*
Sumwhat, to quyte° with the Knightes tale."   *requite*
3120   The Miller, that for-dronken° was al pale,   *because of drink*
So that unnethe° up-on his hors he sat,   *scarcely*
He nolde avalen° neither hood ne hat,   *take off*

---

[1] He wore his cloak tucked up.

	Ne abyde no man for his curteisye,	
	But in Pilates vois[1] he gan to crye,	
3125	And swoor by armes and by blood and bones,	
	"I can° a noble tale for the nones,	*know*
	With which I wol now quyte the Knightes tale."	
	Our Hoste saugh° that he was dronke of ale,	*saw*
	And seyde: "abyd, Robin, my leve° brother,	*dear*
3130	Som bettre man shal telle us first another:	
	Abyd, and lat us werken thriftily."°	*sensibly*
	"By goddes soul," quod he, "that wol nat I;	
	For I wol speke, or elles go my wey."	
	Our Hoste answerde: "tel on, a devel wey!°	*in the devil's name*
3135	Thou art a fool, thy wit is overcome."	
	"Now herkneth,"° quod the Miller, "alle and	*listen*
	some!	
	But first I make a protestacioun	
	That I am dronke, I knowe it by my soun;	
	And therfore, if that I misspeke or seye,	
3140	Wyte° it the ale of Southwerk, I yow preye;	*think*
	For I wol telle a legende and a lyf	
	Bothe of a Carpenter, and of his wyf,	
	How that a clerk hath set the wrightes cappe."[2]	
	The Reve answerde and seyde, "stint thy clappe,°	*chatter*
3145	Lat be thy lewed dronken harlotrye.	
	It is a sinne and eek a greet folye	
	To apeiren° any man, or him diffame,	*injure*
	And eek to bringen wyves in swich fame.	
	Thou mayst y-nogh of othere thinges seyn."	
3150	This dronken Miller spak ful sone ageyn,	
	And seyde, "leve brother Osewold,	
	Who hath no wyf, he is no cokewold.°	*cuckold*
	But I sey nat therfore that thou art oon;	
	Ther been ful gode wyves many oon,	
3155	And ever a thousand gode ayeyns° oon badde,	*against*
	That knowestow wel thy-self, but-if° thou madde.°	*unless / are mad*
	Why artow angry with my tale now?	
	I have a wyf, pardee,° as well as thou,	*by god*
	Yet nolde° I, for the oxen in my plogh,	*would not*
3160	Taken up-on me more than y-nogh,	
	As demen° of my-self that I were oon;	*deeming*
	I wol beleve wel that I am noon.	
	An housbond shal nat been inquisitif	
	Of goddes privetee,° nor of his wyf.	*private matters*
3165	So° he may finde goddes foyson° there,	*so long as / plenty*
	Of the remenant nedeth nat enquere."°	*inquire*
	What sholde I more seyn, but this Millere	
	He nolde his wordes for no man forbere,	

[1] In the medieval mystery plays Pontius Pilate, the governor of Judea when Christ was crucified, spoke loudly and harshly.
[2] I.e., how a clerk got the better of the carpenter.

But tolde his cherles tale in his manere;
3170   Me thinketh that I shal reherce° it here.   *retell*
And ther-fore every gentil wight° I preye,   *genteel person*
For goddes love, demeth nat° that I seye   *do not think*
Of evel entente, but that I moot reherce
Hir tales alle, be they bettre or werse,
3175   Or elles falsen° som of my matere.   *falsify*
And therfore, who-so list it nat y-here,
Turne over the leef, and chese another tale;
For he shal finde y-nowe, grete and smale,
Of storial° thing that toucheth gentillesse,   *historical*
3180   And eek moralitee and holinesse;
Blameth nat me if that ye chese amis.
The Miller is a cherl, ye knowe wel this;
So was the Reve, and othere many mo,
And harlotrye they tolden bothe two.
3185   Avyseth yow° and putte me out of blame;   *be advised*
And eek men shal nat make ernest of game.

Here endeth the prologe.

THE MILLERES TALE

Here biginneth the Millere his tale.

Whylom° ther was dwellinge at Oxenford   *once*
A riche gnof,° that gestes° heeld to bord,°   *knave / guests / board*
And of his craft he was a Carpenter.
3190   With him ther was dwellinge a povre° scoler,   *poor*
Had lerned art, but al his fantasye
Was turned for to lerne astrologye,
And coude a certeyn of conclusiouns
To demen by interrogaciouns,[1]
3195   If that men axed° him in certain houres,   *asked*
Whan that men sholde have droghte or elles
      shoures,
Or if men axed him what sholde bifalle
Of every thing, I may nat rekene hem alle.
   This clerk was cleped° hende° Nicholas;   *named / courteous*
3200   Of derne° love he coude° and of solas;°   *secret / knew / pleasure*
And ther-to he was sleigh and ful privee,°   *secretive*
And lyk a mayden meke for to see.
A chambre hadde he in that hostelrye
Allone, with-outen any companye,
3205   Ful fetisly° y-dight° with herbes swote,°   *fitly / furnished / sweet*
And he him-self as swete as is the rote
Of licorys, or any cetewale.°   *setwall (a spice)*
His Almageste[2] and bokes grete and smale,

---

[1] I.e., and knew how to reach a certain number of conclusions through interrogations.
[2] A treatise on astrology.

His astrelabie,° longinge for° his art,   *astrolabe / belonging to*
3210 His augrim-stones° layen faire a-part   *counting stones*
On shelves couched° at his beddes heed: *placed*
His presse° y-covered with a falding° reed.   *cupboard / woolen cloth*
And al above ther lay a gay sautrye,³
On which he made a nightes melodye
3215 So swetely, that al the chambre rong;
And *Angelus ad virginem*⁴ he song;
And after that he song the kinges note,°   *tune*
Ful often blessed was his mery throte.
And thus this swete clerk his tyme spente
3220 After his freendes finding° and his rente.°   *presents / regular income*
    This Carpenter had wedded newe° a wyf   *recently*
Which that he lovede more than his lyf;
Of eightetene yeer she was of age.
Jalous he was, and heeld hir narwe° in cage,   *closely*
3225 For she was wilde and yong, and he was old,
And demed him-self ben lyk a cokewold.°   *cuckold*
He new nat Catoun,⁵ for his wit was rude,
That bad° man sholde wedde his similitude.   *bade*
Men sholde wedden after° hir estaat,°   *according to / state*
3230 For youthe and elde° is often at debaat.   *old age*
But sith that he was fallen in the snare,
He moste endure, as other folk, his care.
    Fair was this yonge wyf, and ther-with-al
As any wesele° hir body gent° and smal.   *weasel / graceful*
3235 A ceynt° she werede barred° al of silk,   *belt / striped*
A barmclooth° eek as whyt as morne milk   *apron*
Up-on hir lendes,° ful of many a gore.°   *loins / pleat*
Whyt was hir smok° and brouded° al bifore   *smock / embroidered*
And eek bihinde, on hir coler° aboute,   *collar*
3240 Of col-blak silk, with-inne and eek with-oute.
The tapes° of hir whyte voluper°   *ribbons / cap*
Were of the same suyte of° hir coler;   *material as*
Hir filet° brood° of silk, and set ful hye: *headband / broad*
And sikerly° she hadde a likerous° yë.   *certainly / lecherous*
3245 Ful smale° y-pulled° were hir browes two,   *finely / plucked*
And tho were bent, and blake as any sloo.°   *sloe (a plum)*
She was ful more blisful on to see
Than is the newe pere-jonette° tree;   *pear*
And softer than the wolle is of a wether.°   *sheep*
3250 And by hir girdel heeng a purs of lether
Tasseld with silk, and perled° with latoun.°   *studded / brass*
In al this world, to seken up and doun,
There nis no man so wys, that coude thenche°   *think of*
So gay a popelote,° or swich° a wenche.   *doll / such*
3255 Ful brighter was the shyning of hir hewe°   *complexion*

---

³ A psaltery, an ancient stringed instrument.
⁴ "The Angel to the Virgin"
⁵ Dionysius Cato (fourth-century A.D. Roman author) in whose *Distichs* occurs the maxim cited by the Miller.

Than in the tour° the noble° y-forged newe.		*tower / gold coin*
But of hir song, it was as loude and yerne°		*lively*
As any swalwe° sittinge on a berne.		*swallow*
Ther-to she coude skippe and make game,		
3260 As any kide or calf folwinge his dame.		
Hir mouth was swete as bragot° or the meeth,°		*bragget / mead*
Or hord of apples leyd in hey or heeth.°		*heather*
Winsinge° she was, as is a joly colt,		*skittish*
Long as a mast, and upright as a bolt.°		*arrow*
3265 A brooch she baar up-on hir lowe coler,		
As brood as is the bos° of a bocler.°		*boss / shield*
Hir shoes were laced on hir legges hye;		
She was a prymerole,° a pigges-nye°		*primrose / sweetie*
For any lord to leggen° in his bedde,		*lay*
3270 Or yet for any good yeman° to wedde.		*yeoman*
Now sire, and eft° sire, so bifel the cas,		*again*
That on a day this hende Nicholas		
Fil° with this yonge wyf to rage° and pleye,		*happened / romp*
Whyl that hir housbond was at Oseneye,[6]		
3275 As clerkes ben ful subtile and ful queynte;°		*clever*
And prively he caughte hir by the queynte,°		*crotch*
And seyde, "y-wis,° but if ich° have my wille,		*truly / I*
For derne° love of thee, lemman,° I spille."°		*secret / lover / die*
And heeld hir harde by the haunche-bones,°		*hip bones*
3280 And seyde, "lemman, love me al at-ones,°		*at once*
Or I wol dyen, also° god me save!"		*so*
And she sprong as a colt doth in the trave,[7]		
And with hir heed she wryed° faste awey,		*wriggled*
And seyde, "I wol nat kisse thee, by my fey,		
3285 Why, lat be," quod she, "lat be, Nicholas,		
Or I wol crye out harrow° and allas.		*help*
Do wey° your handes for your curteisye!"		*take away*
This Nicholas gan mercy for to crye,		
And spak so faire, and profred hir° so faste,		*propositioned her*
3290 That she hir love him graunted atte laste,		
And swoor hir ooth, by seint Thomas of Kent,[8]		
That she wol been at his comandement,		
Whan that she may hir leyser° wel espye.		*leisure*
"Myn housbond is so ful of jalousye,		
3295 That but ye wayte wel and been privee,°		*secretive*
I woot right wel I nam but deed," quod she.		
"Ye moste been ful derne, as in this cas."		
"Nay ther-of care thee noght," quod Nicholas,		
"A clerk had litherly° biset° his whyle,°		*ill / used / time*
3300 But-if he coude a carpenter bigyle."		
And thus they been acorded and y-sworn		
To wayte a tyme, as I have told biforn.		

[6] Oseney, near Oxford.
[7] A frame used in shoeing a restive horse.
[8] St. Thomas à Becket, who was slain in Canterbury Cathedral in Kent in 1170.

Whan Nicholas had doon thus everydeel,
And thakked° hir aboute the lendes° weel,   *stroked / loins*
3305   He kist hir swete, and taketh his sautrye,
And pleyeth faste, and maketh melodye.
Than fil° it thus, that to the parish-chirche,   *befell*
Cristes owne werkes for to wirche,
This gode wyf wente on an haliday;°   *holy day*
3310   Hir forheed shoon as bright as any day,
So was it wasshen whan she leet° hir werk.   *left*
    Now was ther of that chirche a parish-clerk,
The which that was y-cleped° Absolon.   *called*
Crul° was his heer, and as the gold it shoon,   *curly*
3315   And strouted° as a fanne large and brode;   *spread out*
Ful streight and even lay his joly shode.°   *part*
His rode° was reed, his eyen greye as goos;°   *complexion / goose*
With Powles window corven on his shoos,[9]
In hoses° rede he wente fetisly.°   *stockings / fashionably*
3320   Y-clad he was ful smal° and proprely,   *finely*
Al in a kirtel° of a light wachet;°   *tunic / blue*
Ful faire and thikke been the poyntes° set.   *laces*
And ther-up-on he hadde a gay surplys°   *surplice*
As whyt as is the blosme up-on the rys.°   *bough*
3325   A mery child he was, so god me save,
Wel coude he laten° blood and clippe and shave,   *let*
And make a chartre° of lond or acquitaunce.   *title*
In twenty manere coude he trippe and daunce
After the scole of Oxenforde tho,
3330   And with his legges casten° to and fro,   *leap*
And pleyen songes on a small rubible;°   *fiddle*
Ther-to he song som-tyme a loud quinible;°   *falsetto*
And as wel coude he pleye on his giterne.°   *guitar*
In al the toun nas brewhous ne taverne
3335   That he ne visited with his solas,°   *entertainment*
Ther any gaylard° tappestere° was.   *flirtatious / barmaid*
But sooth to seyn, he was somdel squaymous°   *squeamish*
Of farting, and of speche daungerous.°   *fastidious*
    This Absolon, that jolif was and gay,
3340   Gooth with a sencer° on the haliday,   *censer*
Sensinge the wyves of the parish faste;
And many a lovely look on hem he caste,
And namely on this carpenteres wyf.
To loke on hir him thoughte a mery lyf,
3345   She was so propre and swete and likerous.°   *voluptuous*
I dar wel seyn, if she had been a mous,
And he a cat, he wolde hir hente° anon.   *seize*
    This parish-clerk, this joly Absolon,
Hath in his herte swich a love-longinge,
3350   That of no wyf ne took he noon offringe;
For curteisye, he seyde, he wolde noon.

---

[9] Absolon's fashionable shoes were latticed like the windows of St. Paul's Cathedral in London.

The mone, whan it was night, ful brighte shoon,
And Absolon his giterne hath y-take,
For paramours, he thoghte for to wake.
3355 And forth he gooth, jolif and amorous,
Till he cam to the carpenteres hous
A litel after cokkes hadde y-crowe;
And dressed him up by a shot-windowe°   *shuttered window*
That was up-on the carpenteres wal.
3360 He singeth in his vois gentil and smal,
"Now, dere lady, if thy wille be,
I preye yow that ye wol rewe° on me,"   *have pity*
Ful wel acordaunt° to his giterninge.°   *pitched / guitar-playing*
This carpenter awook, and herde him singe,
3365 And spak un-to his wyf, and seyde anon,
"What! Alison! herestow nat Absolon
That chaunteth thus under our boures° wal?"   *bedroom*
And she answerde hir housbond ther-with-al,
"Yis, god wot, John, I here it every-del."
3370   This passeth forth; what wol ye bet° than wel?   *better*
Fro day to day this joly Absolon
So woweth° hir, that him is wo bigon.   *woos*
He waketh al the night and al the day;
He kempte° hise lokkes brode, and made him   *combed*
        gay;
3375 He woweth hir by menes° and brocage,°   *go-betweens / mediation*
And swoor he wolde been hir owne page;
He singeth, brokkinge° as a nightingale;   *quavering*
He sente hir piment,° meeth,° and spyced ale,   *spiced wine / mead*
And wafres,° pyping hote out of the glede;°   *pastries / coals*
3380 And for she was of toune, he profred mede.°   *payment*
For som folk wol ben wonnen for richesse,
And som for strokes, and som for gentillesse.
        Somtyme, to shewe his lightnesse and
                maistrye,°   *virtuosity*
He pleyeth Herodes on a scaffold hye.[10]
3385 But what availleth him as in this cas?
She loveth so this hende Nicholas,
That Absolon may blowe the bukkes horn,[11]
He ne hadde for his labour but a scorn;
And thus she maketh Absolon hir ape,
3390 And al his ernest turneth til a jape.°   *joke*
Ful sooth is this proverbe, it is no lye,
Men seyn right thus, "alwey the nye slye
Maketh the ferre leve to be looth."[12]
For though that Absolon be wood° or wrooth,°   *mad / wrathful*
3395 By-cause that he fer was from hir sighte,
This nye° Nicholas stood in his lighte.   *nearby*

[10] He acted the part of Herod in a nativity play staged on a high platform.
[11] I.e., Absolon will go unrewarded.
[12] "Always the nigh, sly man makes the far-away lover loathed."

Now bere thee wel, thou hende Nicholas!
For Absolon may waille and singe "allas."
And so bifel it on a Saterday,
3400 This carpenter was goon til° Osenay;   *to*
And hende Nicholas and Alisoun
Acorded been to this conclusioun,
That Nicholas shal shapen him a wyle
This sely° jalous housbond to bigyle;   *naïve*
3405 And if so be the game wente aright,
She sholde slepen in his arm al night,
For this was his desyr and hir also.
And right anon, with-outen wordes mo,
This Nicholas no lenger wolde tarie,
3410 But doth ful softe un-to his chambre carie
Bothe mete and drinke for a day or tweye,°   *two*
And to hir housbonde bad hir for to seye,
If that he axed after Nicholas,
She sholde seye she niste° where he was,   *knew not*
3415 Of al that day she saugh him nat with yë;
She trowed° that he was in maladye,   *believed*
For, for no cry, hir mayde coude him calle;
He nolde answere, for no-thing that mighte falle.
    This passeth forth al thilke° Saterday,   *that*
3420 That Nicholas stille in his chambre lay,
And eet and sleep, or dide what him leste,°   *pleased*
Til Sonday, that the sonne gooth to reste.
    This sely carpenter hath greet merveyle
Of Nicholas, or what thing mighte him eyle,°   *ail*
3425 And seyde, "I am adrad,° by seint Thomas,   *afraid*
It stondeth nat aright with Nicholas.
God shilde° that he deyde sodeynly!   *forbid*
This world is now ful tikel,° sikerly;   *unstable*
I saugh to-day a cors° y-born to chirche   *corpse*
3430 That now, on Monday last, I saugh him wirche.°   *work*
    Go up," quod he un-to his knave anoon,
"Clepe° at his dore, or knokke with a stoon,   *call*
Loke how it is, and tel me boldely."
    This knave gooth him up ful sturdily,
3435 And at the chambre-dore, whyl that he stood,
He cryde and knokked as that he were wood:°   *insane*
"What! how! what do ye, maister Nicholay?
How may ye slepen al the longe day?"
    But al for noght, he herde nat a word;
3440 An hole he fond, ful lowe up-on a bord,
Ther as° the cat was wont in for to crepe;   *where*
And at that hole he looked in ful depe,
And at the laste he hadde of him a sighte.
This Nicholas sat gaping over up-righte,
3445 As he had kyked° on the newe mone.   *gazed*
Adoun he gooth, and tolde his maister sone
In what array he saugh this ilke man.

This carpenter to blessen him bigan,
And seyde, "help us, seinte Frideswyde![13]
3450   A man woot° litel what him shal bityde.   *knows*
This man is falle, with his astromye,
In som woodnesse° or in som agonye;   *madness*
I thoghte ay wel how that it sholde be!
Men sholde nat knowe of goddes privetee.°   *secrets*
3455   Ye, blessed be alwey a lewed° man,   *ignorant*
That noght but only his bileve° can!°   *faith / knows*
So ferde° another clerk with astromye;   *fared*
He walked in the feeldes for to prye
Up-on the sterres, what ther sholde bifalle,
3460   Til he was in a marle-pit y-falle;
He saugh nat that. But yet, by seint Thomas,
Me reweth° sore° of hende Nicholas.   *sorrow / greatly*
He shal be rated of° his studying,   *berated for*
If that I may, by Jesus, hevene king!
3465   Get me a staf, that I may underspore,°   *pry up*
Whyl that thou, Robin, hevest up the dore.
He shal out of his studying, as I gesse"—
And to the chambre-dore he gan him dresse.°   *address*
His knave was a strong carl° for the nones,°   *fellow / task*
3470   And by the haspe he haf° it up atones,°   *heaved / at once*
In-to the floor the dore fil anon.
This Nicholas sat ay as stille as stoon,
And ever gaped upward in-to the eir.
This carpenter wende° he were in despeir,   *thought*
3475   And hente° him by the sholdres mightily,   *grasped*
And shook him harde, and cryde spitously,°   *harshly*
"What! Nicholay! what, how! what! loke adoun!
Awake, and thenk on Cristes passioun;
I crouche° thee from elves and fro wightes!"°   *exorcise / creatures*
3480   Ther-with the night-spel seyde he anon-rightes°   *immediately*
On foure halves° of the hous aboute,   *sides*
And on the threshfold of the dore withoute:—
"Jesu Crist, and sëynt Benedight,°   *St. Benedict*
Blesse this hous from every wikked wight,
3485   For nightes verye,[14] the white *paternoster!*°   *Lord's prayer*
Where wentestow, seynt Petres soster?°   *sister*
And atte laste this hende Nicholas
Gan for to syke° sore, and seyde, "allas!   *sigh*
Shal al the world be lost eftsones° now?"   *again*
3490   This carpenter answerde, "what seystow?
What! thenk on god, as we don, men that
    swinke."°   *work*
This Nicholas answerde, "fecche me drinke;
And after wol I speke in privetee

---

[13] The patron saint of Oxford.
[14] Possibly a contraction of *venerye* meaning "hanky-panky," or else a variant of *werye* meaning "worry"—hence, *for night's worry.*

Of certeyn thing that toucheth me and thee;
3495 I wol telle it non other man, certeyn."
This carpenter goth doun, and comth ageyn,
And broghte of mighty ale a large quart;
And whan that each of hem had dronke his part,
This Nicholas his dore faste shette,
3500 And doun the carpenter by him he sette.
He seyde, "John, myn hoste lief° and dere,   *beloved*
Thou shalt up-on thy trouthe° swere me here,   *word of honor*
That to no wight thou shalt this conseil° wreye;° *advice / betray*
For it is Cristes conseil that I seye,
3505 And if thou telle it man,° thou are forlore,°   *to anyone / lost*
For this vengaunce thou shalt han° therfore,   *have*
That if thou wreye me, thou shalt be wood!"
"Nay, Crist forbede it, for his holy blood!"
Quod tho° this sely man, "I nam no labbe,°   *then / blabber*
3510 Ne, though I seye, I name nat lief° to gabbe.   *likely*
Sey what thou wolt, I shal it never telle
To child ne wyf, by him that harwed° helle!"[15]   *harrowed*
"Now John," quod Nicholas, "I wol nat lye;
I have y-founde in myn astrologye,
3515 As I have loked in the mone bright,
That now, a Monday next, at quarter-night,°   *nearly dawn*
Shal falle a reyn and that so wilde and wood,
That half so greet was never Noës° flood.   *Noah's*
This world," he seyde, "in lasse than in an hour
3520 Shal al be dreynt,° so hidous is the shour;   *drowned*
Thus shal mankynde drenche° and lese° hir lyf."   *drown / lose*
This carpenter answerde, "allas, my wyf!
And shal she drenche? allas! myn Alisoun!"
For sorwe of this he fil almost adoun,
3525 And seyde, "is ther no remedie in this cas?"
"Why, yis, for gode," quod hende Nicholas,
"If thou wolt werken after lore° and reed;°   *learning / advice*
Thou mayst nat werken after thyn owene heed.°   *head*
For thus seith Salomon, that was ful trewe,
3530 'Work al by conseil, and thou shalt nat rewe.'°   *repent*
And if thou werken wolt by good conseil,
I undertake, with-outen mast and seyl,°   *sail*
Yet shal I saven hir and thee and me.
Hastow nat herd how saved was Noë,
3535 Whan that our lord had warned him biforn
That al the world with water sholde be lorn?"°   *lost*
"Yis," quod this carpenter, "ful yore ago."
"Hastow nat herd," quod Nicholas, "also
The sorwe of Noë with his felawshipe,
3540 Er that he mighte gete his wyf to shipe?
Him had be lever,° I dar wel undertake,   *more happy*

---

[15] Many Christians believe that Christ descended into Hell between his crucifixion and his resurrection to bring the just out of Limbo.

At thilke tyme, than alle hise wetheres° blake,   *rams*
That she hadde had a ship hir-self allone.
And ther-fore, wostou° what is best to done?   *do you know*
3545   This asketh haste, and of an hastif° thing   *urgent*
Men may nat preche or maken tarying.
     Anon go gete us faste in-to this in°   *inn*
A kneding-trogh, or elles a kimelin,°   *tub*
For ech of us, but loke that they be large,
3550   In whiche we mowe° swimme° as in a barge,   *may / float*
And han ther-inne vitaille° suffisant   *victuals*
But for a day; fy on the remenant!
The water shal aslake° and goon away   *abate*
Aboute pryme° up-on the nexte day.   *daybreak*
3555   But Robin may nat wite° of this, thy knave,   *know*
Ne eek° thy mayde Gille I may nat save;   *also*
Axe nat why, for though thou aske me,
I wol nat tellen goddes privetee.
Suffiseth thee, but if° thy wittes madde,°   *unless / go mad*
3560   To han° as greet° a grace as Noë hadde.   *have / great*
Thy wyf shal I wel saven, out of doute,
Go now thy wey, and speed thee heeraboute.
     But whan thou hast, for hir and thee and me,
Y-geten us thise kneding-tubbes three,
3565   Than shaltow hange hem in the roof ful hye,
That no man of our purveyaunce° spye.   *preparations*
And whan thou thus hast doon as I have seyd,
And hast our vitaille faire in hem y-leyd,
And eek an ax, to smyte the corde atwo
3570   When that the water comth, that we may go,
And broke an hole an heigh,° up-on the gable,   *on high*
Unto the gardin-ward,° over the stable,   *garden-side*
That we may frely passen forth our way
Whan that the grete shour is goon away—
3575   Than shaltow swimme as myrie, I undertake,
As doth the whyte doke° after hir drake.   *duck*
Than wol I clepe, 'how! Alison! how! John!
Be myrie, for the flood wol passe anon.'
And thou wolt seyn, 'hayl, maister Nicholay!
3580   Good morwe, I se thee wel, for it is day.'
And than shul we be lordes al our lyf
Of al the world, as Noë and his wyf.
     But of o thyng I warne thee ful right,
Be wel avysed, on that ilke night
3585   That we ben entred in-to shippes bord,
That noon of us ne speke nat a word,
Ne clepe, ne crye, but been in his preyere;
For it is goddes owne heste dere.°   *dear behest*
     Thy wyf and thou mote hange fer a-twinne,°   *apart*
3590   For that bitwixe yow shal be no sinne
No more in looking than ther shal in dede;
This ordinance is seyd, go, god thee spede!

Tomorwe at night, whan men ben alle aslepe,
In-to our kneding-tubbes wol we crepe,
3595 And sitten ther, abyding goddes grace.
Go now thy wey, I have no lenger space
To make of this no lenger sermoning.
Men seyn thus, 'send the wyse, and sey no-thing;'[16]
Thou art so wys, it nedeth thee nat teche;
3600 Go, save our lyf, and that I thee biseche."
    This sely carpenter goth forth his wey.
Ful ofte he seith "allas" and "weylawey,"
And to his wyf he tolde his privetee;°   secret
And she was war,° and knew it bet° than he,   aware / better
3605 What al this queynte cast° was for to seye.   device
But nathelees she ferde° as she wolde deye,   pretended
And seyde, "allas! go forth thy wey anon,
Help us to scape,° or we ben lost echon;°   escape / each one
I am thy trewe verray wedded wyf;
3610 Go, dere spouse, and help to save our lyf."
    Lo! which a greet thyng is affeccioun!°   emotion
Men may dye of imaginacioun,
So depe may impressioun be take.
This sely carpenter biginneth quake;
3615 Him thinketh verraily that he may see
Noës flood come walwing° as the see   tumbling
To drenchen Alisoun, his hony dere.
He wepeth, weyleth, maketh sory chere,
He syketh with ful many a sory swogh.°   sound
3620 He gooth and geteth him a kneding-trogh,
And after that a tubbe and a kimelin,
And prively he sente hem to his in,°   house
And heng hem in the roof in privetee.
His owne hand he made laddres three,
3625 To climben by the ronges and the stalkes°   uprights
Un-to the tubbes hanginge in the balkes,°   beams
And hem vitailled,° bothe trogh and tubbe,   stocked
With breed and chese, and good ale in a jubbe,°   jug
Suffysinge right y-nogh as for a day.
3630 But er° that he had maad al this array,°   before / arrangements
He sente his knave, and eek his wenche also,
Up-on his nede° to London for to go.   need or business
And on the Monday, whan it drow to night,
He shette his dore with-oute candel-light,
3635 And dressed° al thing as it sholde be,   set up
And shortly, up they clomben alle three;
They sitten stille wel a furlong-way.[17]
"Now, *Pater-noster*, clom!"° seyde Nicholay,   clam up
And "clom," quod John, and "clom," seyde
        Alisoun.

---

[16] "A word to the wise is enough."
[17] The time it takes to walk a furlong (⅛ mile).

3640	This carpenter seyde his devocioun,°
	And stille he sit, and biddeth his preyere,
	Awaytinge on the reyn, if he it here.
	The dede sleep, for wery bisinesse,
	Fil° on this carpenter right, as I gesse,
3645	Aboute corfew-tyme,° or litel more;
	For travail° of his goost° he groneth sore,
	And eft° he routeth,° for his heed mislay.
	Doun of the laddre stalketh Nicholay.
	And Alisoun, ful softe adoun she spedde;
3650	With-outen wordes mo, they goon to bedde
	Ther-as the carpenter is wont to lye.
	Ther was the revel and the melodye;
	And thus lyth Alison and Nicholas,
	In bisinesse of mirthe and of solas,°
3655	Til that the belle of laudes° gan to ringe,
	And freres in the chauncel° gonne singe.
	This parish-clerk, this amorous Absolon,
	That is for love alwey so wo bigon,
	Up-on the Monday was at Oseneye
3660	With companye, him to disporte and pleye,
	And axed up-on cas° a cloisterer
	Ful prively after John the carpenter;
	And he drough him a-part out of the chirche,
	And seyde, "I noot,° I saugh him here
	nat wirche
3665	Sin Saterday; I trow that he be went
	For timber, ther our abbot hath him sent;
	For he is wont for timber for to go,
	And dwellen at the grange° a day or two;
	Or elles he is at his house, certeyn;
3670	Wher that he be, I can nat sothly° seyn."
	This Absolon ful joly was and light,
	And thoghte, "now is tyme wake° al night;
	For sikirly° I saugh him nat stiringe
	Aboute his dore sin day bigan to springe.
3675	So moot I thryve, I shal, at cokkes crowe,
	Ful prively knokken at his windowe
	That stant ful lowe up-on his boures wal.°
	To Alison now wol I tellen al
	My love-longing, for yet I shal nat misse
3680	That at the leste wey I shal hir kisse.
	Som maner confort shal I have, parfay,°
	My mouth hath icched° al this longe day;
	That is a signe of kissing atte leste.
	Al night me mette° eek, I was at a feste.
3685	Therfor I wol gon slepe an houre or tweye.
	And al the night than wol I wake and pleye."
	Whan that the firste cok hath crowe, anon
	Up rist° this joly lover Absolon,
	And him arrayeth gay, at point-devys.°

Glosses (right margin):

- *prayers*
- *Fell*
- *curfew time (dusk)*
- *suffering / spirit*
- *later / snores*
- *pleasure*
- *lauds (before dawn)*
- *chancel*
- *chance*
- *know not*
- *farm*
- *truthfully*
- *to wake*
- *certainly*
- *bedroom wall*
- *in faith*
- *itched*
- *dreamed*
- *rised*
- *meticulously*

3690   But first he cheweth greyn[18] and lycorys,
To smellen swete, er he had kembd° his heer.   *combed*
Under his tonge a trewe love° he beer,   *a four-leafed herb*
For ther-by wende° he to ben gracious.°   *supposed / attractive*
He rometh to the carpenteres hous,
3695   And stille he stant under the shot-windowe;
Un-to his brest it raughte,° it was so lowe;   *reached*
And softe he cogheth with a semi-soun°—   *low voice*
"What do ye, honey-comb, swete Alisoun?
My faire brid, my swete cinamome,°   *cinnamon*
3700   Awaketh, lemman myn,° and speketh to me!   *my love*
Wel litel thenken ye up-on my wo,
That for your love I swete° ther I go.   *sweat*
No wonder is thogh that I swelte° and swete;   *swelter*
I moorne as doth a lamb after the tete.°   *teat*
3705   Y-wis, lemman, I have swich love-longinge,
That lyk a turtel° trewe is my moorninge;   *turtledove*
I may nat ete na more than a mayde."
    "Go fro the window, Jakke fool," she sayde,
"As help me god, it wol nat be 'com ba° me,'   *kiss*
3710   I love another, and elles I were to blame,
Wel bet than thee, by Jesu, Absolon!
Go forth thy wey, or I wol caste a ston,
And lat me slepe, a twenty devel wey!"
    "Allas," quod Absolon, "and weylawey!
3715   That trewe love was ever so yvel° biset!   *evilly*
Than kisse me, sin° it may be no bet,   *since*
For Jesus love and for the love of me."
    "Wiltow than go thy wey ther-with?" quod she.
    "Ye, certes, lemman," quod this Absolon.
3720   "Thanne make thee redy," quod she, "I come
      anon;"
And un-to Nicholas she seyde stille,°   *softly*
"Now hust,° and thou shalt laughen al thy fille."   *hush*
This Absolon doun sette him on his knees,
And seyde, "I am a lord at all degrees;°   *accounts*
3725   For after this I hope ther cometh more!
Lemman, thy grace, and swete brid, thyn ore!"
    The window she undoth, and that in haste,
"Have do," quod she, "com of, and speed thee
      faste,
Lest that our neighebores thee espye."
3730   This Absolon gan wype his mouth ful drye;
Derk was the night as pich, or as the cole,
And at the window out she putte hir hole,
And Absolon, him fil no bet no wers,
But with his mouth he kiste hir naked ers°   *ass*
3735   Ful savourly,° er he was war° of this.   *savorily / aware*
    Abak he sterte,° and thoghte it was amis,   *started*

---

[18] Grain of Paradise, a spice.

For wel he wiste a womman hath no berd;
He felte a thing al rough and long y-herd,°   *haired*
And seyde, "fy! allas! what have I do?"
3740   "Tehee!" quod she, and clapte the window to;
And Absolon goth forth a sory pas.°   *at a sad pace*
"A berd, a berd!" quod hende Nicholas.
"By goddes *corpus*,° this goth faire and weel!"   *body*
This sely Absolon herde every deel,°   *bit*
3745 And on his lippe he gan for anger byte;
And to him-self he seyde, "I shal thee quyte!"°   *requite*
   Who rubbeth now, who froteth° now his
      lippes   *scrubs*
With dust, with sond, with straw, with clooth,
      with chippes,
But Absolon, that seith ful ofte, "allas!
3750 My soule bitake° I un-to Sathanas,°   *commend / Satan*
But me wer lever° than al this toun," quod he,   *more eager*
"Of this despyt awroken° for to be!   *avenged*
Allas!" quod he, "allas! I ne hadde y-bleynt!"[19]
His hote love was cold and al y-queynt;°   *quenched*
3755 For fro that tyme that he had kiste hir ers,
Of paramours he sette° nat a kers,°   *cared / cress*
For he was heled° of his maladye;   *healed*
Ful ofte paramours he gan deffye,
And weep as dooth a child that is y-bete.°   *beaten*
3760 A softe paas° he wente over the strete   *quietly*
Un-til a smith men cleped daun° Gerveys,   *master*
That in his forge smithed plough-harneys,°   *plough fittings*
He sharpeth shaar° and culter° bisily.   *plowshare / coulter*
This Absolon knokketh al esily,°   *softly*
3765 And seyde, "undo, Gerveys, and that anon."
    "What, who artow?" "It am I, Absolon."
"What, Absolon! for Cristes swete tree,°   *cross*
Why ryse ye so rathe,° ey, *ben'cite!*°   *early / bless me*
What eyleth yow? som gay gerl, god it woot,
3770 Hath broght yow thus up-on the viritoot;
By sëynt Note,[20] ye woot wel what I mene."
    This Absolon ne roghte° nat a bene°   *cared / bean*
Of al his pley, no word agayn he yaf;
He hadde more tow on his distaf[21]
3775 Than Gerveys knew, and seyde, "freend so dere,
That hote culter° in the chimenee here,   *hot iron plow-blade*
As lene° it me, I have ther-with to done,   *Please loan*
And I wol bringe it thee agayn ful sone."
    Gerveys answered, "certes, were it gold,
3780 Or in a poke nobles° alle untold,   *coins in a poke (bag)*
Thou sholdest have, as I am trewe smith;

---

[19] I.e., Alas, that I had not turned aside!
[20] St. Neot, who lived during the ninth century A.D.
[21] More tow on his distaff—hence, more on his mind.

Ey, Cristes foo! what wol ye do ther-with?"
"Ther-of," quod Absolon, "be as be may;
I shal wel telle it thee to-morwe day"—
3785   And caughte the culter by the colde stele.
Ful softe out at the dore he gan to stele,
And wente un-to the carpenteres wal.
He cogheth first, and knokketh ther-with-al
Upon the windowe, right as he dide er.
3790   This Alison answerde, "Who is ther
That knokketh so? I warante° it a theef."   bet
"Why, nay," quod he, "god woot, my swete
    leef,°   beloved
I am thyn Absolon, my dereling!
Of gold," quod he, "I have thee broght a ring;
3795   My moder yaf it me, so god me save,
Ful fyn it is, and ther-to wel y-grave;°   engraved
This wol I yeve thee, if thou me kisse!"
This Nicholas was risen for to pisse,
And thoghte he wolde amenden° al the jape,°   improve / joke
3800   He sholde kisse his ers er that he scape.
And up the windowe dide he hastily,
And out his ers he putteth prively
Over the buttok, to the haunche-bon;°   thigh-bone
And ther-with spak this clerk, this Absolon,
3805   "Spek, swete brid, I noot nat wher thou art."
This Nicholas anon leet flee° a fart,   fly
As greet as it had been a thonder-dent,°   thunderclap
That with the strook he was almost y-blent;°   blinded
And he was redy with his iren hoot,
3810   And Nicholas amidde the ers he smoot.°   smote
Of gooth° the skin an hande-brede° aboute,   off goes / handsbreadth
The hote culter brende so his toute,°   rump
And for the smert he wende for° to dye.   hoped
As he were wood,° for wo he gan to crye—   out of his mind
3815   "Help! water! water! help, for goddes herte!"
This carpenter out of his slomber sterte,
And herde oon cryen "water" as he were wood,
And thoghte, "Allas! now comth Nowélis flood!"
He sit him up with-outen wordes mo,
3820   And with his ax he smoot the corde a-two,
And doun goth al; he fond neither to selle,
Ne breed ne ale, til he cam to the selle
Up-on the floor;²² and ther aswowne° he lay.   unconscious
Up sterte hir Alison, and Nicholay,
3825   And cryden "out" and "harrow" in the strete.
The neighebores, bothe smale and grete,
In ronnen, for to gauren° on this man,   stare
That yet aswowne he lay, bothe pale and wan;
For with the fal he brosten° hadde his arm;   broken

²² He found time to sell neither bread nor ale until he hit the floor.

3830   But stonde he moste un-to his owne harm.
        For whan he spak, he was anon° bore doun°   *at once / borne down*
        With hende Nicholas and Alisoun.
        They tolden every man that he was wood,
        He was agast so of "Nowélis flood"
3835   Thurgh fantasye, that of his vanitee
        He hadde y-boght him kneding-tubbes three.
        And hadde hem hanged in the roof above;
        And that he preyed hem, for goddes love,
        To sitten in the roof, *par companye.*°   *for company*
3840   The folk gan laughen at his fantasye;
        In-to the roof they kyken° and they gape,   *gaze*
        And turned al his harm un-to a jape.
        For what so that this carpenter answerde,
        It was for noght, no man his reson herde;
3845   With othes° grete he was so sworn adoun,   *oaths, curses*
        That he was holden wood in al the toun;
        For every clerk anon-right heeld with other.
        They seyde, "the man is wood, my leve brother;"
        And every wight gan laughen of this stryf.°   *strife*
3850   Thus swyved° was the carpenteres wyf,   *seduced*
        For al his keping and his jalousye;
        And Absolon hath kist hir nether° yë;   *bottom*
        And Nicholas is scalded in the toute.°   *rump*
        This tale is doon, and god save al the route!°   *company*

                                                    [ca. 1390]

❧ RENAISSANCE POETRY ❧

John Skelton   *1460–1529*

TO MISTRESS
MARGARET HUSSEY

Merry Margaret,
As midsummer flower,
Gentle as falcon
Or hawk of the tower.
5   With solace and gladness,
Much mirth and no madness,
All good and no badness,
So joyously,
So maidenly,
10   So womanly
Her demeaning
In every thing—
Far, far passing
That I can endite,[1]
15   Or suffice to write
Of Merry Margaret,
As midsummer flower,
Gentle as falcon,
Or hawk of the tower;
20   As patient and still
And as full of good will,
As fair Isaphill.[2]
Coriander,[3]
Sweet pomander,[4]
25   Good Cassander;[5]
Steadfast of thought,
Well made, well wrought;
Far may be sought,
Ere that ye can find,
30   So courteous, so kind,
As merry Margaret,
This midsummer flower:
Gentle as falcon
Or hawk of the tower.

[1523]

[1] Say.
[2] Hypsipyle, Queen of Lemnos (an island in the Aegean Sea), was praised in Boccaccio's *Of Famous Women* for her kindness to her father and children.
[3] An aromatic, medicinal herb.   [4] A perfumed ball.
[5] Cassandra, whose prophesies were always accurate but never believed.

Sir Thomas Wyatt   *1503–1542*

"MY GALLEY, CHARGÈD WITH FORGETFULNESS"[1]

My galley, chargèd with forgetfulness,
   Through sharp seas, in winter nights, doth pass
   'Tween rock and rock; and eke° mine enemy, alas,   *also*
That is my lord, steereth with cruelness.
5   And, every oar, a thought in readiness,
   As though that death were light in such a case.
   An endless wind doth tear the sail apace,
Of forcèd sighs, and trusty fearfulness.
A rain of tears, a cloud of dark disdain,
10   Hath done the wearied cords great hinderance,
   Wreathèd with error, and eke with ignorance.
The stars be hid, that led me to this pain.
   Drownèd is reason, that should me comfort;[2]
   And I remain, despairing of the port.

                      [posthumous, 1557]

Edmund Spenser   *1552–1599*

THE FAERIE QUEENE

FROM *Book I, Canto I*

A Gentle Knight was pricking° on the plaine,   *spurring*
   Y cladd in mightie armes and silver shielde,
   Wherein old dints of deepe wounds did remaine,
   The cruell markes of many a bloudy fielde;
5   Yet armes till that time did he never wield:
   His angry steede did chide his foming bitt,
   As much disdayning to the curbe to yield:
   Full jolly° knight he seemd, and faire did sitt,   *handsome*
As one for knightly giusts° and fierce encounters fitt.   *jousts*

10   But on his brest a bloudie Crosse he bore,
   The deare remembrance of his dying Lord,
   For whose sweete sake that glorious badge he wore,
   And dead as living ever him ador'd:
   Upon his shield the like was also scor'd,
15   For soveraine° hope, which in his helpe he had: *powerful*
   Right faithful true he was in deede and word,

---

[1] In Richard Tottel's *Songs and Sonnets* (1557) this poem is given the title "The Lover Compareth His State to a Ship in Perilous Storm Tossed on the Sea."
[2] Some versions of the poem read "consort" for "comfort."

But of his cheere° did seeme too solemne sad;   *expression*
Yet nothing did he dread, but ever was ydrad.°   *dreaded*

20
Upon a great adventure he was bond,°   *bound*
   That greatest *Gloriana* to him gave,
   That greatest Glorious Queene of *Faerie* lond,
   To winne him worship, and her grace to have,
   Which of all earthly things he most did crave;
25
   And ever as he rode, his hart did earne°   *yearn*
   To prove his puissance° in battell brave   *might*
   Upon his foe, and his new force to learne;
Upon his foe, a Dragon horrible and stearne.

A lovely Ladie rode him faire beside,
   Upon a lowly Asse more white then snow,
30
   Yet she much whiter, but the same did hide
   Under a vele,° that wimpled° was full low,   *veil / folded*
   And over all a blacke stole she did throw,
   As one that inly mournd: so was she sad,
   And heavie sat upon her palfrey° slow: *a gentle horse*
35
   Seemed in heart some hidden care she had,
And by her in a line° a milke white lambe she lad.°   *leash / led*

So pure an innocent, as that same lambe,
   She was in life and every vertuous lore,
   And by descent from Royall lynage came
40
   Of ancient Kings and Queenes, that had of yore
   Their scepters stretcht from East to Westerne shore,
   And all the world in their subjection held;
   Till that infernal feend with foule uprore
   Forwasted° all their land, and them expeld: *destroyed*
45
Whom to avenge, she had this Knight from far
   compeld.°   *summoned*

Behind her farre away a Dwarfe did lag,
   That lasie seemd in being ever last,
   Or wearièd with bearing of her bag
   Of needments at his backe. Thus as they past,
50
   The day with cloudes was suddeine overcast,
   And angry *Jove* an hideous storme of raine
   Did poure into his Lemans lap° so fast,   *lover's lap (earth)*
   That every wight° to shrowd° it did constrain,   *creature / shelter*
And this faire couple eke° to shroud themselves were   *also*
   fain.°   *eager*

55
Enforst° to seeke some covert° nigh at hand,   *Forced / cover*
   A shadie grove not far away they spide,
   That promist ayde the tempest to withstand:
   Whose loftie trees yclad with sommers pride,
   Did spred so broad, that heavens light did hide,
60
   Not perceable° with power of any starre: *pierceable*

And all within were pathes and alleies wide,
  With footing worne, and leading inward farre:
Faire harbour that them seems; so in they entred arre.

And foorth they passe, with pleasure forward led,
65   Joying to heare the birdes sweete harmony,
  Which therein shrouded from the tempest dred,
  Seemd in their song to scorne the cruell sky.
  Much can° they prayse the trees so straight and hy,   *did*
  The sayling Pine, the Cedar proud and tall,
70 The vine-prop Elme, the Poplar never dry,
  The builder Oake, sole king of forrests all,
The Aspine good for staves, the Cypresse funerall.

The Laurell, meed° of mightie Conquerors   *reward*
  And Poets sage, the Firre that weepeth still,°   *always*
75 The Willow worne of forlorne Paramours,
  The Eugh° obedient to the benders will,   *yew*
  The Birch for shaftes, the Sallow° for the mill,   *goat willow*
  The Mirrhe sweete bleeding in the bitter wound,[1]
  The warlike Beech, the Ash for nothing ill,
80 The fruitfull Olive, and the Platane° round,   *plane tree*
The carver Holme,° the Maple seeldom inward sound.   *holm oak*

Led with delight, they thus beguile the way,
  Untill the blustring storme is overblowne;
  When weening° to returne, whence they did stray,   *thinking*
85 They cannot finde that path, which first was showne,
  But wander too and fro in wayes unknowne,
  Furthest from end then, when they neerest weene,° *think themselves*
  That makes them doubt, their wits be not their owne:
  So many pathes, so many turnings seene,
90 That which of them to take, in diverse doubt they been.

At last resolving forward still to fare,
  Till that some end they finde or° in or out,   *either*
  That path they take, that beaten seemd most bare,
  And like to lead the labyrinth about;°   *without*
95 Which when by tract° they hunted had throughout,   *lapse of time*
  At length it brought them to a hollow cave,
  Amid the thickest woods. The Champion stout
  Eftsoones° dismounted from his courser brave,   *Then*
And to the Dwarfe a while his needlesse spere he gave.

100 Be well aware, quoth then that Ladie milde,
  Least suddaine mischiefe ye too rash provoke:
  The danger hid, the place unknowne and wilde,
  Breedes dreadfull doubts: Oft fire is without smoke,
  And perill without show: therefore your stroke

---

[1] Myrrh is obtained from cuts ("wounds") in the tree's bark.

105 Sir knight with-hold, till further triall made.
Ah Ladie (said he) shame were to revoke
The forward footing for° an hidden shade: *on account of*
Vertue gives her selfe light, through darkenesse for to
    wade.

Yea but (quoth she) the perill of this place
110 I better wot° then you, though now too late   *know*
To wish you backe returne with foule disgrace,
Yet wisedome warnes, whilest foot is in the gate,
To stay the steppe, ere forcèd to retrate.°   *retreat*
This is the wandring wood, this *Errours den,*
115 A monster vile, whom God and man does hate:
Therefore I read° beware. Fly fly (quoth then   *advise*
The fearefull Dwarfe:) this is no place for living men.

But full of fire and greedy hardiment,
The youthfull knight could not for ought be staide,
120 But forth unto the darksome hole he went,
And lookèd in: his glistring armor made
A litle glooming light, much like a shade,
By which he saw the ugly monster plaine,
Halfe like a serpent horribly displaide,
125 But th'other halfe did womans shape retaine,
Most lothsom, filthie, foule, and full of vile disdaine.

And as she lay upon the durtie ground,
Her huge long taile her den all overspred,
Yet was in knots and many boughtes° upwound,   *coils*
130 Pointed with mortall sting. Of her there bred
A thousand yong ones, which she dayly fed,
Sucking upon her poisonous dugs, eachone
Of sundry shapes, yet all ill favorèd:
Soone as that uncouth° light upon them shone,   *unfamiliar*
135 Into her mouth they crept, and suddain all were gone.

Their dam upstart, out of her den effraide,°   *frightened*
And rushed forth, hurling her hideous taile
About her cursèd head, whose folds displaid
Were stretcht now forth at length without entraile.°   *windings*
140 She lookt about, and seeing one in mayle
Armèd to point,° sought back to turne againe;   *to the teeth*
For light she hated as the deadly bale,°   *harm*
Ay° wont in desert darknesse to remaine,   *Always*
Where plaine none might her see, nor she see any
    plaine.

145 Which when the valiant Elfe° perceiv'd, he lept   *fairy knight*
As Lyon fierce upon the flying pray,
And with his trenchand° blade her boldly kept   *sharp*
From turning backe, and forcèd her to stay:

	Therewith enrag'd she loudly gan to bray,	
150	And turning fierce, her speckled taile advaunst,	
	Threatning her angry sting, him to dismay:	
	Who nought aghast, his mightie hand enhaunst:°	*lifted*
	The stroke down from her head unto her shoulder glaunst.°	*glanced*

Therewith enrag'd she loudly gan to bray,
And turning fierce, her speckled taile advaunst,
Threatning her angry sting, him to dismay:
Who nought aghast, his mightie hand enhaunst:°   *lifted*
The stroke down from her head unto her shoulder
  glaunst.°   *glanced*

Much daunted with that dint,° her sence was dazd,   *stroke*
  Yet kindling rage, her selfe she gathered round,
  And all attonce her beastly body raizd
  With doubled forces high above the ground:
  Tho° wrapping up her wrethèd sterne° arownd,   *Then / tail*
  Lept fierce upon his shield, and her huge traine°   *tail*
  All suddenly about his body wound,
  That hand or foot to stirre he strove in vaine:
God helpe the man so wrapt in *Errours* endlesse traine.°   *course*

His Lady sad to see his sore constraint,
  Cride out, Now now Sir knight, shew what ye bee,
  Add faith unto your force, and be not faint:
  Strangle her, else she sure will strangle thee.
  That when he heard, in great perplexitie,
  His gall did grate for griefe° and high disdaine,   *wrath*
  And knitting all his force got one hand free,
  Wherewith he grypt her gorge with so great paine,
That soone to loose her wicked bands did her constraine.

Therewith she spewd out of her filthy maw°   *gut*
  A floud of poyson horrible and blacke,
  Full of great lumpes of flesh and gobbets° raw,   *fragments*
  Which stunck so vildly,° that it forst him slacke   *vilely*
  His grasping hold, and from her turne him backe:
  Her vomit full of bookes and papers was,
  With loathly frogs and toades, which eyes did lacke,
  And creeping sought way in the weedy gras:
Her filthy parbreake° all the place defilèd has.   *vomit*

As when old father *Nilus* gins to swell
  With timely pride above the *Aegyptian* vale,
  His fattie° waves do fertile slime outwell,   *greasy*
  And overflow each plaine and lowly dale:
  But when his later spring° gins to avale,°   *flood / abate*
  Huge heapes of mudd he leaves, wherein there
    breed
  Ten thousand kindes of creatures, partly male
  And partly female of his fruitfull seed;
Such ugly monstrous shapes elsewhere may no man
  reed.°   *see*

The same so sore annoyèd has the knight,
  That welnigh chokèd with the deadly stinke,
  His forces faile, ne° can no longer fight.

nor

Whose corage when the feend perceiv'd to shrinke,
She pourèd forth out of her hellish sinke
195   Her fruitfull cursèd spawne of serpents small,
Deformèd monsters, fowle, and blacke as inke,
Which swarming all about his legs did crall,
And him encombred sore, but could not hurt at all.

As gentle Shepheard in sweete even-tide,
200   When ruddy *Phœbus* gins to welke° in west,   *sink*
High on an hill, his flocke to vewen° wide,   *view*
Markes which do byte their hasty supper best;
A cloud of combrous gnattes do him molest,
All striving to infixe their feeble stings,
205   That from their noyance° he no where can rest,   *annoyance*
But with his clownish hands their tender wings
He brusheth oft, and oft doth mar their murmurings.

Thus ill bestedd,° and fearefull more of shame,   *situated*
Then of the certaine perill he stood in,
210   Halfe furious° unto his foe he came,   *mad*
Resolv'd in minde all suddenly to win,
Or soone to lose, before he once would lin;°   *cease*
And strooke at her with more than manly force,
That from her body full of filthie sin
215   He raft° her hatefull head without remorse;   *cut off*
A streame of cole bloud forth gushed from her corse.°   *corpse*

Her scattred brood, soone as their Parent deare
They saw so rudely falling to the ground,
Groning full deadly, all with troublous feare,
220   Gathred themselves about her body round,
Weening their wonted entrance to have found
At her wide mouth: but being there withstood
They flockèd all about her bleeding wound,
And suckèd up their dying mothers blood,
225   Making her death their life, and eke her hurt their
    good.

That detestàble sight him much amazde,
To see th'unkindly Impes° of heaven accurst,   *young demons*
Devoure their dam;° on whom while so he gazd,   *mother*
Having all satisfide their bloudy thurst,
230   Their bellies swolne he saw with fulnesse burst,
And bowels gushing forth: well worthy end
Of such as drunke her life, the which them nurst;
Now needeth him no lenger labour spend,
His foes have slaine themselves, with whom he should
    contend.

235   His Ladie seeing all, that chaunst, from farre
Approcht in hast to greet his victorie,
And said, Faire knight, borne under happy starre,

Who see your vanquisht foes before you lye;
Well worthy be you of that Armorie,°   *coat of arms*
240   Wherein ye have great glory wonne this day,
And proov'd your strength on a strong enimie,
Your first adventure: many such I pray,
And henceforth ever wish, that like succeed it may.

[1590]

"ONE DAY I WROTE HER NAME UPON THE STRAND"

One day I wrote her name upon the strand,°   *beach*
But came the waves and washed it away:
Again I wrote it with a second hand,
But came the tide and made my pains his prey.
5   "Vain man," said she, "that doest in vain assay,
A mortal thing so to immortalize,
For I myself shall like to this decay,
And eek° my name be wiped out likewise."   *also*
"Not so," quod° I, "let baser things devise   *said*
10   To die in dust, but you shall live by fame:
My verse your virtues rare shall eternize,
And in the heavens write your glorious name.
Where whenas death shall all the world subdue,
Our love shall live, and later life renew."

[1595]

Sir Walter Ralegh   *1552–1618*

[THE NYMPH'S REPLY TO THE SHEPHERD][1]

If all the world and love were young,
And truth in every shepherd's tongue,
These pretty pleasures might me move
To live with thee and be thy love.

5   Time drives flocks from field to fold;
When rivers rage and rocks grow cold;
And Philomel[2] becometh dumb;
The rest complain of cares to come.

The flowers do fade, and wanton fields
10   To wayward winter reckoning yields:

---

[1] This poem was written in answer to Christopher Marlowe's "The Passionate Shepherd to His Love" (1599).
[2] One of the myths in Ovid's *Metamorphoses* (ca. 8 A.D.) relates that Philomel's tongue was cut out by her brother-in-law Tereus, who wished to silence her complaints and keep her from revealing that he had raped her.

A honey tongue, a heart of gall,
Is fancy's spring, but sorrow's fall.

Thy gowns, thy shoes, thy beds of roses,
Thy cap, thy kirtle,° and thy posies,   *dress*
15   Soon break, soon wither, soon forgotten:
In folly ripe, in reason rotten.

Thy belt of straw and ivy-buds,
Thy coral clasps and amber studs,—
All these in me no means can move
20   To come to thee and be thy love.

But could youth last, and love still breed,
Had joys no date, nor age no need,
Then these delights my mind might move
To live with thee and be thy love.

                    [1600]

[EPITAPH]

Even such is time, that takes in trust
Our youth, our joys, our all we have,
And pays us but with earth and dust;
   Who in the dark and silent grave,
5   When we have wandered all our ways,
Shuts up the story of our days;
But from this earth, this grave, this dust,
My God shall raise me up, I trust.

            [posthumous, 1628]

Sir Philip Sidney   *1554–1586*

"LEAVE ME, O LOVE, WHICH REACHEST BUT TO DUST"

Leave me, O love, which reachest but to dust,
And thou, my mind, aspire to higher things!
Grow rich in that which never taketh rust:
Whatever fades, but fading pleasure brings.
5   Draw in thy beams, and humble all thy might
To that sweet yoke where lasting freedoms be;
Which breaks the clouds and opens forth the light
That doth both shine and give us sight to see.
O take fast hold! let that light be thy guide
10   In this small course which birth draws out to death,
And think how evil becometh him to slide

Who seeketh heaven, and comes of heavenly breath.
Then farewell, world! thy uttermost I see:
Eternal Love, maintain thy life in me!

[posthumous, 1598]

"THOU BLIND MAN'S MARK"

Thou blind man's mark, thou fool's self-chosen snare,
Fond fancy's scum, and dregs of scattered thought;
Band of all evils, cradle of causeless care;
Thou web of will, whose end is never wrought;
5   Desire, desire! I have too dearly bought,
With price of mangled mind, thy worthless ware;
Too long, too long, asleep thou hast me brought,
Who should my mind to higher things prepare.
But yet in vain thou hast my ruin sought;
10 In vain thou madest me to vain things aspire;
In vain thou kindlest all thy smoky fire;
For virtue hath this better lesson taught,—
Within myself to seek my only hire,
Desiring nought but how to kill desire.

[posthumous, 1598]

Chidiock Tichborne   *1558?–1586*

TICHBORNE'S ELEGY, WRITTEN WITH HIS OWN HAND IN THE TOWER BEFORE HIS EXECUTION[1]

My prime of youth is but a frost of cares,
　My feast of joy is but a dish of pain,
My crop of corn° is but a field of tares,°   *wheat / weeds*
　And all my good is but vain hope of gain;
5　　The day is past, and yet I saw no sun,
　　And now I live, and now my life is done.

My tale was heard and yet it was not told,
　My fruit is fallen, yet my leaves are green,
My youth is spent and yet I am not old,
10　I saw the world and yet I was not seen;
　　My thread is cut and yet it is not spun,
　　And now I live, and now my life is done.

I sought my death and found it in my womb,
　I looked for life and saw it was a shade,
15　I trod the earth and knew it was my tomb,

[1] On September 20, 1586, Tichborne was hanged and then "disemboweled before life was extinct" for participating in a plot to murder Queen Elizabeth I.

And now I die, and now I was but made;
My glass is full, and now my glass is run,
And now I live, and now my life is done.
[1586]

Christopher Marlowe   *1564–1593*

THE PASSIONATE SHEPHERD TO HIS LOVE

Come live with me and be my love;
And we will all the pleasures prove°   *test*
That hills and valleys, dales and fields,
Or woods or steepy mountain yields.

5   And we will sit upon the rocks,
And see the shepherds feed their flocks
By shallow rivers, to whose falls
Melodious birds sing madrigals.°   *songs*

And I will make thee beds of roses
10   And a thousand fragrant posies;
A cap of flowers, and a kirtle°   *dress*
Embroidered all with leaves of myrtle.

A gown made of the finest wool
Which from our pretty lambs we pull;
15   Fair-linèd slippers for the cold,
With buckles of the purest gold.

A belt of straw and ivy-buds
With coral clasps and amber studs:
And if these pleasures may thee move,
20   Come live with me and be my love.

The shepherd swains shall dance and sing
For thy delight each May morning:
If these delights thy mind may move,
Then live with me and be my love.
[posthumous, 1599]

William Shakespeare   *1564–1616*

"IF I PROFANE WITH MY UNWORTHIEST HAND"

[*A Sonnet from* Romeo and Juliet]

ROMEO. *(To Juliet)* If I profane with my unworthiest hand
This holy shrine,° the gentle sin is this;   *i.e., Juliet's hand*

My lips, two blushing pilgrims,° ready stand   *travelers to a shrine*
To smooth that rough touch with a tender kiss.

5 JULIET. Good pilgrim, you do wrong your hand too
    much,
Which mannerly° devotion shows in this;   *well bred*
For saints have hands that pilgrims' hands do
    touch,
And palm to palm is holy palmer's° kiss.   *pilgrim's*
ROMEO. Have not saints lips, and holy palmers too?
10 JULIET. Ay, pilgrim, lips that they must use in prayer.
ROMEO. O! then, dear saint, let lips do what hands do;
    They pray. Grant thou, lest faith turn to despair.
JULIET. Saints do not move, though grant for
    prayer's sake.
ROMEO. Then move not, while my prayers' effect I take.
        [*Kisses her*]

            [1596]

SONNET XVIII

Shall I compare thee to a summer's day?
Thou art more lovely and more temperate:
Rough winds do shake the darling buds of May,
And summer's lease hath all too short a date:
5 Sometime too hot the eye of heaven shines,
And often is his gold complexion dimmed;
And every fair° from fair sometime declines,   *fair woman*
By chance, or nature's changing course,
    untrimmed;°   *stripped of trimmings*
But thy eternal summer shall not fade,
10 Nor lose possession of that fair thou owest;°   *ownest*
Nor shall death brag thou wander'st in his
    shade,
When in eternal lines to time thou growest:
So long as men can breathe, or eyes can see,
So long lives this, and this gives life to thee.

            [1609]

SONNET LV

Not marble, nor the gilded monuments
Of princes, shall outlive this powerful rhyme;
But you shall shine more bright in these contents
Than unswept stone, besmeared with sluttish time.
5 When wasteful war shall statues overturn,
And broils root out the works of masonry;
Nor Mars his sword[1] nor war's quick fire shall burn

---

[1] Mars' sword. Mars is the Roman god of war.

The living record of your memory.
'Gainst death and all-oblivious enmity
10 Shall you pace forth; your praise shall still find
    room,
Even in the eyes of all posterity
That wear this world out to the ending doom.°   *Judgment Day*
So till the judgment that yourself arise,
You live in this, and dwell in lovers' eyes.

                        [1609]

SONNET LXV

Since brass, nor stone, nor earth, nor boundless sea,
But sad mortality o'er-sways their power,
How with this rage shall beauty hold a plea,°   *defense in law*
Whose action° is no stronger than a flower?   *legal action*
5 O how shall summer's honey breath hold out
Against the wreckful siege of battering days,
When rocks impregnable are not so stout,
Nor gates of steel so strong, but time decays?
O fearful meditation! where, alack!
10 Shall time's best jewel from time's chest lie hid?
Or what strong hand can hold his swift foot back?
Or who his spoil of beauty can forbid?
O none, unless this miracle have might,
That in black ink my love may still shine bright.

                        [1609]

SONNET CXVI

Let me not to the marriage of true minds
Admit impediments.[1] Love is not love
Which alters when it alteration finds,
Or bends with the remover to remove:
5 O no! it is an ever-fixèd mark,
That looks on tempests, and is never shaken;
It is the star to every wandering bark,°   *ship*
Whose worth's unknown, although his height° be taken.   *altitude*
Love's not time's fool, though rosy lips and cheeks
10 Within his bending sickle's compass° come;   *reach*
Love alters not with his brief hours and weeks,
But bears° it out even to the edge of doom.   *lasts*
If this be error, and upon me proved,
I never writ, nor no man ever loved.

                        [1609]

---

[1] Hindrances. Shakespeare is alluding to the words used in the Anglican marriage service.

SONNET CXXIX

The expense° of spirit in a waste° of shame   *draining / wasteland*
Is lust in action; and till action, lust
Is perjured, murderous, bloody, full of blame,
Savage, extreme, rude, cruel, not to trust;
5   Enjoyed no sooner, but despisèd straight;
Past reason hunted; and no sooner had,
Past reason hated, as a swallowed bait,
On purpose laid to make the taker mad:
Mad in pursuit, and in possession so;
10   Had, having, and in quest to have, extreme;
A bliss in proof,° —and proved, a very woe;   *the act (of coition)*
Before, a joy proposed; behind, a dream:
All this the world well knows; yet none
    knows well
To shun the heaven that leads men to this hell.
                     [1609]

SONNET CXXX

My mistress' eyes are nothing like the sun;
Coral is far more red than her lips' red:
If snow be white, why then her breasts are dun;°   *dull brown*
If hairs be wires, black wires grow on her head.
5   I have seen roses damasked,° red and white,   *blush-colored*
But no such roses see I in her cheeks;
And in some perfumes is there more delight
Than in the breath that from my mistress reeks.
I love to hear her speak,—yet well I know
10   That music hath a far more pleasing sound;
I grant I never saw a goddess go,°—   *walk*
My mistress, when she walks, treads on the ground;
And yet, by heaven, I think my love as rare
As any she bely'd° with false compare.   *proved false*
                     [1609]

SONNET CXLVI

Poor soul, the centre of my sinful earth,
Fooled by[1] these rebel powers that thee
    array,°   *dress*
Why dost thou pine within, and suffer dearth,
Painting thy outward walls so costly gay?
5   Why so large cost, having so short a lease,

[1] "Fooled by" is an emendation; the first edition repeats the last three words of line 1.

Dost thou upon thy fading mansion spend?
Shall worms, inheritors of this excess,
Eat up thy charge? Is this thy body's end?
Then, soul, live thou upon thy servant's loss,
And let that° pine to aggravate° thy store;   *the body / increase*
Buy terms° divine in selling hours of dross;°   *periods of time / refuse*
Within be fed, without be rich no more:
So shall thou feed on death, that feeds on
    men,
And, death once dead, there's no more dying
    then.

                                [1609]

"FEAR NO MORE THE HEAT O' TH' SUN"

[*A Song in* Cymbeline]

Fear no more the heat o' th' sun,
  Nor the furious winter's rages;
Thou thy worldly task hast done,
  Home art gone, and ta'en thy wages:
Golden lads and girls all must,
As chimney-sweepers, come to dust.

Fear no more the frown o' th' great,
  Thou art past the tyrant's stroke;
Care no more to clothe and eat,
  To thee the reed is as the oak.
The sceptre, learning, physic, must
All follow this, and come to dust.

Fear no more the lightning-flash,
  Nor th' all-dreaded thunder stone;[1]
Fear not slander, censure rash,
  Thou hast finished joy and moan.
All lovers young, all lovers must
Consign° to thee, and come to dust.   *deliver (themselves)*

No exorciser harm thee!
Nor no witchcraft charm thee!
Ghost unlaid forbear thee!
Nothing ill come near thee!
Quiet consummation have,
And renownèd be thy grave!

                                [1610]

---

[1] Falling stones were believed to cause the sound of thunder.

"FULL FATHOM FIVE"

[*A Song in* The Tempest]

Full fathom five thy father lies;
   Of his bones are coral made;
Those are pearls that were his eyes:
   Nothing of him that doth fade,
5 But doth suffer a sea change
Into something rich and strange.
Sea nymphs hourly ring his knell:
   Ding-dong.
Hark! now I hear them—Ding-dong, bell.
                       [1612]

"WHERE THE BEE SUCKS, THERE SUCK I"

[*A Song in* The Tempest]

Where the bee sucks, there suck I:
In a cowslip's[1] bell I lie;
There I couch when owls do cry.
On the bat's back I do fly
5 After summer merrily.
Merrily, merrily shall I live now
Under the blossom that hangs on the bough.
                       [1612]

Thomas Campion   *1567–1620*

MY SWEETEST LESBIA[2]

My sweetest Lesbia, let us live and love.
And, though the sager sort our deeds reprove,
Let us not weigh them. Heaven's great lamps do dive
Into their west, and straight again revive.
5 But soon as once set is our little light,
Then must we sleep one ever-during° night.   *everlasting*

If all would lead their lives in love like me,
Then bloody swords and armor should not be.

---

[1] An English herb with yellow flowers.
[2] The Roman poet Catullus (87–ca. 54 B.C.), whom Campion imitated in this poem, often addressed his poetry to Lesbia. The name has no connection with the word *Lesbian,* which was originally used to describe the homosexual followers of the Greek poetess Sappho (ca. 600 B.C.) on the island of Lesbos in the Aegean Sea.

No drum nor trumpet peaceful sleeps should move,
10 Unless alarm came from the camp of Love.
But fools do live and waste their little light,
And seek with pain their ever-during night.

When timely death my life and fortune ends,
Let not my hearse be vexed with mourning friends.
15 But let all lovers, rich in triumph, come
And with sweet pastimes grace my happy tomb.
And, Lesbia, close up thou my little light,
And crown with love my ever-during night.

[1601]

WHEN TO HER LUTE CORINNA SINGS

When to her lute Corinna sings,
Her voice revives the leaden strings,
And doth in highest notes appear
As any challenged echo clear.
5 But when she doth of mourning speak,
Even with her sighs the strings do break.

And as her lute doth live or die,
Led by her passion, so must I.
For when of pleasure she doth sing,
10 My thoughts enjoy a sudden spring;
But if she doth of sorrow speak,
Even from my heart the strings do break.

[1601]

SEVENTEENTH-CENTURY POETRY

John Donne   *1572–1631*

THE GOOD-MORROW

I wonder by my troth, what thou and I
  Did, till we loved? Were we not weaned till then,
But sucked on country pleasures, childishly?
  Or snorted we in the seven sleepers' den?[1]
5   'Twas so; but this,° all pleasures fancies be.   *except for love*
If ever any beauty I did see,
Which I desired, and got, 'twas but a dream of thee.

And now good morrow to our waking souls,
  Which watch not one another out of fear;
10   For love, all love of other sights controls,
  And makes one little room, an everywhere.
Let sea-discoverers to new worlds have gone,
Let maps to others, worlds on worlds have shown,
Let us possess one world; each hath one, and is one.

15   My face in thine eye, thine in mine appears,
  And true plain hearts do in the faces rest;
Where can we find two better hemispheres
  Without sharp° north, without declining west?   *cold*
Whatever dies, was not mixed equally;[2]
20   If our two loves be one, or, thou and I
Love so alike that none do slacken, none can die.
                         [posthumous, 1633]

A VALEDICTION: FORBIDDING MOURNING

As virtuous men pass mildly away,
And whisper to their souls to go,
Whilst some of their sad friends do say,
"The breath goes now," and some say, "No,"

5   So let us melt and make no noise,
No tear-floods, nor sigh-tempests move;

---

[1] Seven young Christians supposedly slept for 187 years after being walled up in a cave in 249 A.D. during the reign of the Roman emperor Decius.
[2] In medieval philosophy death was a result of an imperfect mixture of elements; when the elements are perfectly balanced, immortality should be possible.

'Twere profanation of our joys
To tell the laity our love.

10 Moving of th' earth brings harm and fears;
Men reckon what it did and meant.
But trepidation of the spheres,
Though greater far, is innocent.

Dull sùblunary lovers' love
15 (Whose soul is sense) cannot admit
Absence, because it doth remove
Those things which elemented it.

But we by a love so much refined
That ourselves know not what it is,
Inter-assurèd of the mind,
20 Care less eyes, lips, and hands to miss.

Our two souls, therefore, which are one,
Though I must go, endure not yet
A breach, but an expansion,
Like gold to airy thinness beat.

25 If they be two, they are two so
As stiff twin compasses are two;
Thy soul, the fixed foot, makes no show
To move, but doth if th' other do.

And though it in the center sit,
30 Yet when the other far doth roam,
It leans and hearkens after it,
And grows erect as that comes home.

Such wilt thou be to me, who must,
Like th' other foot, obliquely run;
35 Thy firmness makes my circle just,
And makes me end where I begun.

[posthumous, 1633]

THE SUN RISING

Busy old fool, unruly sun,
Why dost thou thus,
Through windows, and through curtains call on us?
Must to thy motions lovers' seasons run?
5 Saucy pedantic wretch, go chide
Late school-boys, and sour prentices.° *apprentices*
Go tell court-huntsmen that the King will ride.
Call country ants to harvest offices;
Love, all alike, no season knows, nor clime,
10 Nor hours, days, months, which are the rags of time.

Thy beams, so reverend and strong
   Why shouldst thou think?
I could eclipse and cloud them with a wink,
But that I would not lose her sight so long:
   If her eyes have not blinded thine,
      Look, and tomorrow late, tell me
   Whether both the Indias[1] of spice and mine
   Be where thou left'st them, or lie here with me.
Ask for those kings whom thou saw'st yesterday,
And thou shalt hear, All here in one bed lay.

She is all states, and all princes, I,
   Nothing else is.
Princes do but play us; compared to this,
All honor's mimic;° all wealth alchemy.[2]   *mimicry*
   Thou, sun, art half as happy as we,
      In that the world's contracted thus;
   Thine age asks ease, and since thy duties be
   To warm the world, that's done in warming us.
Shine here to us, and thou art everywhere;
This bed thy center is, these walls, thy sphere.
                            [posthumous, 1633]

THE CANONIZATION

For God's sake hold your tongue, and let me love,
   Or chide my palsy, or my gout,
My five grey hairs, or ruined fortunes flout;
With wealth your state, your mind with arts
                  improve,
      Take you a course,° get you a place,°   *direction / appointment*
      Observe His Honor or his Grace,
   Or the king's real or his stamped face°   *i.e., on a coin*
      Contemplate; what you will, approve,°   *try out*
         So you will let me love.

Alas, alas! who's injured by my love?
   What merchant's ships have my sighs drowned?
Who says my tears have overflowed his ground?
When did my colds a forward spring remove?
      When did the heats, which my veins fill,
      Add one more to the plaguy bill?[1]
Soldiers find wars, and lawyers find out still

---

[1] The East Indies were noted for spices; the West Indies for gold and silver mines.
[2] The pseudo-science of turning base metal into gold—hence, in this context, "fraudulent" or "phoney."
[1] Deaths from the plague were recorded in a weekly bill or list.

Litigious men, which quarrels move,
Though she and I do love.

Call us what you will, we are made such by love;
20   Call her one, me another fly;
We are tapers too, and at our own cost die;
And we in us find th' eagle and the dove;
The phoenix riddle hath more wit
By us; we two being one, are it:[2]
25 So to one neutral thing both sexes fit.
We die and rise the same, and prove
Mysterious by this love.

We can die by it, if not live by love.
And if unfit for tomb and hearse
30 Our legend be, it will be fit for verse;
And if no piece of chronicle we prove,
We'll build in sonnets pretty rooms.
As well a well-wrought urn becomes
The greatest ashes, as half-acre tombs;
35   And by these hymns all shall approve°   *certify*
Us canonized for love:

And thus invoke° us: "You whom reverend love   *pray to*
Made one another's hermitage;
You to whom love was peace, that now is rage,
40 Who did the whole world's soul contract, and
            drove
Into the glasses° of your eyes,   *reflecting surfaces*
(So made such mirrors, and such spies,
That they did all to you epitomize)[3]
Countries, towns, courts: beg from above
45   A pattern of your love."[4]

[posthumous, 1633]

THE RELIQUE

When my grave is broke up again
Some second guest to entertain,
(For graves have learned that woman-head,°   *female trait*
To be to more than one a bed)
5   And he that digs it, spies

---

[2] The mythological phoenix lights its own funeral pyre, is consumed by the fire, and then is resurrected from its own ashes. Donne's lovers repeat this cycle through their desire, gratification, sexual exhaustion, and renewed desire.

[3] Donne's lovers see reflected in each other's eyes not only themselves, but also (more figuratively than literally) a background of countries, towns, and courts; therefore they have found in each other an epitome of the whole world.

[4] I.e., Donne and his mistress, as saints of love, should beg God to send to earth a model of their love.

A bracelet of bright hair about the bone,
    Will he not let us alone,
And think that there a loving couple lies
Who thought that this device might be some way
To make their souls, at the last busy day,
Meet at this grave, and make a little stay?

    If this fall in a time, or land,
    Where mis-devotion° doth command,   *idolatry*
    Then he that digs us up will bring
    Us to the bishop, and the king,
    To make us reliques; then
Thou shalt be a Mary Magdalen, and I
    A something else thereby;
All women shall adore us, and some men;
And since at such time miracles are sought,
I would have that age by this paper taught
What miracles we harmless lovers wrought.

    First we loved well and faithfully,
    Yet knew not what we loved, nor why;
    Diff'rence of sex no more we knew,
    Than our guardian angels do;
    Coming and going we
Perchance might kiss, but not between those meals;
    Our hands ne'er touched the seals,
Which Nature, injured by late law, set free:
These miracles we did; but now, alas!
All measure and all language I should pass,
Should I tell what a miracle she was.
                           [posthumous, 1633]

"DEATH BE NOT PROUD"

Death, be not proud, though some have called thee
Mighty and dreadful, for thou art not so;
For those, whom thou think'st thou dost overthrow,
Die not, poor death; nor yet canst thou kill me.
From rest and sleep, which but thy picture° be,   *image, representation*
Much pleasure; then from thee much more must flow:
And soonest our best men with thee do go,
Rest of their bones, and soul's delivery.
Thou art slave to fate, chance, kings, and desperate
    men,
And dost with poison, war, and sickness dwell,
And poppy° or charms can make us sleep as well,   *opium*
And better than thy stroke. Why swell'st thou then?
One short sleep past, we wake eternally;
And death shall be no more; Death, thou shalt die.
                           [posthumous, 1633]

"BATTER MY HEART, THREE-PERSONED GOD"

Batter my heart, three-personed God; for you
As yet but knock, breathe, shine, and seek to mend;
That I may rise and stand, o'erthrow me and bend
Your force, to break, blow, burn, and make me new.
5   I, like an usurped° town to another due,   *seized*
Labor to admit you, but oh, to no end;
Reason, your viceroy° in me, me should defend,   *deputy*
But is captived, and proves weak or untrue;
Yet dearly I love you, and would be loved fain,°   *gladly*
10   But am betrothed unto your enemy:
Divorce me, untie, or break that knot again,
Take me to you, imprison me; for I,
Except you enthrall me, never shall be free;
Nor ever chaste, except you ravish me.

[posthumous, 1633]

Ben Jonson   *1572–1637*

SONG: TO CELIA

Drink to me only with thine eyes,
  And I will pledge° with mine;   *toast you*
Or leave a kiss but in the cup,
  And I'll not look for wine.
5   The thirst, that from the soul doth rise,
  Doth ask a drink divine:
But might I of Jove's nectar sup,
  I would not change for thine.

I sent thee, late, a rosy wreath,
10 Not so much honoring thee,
As giving it a hope, that there
  It could not withered be.
But thou thereon did'st only breathe,
  And sent'st it back to me:
15 Since when, it grows, and smells, I swear,
  Not of itself, but thee.

[1616]

Robert Herrick   *1591–1674*

TO THE VIRGINS, TO MAKE MUCH OF TIME

Gather ye rosebuds while ye may,
  Old Time is still a-flying:

And this same flower that smiles today
    Tomorrow will be dying.

5   The glorious lamp of heaven, the sun,
    The higher he's a-getting,
The sooner will his race be run,
    And nearer he's to setting.

That age is best which is the first,
10   When youth and blood are warmer;
But being spent, the worse, and worst
    Times still succeed the former.

Then be not coy, but use your time,
    And while ye may, go marry:
15 For having lost but once your prime,
    You may for ever tarry.

               [1648]

THE NIGHT-PIECE: TO JULIA

Her eyes the glow-worm° lend thee,   *larva of the firefly*
The shooting stars attend thee;
    And the elves also,
    Whose little eyes glow
5 Like the sparks of fire, befriend thee.

No Will-o'-the-wisp° mislight thee,   *swamp fire*
Nor snake or slow-worm° bite thee;   *lizard*
    But on, on thy way,
    Not making a stay,
10 Since ghost there's none to affright thee.

Let not the dark thee cumber:°   *encumber*
What though the moon does slumber?
    The stars of the night
    Will lend thee their light
15 Like tapers clear without number.

Then, Julia, let me woo thee,
Thus, thus to come unto me;
    And when I shall meet
    Thy silv'ry feet,
20 My soul I'll pour into thee.

               [1648]

TO DAFFODILS

Fair daffodils, we weep to see
    You haste away so soon;

As yet the early-rising sun
  Has not attained his noon.
5   Stay, stay
    Until the hasting day
          Has run
  But to the evensong;
And, having prayed together, we
10   Will go with you along.

We have short time to stay, as you,
  We have as short a spring;
As quick a growth to meet decay,
  As you, or anything.
15   We die
  As your hours do, and dry
          Away
  Like to the summer's rain;
Or as the pearls of morning's dew,
20   Ne'er to be found again.

                [1648]

TO DAISIES, NOT TO SHUT SO SOON

Shut not so soon; the dull-eyed night
  Has not as yet begun
To make a seizure on the light,
  Or to seal up the sun.

5 No marigolds yet closèd are,
  No shadows great appear;
Nor doth the early shepherd's star
  Shine like a spangle here.

Stay but till my Julia close
10   Her life-begetting eye,
And let the whole world then dispose
  Itself to live or die.

                [1648]

THE RESURRECTION POSSIBLE AND PROBABLE

For each one body that i' th' earth is sown
There's an uprising but of one for one,
But for each grain° that in the ground is thrown   *head of wheat*
Threescore or fourscore spring up thence for one;
5 So that the wonder is not half so great
Of ours, as is the rising of the wheat.

                [1648]

UPON JULIA'S VOICE

So smooth, so sweet, so silvery is thy voice,
As, could they hear, the Damned would make no noise,
But listen to thee (walking in thy chamber)
Melting melodious words to Lutes of Amber.

[1648]

George Herbert   *1593–1633*

THE PULLEY

When God at first made man,
Having a glass of blessings standing by—
"Let us," said He, "pour on him all we can;
Let the world's riches, which dispersèd lie,
5   Contract into a span."°   *a handspan*

So strength first made a way,
Then beauty flowed, then wisdom, honor, pleasure:
When almost all was out, God made a stay,
Perceiving that, alone of all his treasure,
10   Rest in the bottom lay.

"For if I should," said He,
"Bestow this jewel also on my creature,
He would adore my gifts instead of me,
And rest in nature, not the God of nature;
15   So both should losers be.

"Yet let him keep the rest,
But keep them with repining restlessness;
Let him be rich and weary, that at least,
If goodness lead him not, yet weariness
20   May toss him to my breast."

[1633]

LOVE

Love bade me welcome: yet my soul drew back,
      Guilty of dust and sin.
But quick-eyed Love, observing me grow slack
      From my first entrance in,
5 Drew nearer to me, sweetly questioning
      If I lacked anything.

"A guest," I answered, "worthy to be here:"
      Love said, "You shall be he."

> "I, the unkind, ungrateful? Ah, my dear,
> 10   I cannot look on thee."
> Love took my hand and smiling did reply,
>   "Who made the eyes but I?"
>
> "Truth, Lord; but I have marred them; let my shame
>   Go where it doth deserve."
> 15 "And know you not," says Love, "who bore the blame?"
>   "My dear, then I will serve."
> "You must sit down," says Love, "and taste my meat."
>   So I did sit and eat.

[1633]

Edmund Waller *1606–1687*

GO, LOVELY ROSE

> Go, lovely Rose—
> Tell her that wastes her time and me,
> That now she knows,
> When I resemble° her to thee,   *compare*
> 5 How sweet and fair she seems to be.
>
> Tell her that's young,
> And shuns to have her graces spied,
> That hadst thou sprung
> In deserts where no men abide,
> 10 Thou must have uncommended died.
>
> Small is the worth
> Of beauty from the light retired:
> Bid her come forth,
> Suffer herself to be desired,
> 15 And not blush so to be admired.
>
> Then die—that she
> The common fate of all things rare
> May read in thee;
> How small a part of time they share
> 20 That are so wondrous sweet and fair!

[1645]

ON A GIRDLE

> That which her slender waist confined
> Shall now my joyful temples bind;
> No monarch but would give his crown,
> His arms might do what this had done.

5   It was my heaven's extremest sphere,
     The pale° which held that lovely deer: *encircling fence*
     My joy, my grief, my hope, my love,
     Did all within this circle move.

     A narrow compass! and yet there
10   Dwelt all that's good, and all that's fair!
     Give me but what this ribband° bound,   *ribbon*
     Take all the rest the sun goes round!
                                        [1686]

John Milton   *1608–1674*

PARADISE LOST

FROM *Book 1*

     Of man's first disobedience and the fruit[1]
     Of that forbidden tree, whose mortal taste
     Brought death into the world and all our woe,
     With loss of Eden, till one greater Man°   *Christ*
5   Restore us and regain the blissful seat,
     Sing heavenly Muse, that on the secret top
     Of Oreb, or of Sinai,[2] didst inspire
     That shepherd, who first taught the chosen seed,
     In the beginning how the heavens and earth
10   Rose out of Chaos; or if Sion hill[3]
     Delight thee more, and Siloa's brook that flowed
     Fast by the oracle of God; I thence
     Invoke thy aid to my advent'rous song,
     That with no middle flight intends to soar
15   Above th' Aonian mount,[4] while it pursues
     Things unattempted yet in prose or rhyme.
         And chiefly thou, O Spirit,° that dost prefer   *the Holy Spirit*
     Before all temples th' upright heart and pure,
     Instruct me, for thou know'st; thou from the first
20   Wast present, and with mighty wings outspread
     Dove-like sat'st brooding on the vast abyss,
     And mad'st it pregnant:[5] what in me is dark
     Illumine, what is low raise and support;
     That to the height of this great argument°   *theme*
25   I may assert eternal Providence,

[1] I.e., the forbidden apple, but also the result (or "fruit") of Adam and Eve's disobedience.
[2] Both are names for Mt. Sinai where Moses heard the word of God.
[3] Zion hill and Siloam brook are near the temple (the "oracle of God") in Jerusalem.
[4] Mt. Helicon, home of the Muses.
[5] An allusion to Genesis 1:2.

And justify the ways of God to men.
   Say first, for heaven hides nothing from thy view,
Nor the deep tract of hell; say first, what cause
Moved our grand parents in that happy state,
30   Favored of heaven so highly, to fall off
From their Creator, and transgress his will
For one restraint, lords of the world besides?
Who first seduced them to that foul revolt?
Th' infernal serpent; he it was, whose guile,
35   Stirred up with envy and revenge, deceived
The mother of mankind, what time° his pride   *when*
Had cast him out from heaven, with all his host
Of rebel angels, by whose aid aspiring
To set himself in glory above his peers,
40   He trusted to have equalled the Most High,
If he opposed; and with ambitious aim
Against the throne and monarchy of God
Raised impious war in heaven and battle proud,
With vain attempt. Him the Almighty Power
45   Hurled headlong flaming from th' ethereal sky,
With hideous ruin and combustion, down
To bottomless perdition, there to dwell
In adamantine° chains and penal fire,   *unbreakable*
Who durst° defy th' Omnipotent to arms.   *dared to*
50   Nine times the space that measures day and night
To mortal men, he with his horrid crew
Lay vanquished, rolling in the fiery gulf,
Confounded though immortal: but his doom
Reserved him to more wrath; for now the thought
55   Both of lost happiness and lasting pain
Torments him; round he throws his baleful eyes,
That witnessed huge affliction and dismay,
Mixed with obdurate pride and steadfast hate.
At once, as far as angels ken,° he views   *vision*
60   The dismal situation waste and wild;
A dungeon horrible, on all sides round,
As one great furnace, flamed; yet from those flames
No light, but rather darkness visible
Served only to discover sights of woe,
65   Regions of sorrow, doleful shades, where peace
And rest can never dwell, hope never comes,
That comes to all; but torture without end
Still urges, and a fiery deluge, fed
With ever-burning sulphur unconsumed.
70   Such place eternal justice had prepared
For those rebellious; here their prison ordained
In utter darkness, and their portion set
As far removed from God and light of heaven,
As from the center thrice to th' utmost pole.
75   O how unlike the place from whence they fell!

There the companions of his fall, o'erwhelmed
With floods and whirlwinds of tempestuous fire,
He soon discerns, and welt'ring° by his side   *wallowing*
One next himself in power, and next in crime,
80   Long after known in Palestine, and named
Beëlzebub:[6] To whom th' arch-enemy,
And thence in heaven called Satan, with bold words
Breaking the horrid silence, thus began:
      "If thou beest he—But O how fallen! how
            changed
85   From him, who in the happy realms of light,°   *heaven*
Clothed with transcendent brightness, didst outshine
Myriads, though bright! if he, whom mutual league,
United thoughts and counsels, equal hope
And hazard in the glorious enterprize,
90   Joined with me once, now misery hath joined
In equal ruin: into what pit thou seest
From what height fallen; so much the stronger
            proved
He with his thunder. And till then who knew
The force of those dire arms? Yet not for those,
95   Nor what the potent victor in his rage
Can else inflict, do I repent, or change,
Though changed in outward luster, that fixed mind,
And high disdain from sense of injured merit,
That with the Mightiest raised me to contend,
100   And to the fierce contention brought along
Innumerable force of spirits armed,
That durst dislike his reign; and, me preferring,
His utmost power with adverse power opposed
In dubious battle on the plains of heaven,
105   And shook his throne. What though the field be
            lost?
All is not lost; th' unconquerable will,
And study° of revenge, immortal hate   *pursuit*
And courage never to submit or yield,
And what is else not to be overcome;
110   That glory never shall his wrath or might
Extort from me. To bow and sue for grace
With suppliant knee, and deify his power,
Who from the terror of this arm so late
Doubted° his empire, that were low indeed;   *Feared for*
115   That were an ignominy and shame beneath
This downfall; since, by fate, the strength of gods
And this empyreal° substance cannot fail;   *heavenly*
Since through experience of this great event,
In arms not worse, in foresight much advanced,
120   We may with more successful hope resolve

---

[6] A sun god worshipped in ancient Palestine—here Satan's lieutenant.

To wage by force or guile eternal war,
Irreconcileable to our grand foe,
Who now triumphs, and in th' excess of joy
Sole reigning holds the tyranny of heaven."

[1667]

"WHEN I CONSIDER HOW MY LIGHT IS SPENT"

When I consider how my light is spent[1]
  Ere half my days, in this dark world and wide,
  And that one talent° which is death to hide,   *i.e., writing*
  Lodged with me useless, though my soul more bent
5 To serve therewith my maker, and present
  My true account, lest he returning chide.
  "Doth God exact day-labor, light denied?"
  I fondly° ask; but patience, to prevent   *foolishly*
That murmur, soon replies, "God doth not need
10   Either man's work, or his own gifts; who best
  Bear his mild yoke, they serve him best: his state
Is kingly; thousands at his bidding speed,
  And post o'er land and ocean without rest;
  They also serve who only stand and wait."

[1673]

ON THE LATE MASSACRE IN PIEDMONT[2]

Avenge, O Lord, thy slaughtered saints, whose bones
  Lie scattered on the Alpine mountains cold;
  Even them who kept thy truth so pure of old,
  When all our fathers worshipped stocks and
    stones,°   *graven images*
5 Forget not: in thy book record their groans
  Who were thy sheep, and in their ancient fold
  Slain by the bloody Piemontese that rolled
  Mother with infant down the rocks. Their moans
The vales° redoubled to the hills, and they   *valleys*
10   To Heaven. Their martyred blood and ashes sow
  O'er all the Italian fields, where still doth sway
The triple tyrant;° that from these may grow   *the Pope*
  A hundred fold, who having learned thy way
  Early may fly the Babylonian woe.[3]

[1673]

---

[1] Milton gradually lost his vision between 1644 and 1652.
[2] On April 24, 1655, the Protestants living in the Alpine villages of the Piedmont (northern Italy and southern France) were slaughtered by the Catholic soldiers of neighboring Savoy.
[3] Milton and other Puritans often associated the Catholic Church with the "whore of Babylon" (Revelations 17).

Sir John Suckling   *1609–1642*

[THE CONSTANT LOVER]

Out upon it! I have loved
  Three whole days together!
And am like to love three more,
  If it prove fair weather.

5   Time shall moult away his wings
  Ere he shall discover
In the whole wide world again
  Such a constant lover.

But the spite° on 't is, no praise   *chagrin*
10 Is due at all to me:
Love with me had made no stays,
  Had it any been but she.

Had it any been but she,
  And that very face,
15 There had been at least ere this
  A dozen dozen in her place.
           [posthumous, 1659]

Richard Lovelace   *1618–1657*

TO LUCASTA, GOING TO THE WARS

Tell me not, sweet, I am unkind,
  That from the nunnery
Of thy chaste breast and quiet mind
  To war and arms I fly.

5   True, a new mistress now I chase,
  The first foe in the field;
And with a stronger faith embrace
  A sword, a horse, a shield.

Yet this inconstancy is such
10 As thou too shalt adore;
I could not love thee, dear, so much,
  Loved I not honor more.
           [1649]

TO ALTHEA, FROM PRISON

When Love with unconfinèd wings
  Hovers within my gates,
And my divine Althea brings
  To whisper at the grates;
5   When I lie tangled in her hair
  And fettered to her eye,
The birds that wanton in the air
  Know no such liberty.

When flowing cups run swiftly round
10   With no allaying Thames,[1]
Our careless heads with roses bound,
  Our hearts with loyal flames;
When thirsty grief in wine we steep,
  When healths and draughts go free—
15 Fishes that tipple in the deep
  Know no such liberty.

When, like committed° linnets,° I   *caged / songbirds*
  With shriller throat shall sing
The sweetness, mercy, majesty,
20   And glories of my King;
When I shall voice aloud how good
  He is, how great should be,
Enlargèd winds, that curl the flood,
  Know no such liberty.

25 Stone walls do not a prison make,
  Nor iron bars a cage;
Minds innocent and quiet take
  That for an hermitage;
If I have freedom in my love
30   And in my soul am free,
Angels alone, that soar above,
  Enjoy such liberty.

                    [1649]

TO AMARANTHA, THAT SHE WOULD DISHEVEL HER HAIR

Amarantha sweet and fair,
Ah, braid no more that shining hair!

---

[1] I.e., undiluted with water.

As my curious hand or eye
Hovering round thee, let it fly!

5   Let it fly as unconfined
As its calm ravisher the wind,
Who hath left his darling, th' East,
To wanton o'er that spicy nest.

Every tress must be confest,
10   But neatly tangled at the best;
Like a clew° of golden thread   *ball*
Most excellently ravellèd.

Do not then wind up that light
In ribbands, and o'ercloud in night,
15   Like the Sun in 's early ray;
But shake your head, and scatter day!

See, 'tis broke! Within this grove,
The bower and the walks of love,
Weary lie we down and rest
20   And fan each other's panting breast.

Here we'll strip and cool our fire
In cream below, in milk-baths higher;
And when all wells are drawn dry,
I'll drink a tear out of thine eye,

25   Which our very joys shall leave,
That sorrows thus we can deceive;
Or our very sorrows weep,
That joys so ripe so little keep.

[1649]

Andrew Marvell   *1621–1678*

TO HIS COY MISTRESS

Had we but world enough, and time,
This coyness, lady, were no crime
We would sit down and think which way
To walk, and pass our long love's day.
5   Thou by the Indian Ganges' side
Shouldst rubies find: I by the tide
Of Humber[1] would complain. I would
Love you ten years before the Flood,

---

[1] The Humber River flowing past Hull, a city in the North of England, where Marvell lived.

And you should, if you please, refuse
10 Till the conversion of the Jews.[2]
My vegetable love should grow
Vaster than empires, and more slow;
An hundred years should go to praise
Thine eyes and on thy forehead gaze;
15 Two hundred to adore each breast,
But thirty thousand to the rest;
An age at least to every part,
And the last age should show your heart.
For, lady, you deserve this state,[3]
20 Nor would I love at lower rate.
　　But at my back I always hear
Time's wingèd chariot hurrying near;
And yonder all before us lie
Deserts of vast eternity.
25 Thy beauty shall no more be found,
Nor, in thy marble vault, shall sound
My echoing song: then worms shall try
That long preserved virginity,
And your quaint honor turn to dust,
30 And into ashes all my lust:
The grave's a fine and private place,
But none, I think, do there embrace.
　　Now therefore, while the youthful hue
Sits on thy skin like morning dew,
35 And while thy willing soul transpires
At every pore with instant fires,[4]
Now let us sport us while we may,
And now, like amorous birds of prey,
Rather at once our time devour
40 Than languish in his slow-chapt[5] power.
Let us roll all our strength and all
Our sweetness up into one ball,
And tear our pleasures with rough strife
Thorough the iron gates of life:
45 Thus, though we cannot make our sun
Stand still, yet we will make him run.

[posthumous, 1681]

THE DEFINITION OF LOVE

My love is of a birth as rare
As 'tis, for object, strange and high;

---

[2] According to traditional Christian beliefs, this is to take place just before the Last Judgment.
[3] Stateliness.
[4] I.e., while your willing soul reveals itself through your blushes ("instant fires").
[5] Slow-jawed—hence, slowly destroying.

It was begotten by despair,
Upon impossibility.

5   Magnanimous despair alone
Could show me so divine a thing,
Where feeble hope could ne'er have flown,
But vainly flapped its tinsel wing.

And yet I quickly might arrive
10   Where my extended soul is fixed;[1]
But fate does iron wedges drive,
And always crowds itself betwixt.

For fate with jealous eye does see
Two perfect loves, nor lets them close,[2]
15   Their union would her ruin be,
And her tyrannic power depose.

And therefore her decrees of steel
Us as the distant poles have placed,
(Though Love's whole world on us doth wheel)
20   Not by themselves to be embraced,

Unless the giddy heaven fall,
And earth some new convulsion tear,
And, us to join, the world should all
Be cramped into a planisphere.[3]

25   As lines, so loves oblique may well
Themselves in every angle greet:[4]
But ours, so truly parallel,
Though infinite, can never meet.

Therefore the love which us doth bind,
30   But fate so enviously debars,
Is the conjunction of the mind,
And opposition of the stars.

                                    [posthumous, 1681]

Katherine Philips   *1631–1664*

AGAINST LOVE

Hence, Cupid! with your cheating toys.
Your real Griefs, and painted Joys,

---

[1] Marvell imagines his soul extending out and fixed upon his mistress.
[2] Come together.
[3] A sphere flattened so that the north and south poles touch.
[4] Oblique or non-parallel lines eventually intersect, just as imperfect, sinful lovers do.

Your Pleasure which itself destroys.
Lovers like men in fevers burn and rave,
And only what will injure them do crave.
Men's weakness makes Love so severe,
They give him power by their fear,
And make the shackles which they wear.
Who to another does his heart submit;
Makes his own Idol, and then worships it.
Him whose heart is all his own,
Peace and liberty does crown;
He apprehends no killing frown.
He feels no raptures which are joys diseased,
And is not much transported, but still pleased.

[1664]

John Dryden   *1631–1700*

ALEXANDER'S FEAST

or, The Power of Music;
An Ode in Honour of St. Cecilia's Day

'Twas at the royal feast for Persia won
     By Philip's warlike son:[1]
     Aloft in awful state
     The godlike hero sate
     On his imperial throne:
His valiant peers were placed around;
Their brows with roses and with myrtles bound:
     (So should desert in arms be crowned.)
The lovely Thais, by his side,
Sat like a blooming Eastern bride
In flower of youth and beauty's pride.
     Happy, happy, happy pair!
     None but the brave,
     None but the brave,
     None but the brave deserves the fair.

CHORUS
Happy, happy, happy pair!
None but the brave,
None but the brave,
None but the brave deserves the fair.

II

     Timotheus, placed on high
     Amid the tuneful choir,

[1] Alexander the Great (356–323 B.C.), son of King Philip II of Macedonia, defeated the Persian Emperor Darius III and occupied his capital city in 331 B.C.

With flying fingers touched the lyre:
The trembling notes ascend the sky,
   And heavenly joys inspire.
25 The song began from Jove,[2]
Who left his blissful seats above,
(Such is the power of mighty love.)
A dragon's fiery form belied the god:
Sublime on radiant spires° he rode,   *shining coils*
30   When he to fair Olympia pressed;
   And while he sought her snowy breast:
Then, round her slender waist he curled,
And stamped an image of himself, a sovereign of the
   world.
The listening crowd admire° the lofty sound;   *marvel at*
35 "A present deity," they shout around;
"A present deity," the vaulted roofs rebound:
     With ravished ears
     The monarch hears,
     Assumes the god,
40   Affects to nod,
And seems to shake the spheres.[3]

CHORUS

*   With ravished ears*
*   The monarch hears,*
*   Assumes the god,*
45 *   Affects to nod,*
And seems to shake the spheres.

III

The praise of Bacchus[4] then the sweet musician sung,
   Of Bacchus ever fair and ever young:
    "The jolly god in triumph comes;
50   Sound the trumpets; beat the drums;
    Flushed with a purple grace
    He shows his honest face:
Now give the hautboys° breath; he comes, he comes.   *oboes*
   Bacchus, ever fair and young.
55   Drinking joys did first ordain;
Bacchus' blessings are a treasure,
Drinking is the soldier's pleasure:
    Rich the treasure,
    Sweet the pleasure,
60   Sweet is pleasure after pain."

---

[2] Here and in the subsequent lines Timotheus relates the mythological account of Alexander's birth. Supposedly, Jove in the form of a dragon mated with Alexander's mother, Olympias.
[3] The nods of Jove were thought to cause earthquakes ("shake the spheres").
[4] The Roman name of the god of wine (Dionysos in Greek).

CHORUS

Bacchus' blessings are a treasure,
Drinking is the soldier's pleasure:
Rich the treasure,
Sweet the pleasure,
65 *Sweet is pleasure after pain.*

IV

Soothed with the sound, the king grew vain;
Fought all his battles o'er again;
And thrice he routed all his foes; and thrice he slew
the slain.
The master[5] saw the madness rise;
70 His glowing cheeks, his ardent eyes;
And, while he heaven and earth defied,
Changed his hand and checked his pride.
He chose a mournful Muse,
Soft pity to infuse:
75 He sung Darius great and good,
By too severe a fate,
Fallen, fallen, fallen, fallen,
Fallen from his high estate,
And weltering in his blood;
80 Deserted, at his utmost need,
By those his former bounty fed;
On the bare earth exposed he lies,
With not a friend to close his eyes.
With downcast looks the joyless victor sate,
85 Revolving in his altered soul
The various turns of chance below;
And, now and then, a sigh he stole;
And tears began to flow.

CHORUS

Revolving in his altered soul
90 *The various turns of chance below;*
And, now and then, a sigh he stole;
And tears began to flow.

V

The mighty master smiled to see
That love was in the next degree:
95 'Twas but a kindred sound to move,
For pity melts the mind to love.
Softly sweet, in Lydian measures,[6]
Soon he soothed his soul to pleasures.
"War," he sung, "is toil and trouble;
100 Honor but an empty bubble.

___

[5] Timotheus.
[6] Soft and voluptuous melodies.

     Never ending, still beginning,
    Fighting still, and still destroying,
     If the world be worth thy winning,
    Think, O think it worth enjoying.
105   Lovely Thais sits beside thee,
     Take the good the gods provide thee."
The many rend the skies with loud applause;
So Love was crowned, but Music won the cause.
  The prince, unable to conceal his pain,
110   Gazed on the fair
      Who caused his care,
   And sighed and looked, sighed and looked,
Sighed and looked, and sighed again:
At length, with love and wine at once oppressed,
115 The vanquished victor sunk upon her breast.

CHORUS

The prince, unable to conceal his pain,
   Gazed on the fair
   Who caused his care,
  And sighed and looked, sighed and looked,
120 *Sighed and looked, and sighed again:*
At length, with love and wine at once oppressed,
The vanquished victor sunk upon her breast.

VI

Now strike the golden lyre again:
A louder yet, and yet a louder strain.
125 Break his bands of sleep asunder,
And rouse him, like a rattling peal of thunder.
    Hark, hark, the horrid sound
     Has raised up his head:
     As awaked from the dead,
130   And amazed, he stares around.
"Revenge, revenge!" Timotheus cries,
   "See the Furies[7] arise!
   See the snakes that they rear,
   How they hiss in their hair,
135 And the sparkles that flash from their eyes!
    Behold a ghastly band,
    Each a torch in his hand!
Those are Grecian ghosts that in battle were slain,
     And unburied remain
140   Inglorious on the plain:
    Give the vengeance due
    To the valiant crew.
Behold how they toss their torches on high,
    How they point to the Persian abodes,
145 And glittering temples of their hostile gods!"

[7] The snaky-haired female spirits of revenge.

The princes applaud with a furious joy;
And the king seized a flambeau° with zeal to destroy;   *torch*
    Thais led the way,
    To light him to his prey,
150   And, like another Helen, fired another Troy.[8]

CHORUS

And the king seized a flambeau with zeal to destroy;
    Thais led the way,
    To light him to his prey,
And, like another Helen, fired another Troy.

VII

155   Thus, long ago,
   Ere heaving bellows learned to blow,
    While organs yet were mute;
   Timotheus, to his breathing flute,
      And sounding lyre,
160   Could swell the soul to rage or kindle soft desire.
    At last, divine Cecilia[9] came,
    Inventress of the vocal frame,°   *organ*
The sweet enthusiast, from her sacred store,
   Enlarged the former narrow bounds,
165   And added length[10] to solemn sounds,
With nature's mother wit and arts unknown before.
   Let old Timotheus yield the prize,
    Or both divide the crown;
   He raised a mortal to the skies;
170   She drew an angel down.[11]

GRAND CHORUS

    At last, divine Cecilia came,
    Inventress of the vocal frame;
The sweet enthusiast, from her sacred store,
   Enlarged the former narrow bounds,
175   *And added length to solemn sounds,*
With nature's mother wit and arts unknown before.
   Let old Timotheus yield the prize,
    Or both divide the crown;
   He raised a mortal to the skies;
180   *She drew an angel down.*

[1697]

---

[8] Having married Menelaus (a Greek king), Helen eloped with Paris (a Trojan prince), providing the cause for the wars celebrated by the poet Homer that ultimately led to the burning of Troy.

[9] The patron saint of music.

[10] I.e., lengthy, sustained notes from the organ.

[11] The beauty of St. Cecilia's music was said to have drawn an angel down to earth, thinking that such beautiful music could only have come from heaven.

EIGHTEENTH-CENTURY POETRY

Matthew Prior   *1664–1721*

AN EPITAPH

Interred beneath this marble stone
Lie sauntering Jack and idle Joan.
While rolling threescore years and one
Did round this globe their courses run;
5 If human things went ill or well;
If changing empires rose or fell;
The morning passed, the evening came,
And found this couple still the same.
They walked and ate, good folks: what then?
10 Why then they walked and ate again.
They soundly slept the night away;
They did just nothing all the day;
And having buried children four,
Would not take pains to try for more.
15 Nor sister either had, nor brother:
They seemed just tallied° for each other.   *fit*
   Their moral° and economy°   *morals / parsimony*
Most perfectly they made agree:
Each virtue kept its proper bound,
20 Nor trespassed on the other's ground.
Nor fame, nor censure they regarded:
They neither punished, nor rewarded.
He cared not what the footmen did;
Her maids she neither praised, nor chid:°   *scolded*
25 So every servant took his course;
And bad at first, they all grew worse.
Slothful disorder filled his stable,
And sluttish plenty decked her table.
Their beer was strong; their wine was port;
30 Their meal was large; their grace was short.
They gave the poor the remnant-meat
Just when it grew not fit to eat.
   They paid the church and parish rate,°   *tax*
And took, but read not the receipt;
35 For which they claimed their Sunday's due
Of slumbering in an upper pew.
   No man's defects sought they to know,
So never made themselves a foe.

No man's good deeds did they commend,
40 So never raised themselves a friend.
Nor cherished they relations poor:
That might decrease their present store;
Not barn nor house did they repair:
That might oblige their future heir.
45   They neither added, nor confounded.°   *squandered*
They neither wanted, nor abounded.
Each Christmas they accompts° did clear;   *accounts*
And wound their bottom round the year.[1]
Nor tear nor smile did they employ
50 At news of public grief or joy.
When bells were rung and bonfires made,
If asked, they ne'er denied their aid:
Their jug was to the ringers carried,
Whoever either died, or married.
55 Their billet° at the fire was found,   *firewood*
Whoever was deposed, or crowned.
    Nor good, nor bad, nor fools, nor wise;
They would not learn, nor could advise;
Without love, hatred, joy, or fear,
60 They led—a kind of—as it were;
Nor wished, nor cared, nor laughed, nor cried:
And so they lived; and so they died.
                                        [1718]

Jonathan Swift   *1667–1745*

A DESCRIPTION OF THE MORNING

Now hardly here and there a hackney-coach°   *carriage for hire*
Appearing, showed the ruddy morn's approach.
Now Betty from her master's bed had flown,
And softly stole to discompose her own;
5 The slip-shod 'prentice from his master's door
Had pared° the dirt and sprinkled° round the floor.   *diminished / moistened*
Now Moll had whirled her mop with dext'rous airs,
Prepared to scrub the entry and the stairs.
The youth with broomy stumps began to trace°   *search for old nails*
10 The kennel-edge,° where wheels had worn the place.   *gutter.*
The small-coal man° was heard with cadence deep,   *charcoal vendor*
Till drowned in shriller notes of chimney-sweep:
Duns° at his lordship's gate began to meet;   *bill collectors*
And brickdust Moll had screamed through half
        the street.[2]
15 The turnkey now his flock returning sees,

[1] I.e., continued to unwind the thread of their lives throughout the year.
[2] Moll sells brick dust for use as a scouring powder.

Duly let out a-nights to steal for fees:[3]
The watchful bailiffs take their silent stands,
And schoolboys lag with satchels in their hands.

[1709]

John Gay   *1685–1732*

MY OWN EPITAPH

Life is a jest; and all things show it.
I thought so once; but now I know it.
[1720]

THE MAN AND THE FLEA

Whether on earth, in air, or main,°   *open sea*
Sure every thing alive is vain!
   Does not the hawk all fowls survey,
As destined only for his prey?
5   And do not tyrants, prouder things,
Think men were born for slaves to kings?
   When the crab views the pearly strands,°   *beaches*
Or Tagus,[1] bright with golden sands,
Or crawls beside the coral grove,
10   And hears the ocean roll above;
"Nature is too profuse," says he,
"Who gave all these to pleasure me!"
   When bord'ring pinks and roses bloom,
And every garden breathes perfume,
15   When peaches glow with sunny dyes,
Like Laura's cheek, when blushes rise;
When with huge figs the branches bend;
When clusters from the vine depend;
The snail looks round on flower and tree,
20   And cries, "All these were made for me!"
   "What dignity's in human nature,"
Says Man, the most conceited creature,
As from a cliff he cast his eye,
And viewed the sea and arched sky!
25   The sun was sunk beneath the main,
The moon, and all the starry train
Hung the vast vault of heaven. The Man

---

[3] The jailer lets his prisoners out to steal during the night and then collects a fee from them as
   they return in the morning.
[1] The Tagus River flows through central Spain and Portugal to the Atlantic.

His contemplation thus began.
   "When I behold this glorious show,
30   And the wide watry world below,
The scaly people of the main,
The beasts that range the wood or plain,
The winged inhabitants of air,
The day, the night, the various year,
35   And know all these by heaven designed
As gifts to pleasure human kind,
I cannot raise my worth too high;
Of what vast consequence am I!"
   "Not of th' importance you suppose,"
40   Replies a Flea upon his nose:
"Be humble, learn thyself to scan;°   *analyze*
Know, pride was never made for man.
'Tis vanity that swells thy mind.
What, heaven and earth for thee designed!
45   For thee! Made only for our need;
That more important Fleas might feed."
                         [1727]

Alexander Pope   *1688–1744*

AN ESSAY ON CRITICISM

FROM *Part 2*

A little learning is a dangerous thing;
Drink deep, or taste not the Pierian spring.[1]
There shallow draughts intoxicate the brain,
And drinking largely sobers us again.
Fired at first sight with what the Muse imparts,
220   In fearless youth we tempt the heights of arts,
While from the bounded level of our mind,
Short views we take, nor see the lengths behind,
But more advanced, behold with strange surprise
New, distant scenes of endless science° rise!   *knowledge*
225   So pleased at first, the towering Alps we try,
Mount o'er the vales, and seem to tread the sky;
The eternal snows appear already past,
And the first clouds and mountains seem the last:
But those attained, we tremble to survey
230   The growing labors of the lengthened way,
The increasing prospect tires our wandering eyes,
Hills peep o'er hills, and Alps on Alps arise!
                         [1711]

[1] A spring sacred to the Muses.

AN ESSAY ON MAN

FROM *Epistle II*

I. Know then thyself, presume not God to scan;°   *scrutinize*
The proper study of mankind is Man.
Placed on this isthmus of a middle state,
A being darkly wise, and rudely° great;   *crudely*
With too much knowledge for the Sceptic side,
With too much weakness for the Stoic's pride,
He hangs between; in doubt to act, or rest,
In doubt to deem himself a god, or beast;
In doubt his mind or body to prefer,
Born but to die, and reasoning but to err;
Alike in ignorance, his reason such,
Whether he thinks too little, or too much:
Chaos of thought and passion, all confused;
Still by himself abused, or disabused;
Created half to rise, and half to fall;
Great lord of all things, yet a prey to all;
Sole judge of truth, in endless error hurled:
The glory, jest, and riddle of the world!

[1733]

Thomas Gray   *1716–1771*

ELEGY WRITTEN IN A COUNTRY CHURCHYARD

The curfew tolls the knell of parting day,
  The lowing herd wind slowly o'er the lea,°   *meadow*
The plowman homeward plods his weary way,
  And leaves the world to darkness and to me.

Now fades the glimmering landscape on the sight,
  And all the air a solemn stillness holds,
Save where the beetle wheels his droning flight,
  And drowsy tinklings lull the distant folds;

Save that from yonder ivy-mantled tower
  The moping owl does to the moon complain
Of such as, wand'ring near her secret bower,
  Molest her ancient solitary reign.

Beneath those rugged elms, the yew-tree's shade,
  Where heaves the turf in many a mould'ring heap,
Each in his narrow cell for ever laid,
  The rude° forefathers of the hamlet sleep.   *rugged*

The breezy call of incense-breathing Morn,
　　The swallow twitt'ring from the straw-built shed,
The cock's shrill clarion, or the echoing horn,
20　　No more shall rouse them from their lowly bed.

For them no more the blazing hearth shall burn,
　　Or busy housewife ply her evening care:
No children run to lisp their sire's return,
　　Or climb his knees the envied kiss to share.

25 Oft did the harvest to their sickle yield,
　　Their furrow oft the stubborn glebe° has broke:　　　　*field*
How jocund did they drive their team afield!
　　How bowed the woods beneath their sturdy stroke!

Let not Ambition mock their useful toil,
30　　Their homely joys, and destiny obscure;
Nor Grandeur hear with a disdainful smile
　　The short and simple annals of the poor.

The boast of heraldry, the pomp of power,
　　And all that beauty, all that wealth e'er gave,
35 Awaits alike th' inevitable hour:
　　The paths of glory lead but to the grave.

Nor you, ye proud, impute to these the fault,
　　If Memory o'er their tomb no trophies° rise,　　　　*monuments*
Where through the long-drawn aisle and fretted° vault　　*decorated*
40　　The pealing anthem swells the note of praise.

Can storied urn or animated° bust　　　　　　　　　　*lifelike*
　　Back to its mansion call the fleeting breath?
Can Honor's voice provoke° the silent dust,　　　　　　*arouse*
　　Or Flatt'ry soothe the dull cold ear of death?

45 Perhaps in this neglected spot is laid
　　Some heart once pregnant with celestial fire;
Hands, that the rod of empire might have swayed,
　　Or waked to ecstasy the living lyre.

But Knowledge to their eyes her ample page
50　　Rich with the spoils of time did ne'er unroll;
Chill Penury° repressed their noble rage,　　　　　　　*poverty*
　　And froze the genial current of the soul.

Full many a gem of purest ray serene
　　The dark unfathomed caves of ocean bear:
55 Full many a flower is born to blush unseen,
　　And waste its sweetness on the desert air.

Some village Hampden[1] that with dauntless breast
   The little tyrant of his fields withstood,
Some mute inglorious Milton here may rest,
60   Some Cromwell guiltless of his country's blood.

Th' applause of list'ning senates to command,
   The threats of pain and ruin to despise,
To scatter plenty o'er a smiling land,
   And read their history in a nation's eyes,

65   Their lot forbade; nor circumscribed alone
   Their growing virtues, but their crimes confined;
Forbade to wade through slaughter to a throne.
   And shut the gates of mercy on mankind,

The struggling pangs of conscious truth to hide,
70   To quench the blushes of ingenuous shame,
Or heap the shrine of Luxury and Pride
   With incense kindled at the Muse's flame.

Far from the madding° crowd's ignoble strife   *raving*
   Their sober wishes never learned to stray;
75 Along the cool sequestered vale of life
   They kept the noiseless tenor of their way.

Yet even these bones from insult to protect
   Some frail memorial still erected nigh,
With uncouth rhymes and shapeless sculpture decked,°   *decorated*
80   Implores the passing tribute of a sigh.

Their name, their years, spelt by th' unlettered muse,
   The place of fame and elegy supply:
And many a holy text around she strews,
   That teach the rustic moralist to die.

85 For who, to dumb Forgetfulness a prey,
   This pleasing anxious being e'er resigned,
Left the warm precincts of the cheerful day,
   Nor cast one longing lingering look behind?

On some fond breast the parting soul relies,
90   Some pious drops the closing eye requires;
E'en from the tomb the voice of Nature cries,
   E'en in our ashes live their wonted fires.

---

[1] John Hampden (1594–1643), a member of the English House of Commons, forcefully opposed Charles I. John Milton (1608–1674), the author of *Paradise Lost,* wrote vigorously against the divine right of kings to rule and became Cromwell's spokesman. Oliver Cromwell (1599–1658) led the forces that deposed Charles I; he subsequently became the Puritan dictator of England.

For thee, who, mindful of th' unhonored dead,
    Dost in these lines their artless tale relate;
95 If chance, by lonely contemplation led,
    Some kindred spirit shall inquire thy fate,

Haply some hoary-headed° swain may say,   *gray-haired*
    "Oft have we seen him at the peep of dawn
Brushing with hasty steps the dews away
100   To meet the sun upon the upland lawn.

"There at the foot of yonder nodding beech
    That wreathes its old fantastic roots so high,
His listless length at noontide would he stretch,
    And pore upon the brook that babbles by.

105 "Hard by yon wood, now smiling as in scorn,
    Mutt'ring his wayward fancies he would rove,
Now drooping, woeful wan, like one forlorn,
    Or crazed with care, or crossed in hopeless love.

"One morn I missed him on the customed hill,
110   Along the heath and near his fav'rite tree;
Another came; nor yet beside the rill,
    Nor up the lawn, nor at the wood was he;

"The next with dirges due in sad array
    Slow through the church-way path we saw him borne.
115 Approach and read (for thou canst read) the lay
    Graved on the stone beneath yon agèd thorn:"

The Epitaph

Here rests his head upon the lap of Earth
    A youth to Fortune and to Fame unknown.
Fair Science° frowned not on his humble birth,   *knowledge*
120   *And Melancholy marked him for her own.*

Large was his bounty, and his soul sincere,
    Heaven did a recompense as largely send:
He gave to Mis'ry all he had, a tear,
    He gained from Heaven ('twas all he wished) a friend.

125 *No farther seek his merits to disclose,*
    Or draw his frailties from their dread abode
(There they alike in trembling hope repose),
    The bosom of his Father and his God.

                                 [1751]

William Blake   *1757–1827*

FROM *Songs of Innocence*

THE LITTLE BLACK BOY

My mother bore me in the southern wild,
    And I am black, but O, my soul is white!
White as an angel is the English child,
    But I am black, as if bereaved° of light.   *robbed*

5   My mother taught me underneath a tree,
        And, sitting down before the heat of day,
    She took me on her lap and kissèd me,
        And, pointing to the east, began to say:

    "Look at the rising sun: there God does live,
10   And gives his light, and gives his heat away,
    And flowers and trees and beasts and men receive
        Comfort in morning, joy in the noonday.

    "And we are put on earth a little space,
        That we may learn to bear the beams of love;
15 And these black bodies and this sunburnt face
        Are but a cloud, and like a shady grove.

    "For when our souls have learned the heat to bear,
        The cloud will vanish, we shall hear his voice,
    Saying, 'Come out from the grove, my love and care,
20   And round my golden tent like lambs rejoice.' "

    Thus did my mother say, and kissèd me,
        And thus I say to little English boy.
    When I from black and he from white cloud free,
        And round the tent of God like lambs we joy,

25 I'll shade him from the heat till he can bear
        To lean in joy upon our Father's knee;
    And then I'll stand and stroke his silver hair,
        And be like him, and he will then love me.

                                                                            [1789]

THE CHIMNEY SWEEPER

When my mother died I was very young,
And my father sold me while yet my tongue
Could scarcely cry " 'weep! 'weep! 'weep! 'weep!"
So your chimneys I sweep and in soot I sleep.

5   There's little Tom Dacre, who cried when his head
    That curled like a lamb's back, was shaved, so I said,
    "Hush, Tom! never mind it, for when your head's bare,
    You know that the soot cannot spoil your white hair."

    And so he was quiet, and that very night,
10 As Tom was a-sleeping he had such a sight!
    That thousands of sweepers, Dick, Joe, Ned, and Jack,
    Were all of them locked up in coffins of black;

    And by came an angel who had a bright key,
    And he opened the coffins and set them all free;
15 Then down a green plain, leaping, laughing they run,
    And wash in a river and shine in the sun;

    Then naked and white, all their bags left behind,
    They rise upon clouds and sport in the wind.
    And the angel told Tom, if he'd be a good boy,
20 He'd have God for his father and never want joy.

    And so Tom awoke; and we rose in the dark
    And got with our bags and our brushes to work.
    Tho' the morning was cold, Tom was happy and warm;
    So if all do their duty, they need not fear harm.

                                          [1789]

FROM *Songs of Experience*

THE CHIMNEY SWEEPER

    A little black thing among the snow:
    Crying weep, weep, in notes of woe!
    Where are thy father and mother? Say?
    They are both gone up to the church to pray.

5   Because I was happy upon the heath,
    And smiled among the winter's snow:
    They clothed me in the clothes of death,
    And taught me to sing the notes of woe.

    And because I am happy, and dance and sing,
10 They think they have done me no injury:
    And are gone to praise God and his priest and king
    Who make up a heaven of our misery.

                                          [1794]

THE SICK ROSE

    O Rose thou art sick.
    The invisible worm,

That flies in the night
In the howling storm:

5 Has found out thy bed
Of crimson joy:
And his dark secret love
Does thy life destroy.
                    [1794]

THE TYGER

Tyger, Tyger, burning bright
In the forests of the night,
What immortal hand or eye
Could frame thy fearful symmetry?

5 In what distant deeps or skies
Burnt the fire of thine eyes?
On what wings dare he aspire?
What the hand dare seize the fire?

And what shoulder and what art
10 Could twist the sinews of thy heart?
And, when thy heart began to beat,
What dread hand and what dread feet?

What the hammer? What the chain?
In what furnace was thy brain?
15 What the anvil? What dread grasp
Dare its deadly terrors clasp?

When the stars threw down their spears,
And watered heaven with their tears,
Did He smile his work to see?
20 Did He who made the lamb make thee?

Tyger, Tyger, burning bright
In the forests of the night,
What immortal hand or eye
Dare frame thy fearful symmetry?
                    [1794]

LONDON

I wander thro' each chartered street,
Near where the chartered° Thames does flow,   *bound*
And mark in every face I meet
Marks of weakness, marks of woe.

5 In every cry of every man,
In every infant's cry of fear,
In every voice, in every ban,
The mind-forged manacles I hear.

How the chimney-sweeper's cry
10 Every black'ning church appalls,
And the hapless soldier's sigh,
Runs in blood down palace walls.

But most thro' midnight streets I hear
How the youthful harlot's curse
15 Blasts the new-born infant's tear
And blights with plagues the marriage hearse.

[1794]

Robert Burns   *1759–1796*

TO A MOUSE, ON TURNING HER UP IN HER NEST WITH THE PLOUGH, NOVEMBER, 1785

Wee, sleekit,° cow'rin', tim'rous beastie,   *sleek*
O what a panic's in thy breastie!
Thou need na start awa sae hasty,
     Wi' bickering brattle!°   *scamper*
5 I wad be laith to rin an' chase thee
     Wi' murd'ring pattle!°   *small spade*

I'm truly sorry man's dominion
Has broken Nature's social union,
An' justifies that ill opinion
10   Which makes thee startle
At me, thy poor earth-born companion,
     An' fellow-mortal!

I doubt na, whiles,° but thou may thieve;   *at times*
What then? poor beastie, thou maun live!
15 A daimen-icker° in a thrave°   *odd ear / thousand*
     'S a sma' request:
I'll get a blessin' wi' the lave,°   *remnant*
     And never miss 't!

Thy wee bit housie, too, in ruin!
20 Its silly wa's° the win's are strewin'!   *walls*
An' naething, now, to big° a new ane,   *build*
     O' foggage° green!   *foliage*
An' bleak December's winds ensuin',
     Baith snell° an' keen!   *bitter*

25 Thou saw the fields laid bare and waste.
An' weary winter comin' fast,
An' cozie here, beneath the blast,
     Thou thought to dwell,
Till crash! the cruel coulter° past   *plow*
30   Out-thro' thy cell.

That wee bit heap o' leaves an' stibble
Has cost thee mony a weary nibble!
Now thou's turn'd out, for a' thy trouble,
     But° house or hald,°   *Without / hold*
35 To thole° the winter's sleety dribble,   *suffer*
     An' cranreuch° cauld!   *frozen dew*

But, Mousie, thou art no thy lane,°   *not alone*
In proving foresight may be vain:
The best laid schemes o' mice an' men
40   Gang aft a-gley,°   *awry*
An' lea'e us nought but grief an' pain
     For promis'd joy.

Still thou art blest compar'd wi' me!
The present only toucheth thee:
45 But oh! I backward cast my e'e
     On prospects drear!
An' forward tho' I canna see,
     I guess an' fear!
              [1786]

TAM O' SHANTER

When chapman billies° leave the street,   *fellow peddlers*
And drouthy° neibors° neibors meet,   *thirsty / neighbors*
As market-days are wearing late,
An' folk begin to tak the gate;
5 While we sit bousing at the nappy,°   *ale*
An' getting fou° and unco° happy,   *drunk / very*
We think na on the lang Scots miles,
The mosses, waters, slaps,° and styles,°   *gates / steps over walls*
That lie between us and our hame,
10 Where sits our sulky sullen dame,
Gathering her brows like gathering storm,
Nursing her wrath to keep it warm.
   This truth fand honest Tam o' Shanter,
As he frae Ayr[1] ae night did canter—
15 (Auld Ayr, wham ne'er a town surpasses
For honest men and bonnie lasses).
   O Tam! hadst thou but been sae wise

---

[1] A county seat in southwestern Scotland.

As ta'en thy ain wife Kate's advice!
She tauld thee weel thou was a skellum,°   *bum*
20 A bletherin', blusterin', drunken blellum,°   *babbler*
That frae November till October,
Ae market-day thou was na sober;
That ilka° melder° wi' the miller   *each / load of grain*
Thou sat as lang as thou had siller;°   *silver*
25 That every naig° was ca'd° a shoe on,   *nag / hammered*
The smith and thee gat roarin' fou on;
That at the Lord's house, even on Sunday,
Thou drank wi' Kirkton Jean till Monday.
She prophesied that, late or soon,
30 Thou would be found deep drown'd in Doon;[2]
Or catch'd wi' warlocks in the mirk
By Alloway's auld haunted kirk.
    Ah, gentle dames! it gars me greet°   *makes me weep*
To think how mony counsels sweet,
35 How mony lengthen'd sage advices,
The husband frae the wife despises!
    But to our tale: Ae market night,
Tam had got planted unco right,
Fast by an ingle,° bleezing° finely,   *fireplace / blazing*
40 Wi' reaming swats,° that drank divinely;   *foaming ale*
And at his elbow, Souter° Johnny,   *Cobbler*
His ancient, trusty, drouthy crony;
Tam lo'ed him like a very brither;
They had been fou for weeks thegither.
45 The night drave on wi' sangs and clatter.
And aye the ale was growing better:
The landlady and Tam grew gracious,
Wi' favours secret, sweet, and precious;
The souter tauld his queerest stories;
50 The landlord's laugh was ready chorus:
The storm without might rair and rustle,
Tam did na mind the storm a whistle.
    Care, mad to see a man sae happy,
E'en drown'd himsel amang the nappy.
55 As bees flee hame wi' lades° o' treasure,   *loads*
The minutes wing'd their way wi' pleasure;
Kings may be blest, but Tam was glorious,
O'er a' the ills o' life victorious!
    But pleasures are like poppies spread—
60 You seize the flow'r, its bloom is shed;
Or like the snow falls in the river—
A moment white, then melts for ever;
Or like the borealis[3] race,
That flit ere you can point their place;
65 Or like the rainbow's lovely form

---

[2] The River Doon that flows by Alloway church ("kirk").
[3] Northern lights.

Evanishing amid the storm.
Nae man can tether time nor tide;
The hour approaches Tam maun° ride;   *must*
That hour, o' night's black arch the key-stane,
70   That dreary hour, he mounts his beast in;
And sic a night he taks the road in,
As ne'er poor sinner was abroad in.
    The wind blew as 'twad blawn its last;
The rattling show'rs rose on the blast;
75   The speedy gleams the darkness swallow'd;
Loud, deep, and lang, the thunder bellow'd:
That night, a child might understand,
The Deil had business on his hand.
    Weel mounted on his gray mare, Meg,
80   A better never lifted leg,
Tam skelpit° on thro' dub° and mire,   *hurried / puddle*
Despising wind, and rain, and fire;
Whiles holding fast his gude blue bonnet;
Whiles crooning o'er some auld Scots sonnet;
85   Whiles glow'ring round wi' prudent cares,
Lest bogles° catch him unawares.   *goblins*
Kirk-Alloway was drawing nigh,
Whare ghaists and houlets° nightly cry.   *owls*
    By this time he was cross the ford,
90   Where in the snaw the chapman smoor'd;°   *peddler smothered*
And past the birks° and meikle stane,°   *birches / huge stone*
Where drunken Charlie brak's neck-bane;
And thro' the whins,° and by the cairn,°   *shrubs / heap of stones*
Where hunters fand the murder'd bairn;°   *child*
95   And near the thorn, aboon the well,
Where Mungo's mither hang'd hersel.
Before him Doon pours all his floods;
The doubling storm roars thro' the woods;
The lightnings flash from pole to pole;
100 Near and more near the thunders roll:
When, glimmering thro' the groaning trees,
Kirk-Alloway seem'd in a bleeze;
Thro' ilka bore° the beams were glancing;   *chink*
And loud resounded mirth and dancing.
105   Inspiring bold John Barleycorn![4]
What dangers thou canst make us scorn!
Wi' tippenny,° we fear nae evil;   *twopenny ale*
Wi' usquebae,° we'll face the devil!   *whisky*
The swats sae ream'd in Tammie's noddle,
110 Fair play, he car'd na deils a boddle![5]
But Maggie stood right sair° astonish'd,   *sore (= very)*
Till, by the heel and hand admonish'd,
She ventur'd forward on the light;

---

[4] A personification of ale.
[5] In truth, he cared not a bit for devils!

	And, vow! Tam saw an unco° sight!	*strange*
115	Warlocks and witches in a dance!	
	Nae cotillon brent new frae° France,	*brand new from*
	But hornpipes, jigs, strathspeys,[6] and reels,	
	Put life and mettle in their heels.	
	A winnock-bunker° in the east,	*window seat*
120	There sat auld Nick, in shape o' beast—	
	A touzie tyke,° black, grim, and large!	*shaggy cur*
	To gie them music was his charge:	
	He screw'd the pipes and gart them skirl.[7]	
	Till roof and rafters a' did dirl.°	*vibrate*
125	Coffins stood round like open presses,	
	That shaw'd the dead in their last dresses:	
	And by some devilish cantraip° sleight	*magic*
	Each in its cauld hand held a light,	
	By which heroic Tam was able	
130	To note upon the haly table	
	A murderer's banes in gibbet-airns;°	*gallows chains*
	Twa span-lang,° wee, unchristen'd bairns;	*span-long (about 9″)*
	A thief new-cutted frae the rape—	
	Wi' his last gasp his gab° did gape;	*mouth*
135	Five tomahawks, wi' blude red rusted;	
	Five scymitars, wi' murder crusted;	
	A garter, which a babe had strangled;	
	A knife, a father's throat had mangled,	
	Whom his ain son o' life bereft—	
140	The gray hairs yet stack to the heft;	
	Wi' mair of horrible and awfu',	
	Which even to name wad be unlawfu'.	
	As Tammie glowr'd, amaz'd, and curious,	
	The mirth and fun grew fast and furious:	
145	The piper loud and louder blew;	
	The dancers quick and quicker flew;	
	They reel'd, they set, they cross'd, they cleekit,°	*linked arms*
	Till ilka carlin° swat and reekit,	*hag*
	And coost her duddies to the wark,[8]	
150	And linkit at it in her sark!°	*slip*
	Now Tam, O Tam! had thae been queans,°	*maidens*
	A' plump and strapping in their teens;	
	Their sarks, instead o' creeshie flannen,°	*greasy flannel*
	Been snaw-white seventeen hunder linen!°	*very fine linen*
155	Thir breeks° o' mine, my only pair,	*these breeches*
	That ance were plush, o' gude blue hair,	
	I wad hae gi'en them off my hurdies,°	*hips*
	For ae blink o' the bonnie burdies!	
	But wither'd beldams, auld and droll,	
160	Rigwoodie° hags wad spean° a foal,	*boney / wean (by fright)*

[6] A lively Scottish dance for couples.
[7] He twisted the bagpipes and made them shriek.
[8] And cast off her duds (clothes) for the sake of the work.

Louping° and flinging on a crummock,°   *leaping / crooked staff*
I wonder didna turn thy stomach.
    But Tam kent° what was what fu' brawlie°   *knew / well*
There was ae winsome wench and walie°   *voluptuous*
That night enlisted in the core,
Lang after kent° on Carrick shore!   *known*
(For mony a beast to dead she shot,
And perish'd mony a bonnie boat,
And shook baith meikle corn and bear,°   *barley*
And kept the country-side in fear.)
Her cutty sark,° o' Paisley harn,°   *short slip / yarn*
That while a lassie she had worn,
In longitude tho' sorely scanty,
It was her best, and she was vauntie.°   *vain*
Ah! little kent thy reverend grannie
That sark she coft° for her wee Nannie   *bought*
Wi' twa pund Scots ('twas a' her riches)
Wad ever grac'd a dance of witches!
    But here my muse her wing maun cour;°   *curb*
Sic flights are far beyond her pow'r—
To sing how Nannie lap and flang,
(A souple jade she was, and strang);
And how Tam stood, like ane bewitch'd,
And thought his very een enrich'd;
Even Satan glowr'd, and fidg'd fu' fain,°   *fidgeted very eagerly*
And hotch'd° and blew wi' might and main: *hitched*
Till first ae caper, syne° anither,   *then*
Tam tint° his reason a' thegither,   *lost*
And roars out 'Weel done, Cutty-sark!'
And in an instant all was dark!
And scarcely had he Maggie rallied,
When out the hellish legion sallied.
    As bees bizz out wi' angry fyke°   *fuss*
When plundering herds assail their byke,°   *hive*
As open pussie's mortal foes
When pop! she starts before their nose,
As eager runs the market-crowd,
When 'Catch the thief!' resounds aloud.
So Maggie runs; the witches follow,
Wi' mony an eldritch° skriech and hollow.   *frightful*
    Ah, Tam! ah, Tam! thou'll get thy fairin'!
In hell they'll roast thee like a herrin'!
In vain thy Kate awaits thy comin'!
Kate soon will be a woefu' woman!
Now do thy speedy utmost, Meg,
And win the key-stane o' the brig:°   *bridge*
There at them thou thy tail may toss,
A running stream they darena cross.
But ere the key-stane she could make,
The fient° a tail she had to shake!   *devil a bit of*
For Nannie, far before the rest,

Hard upon noble Maggie prest,
And flew at Tam wi' furious ettle,°   *design*
But little wist she Maggie's mettle!
215 Ae spring brought off her master hale,
But left behind her ain gray tail:
The carlin claught° her by the rump,   *clutched*
And left poor Maggie scarce a stump.
    Now, wha this tale o' truth shall read,
220 Each man and mother's son, take heed;
Whene'er to drink you are inclin'd,
Or cutty-sarks run in your mind,
Think! ye may buy the joys o'er dear,
Remember Tam o' Shanter's mare.

(1791]

A RED, RED ROSE

O, my luve is like a red, red rose
    That's newly sprung in June:
O, my luve is like the melodie
    That's sweetly play'd in tune.

5 So fair art thou, my bonnie lass,
    So deep in luve am I:
And I will luve thee still, my dear,
    Till a' the seas gang dry.

Till a' the seas gang dry, my dear,
10   And the rocks melt wi' the sun:
And I will luve thee still, my dear,
    While the sands o' life shall run.

And fair thee weel, my only luve,
    And fair thee weel awhile!
15 And I will come again, my luve,
    Tho' it were ten thousand mile.

[1796]

FOR A' THAT AND A' THAT

Is there, for honest poverty,
    That hings his head, and a' that;
The coward-slave, we pass him by,
    We dare be poor for a' that!
5   For a' that, and a' that,
       Our toils obscure, and a' that,
    The rank is but the guinea's stamp,
     The man's the gowd° for a' that.   *gold*

What though on hamely fare we dine,
10   Wear hoddin-grey,° and a' that;   *coarse, undyed wool*
Gie fools their silks, and knaves their wine,
      A man's a man for a' that.
          For a' that, and a' that,
              Their tinsel show, and a' that;
15   The honest man, tho' e'er sae poor,
              Is king o' men for a' that.

Ye see yon birkie,° ca'd a lord,   *young fellow*
      Wha struts, and stares, and a' that;
Tho' hundreds worship at his word,
20   He's but a coof° for a' that.   *numbskull*
          For a' that, and a' that,
              His ribband, star,° and a' that,   *star of knighthood*
          The man of independent mind,
              He looks and laughs at a' that.

25 A prince can mak a belted knight,
      A marquis, duke, and a' that;
But an honest man's aboon° his might,   *above*
      Guid faith, he mauna fa'° that!   *mustn't claim*
          For a' that, and a' that,
30   Their dignities, and a' that,
          The pith o' sense, and pride o' worth,
              Are higher rank than a' that.

Then let us pray that come it may,
      As come it will for a' that,
35 That sense and worth, o'er a' the earth,
      Shall bear the gree,° and a' that.   *prize*
          For a' that and a' that,
              It's coming yet, for a' that,
          That man to man, the warld o'er,
40   Shall brothers be for a' that.
                              [1795]

NINETEENTH-CENTURY POETRY

William Wordsworth *1770–1850*

LINES

Composed a Few Miles Above Tintern Abbey
on Revisiting the Banks of the Wye During a Tour. July 13, 1798

Five years have passed; five summers, with the length
Of five long winters! and again I hear
These waters, rolling from their mountain-springs
With a soft inland murmur. —Once again
5 Do I behold these steep and lofty cliffs,
That on a wild secluded scene impress
Thoughts of more deep seclusion; and connect
The landscape with the quiet of the sky.
The day is come when I again repose
10 Here, under this dark sycamore, and view
These plots of cottage-ground, these orchard-tufts,
Which at this season, with their unripe fruits,
Are clad in one green hue, and lose themselves
'Mid groves and copses. Once again I see
15 These hedge-rows, hardly hedge-rows, little lines
Of sportive wood run wild: these pastoral farms,
Green to the very door; and wreaths of smoke
Sent up, in silence, from among the trees!
With some uncertain notice, as might seem
20 Of vagrant dwellers in the houseless woods,
Or of some hermit's cave, where by his fire
The hermit sits alone.
                      These beauteous forms,
Through a long absence, have not been to me
As is a landscape to a blind man's eye:
25 But oft, in lonely rooms, and 'mid the din
Of towns and cities, I have owed to them
In hours of weariness, sensations sweet,
Felt in the blood, and felt along the heart;
And passing even into my purer mind,
30 With tranquil restoration:°—feelings too   *recollection*
Of unremembered pleasure: such, perhaps,
As have no slight or trivial influence
On that best portion of a good man's life,
His little, nameless, unremembered, acts
35 Of kindness and of love. Nor less, I trust,

235

To them I may have owed another gift,
Of aspect more sublime; that blessed mood
In which the burthen of the mystery,
In which the heavy and the weary weight
40   Of all this unintelligible world,
Is lightened:—that serene and blessed mood,
In which the affections gently lead us on,—
Until, the breath of this corporeal frame
And even the motion of our human blood
45   Almost suspended, we are laid asleep
In body, and become a living soul:
While with an eye made quiet by the power
Of harmony, and the deep power of joy,
We see into the life of things.
                                                      If this
50   Be but a vain belief, yet, oh! how oft—
In darkness and amid the many shapes
Of joyless daylight; when the fretful stir
Unprofitable, and the fever of the world,
Have hung upon the beatings of my heart—
55   How oft, in spirit, have I turned to thee,
O sylvan Wye! thou wanderer through the woods,
How often has my spirit turned to thee!

    And now, with gleams of half-extinguished thought,
With many recognitions dim and faint,
60   And somewhat of a sad perplexity,
The picture of the mind revives again:
While here I stand, not only with the sense
Of present pleasure, but with pleasing thoughts
That in this moment there is life and food
65   For future years. And so I dare to hope,
Though changed, no doubt, from what I was when
      first
I came along these hills; when like a roe°   *a small deer*
I bounded o'er the mountains, by the sides
Of the deep rivers, and the lonely streams,
70   Wherever nature led: more like a man
Flying from something that he dreads than one
Who sought the thing he loved. For nature then
(The coarser pleasures of my boyish days,
And their glad animal movements all gone by)
75   To me was all in all.—I cannot paint
What then I was. The sounding cataract°   *waterfall*
Haunted me like a passion: the tall rock,
The mountain, and the deep and gloomy wood,
Their colors and their forms, were then to me
80   An appetite; a feeling and a love,
That had no need of a remoter charm,
By thought supplied, nor any interest
Unborrowed from the eye.—That time is past,
And all its aching joys are now no more,

85 And all its dizzy raptures. Not for this
Faint I, nor mourn nor murmur; other gifts
Have followed; for such loss, I would believe,
Abundant recompense. For I have learned
To look on nature, not as in the hour
90 Of thoughtless youth; but hearing oftentimes
The still, sad music of humanity,
Nor harsh nor grating, though of ample power
To chasten and subdue. And I have felt
A presence that disturbs me with the joy
95 Of elevated thoughts; a sense sublime
Of something far more deeply interfused,
Whose dwelling is the light of setting suns,
And the round ocean and the living air,
And the blue sky, and in the mind of man:
100 A motion and a spirit, that impels
All thinking things, all objects of all thought,
And rolls through all things. Therefore am I still
A lover of the meadows and the woods,
And mountains; and of all that we behold
105 From this green earth; of all the mighty world
Of eye, and ear,—both what they half create,
And what perceive; well pleased to recognize
In nature and the language of the sense
The anchor of my purest thoughts, the nurse,
110 The guide, the guardian of my heart, and soul
Of all my moral being.
                              Nor perchance,
If I were not thus taught, should I the more
Suffer my genial spirits° to decay: *creative powers*
For thou art with me here upon the banks
115 Of this fair river; thou my dearest Friend,°   *his sister Dorothy*
My dear, dear Friend; and in thy voice I catch
The language of my former heart, and read
My former pleasures in the shooting lights
Of thy wild eyes. Oh! yet a little while
120 May I behold in thee what I was once,
My dear, dear Sister! and this prayer I make,
Knowing that Nature never did betray
The heart that loved her; 'tis her privilege,
Through all the years of this our life, to lead
125 From joy to joy: for she can so inform
The mind that is within us, so impress
With quietness and beauty, and so feed
With lofty thoughts, that neither evil tongues,
Rash judgments, nor the sneers of selfish men,
130 Nor greetings where no kindness is, nor all
The dreary intercourse of daily life,
Shall e'er prevail against us, or disturb
Our cheerful faith, that all which we behold
Is full of blessings. Therefore let the moon
135 Shine on thee in thy solitary walk;

And let the misty mountain-winds be free
To blow against thee: and, in after years,
When these wild ecstasies shall be matured
Into a sober pleasure; when thy mind
140 Shall be a mansion for all lovely forms,
Thy memory be as a dwelling-place
For all sweet sounds and harmonies; oh! then,
If solitude, or fear, or pain, or grief,
Should be thy portion, with what healing thoughts
145 Of tender joy wilt thou remember me,
And these my exhortations! Nor, perchance—
If I should be where I no more can hear
Thy voice, nor catch from thy wild eyes these gleams
Of past existence—wilt thou then forget
150 That on the banks of this delightful stream
We stood together; and that I, so long
A worshipper of Nature, hither came
Unwearied in that service: rather say
With warmer love—oh! with far deeper zeal
155 Of holier love. Nor wilt thou then forget,
That after many wanderings, many years
Of absence, these steep woods and lofty cliffs,
And this green pastoral landscape, were to me
More dear, both for themselves and for thy sake!

[1798]

"SHE DWELT AMONG THE UNTRODDEN WAYS"

She dwelt among the untrodden ways
    Beside the springs of Dove,
A maid whom there were none to praise
    And very few to love:

5 A violet by a mossy stone
    Half hidden from the eye!
Fair as a star, when only one
    Is shining in the sky.

She lived unknown, and few could know
10   When Lucy ceased to be;
But she is in her grave, and oh,
    The difference to me!

[1800]

I WANDERED LONELY AS A CLOUD

I wandered lonely as a cloud
    That floats on high o'er vales and hills,
When all at once I saw a crowd,
    A host, of golden daffodils;

Beside the lake, beneath the trees,
Fluttering and dancing in the breeze.

Continuous as the stars that shine
  And twinkle on the Milky Way,
They stretched in never-ending line
  Along the margin of a bay:
Ten thousand saw I at a glance,
Tossing their heads in sprightly dance.

The waves beside them danced, but they
  Out-did the sparkling waves in glee:
A poet could not but be gay,
  In such a jocund company:
I gazed—and gazed—but little thought
What wealth the show to me had brought:

For oft, when on my couch I lie
  In vacant or in pensive mood,
They flash upon that inward eye
  Which is the bliss of solitude;
And then my heart with pleasure fills,
And dances with the daffodils.

                                    [1807]

"SHE WAS A PHANTOM OF DELIGHT"

She was a phantom of delight
When first she gleamed upon my sight;
A lovely apparition, sent
To be a moment's ornament;
Her eyes as stars of twilight fair;
Like twilight's, too, her dusky hair;
But all things else about her drawn
From May-time and the cheerful dawn;
A dancing shape, an image gay,
To haunt, to startle, and waylay.

I saw her upon nearer view,
A spirit, yet a woman too!
Her household motions light and free,
And steps of virgin liberty;
A countenance in which did meet
Sweet records, promises as sweet;
A creature not too bright or good
For human nature's daily food;
For transient sorrows, simple wiles,
Praise, blame, love, kisses, tears, and smiles.

And now I see with eye serene
The very pulse of the machine;

A being breathing thoughtful breath,
A traveller between life and death;
25 The reason firm, the temperate will,
Endurance, foresight, strength, and skill;
A perfect woman, nobly planned,
To warn, to comfort, and command;
And yet a spirit still, and bright
30 With something of angelic light.

[1807]

THE SOLITARY REAPER

Behold her, single in the field,
Yon solitary Highland Lass!
Reaping and singing by herself;
Stop here, or gently pass!
5 Alone she cuts and binds the grain,
And sings a melancholy strain;
O listen! for the vale profound
Is overflowing with the sound.

No nightingale did ever chaunt
10 More welcome notes to weary bands
Of travellers in some shady haunt,
Among Arabian sands:
A voice so thrilling ne'er was heard
In spring-time from the cuckoo-bird,
15 Breaking the silence of the seas
Among the farthest Hebrides.[1]

Will no one tell me what she sings?—
Perhaps the plaintive numbers flow
For old, unhappy, far-off things,
20 And battles long ago:
Or is it some more humble lay,
Familiar matter of today?
Some natural sorrow, loss, or pain,
That has been, and may be again?

25 Whate'er the theme, the maiden sang
As if her song could have no ending;
I saw her singing at her work,
And o'er the sickle bending:—
I listened, motionless and still;
30 And, as I mounted up the hill,
The music in my heart I bore,
Long after it was heard no more.

[1807]

[1] A group of islands west of Scotland.

COMPOSED UPON WESTMINSTER BRIDGE, SEPTEMBER 3, 1802

Earth has not anything to show more fair:
　　Dull would he be of soul who could pass by
　　A sight so touching in its majesty:
This city now doth like a garment wear
5　The beauty of the morning; silent, bare,
　　Ships, towers, domes, theaters, and temples lie
　　Open unto the fields, and to the sky;
All bright and glittering in the smokeless air.
Never did sun more beautifully steep
10　　In his first splendor, valley, rock, or hill;
Ne'er saw I, never felt, a calm so deep!
　　The river glideth at his own sweet will:
Dear God! the very houses seem asleep;
　　And all that mighty heart is lying still!

[1807]

"THE WORLD IS TOO MUCH WITH US"

The world is too much with us; late and soon,
　　Getting and spending, we lay waste our powers:
　　Little we see in Nature that is ours;
We have given our hearts away, a sordid boon:
5　This sea that bares her bosom to the moon;
　　The winds that will be howling at all hours,
　　And are up-gathered now like sleeping flowers;
For this, for everything, we are out of tune;
It moves us not.—Great God! I'd rather be
10　　A pagan suckled in a creed outworn;
So might I, standing on this pleasant lea,° 　　　　　　　*meadow*
　　Have glimpses that would make me less forlorn;
Have sight of Proteus[1] rising from the sea;
　　Or hear old Triton[2] blow his wreathèd horn.

[1807]

Samuel Taylor Coleridge　*1772–1834*

KUBLA KHAN

In Xanadu did Kubla Khan
　　A stately pleasure-dome decree:
Where Alph, the sacred river, ran

---

[1] A Greek sea god capable of changing shapes at will.
[2] A Greek sea god often depicted with a conch-shell trumpet.

Through caverns measureless to man
    Down to a sunless sea.
So twice five miles of fertile ground
With walls and towers were girdled round:
And there were gardens bright with sinuous rills
Where blossomed many an incense-bearing tree;
And here were forests ancient as the hills,
Enfolding sunny spots of greenery.

But O, that deep romantic chasm which slanted
Down the green hill athwart a cedarn cover!°   *across a cedar woods*
A savage place! as holy and enchanted
As e'er beneath a waning moon was haunted
By woman wailing for her demon-lover!
And from this chasm, with ceaseless turmoil
        seething
As if this earth in fast thick pants were
        breathing,
A mighty fountain momently° was forced;   *every moment*
Amid whose swift half-intermitted burst
Huge fragments vaulted like rebounding hail,
Or chaffy grain beneath the thresher's flail:
And 'mid these dancing rocks at once and ever
It flung up momently the sacred river.
Five miles meandering with a mazy motion
Through wood and dale the sacred river ran,
Then reached the caverns measureless to man,
And sank in tumult to a lifeless ocean:
And 'mid this tumult Kubla heard from far
Ancestral voices prophesying war!
    The shadow of the dome of pleasure
        Floated midway on the waves;
    Where was heard the mingled measure
        From the fountain and the caves.
It was a miracle of rare device,
A sunny pleasure-dome with caves of ice!

A damsel with a dulcimer
    In a vision once I saw:
It was an Abyssinian maid,
    And on her dulcimer she played,
Singing of Mount Abora.
Could I revive within me,
    Her symphony and song,
To such a deep delight 'twould win me,
That with music loud and long,
I would build that dome in air,
That sunny dome! those caves of ice!
And all who heard should see them there,
And all should cry, Beware! Beware!
His flashing eyes, his floating hair!
Weave a circle round him thrice,

And close your eyes with holy dread,
For he on honey-dew hath fed,
And drunk the milk of Paradise.

[1816]

WORK WITHOUT HOPE

[*Lines Composed 21st* February 1825]

All Nature seems at work. Slugs leave their lair—
The bees are stirring—birds are on the wing—
And Winter, slumbering in the open air,
Wears on his smiling face a dream of Spring!
5   And I, the while, the sole unbusy thing,
Nor honey make, nor pair, nor build, nor sing.

Yet well I ken° the banks where amaranths[1] blow,   *know*
Have traced the fount whence streams of nectar flow.
Bloom, O ye amaranths! bloom for whom ye may,
10   For me ye bloom not! Glide, rich streams, away!
With lips unbrightened, wreathless brow, I stroll:
And would you learn the spells that drowse my soul?
Work without hope draws nectar in a sieve,
And hope without an object cannot live.

[1828]

ON DONNE'S POETRY

With Donne, whose muse on dromedary° trots,   *camel*
Wreathe iron pokers into truelove knots;
Rhyme's sturdy cripple, fancy's maze and clue,
Wit's forge and fire-blast, meaning's press and screw.

[posthumous, 1836]

Leigh Hunt   *1784–1859*

RONDEAU

Jenny kissed me when we met,
    Jumping from the chair she sat in;
Time, you thief, who love to get
    Sweets into your list, put that in!
5   Say I'm weary, say I'm sad,
    Say that health and wealth have missed me,

---

[1] Mythical ever-blooming flowers.

Say I'm growing old, but add,
    Jenny kissed me.

[1838]

George Gordon, Lord Byron   *1788–1824*

THE DESTRUCTION OF SENNACHERIB[1]

The Assyrian came down like the wolf on the fold,
And his cohorts were gleaming in purple and gold;
And the sheen of their spears was like stars on the sea,
When the blue wave rolls nightly on deep Galilee.

5   Like the leaves of the forest when summer is green,
That host with their banners at sunset were seen:
Like the leaves of the forest when autumn hath blown,
That host on the morrow lay withered and strown.

For the Angel of Death spread his wings on the blast,
10   And breathed in the face of the foe as he passed;
And the eyes of the sleepers waxed deadly and chill,
And their hearts but once heaved, and for ever grew still!

And there lay the steed with his nostril all wide,
But through it there rolled not the breath of his pride;
15   And the foam of his gasping lay white on the turf,
And cold as the spray of the rock-beating surf.

And there lay the rider distorted and pale,
With the dew on his brow and the rust on his mail;
And the tents were all silent, the banners alone,
20   The lances unlifted, the trumpet unblown.

And the widows of Ashur° are loud in their wail,   *Assyria*
And the idols are broke in the temple of Baal;°   *a sun god*
And the might of the Gentile,° unsmote by the sword,   *non-Jew*
Hath melted like snow in the glance of the Lord!

[1815]

DON JUAN

Fragment on the back of the Poet's MS. of Canto 1

I would to heaven that I were so much clay,
    As I am blood, bone, marrow, passion, feeling—

---

[1] King of Assyria. See II Kings 19.

Because at least the past were passed away—
   And for the future—(but I write this reeling,
Having got drunk exceedingly today,
   So that I seem to stand upon the ceiling)
I say—the future is a serious matter—
And so—for God's sake—hock° and soda-water!   *a white wine*

FROM *Canto 1*

CCXVIII

What is the end of Fame? 'tis but to fill
   A certain portion of uncertain paper:
Some liken it to climbing up a hill,
   Whose summit, like all hills, is lost in vapor;
For this men write, speak, preach, and heroes kill,
   And bards burn what they call their "midnight
      taper,"
To have, when the original is dust,
A name, a wretched picture, and worse bust.

[1819]

FROM *Canto 2*

CLXXIX

Man, being reasonable, must get drunk;
   The best of life is but intoxication:
Glory, the grape, love, gold, in these are sunk
   The hopes of all men, and of every nation;
Without their sap, how branchless were the trunk
   Of life's strange tree, so fruitful on occasion:
But to return—Get very drunk: and when
You wake with headache, you shall see what then.

. . . .

CXCVI

An infant when it gazes on a light,
   A child the moment when it drains the breast,
A devotee when soars the Host° in sight,   *Eucharist*
   An Arab with a stranger for a guest,
A sailor when the prize has struck° in fight,   *surrendered*
   A miser filling his most hoarded chest,
Feel rapture; but not such true joy are reaping
As they who watch o'er what they love while sleeping.

CXCVII

For there it lies so tranquil, so beloved,
   All that it hath of life with us is living;
So gentle, stirless, helpless, and unmoved,
   And all unconscious of the joy 'tis giving;
All it hath felt, inflicted, passed, and proved,
   Hushed into depths beyond the watcher's diving;

15   There lies the thing we love with all its errors
            And all its charms, like death without its terrors.

                                                             [1819]

                              FROM *Canto 3*

                                    V
            'Tis melancholy, and a fearful sign
                Of human frailty, folly, also crime,
            That love and marriage rarely can combine,
                Although they both are born in the same clime;
5   Marriage from love, like vinegar from wine—
                A sad, sour, sober beverage—by time
            Is sharpened from its high celestial flavor
            Down to a very homely household savor.

                                   VI
            There's something of antipathy, as 'twere,
10   Between their present and their future state;
            A kind of flattery that's hardly fair
                Is used until the truth arrives too late—
            Yet what can people do, except despair?
                The same things change their names at such a rate;
15   For instance—passion in a lover's glorious,
            But in a husband is pronounced uxorious.°   *too fond*

                                  VII
            Men grow ashamed of being so very fond;
                They sometimes also get a little tired
            (But that, of course, is rare), and then despond:
20   The same things cannot always be admired,
            Yet 'tis "so nominated in the bond,"[1]
                That both are tied till one shall have expired.
            Sad thought! to lose the spouse that was adorning
            Our days, and put one's servants into mourning.

                                  VIII
25   There's doubtless something in domestic doings
                Which forms, in fact, true love's antithesis;
            Romances paint at full length people's wooings,
                But only give a bust of marriages;
            For no one cares for matrimonial cooings,
30   There's nothing wrong in a connubial° kiss: *marital*
            Think you, if Laura had been Petrarch's wife,
            He would have written sonnets all his life?[2]

[1] The bond of marriage. See Shakespeare's *The Merchant of Venice,* Act 4, Scene 1.
[2] The Italian poet Petrarch (1304–1374) wrote a famous cycle of sonnets to Laura. In his manuscript
  Byron gave a more risqué twist to these lines:
    Had Petrarch's passion led to Petrarch's wedding,
    How many sonnets had ensued the bedding?

IX

All tragedies are finished by a death,
    All comedies are ended by a marriage;
35   The future states of both are left to faith,
    For authors fear description might disparage
The worlds to come of both, or fall beneath,
    And then both worlds would punish their miscarriage;
So leaving each their priest and prayer-book ready,
40   They say no more of Death or of the Lady.

. . . .

LXXXVIII

But words are things, and a small drop of ink,
    Falling like dew, upon a thought, produces
That which makes thousands, perhaps millions, think;
    'Tis strange, the shortest letter which man uses
5   Instead of speech, may form a lasting link
    Of ages; to what straits old Time reduces
Frail man, when paper—even a rag like this,
Survives himself, his tomb, and all that's his.

[1821]

FROM *Canto II*

I

When Bishop Berkeley[1] said "there was no matter"
    And proved it—'twas no matter what he said:
They say his system 'tis in vain to batter,
    Too subtle for the airiest human head;
5   And yet who can believe it? I would shatter
    Gladly all matters down to stone or lead,
Or adamant, to find the world a spirit,
And wear my head, denying that I wear it.

[1823]

FROM *Canto 14*

I

If from great nature's or our own abyss
    Of thought we could but snatch a certainty,
Perhaps mankind might find the path they miss—
    But then 'twould spoil much good philosophy.
5   One system eats another up, and this
    Much as old Saturn ate his progeny;[2]
For when his pious consort gave him stones
In lieu of sons, of these he made no bones.

---

[1] Bishop George Berkeley (1685–1753) was an Irish philosopher who argued that physical objects exist only in the mind of the perceiver and in the mind of God.

[2] Saturn is the Roman name for Cronus, a Titan who was warned that he would be destroyed by his own children. Therefore he ate each of his offspring at birth until one, Zeus, was concealed from him and later forced his father to vomit forth the other gods.

II

But System doth reverse the Titan's breakfast,
   And eats her parents, albeit the digestion
Is difficult: Pray tell me, can you make fast,
   After due search, your faith to any question?
Look back o'er ages, ere unto the stake fast
   You bind yourself, and call some mode the best one.
Nothing more true than *not* to trust your senses;
And yet what are your other evidences?

III

For me, I know nought; nothing I deny,
   Admit, reject, contemn;° and what know *you,*   *scorn*
Except perhaps that you were born to die?
   And both may after all turn out untrue.
An age may come, Font° of Eternity,   *beginning*
   When nothing shall be either old or new.
Death, so called, is a thing which makes men weep,
And yet a third of life is passed in sleep.

IV

A sleep without dreams, after a rough day
   Of toil, is what we covet most; and yet
How clay shrinks back from more quiescent clay!
   The very Suicide that pays his debt
At once without instalments (an old way
   Of paying debts, which creditors regret)
Lets out impatiently his rushing breath,
Less from disgust of life than dread of death.

Percy Bysshe Shelley   *1792–1822*

MONT BLANC[1]

Lines Written in the Vale of Chamouni

I

The everlasting universe of things
Flows through the mind, and rolls its rapid waves,
Now dark, now glittering, now reflecting gloom,

---

[1] "The poem was composed under the immediate impression of the deep and powerful feelings excited by the objects which it attempts to describe; and, as an undisciplined overflowing of the soul, rests its claim to approbation on an attempt to imitate the untamable wildness and inaccessible solemnity from which those feelings sprang." [Shelley's note.]
   The "objects" were Mont Blanc (the highest mountain in Europe) and the river Arve that descends from the mountain's inaccessible glaciers through the valley of Chamonix in southeastern France.

Now lending splendor, where from secret springs
The source of human thought its tribute brings
Of waters,—with a sound but half its own,
Such as a feeble brook will oft assume
In the wild woods, among the mountains lone,
Where waterfalls around it leap forever,
Where woods and winds contend, and a vast river
Over its rocks ceaselessly bursts and raves.

II

Thus thou, Ravine of Arve—dark, deep Ravine—
Thou many-colored, many-voicèd vale,
Over whose pines, and crags, and caverns sail
Fast cloud-shadows, and sunbeams! awful scene,
Where Power in likeness of the Arve comes down
From the ice-gulfs that grid his secret throne
Bursting through these dark mountains like the flame
Of lightning through the tempest! thou dost lie,—
Thy giant brood of pines around thee clinging,
Children of elder time, in whose devotion
The chainless winds still come and ever came
To drink their odors, and their mighty swinging
To hear—an old and solemn harmony;
Thine earthly rainbows stretched across the sweep
Of the ethereal waterfall, whose veil
Robes some unsculptured image; the strange sleep
Which when the voices of the desert fail
Wraps all in its own deep eternity;
Thy caverns echoing to the Arve's commotion—
A loud, lone sound no other sound can tame.
Thou art pervaded with that ceaseless motion,
Thou art the path of that unresting sound,
Dizzy Ravine! and when I gaze on thee,
I seem as in a trance sublime and strange
To muse on my own separate fantasy,
My own, my human mind, which passively
Now renders and receives fast influencings,
Holding an unremitting interchange
With the clear universe of things around;
One legion of wild thoughts, whose wandering wings
Now float above thy darkness, and now rest,
Where that or thou art no unbidden guest,
In the still cave of the witch Poesy,
Seeking among the shadows that pass by—
Ghosts of all things that are—some shade of thee,
Some phantom, some faint image; till the breast
From which they fled recalls them, thou art there!

III

Some say that gleams of a remoter world
Visit the soul in sleep,—that death is slumber,

And that its shapes the busy thoughts outnumber
Of those who wake and live. I look on high;
Has some unknown Omnipotence unfurled
The veil of life and death? or do I lie
55   In dream, and does the mightier world of sleep
Spread far around and inaccessibly
Its circles? For the very spirit fails,
Driven like a homeless cloud from steep to steep
That vanishes among the viewless gales!
60   Far, far above, piercing the infinite sky,
Mont Blanc appears,—still, snowy and serene—
Its subject mountains their unearthly forms
Pile around it, ice and rock; broad vales between
Of frozen floods, unfathomable deeps,
65   Blue as the overhanging heaven, that spread
And wind among the accumulated steeps;
A desert peopled by the storms alone,
Save when the eagle brings some hunter's bone,
And the wolf tracks her there. How hideously
70   Its shapes are heaped around! rude, bare and high,
Ghastly, and scarred, and riven.—Is this the scene
Where the old Earthquake-dæmon taught her young
Ruin? Were these their toys? or did a sea
Of fire envelop once this silent snow?
75   None can reply—all seems eternal now.
The wilderness has a mysterious tongue
Which teaches awful doubt, or faith so mild,
So solemn, so serene, that man may be
But for such faith with Nature reconciled;[2]
80   Thou hast a voice, great Mountain, to repeal
Large codes of fraud and woe;[3] not understood
By all, but which the wise, and great, and good,
Interpret, or make felt, or deeply feel.

IV
The fields, the lakes, the forests and the streams,
85   Ocean, and all the living things that dwell
Within the dædal° earth; lightning, and rain,   *varied*
Earthquake, and fiery flood, and hurricane,
The torpor of the year when feeble dreams
Visit the hidden buds or dreamless sleep
90   Holds every future leaf and flower, the bound
With which from that detested trance they leap,
The works and ways of man, their death and birth,
And that of him and all that his may be,—

---

[2] The wilderness teaches either scepticism about the existence of God or (less acceptable to Shelley) a simple, Wordsworthian faith "that all which we behold / Is full of blessings" (*Tintern Abbey*, lines 133–134).
[3] The "voice" of the mountain contradicts the commonly held social and religious codes.

All things that move and breathe with toil and sound
95 Are born and die, revolve, subside and swell;
Power dwells apart in its tranquillity,
Remote, serene, and inaccessible;—
And *this,* the naked countenance of earth
On which I gaze, even these primeval mountains,
100 Teach the adverting° mind. The glaciers creep,   observing
Like snakes that watch their prey, from their far fountains,
Slow rolling on; there many a precipice
Frost and the sun in scorn of mortal power
Have piled—dome, pyramid and pinnacle,
105 A city of death, distinct with many a tower
And wall impregnable of beaming ice;
Yet not a city, but a flood of ruin
Is there, that from the boundaries of the sky
Rolls its perpetual stream; vast pines are strewing
110 Its destined path, or in the mangled soil
Branchless and shattered stand; the rocks, drawn down
From yon remotest waste, have overthrown
The limits of the dead and living world,
Never to be reclaimed. The dwelling-place
115 Of insects, beasts and birds, becomes its spoil,
Their food and their retreat forever gone;
So much of life and joy is lost. The race
Of man flies far in dread; his work and dwelling
Vanish, like smoke before the tempest's stream,
120 And their place is not known. Below, vast caves
Shine in the rushing torrents' restless gleam,
Which from those secret chasms in tumult welling
Meet in the vale; and one majestic river,
The breath and blood of distant lands, forever
125 Rolls its loud waters to the ocean waves,
Breathes its swift vapors to the circling air.

                                    V
Mont Blanc yet gleams on high: the power is there,
The still and solemn power of many sights
And many sounds, and much of life and death.
130 In the calm darkness of the moonless nights,
In the lone glare of day, the snows descend
Upon that mountain; none beholds them there,
Nor when the flakes burn in the sinking sun,
Or the star-beams dart through them; winds contend
135 Silently there, and heap the snow, with breath
Rapid and strong, but silently! Its home
The voiceless lightning in these solitudes
Keeps innocently, and like vapor broods
Over the snow. The secret strength of things,
140 Which governs thought, and to the infinite dome
Of heaven is as a law, inhabits thee!
And what were thou, and earth, and stars, and sea,

If to the human mind's imaginings
Silence and solitude were vacancy?[4]

[1817]

ODE TO THE WEST WIND[1]

I

O wild west wind, thou breath of autumn's being,
Thou, from whose unseen presence the leaves dead
Are driven, like ghosts from an enchanter fleeing,

5   Yellow, and black, and pale, and hectic red
Pestilence-stricken multitudes: O thou,
Who chariotest to their dark wintry bed

The wingèd seeds, where they lie cold and low,
Each like a corpse within its grave, until
Thine azure sister of the spring shall blow

10   Her clarion o'er the dreaming earth, and fill
(Driving sweet buds like flocks to feed in air)
With living hues and odors plain and hill:

Wild Spirit, which art moving everywhere;
Destroyer and preserver; hear, oh, hear!

II

15   Thou on whose stream, mid the steep sky's commotion,
Loose clouds like earth's decaying leaves are shed,
Shook from the tangled boughs of heaven and ocean,

Angels of rain and lightning: there are spread
On the blue surface of thine airy surge,
20   Like the bright hair uplifted from the head

Of some fierce Mænad,[2] even from the dim verge
Of the horizon to the zenith's height,
The locks of the approaching storm. Thou dirge

[4] Shelley concludes by asking what importance the silent and solitary power of Mont Blanc would
have if the human mind were incapable of imagination.
[1] "This poem was conceived and chiefly written in a wood that skirts the Arno, near Florence,
and on a day when that tempestuous wind, whose temperature is at once mild and animating,
was collecting the vapors which pour down the autumnal rains. They began, as I foresaw, at
sunset with a violent tempest of hail and rain, attended by that magnificent thunder and lightning
peculiar to the Cisalpine regions.
  "The phenomenon alluded to at the conclusion of the third stanza is well known to naturalists.
The vegetation at the bottom of the sea, of rivers, and of lakes, sympathizes with that of the
land in the change of seasons, and is consequently influenced by the winds which announce it."
[Shelley's note.]
[2] A frenzied female follower of Bacchus, the Greek god of wine.

Of the dying year, to which this closing night
25 Will be the dome of a vast sepulchre,
Vaulted with all thy congregated might

Of vapors, from whose solid atmosphere
Black rain, and fire, and hail will burst: oh, hear!

III

Thou who didst waken from his summer dreams
30 The blue Mediterranean, where he lay,
Lulled by the coil of his crystalline streams,

Beside a pumice isle[3] in Baiæ's bay,[4]
And saw in sleep old palaces and towers
Quivering within the wave's intenser day,

35 All overgrown with azure moss and flowers
So sweet the sense faints picturing them! Thou
For whose path the Atlantic's level powers

Cleave themselves into chasms, while far below
The sea-blooms and the oozy woods which wear
40 The sapless foliage of the ocean know

Thy voice, and suddenly grow gray with fear,
And tremble and despoil themselves: oh, hear!

IV

If I were a dead leaf thou mightest bear;
If I were a swift cloud to fly with thee;
45 A wave to pant beneath thy power, and share

The impulse of thy strength, only less free
Than thou, O uncontrollable! If even
I were as in my boyhood, and could be

The comrade of thy wanderings over heaven,
50 As then, when to outstrip thy skyey speed
Scarce seemed a vision; I would ne'er have striven

As thus with thee in prayer in my sore need.
Oh, lift me as a wave, a leaf, a cloud!
I fall upon the thorns of life! I bleed!

55 A heavy weight of hours has chained and bowed
One too like thee: tameless, and swift, and proud.

---

[3] An island of volcanic stone.   [4] Near Naples.

V

Make me thy lyre, even as the forest is:
What if my leaves are falling like its own!
The tumult of thy mighty harmonies

60   Will take from both a deep, autumnal tone,
Sweet though in sadness. Be thou, Spirit fierce,
My spirit! Be thou me, impetuous one!

Drive my dead thoughts over the universe
Like withered leaves to quicken a new birth!
65   And, by the incantation of this verse,

Scatter, as from an unextinguished hearth
Ashes and sparks, my words among mankind!
Be through my lips to unawakened earth

The trumpet of a prophecy! O Wind,
70   If winter comes, can spring be far behind?

                                                              [1820]

SONNET

Lift not the painted veil which those who live
Call Life: though unreal shapes be pictured there,
And it but mimic all we would believe
With colors idly spread—behind, lurk Fear
5   And Hope, twin Destinies; who ever weave
Their shadows, o'er the chasm, sightless and drear.
I knew one who had lifted it—he sought,
For his lost heart was tender, things to love,
But found them not, alas! nor was there aught
10   The world contains, the which he could approve.
Through the unheeding many he did move,
A splendor among shadows, a bright blot
Upon this gloomy scene, a Spirit that strove
For truth, and like the Preacher found it not.
                                                              [1824]

John Keats   *1795–1821*

ODE TO A NIGHTINGALE

I

My heart aches, and a drowsy numbness pains
   My sense, as though of hemlock I had drunk,
Or emptied some dull opiate to the drains

One minute past, and Lethe-wards[1] had sunk:
5   'T is not through envy of thy happy lot,
        But being too happy in thine happiness,—
            That thou, light-wingèd Dryad[2] of the trees,
                In some melodious plot
        Of beechen green, and shadows numberless,
10   Singest of summer in full-throated ease.

                                    II
    O for a draught of vintage! that hath been
        Cooled a long age in the deep-delved earth,
    Tasting of Flora[3] and the country-green,
        Dance, and Provençal song,[4] and sunburnt mirth!
15   O for a beaker full of the warm South,
        Full of the true, the blushful Hippocrene,[5]
            With beaded bubbles winking at the brim,
                And purple-stainèd mouth;
        That I might drink, and leave the world unseen,
20   And with thee fade away into the forest dim:

                                    III
    Fade far away, dissolve, and quite forget
        What thou among the leaves hast never known,
    The weariness, the fever, and the fret
        Here, where men sit and hear each other groan;
25   Where palsy shakes a few, sad, last gray hairs,
        Where youth grows pale, and spectre-thin, and dies;
            Where but to think is to be full of sorrow
                And leaden-eyed despairs,
        Where Beauty cannot keep her lustrous eyes,
30   Or new Love pine at them beyond tomorrow.

                                    IV
    Away! away! for I will fly to thee,
        Not charioted by Bacchus and his pards,[6]
    But on the viewless wings of Poesy,
        Though the dull brain perplexes and retards:
35   Already with thee! tender is the night,
        And haply the Queen-Moon is on her throne,
            Clustered around by all her starry Fays;°   *fairies*
                But here there is no light,
        Save what from heaven is with the breezes blown
40   Through verdurous glooms and winding mossy
                ways.

[1] Toward Lethe, the river of forgetfulness in the Underworld.
[2] Wood nymph.   [3] The goddess of flowers.
[4] The medieval troubadors of Provence in southern France were famous for their songs.
[5] A mythological fountain whose waters bring poetic inspiration.
[6] Bacchus, the god of wine, rode in a chariot drawn by leopards.

V

I cannot see what flowers are at my feet,
   Nor what soft incense hangs upon the boughs,
But, in embalmèd° darkness, guess each sweet   *sweet smelling*
   Wherewith the seasonable month endows
45 The grass, the thicket, and the fruit-tree wild;
   White hawthorn, and the pastoral eglantine;
      Fast fading violets covered up in leaves;
        And mid-May's eldest child,
   The coming musk-rose, full of dewy wine,
50   The murmurous haunt of flies on summer eves.

VI

Darkling[7] I listen; and, for many a time
   I have been half in love with easeful Death,
Called him soft names in many a musèd rhyme,
   To take into the air my quiet breath;
55 Now more than ever seems it rich to die,
   To cease upon the midnight with no pain,
      While thou art pouring forth thy soul abroad
        In such an ecstasy!
   Still wouldst thou sing, and I have ears in vain—
60 To thy high requiem become a sod.

VII

Thou wast not born for death, immortal Bird!
   No hungry generations tread thee down;
The voice I hear this passing night was heard
   In ancient days by emperor and clown:
65 Perhaps the self-same song that found a path
   Through the sad heart of Ruth,[8] when, sick for home,
      She stood in tears amid the alien corn;
        The same that oft-times hath
   Charmed magic casements, opening on the foam
70   Of perilous seas, in faery lands forlorn.

VIII

Forlorn! the very word is like a bell
   To toll me back from thee to my sole self!
Adieu! the fancy cannot cheat so well
   As she is famed to do, deceiving elf.
75 Adieu! adieu! thy plaintive anthem fades
   Past the near meadows, over the still stream,
      Up the hill-side; and now 't is buried deep
        In the next valley-glades:
   Was it a vision, or a waking dream?
80   Fled is that music:—do I wake or sleep?

[1819]

---

[7] In the dark.
[8] A young widow in the Bible, Ruth 2.

ODE ON A GRECIAN URN

I

Thou still unravished bride of quietness,
　　Thou foster-child of Silence and slow Time,
Sylvan historian, who canst thus express
　　A flowery tale more sweetly than our rhyme:
5　What leaf-fringed legend haunts about thy shape
　　　Of deities or mortals, or of both,
　　　　In Tempe[1] or the dales of Arcady?[2]
　　What men or gods are these? What maidens loth?
What mad pursuit? What struggle to escape?
10　　　What pipes and timbrels? What wild ecstasy?

II

Heard melodies are sweet, but those unheard
　　Are sweeter; therefore, ye soft pipes, play on;
Not to the sensual ear, but, more endeared
　　Pipe to the spirit ditties of no tone:
15　Fair youth, beneath the trees, thou canst not leave
　　Thy song, nor ever can those trees be bare;
　　　Bold lover, never, never canst thou kiss,
Though winning near the goal—yet, do not grieve;
　　　She cannot fade, though thou hast not thy bliss,
20　For ever wilt thou love, and she be fair!

III

Ah, happy, happy boughs! that cannot shed
　　Your leaves, nor ever bid the spring adieu;
And, happy melodist, unwearièd,
　　For ever piping songs for ever new;
25　More happy love! more happy, happy love!
　　For ever warm and still to be enjoyed,
　　　For ever panting, and for ever young;
All breathing human passion far above,
　　That leaves a heart high-sorrowful and cloyed,
30　　A burning forehead, and a parching tongue.

IV

Who are these coming to the sacrifice?
　　To what green altar, O mysterious priest,
Lead'st thou that heifer lowing at the skies,
　　And all her silken flanks with garlands drest?
35　What little town by river or sea shore,
　　Or mountain-built with peaceful citadel,
　　　Is emptied of this folk, this pious morn?
And, little town, thy streets for evermore

---

[1] A valley in Greece famous for its beauty.
[2] Arcadia, a region in ancient Greece, often used to represent the perfect pastoral environment.

Will silent be; and not a soul to tell
 Why thou art desolate, can e'er return.

V

O Attic shape! Fair attitude! with brede°   *ornamentation*
 Of marble men and maidens overwrought,
With forest branches and the trodden weed;
 Thou, silent form, dost tease us out of thought
As doth eternity: Cold pastoral!
 When old age shall this generation waste,
  Thou shalt remain, in midst of other woe
  Than ours, a friend to man, to whom thou say'st,
"Beauty is truth, truth beauty,"—that is all
 Ye know on earth, and all ye need to know.
[1820]

TO AUTUMN

I

Season of mists and mellow fruitfulness,
 Close bosom-friend of the maturing sun;
Conspiring with him how to load and bless
 With fruit the vines that round the thatch-eaves run;
To bend with apples the mossed cottage-trees,
 And fill all fruit with ripeness to the core;
  To swell the gourd, and plump the hazel shells
 With a sweet kernel; to set budding more,
And still more, later flowers for the bees,
Until they think warm days will never cease,
  For summer has o'er-brimmed their clammy cells.

II

Who hath not seen thee oft amid thy store?
 Sometimes whoever seeks abroad may find
Thee sitting careless on a granary floor,
 Thy hair soft-lifted by the winnowing wind;
Or on a half-reaped furrow sound asleep,
 Drowsed with the fume of poppies, while thy hook
  Spares the next swath and all its twinèd flowers:
And sometimes like a gleaner thou dost keep
 Steady thy laden head across a brook;
 Or by a cider-press, with patient look,
  Thou watchest the last oozings hours by hours.

III

Where are the songs of spring? Ay, where are they?
 Think not of them, thou hast thy music too,—
While barred clouds bloom the soft-dying day,
 And touch the stubble-plains with rosy hue;

Then in a wailful choir the small gnats mourn
    Among the river sallows,° borne aloft   *willows*
    Or sinking as the light wind lives or dies;
30 And full-grown lambs loud bleat from hilly bourn;°   *territory*
    Hedge-crickets sing; and now with treble soft
    The redbreast whistles from a garden-croft,°   *a garden plot*
    And gathering swallows twitter in the skies.

[1820]

ODE ON MELANCHOLY

I

No, no! go not to Lethe,[1] neither twist
    Wolf's-bane, tight-rooted, for its poisonous wine;
Nor suffer thy pale forehead to be kissed
    By nightshade, ruby grape of Proserpine,[2]
5 Make not your rosary of yew-berries,
    Nor let the beetle, or the death-moth be
      Your mournful Psyche, nor the downy owl
A partner in your sorrow's mysteries;
    For shade to shade will come too drowsily,
10   And drown the wakeful anguish of the soul.

II

But when the melancholy fit shall fall
    Sudden from heaven like a weeping cloud,
That fosters the droop-headed flowers all,
    And hides the green hills in an April shroud;
15 Then glut thy sorrow on a morning rose,
    Or on the rainbow of the salt-sand wave,
      Or on the wealth of globèd peonies;
Or if thy mistress some rich anger shows,
    Emprison her soft hand, and let her rave,
20   And feed deep, deep upon her peerless eyes.

III

She dwells with Beauty—Beauty that must die;
    And Joy, whose hand is ever at his lips
Bidding adieu; and aching Pleasure nigh,
    Turning to poison while the bee-mouth sips:
25 Aye, in the very temple of Delight
    Veiled Melancholy has her sovran shrine,
      Though seen of none save him whose strenuous tongue

---

[1] The river of forgetfulness in the Underworld.
[2] In Roman mythology Proserpine is the queen of the Underworld. Wolf's-bane (line 2) and nightshade (line 4) are poisonous plants. Yew-berries (line 5), the beetle (line 6), and the death-moth (line 6) are all associated with death. Psyche (line 7), or the butterfly, personifies the soul in Greek mythology.

Can burst Joy's grape against his palate fine;
   His soul shall taste the sadness of her might,
30   And be among her cloudy trophies hung.

                                     [1820]

"BRIGHT STAR, WOULD I WERE STEADFAST AS THOU ART!"

Bright star, would I were steadfast as thou art!
   Not in lone splendor hung aloft the night,
And watching, with eternal lids apart,
   Like Nature's patient sleepless Eremite,°   *hermit*
5 The moving waters at their priestlike task
   Of pure ablution° round earth's human   *washing, purifying*
     shores
Or gazing on the new soft fallen mask
   Of snow upon the mountains and the moors:
No—yet still steadfast, still unchangeable,
10   Pillowed upon my fair love's ripening breast,
To feel for ever its soft fall and swell,
   Awake for ever in a sweet unrest,
Still, still to hear her tender-taken breath,
And so live ever—or else swoon to death.

                        [posthumous, 1838]

"IF BY DULL RHYMES OUR ENGLISH MUST BE CHAINED"

If by dull rhymes our English must be chained,
   And, like Andromeda,[1] the sonnet sweet
Fettered, in spite of pained loveliness;
Let us find out, if we must be constrained,
5   Sandals more interwoven and complete
To fit the naked foot of poesy;
Let us inspect the lyre, and weigh the stress
Of every chord, and see what may be gained
   By ear industrious, and attention meet;
10 Misers of sound and syllable, no less
Than Midas[2] of his coinage, let us be
   Jealous of dead leaves in the bay-wreath crown:
So, if we may not let the Muse be free,

---

[1] Chained to a rock as a sacrifice to a sea monster, Andromeda in Greek mythology was saved at the last moment by Perseus.
[2] The miserly King Midas is a character in Greek mythology who was granted his wish that everything he touched should turn to gold.

She will be bound with garlands of her own.
[posthumous, 1848]

"WHEN I HAVE FEARS THAT I MAY CEASE TO BE"

When I have fears that I may cease to be
  Before my pen has gleaned my teeming brain,
Before high pilèd books, in charactry,°   *letters*
  Hold like rich garners° the full-ripened grain;   *granaries*
5 When I behold, upon the night's starred face,
  Huge cloudy symbols of a high romance,
And think that I may never live to trace
  Their shadows, with the magic hand of chance;
And when I feel, fair creature of an hour!
10   That I shall never look upon thee more,
Never have relish in the faery power
  Of unreflecting love;—then on the shore
Of the wide world I stand alone, and think
Till love and fame to nothingness do sink.
[posthumous, 1848]

Ralph Waldo Emerson   *1803–1882*

EACH AND ALL

Little thinks, in the field, yon red-cloaked clown[1]
Of thee from the hill-top looking down;
The heifer that lows in the upland farm,
Far-heard, lows not thine ear to charm;
5 The sexton, tolling his bell at noon,
Deems not that great Napoleon
Stops his horse, and lists with delight,
Whilst his files sweep round yon Alpine height;
Nor knowest thou what argument
10 Thy life to thy neighbor's creed has lent.
All are needed by each one;
Nothing is fair or good alone.
I thought the sparrow's note from heaven,
Singing at dawn on the alder bough;
15 I brought him home, in his nest, at even;
He sings the song, but it cheers not now,
For I did not bring home the river and sky;—
He sang to my ear,—they sang to my eye.
The delicate shells lay on the shore;

---

[1] A farmer or peasant.

20 The bubbles of the latest wave
Fresh pearls to their enamel gave,
And the bellowing of the savage sea
Greeted their safe escape to me.
I wiped away the weeds and foam,
25 I fetched my sea-born treasures home;
But the poor, unsightly, noisome things
Had left their beauty on the shore
With the sun and the sand and the wild uproar.
The lover watched his graceful maid,
30 As 'mid the virgin train she strayed,
Nor knew her beauty's best attire
Was woven still by the snow-white choir.
At last she came to his hermitage,
Like the bird from the woodlands to the cage;—
35 The gay enchantment was undone,
A gentle wife, but fairy none.
Then I said, "I covet truth;
Beauty is unripe childhood's cheat;
I leave it behind with the games of youth:"—
40 As I spoke, beneath my feet
The ground-pine curled its pretty wreath,
Running over the club-moss burrs;
I inhaled the violet's breath;
Around me stood the oaks and firs;
45 Pine-cones and acorns lay on the ground;
Over me soared the eternal sky,
Full of light and of deity;
Again I saw, again I heard,
The rolling river, the morning bird;—
50 Beauty through my senses stole;
I yielded myself to the perfect whole.

[1839]

THE SNOW-STORM

Announced by all the trumpets of the sky,
Arrives the snow, and, driving o'er the fields,
Seems nowhere to alight: the whited air
Hides hills and woods, the river, and the heaven,
5 And veils the farm-house at the garden's end.
The sled and traveller stopped, the courier's feet
Delayed, all friends shut out, the housemates sit
Around the radiant fireplace, enclosed
In a tumultuous privacy of storm.

10 Come see the north wind's masonry.
Out of an unseen quarry evermore
Furnished with tile, the fierce artificer
Curves his white bastions with projected roof

Round every windward stake, or tree, or door.
15 Speeding, the myriad-handed, his wild work
So fanciful, so savage, nought cares he
For number or proportion. Mockingly,
On coop or kennel he hangs Parian[1] wreaths;
A swan-like form invests the hidden thorn;
20 Fills up the farmer's lane from wall to wall,
Maugre° the farmer's sighs; and at the gate   *Despite*
A tapering turret overtops the work.
And when his hours are numbered, and the world
Is all his own, retiring, as he were not,
25 Leaves, when the sun appears, astonished Art
To mimic in slow structures, stone by stone,
Built in an age, the mad wind's night-work,
The frolic architecture of the snow.

[1841]

DAYS

Daughters of Time, the hypocritic Days,
Muffled and dumb like barefoot dervishes,[1]
And marching single in an endless file,
Bring diadems° and fagots° in their hands.   *crowns / bundles of sticks*
5 To each they offer gifts after his will,
Bread, kingdoms, stars, and sky that holds
    them all.
I, in my pleached garden,[2] watched the pomp,
Forgot my morning wishes, hastily
Took a few herbs and apples, and the Day
10 Turned and departed silent. I, too late,
Under her solemn fillet° saw the scorn.   *headband*

[1857]

BRAHMA[1]

If the red slayer think he slays,
    Or if the slain think he is slain,
They know not well the subtle ways
    I keep, and pass, and turn again.

5 Far or forgot to me is near;
    Shadow and sunlight are the same;
The vanished gods to me appear;
    And one to me are shame and fame.

---

[1] A famous type of white marble from the Greek islands of Paros.
[1] Moslem ascetics who achieve ecstasy by performing whirling dances.
[2] A type of formal garden in which the trees and bushes have been interlaced.
[1] The supreme god of Hinduism.

10
    They reckon ill who leave me out;
       When me they fly, I am the wings;
    I am the doubter and the doubt,
       And I the hymn the Brahmin sings.

    The strong gods pine for my abode,
       And pine in vain the sacred Seven;[2]
15
    But thou, meek lover of the good!
       Find me, and turn thy back on heaven.

                      [1857]

Elizabeth Barrett Browning   *1806–1861*

"HOW DO I LOVE THEE?
LET ME COUNT THE WAYS"

How do I love thee? Let me count the ways.
I love thee to the depth and breadth and height
My soul can reach, when feeling out of sight
For the ends of Being and ideal Grace.
5
I love thee to the level of every day's
Most quiet need, by sun and candlelight.
I love thee freely, as men strive for right;
I love thee purely, as they turn from praise.
I love thee with the passion put to use
10
In my old griefs, and with my childhood's faith.
I love thee with a love I seemed to lose
With my lost saints—I love thee with the breath,
Smiles, tears, of all my life!—and, if God choose,
I shall but love thee better after death.

                      [1850]

Henry Wadsworth Longfellow   *1807–1882*

MEZZO CAMMIN[1]

Written at Boppard on the Rhine, August 25, 1842
Just Before Leaving for Home

Half of my life is gone, and I have let
   The years slip from me and have not fulfilled

---

[2] The highest saints of Hinduism.
[1] The title (meaning "midway along the journey") is taken from the first line of Dante's *Divine Comedy* (completed in 1321); when he wrote this poem in 1842 at age 35, Longfellow had reached the midpoint of the Biblical "three-score years and ten."

The aspiration of my youth, to build
  Some tower of song with lofty parapet.
5 Not indolence, nor pleasure, nor the fret
  Of restless passions that would not be stilled,
  But sorrow, and a care that almost killed,[2]
  Kept me from what I may accomplish yet;

Though, half-way up the hill, I see the Past
10 Lying beneath me with its sounds and sights,—
  A city in the twilight dim and vast,
With smoking roofs, soft bells, and gleaming lights,—
  And hear above me on the autumnal blast
  The cataract of Death far thundering from the heights.

[1846]

SNOW-FLAKES

Out of the bosom of the Air,
  Out of the cloud-folds of her garments shaken,
Over the woodlands brown and bare,
  Over the harvest-fields forsaken,
5   Silent, and soft, and slow
    Descends the snow.

Even as our cloudy fancies take
  Suddenly shape in some divine expression,
Even as the troubled heart doth make
10 In the white countenance confession,
    The troubled sky reveals
    The grief it feels.

This is the poem of the air,
  Slowly in silent syllables recorded;
15 This is the secret of despair
  Long in its cloudy bosom hoarded,
    Now whispered and revealed
    To wood and field.

[1863]

AFTERMATH[1]

When the summer fields are mown,
When the birds are fledged and flown,

---

[2] The poet's first wife had died in 1835.
[1] The aftermath literally refers to the second or later mowing of a crop of grass which springs
up after the first mowing of early summer.

And the dry leaves strew the path;
With the falling of the snow,
5   With the cawing of the crow,
Once again the fields we mow
    And gather in the aftermath.

Not the sweet, new grass with flowers
Is this harvesting of ours;
10   Not the upland clover bloom;
But the rowen mixed with weeds,
Tangled tufts from marsh and meads,
Where the poppy drops its seeds
    In the silence and the gloom.

                              [1873]

THE TIDE RISES, THE TIDE FALLS

The tide rises, the tide falls,
The twilight darkens, the curlew° calls;   *shore bird*
Along the sea-sands damp and brown
The traveller hastens toward the town,
5   And the tide rises, the tide falls.

Darkness settles on roofs and walls,
But the sea, the sea in the darkness calls;
The little waves, with their soft, white hands,
Efface the footprints in the sands,
10   And the tide rises, the tide falls.

The morning breaks; the steeds in their stalls
Stamp and neigh, as the hostler° calls;   *stableman*
The day returns, but nevermore
Returns the traveller to the shore,
15   And the tide rises, the tide falls.

                              [1880]

Edgar Allan Poe   *1809–1849*

SONNET—TO SCIENCE

Science! true daughter of Old Time thou art!
    Who alterest all things with thy peering eyes.
Why preyest thou thus upon the poet's heart,
    Vulture, whose wings are dull realities?
5   How should he love thee? or how deem thee wise,
    Who wouldst not leave him in his wandering
To seek for treasure in the jewelled skies,

    Albeit he soared with an undaunted wing?
    Hast thou not dragged Diana from her car?[1]
10   And driven the Hamadryad[2] from the wood
    To seek a shelter in some happier star?
    Hast thou not torn the Naiad from her flood,
    The Elfin from the green grass, and from me
    The summer dream beneath the tamarind[3] tree?

                      [1829]

TO HELEN

    Helen, thy beauty is to me
      Like those Nicéan[1] barks of yore,
    That gently, o'er a perfumed sea,
      The weary, way-worn wanderer bore
5   To his own native shore.

    On desperate seas long wont to roam,
      Thy hyacinth[2] hair, thy classic face,
    Thy Naiad[3] airs have brought me home
      To the glory that was Greece
10   And the grandeur that was Rome.

    Lo! in yon brilliant window-niche
      How statue-like I see thee stand,
    The agate lamp within thy hand!
    Ah, Psyche[4] from the regions which
15   Are Holy Land!

                      [1831]

ELDORADO[1]

    Gaily bedight,
    A gallant knight,
    In sunshine and in shadow,
    Had journeyed long,
5   Singing a song,
    In search of Eldorado.

---

[1] Diana is the Roman goddess of the moon. The moon itself is often pictured as a chariot or "cart" which she drives through the sky.
[2] A woodland nymph of Greek mythology. A Naiad (below) is a nymph associated with lakes, rivers, and fountains.
[3] An exotic tropical evergreen tree with pale green leaves and tiny yellow flowers.
[1] The allusion is unclear.   [2] Curly or wavy.
[3] Nymphs of Greek mythology associated with lakes, rivers, and fountains.
[4] The Greek word for "soul," personified in Greek mythology as a beautiful maiden loved by Cupid.
[1] The legendary kingdom of gold sought after by early Spanish explorers. By Poe's time Eldorado had become synonymous with any elusive land of untold wealth.

But he grew old—
This knight so bold—
And o'er his heart a shadow
10   Fell as he found
No spot of ground
That looked like Eldorado.

And, as his strength
Failed him at length,
15   He met a pilgrim shadow—
"Shadow," said he,
"Where can it be—
This land of Eldorado?"

"Over the Mountains
20   Of the Moon,
Down the Valley of the Shadow,
Ride, boldly ride,"
The shade replied,—
"If you seek for Eldorado!"
                [posthumous, 1850]

Edward FitzGerald   *1809–1883*

FROM THE RUBÁIYÁT OF OMAR KHAYYÁM[1]

Come, fill the Cup, and in the fire of Spring
Your Winter-garment of Repentance fling:
   The Bird of Time has but a little way
To flutter—and the Bird is on the Wing.

5   Whether at Naishápúr or Babylon,
Whether the Cup with sweet or bitter run,
   The Wine of Life keeps oozing drop by drop,
The Leaves of Life keep falling one by one.

A Book of Verses underneath the Bough,
10   A Jug of wine, a Loaf of Bread—and Thou
   Beside me singing in the Wilderness—
Oh, Wilderness were Paradise enow!

Some for the Glories of This World; and some
Sigh for the Prophet's Paradise to come;

---

[1] The 17 quatrains reprinted here are selected from the 97 quatrains in FitzGerald's fourth edition of the *Rubáiyát*. Each quatrain (or *rubais*) is an independent poem—though occasionally (as in lines 21–32) a series of *rubais* may develop related ideas. Omar Khayyám was a Persian poet (ca. 1048–1122) whose *rubais* were translated and adapted by FitzGerald.

15   Ah, take the Cash, and let the Credit go,
Nor heed the rumble of a distant Drum!

The Worldly Hope men set their Hearts upon
Turns Ashes—or it prospers; and anon,
    Like Snow upon the Desert's dusty Face,
20   Lighting a little hour or two—is gone.

Why, all the Saints and Sages who discussed
Of the Two Worlds so wisely—they are thrust
    Like foolish Prophets forth; their Words to Scorn
Are scattered, and their Mouths are stopt with Dust.

25   Myself when young did eagerly frequent
Doctor and Saint, and heard great argument
    About it and about: but evermore
Came out by the same Door where in I went.

With them the seed of Wisdom did I sow,
30   And with mine own hand wrought to make it grow;
    And this was all the Harvest that I reaped—
"I came like Water, and like Wind I go."

Perplext no more with Human or Divine,
Tomorrow's tangle to the winds resign,
35   And lose your fingers in the tresses of
The Cypress-slender Minister of Wine.

You know, my Friends, with what a brave Carouse
I made a Second Marriage in my house;
    Divorced old barren Reason from my Bed,
40   And took the Daughter of the Vine to Spouse.

For "Is" and "Is-not" though with Rule and Line
And "Up-and-down" by Logic I define,
    Of all that one should care to fathom, I
Was never deep in anything but—Wine.

45   O threats of Hell and Hopes of Paradise!
One thing at least is certain—*This* Life flies;
    One thing is certain and the rest is Lies,
The Flower that once has blown for ever dies.

But helpless Pieces of the Game He plays
50   Upon this Chequer-board of Nights and Days;
    Hither and thither moves, and checks, and slays,
And one by one back in the Closet lays.

The Moving Finger writes; and, having writ,
Moves on: nor all your Piety nor Wit
55   Shall lure it back to cancel half a Line,
Nor all your Tears wash out a Word of it.

Yesterday *This* Day's Madness did prepare;
Tomorrow's Silence, Triumph, or Despair:
   Drink! for you know not whence you came, nor why:
60   Drink! for you know not why you go, nor where.

And much as Wine has played the Infidel,
And robbed me of my Robe of Honor—Well,
   I wonder often what the Vintners buy
One half so precious as the stuff they sell.

65   Ah Love! could you and I with Him conspire
To grasp this sorry Scheme of Things entire,
   Would not we shatter it to bits—and then
Remould it nearer to the Heart's Desire!

                       [1859]

Alfred, Lord Tennyson   *1809–1892*

ULYSSES[1]

It little profits that an idle king,
By this still hearth, among these barren crags,
Matched with an aged wife, I mete° and dole°   *allot / give sparingly*
Unequal laws unto a savage race,
5   That hoard, and sleep, and feed, and know not me.
I cannot rest from travel: I will drink
Life to the lees:° all times I have enjoyed   *dregs*
Greatly, have suffered greatly, both with those
That loved me, and alone; on shore, and when
10 Thro' scudding drifts° the rainy Hyades°   *spray / a constellation*
Vexed the dim sea. I am become a name;
For always roaming with a hungry heart
Much have I seen and known: cities of men
And manners, climates, councils, governments,
15 Myself not least, but honored of them all;
And drunk delight of battle with my peers,
Far on the ringing plains of windy Troy.
I am a part of all that I have met;
Yet all experience is an arch wherethro'
20 Gleams that untravelled world, whose margin fades
For ever and for ever when I move.
How dull it is to pause, to make an end,
To rust unburnished, not to shine in use!
As tho' to breathe were life. Life piled on life
25 Were all too little, and of one to me
Little remains: but every hour is saved

---

[1] The poem takes place after Ulysses' return from the Trojan War and after he has had time to grow bored with peace, Penelope, and politics. Ulysses is, of course, the Roman name for Odysseus, the hero of Homer's *Odyssey*.

From that eternal silence, something more,
A bringer of new things; and vile it were
For some three suns° to store and hoard myself,   *years*

30 And this gray spirit yearning in desire
To follow knowledge like a sinking star,
Beyond the utmost bound of human thought.
    This is my son, mine own Telemachus,
To whom I leave the sceptre and the isle—

35 Well-loved of me, discerning to fulfil
This labor, by slow prudence to make mild
A rugged people, and thro' soft degees
Subdue them to the useful and the good.
Most blameless is he, centered in the sphere

40 Of common duties, decent not to fail
In offices of tenderness, and pay
Meet adoration to my household gods,
When I am gone. He works his work, I mine.
    There lies the port; the vessel puffs her sail:

45 There gloom the dark broad seas. My mariners,
Souls that have toiled, and wrought, and thought with me—
That ever with a frolic welcome took
The thunder and the sunshine, and opposed
Free hearts, free foreheads—you and I are old;

50 Old age hath yet his honor and his toil;
Death closes all; but something ere the end,
Some work of noble note, may yet be done,
Not unbecoming men that strove with Gods.
The lights begin to twinkle from the rocks:

55 The long day wanes: the slow moon climbs: the deep
Moans round with many voices. Come, my friends,
'T is not too late to seek a newer world.
Push off, and sitting well in order smite
The sounding furrows; for my purpose holds

60 To sail beyond the sunset, and the baths
Of all the western stars, until I die.
It may be that the gulfs will wash us down:
It may be we shall touch the Happy Isles,°   *Elysium or Paradise*
And see the great Achilles,° whom we knew.   *a Greek hero*

65 Tho' much is taken, much abides; and tho'
We are not now that strength which in old days
Moved earth and heaven, that which we are, we are:
One equal temper of heroic hearts,
Made weak by time and fate, but strong in will

70 To strive, to seek, to find, and not to yield.
                                        [1842]

"BREAK, BREAK, BREAK"

Break, break, break,
    On thy cold gray stones, O Sea!

And I would that my tongue could utter
  The thoughts that arise in me.

5   O well for the fisherman's boy,
  That he shouts with his sister at play!
O well for the sailor lad,
  That he sings in his boat on the bay!

And the stately ships go on
10   To their haven under the hill;
But O for the touch of a vanished hand,
  And the sound of a voice that is still!

Break, break, break,
  At the foot of thy crags, O Sea!
15 But the tender grace of a day that is dead
  Will never come back to me.

                        [1842]

[THE SPLENDOR FALLS]

The splendor falls on castle walls
  And snowy summits old in story;
The long light shakes across the lakes,
  And the wild cataract leaps in glory.
5 Blow, bugle, blow, set the wild echoes flying,
Blow, bugle; answer, echoes, dying, dying, dying.

O, hark, O, hear! how thin and clear,
  And thinner, clearer, farther going!
O, sweet and far from cliff and scar°   *mountainside*
10   The horns of Elfland faintly blowing!
Blow, let us hear the purple glens replying,
Blow, bugle; answer, echoes, dying, dying, dying.

O love, they die in yon rich sky,
  They faint on hill or field or river;
15 Our echoes roll from soul to soul,
  And grow forever and forever.
Blow, bugle, blow, set the wild echoes flying,
And answer, echoes, answer, dying, dying, dying.

                        [1850]

THE EAGLE: A FRAGMENT

He clasps the crag with crooked hands;
Close to the sun in lonely lands,
Ringed with the azure world, he stands.

The wrinkled sea beneath him crawls:
5   He watches from his mountain walls,
And like a thunderbolt he falls.

[1851]

"FLOWER IN THE CRANNIED WALL"

Flower in the crannied wall,
I pluck you out of the crannies,
I hold you here, root and all, in my hand.
Little flower—but *if* I could understand
5   What you are, root and all, and all in all,
I should know what God and man is.

[1869]

Robert Browning   *1812–1889*

PORPHYRIA'S LOVER

The rain set early in to-night,
   The sullen wind was soon awake,
It tore the elm-tops down for spite,
   And did its worst to vex the lake:
5   I listened with heart fit to break;
When glided in Porphyria; straight
   She shut the cold out and the storm,
And kneeled and made the cheerless grate
   Blaze up, and all the cottage warm;
10   Which done, she rose, and from her form
Withdrew the dripping cloak and shawl,
   And laid her soiled gloves by, untied
Her hat, and let the damp hair fall,
   And, last, she sat down by my side
15   And called me. When no voice replied,
She put my arm about her waist,
   And made her smooth white shoulder bare,
And all her yellow hair displaced,
   And, stooping, made my cheek lie there,
20   And spread, o'er all, her yellow hair,
Murmuring how she loved me—she
   Too weak, for all her heart's endeavor,
To set its struggling passion free
   From pride, and vainer ties dissever,
25   And give herself to me forever.
But passion sometimes would prevail,
   Nor could tonight's gay feast restrain
A sudden thought of one so pale
   For love of her, and all in vain:
30   So, she was come through wind and rain.

Be sure I looked up at her eyes
   Happy and proud; at last I knew
Porphyria worshipped me; surprise
   Made my heart swell, and still it grew
35   While I debated what to do.
That moment she was mine, mine, fair,
   Perfectly pure and good: I found
A thing to do, and all her hair
   In one long yellow string I wound
40   Three times her little throat around,
And strangled her. No pain felt she;
   I am quite sure she felt no pain.
As a shut bud that holds a bee,
   I warily oped her lids: again
45   Laughed the blue eyes without a stain.
And I untightened next the tress
   About her neck; her cheek once more
Blushed bright beneath my burning kiss:
   I propped her head up as before,
50   Only, this time my shoulder bore
Her head, which droops upon it still:
   The smiling rosy little head,
So glad it has its utmost will,
   That all it scorned at once is fled,
55   And I, its love, am gained instead!
Porphyria's love: she guessed not how
   Her darling one wish would be heard.
And thus we sit together now,
   And all night long we have not stirred,
60   And yet God has not said a word!

                                                        [1836]

MY LAST DUCHESS[1]

Ferrara

That's my last Duchess painted on the wall,
Looking as if she were alive. I call
That piece a wonder, now: Frà Pandolf's hands
Worked busily a day, and there she stands.
5   Will 't please you sit and look at her? I said
"Frà Pandolf" by design: for never read
Strangers like you that pictured countenance,
The depth and passion of its earnest glance,
But to myself they turned (since none puts by
10   The curtain I have drawn for you, but I)
And seemed as they would ask me, if they durst,
How such a glance came there; so, not the first

---

[1] In 1564 Alphonso II, Duke of Ferrara, actually did negotiate a second marriage after the death (under suspicious circumstances) of his first wife, Lucrezia, at the age of seventeen.

Are you to turn and ask thus. Sir, 't was not
Her husband's presence only, called that spot
15 Of joy into the Duchess' cheek: perhaps
Frà Pandolf chanced to say "Her mantle laps
Over my lady's wrist too much," or "Paint
Must never hope to reproduce the faint
Half-flush that dies along her throat:" such stuff
20 Was courtesy, she thought, and cause enough
For calling up that spot of joy. She had
A heart—how shall I say?—too soon made glad,
Too easily impressed; she liked whate'er
She looked on, and her looks went everywhere.
25 Sir, 't was all one! My favor at her breast,
The dropping of the daylight in the West,
The bough of cherries some officious fool
Broke in the orchard for her, the white mule
She rode with round the terrace—all and each
30 Would draw from her alike the approving speech,
Or blush, at least. She thanked men,—good! but thanked
Somehow—I know not how—as if she ranked
My gift of a nine-hundred-years-old name
With anybody's gift. Who'd stoop to blame
35 This sort of trifling? Even had you skill
In speech—(which I have not)—to make your will
Quite clear to such an one, and say, "Just this
Or that in you disgusts me; here you miss,
Or there exceed the mark"—and if she let
40 Herself be lessoned so, nor plainly set
Her wits to yours, forsooth, and made excuse,
—E'en then would be some stooping; and I choose
Never to stoop. Oh sir, she smiled, no doubt,
Whene'er I passed her; but who passed without
45 Much the same smile? This grew; I gave commands;
Then all smiles stopped together. There she stands
As if alive. Will 't please you rise? We'll meet
The company below, then. I repeat,
The Count your master's known munificence
50 Is ample warrant that no just pretence
Of mine for dowry will be disallowed;
Though his fair daughter's self, as I avowed
At starting, is my object. Nay, we'll go
Together down, sir. Notice Neptune, though,
55 Taming a sea-horse, thought a rarity,
Which Claus of Innsbruck cast in bronze for me?

[1842]

MEETING AT NIGHT

The gray sea and the long black land;
And the low yellow half-moon large and low:
And the startled little waves that leap

In fiery ringlets from their sleep,
As I gain the cove with pushing prow,
And quench its speed i' the slushy sand.

Then a mile of warm sea-scented beach;
Three fields to cross till a farm appears;
A tap at the pane, the quick sharp scratch
And blue spurt of a lighted match,
And a voice less loud, through joys and fears,
Than the two hearts beating each to each!

[1845]

PARTING AT MORNING

Round the cape of a sudden came the sea,
And the sun looked over the mountain's rim:
And straight was a path of gold for him,°   *the sun*
And the need of a world of men for me.

[1845]

SOLILOQUY OF THE SPANISH CLOISTER

I

Gr-rr—there go, my heart's abhorrence!
  Water your damned flower-pots, do!
If hate killed men, Brother Lawrence,
  God's blood, would not mine kill you!
What? your myrtle-bush wants trimming?
  Oh, that rose has prior claims—
Needs its leaden vase filled brimming?
  Hell dry you up with its flames!

II

At the meal we sit together:
  Salve tibi!° I must hear   *Hail to thee!*
Wise talk of the kind of weather,
  Sort of season, time of year:
Not a plenteous cork-crop: scarcely
  Dare we hope oak-galls,[1] *I doubt:*
What's the Latin name for "parsley"?
  What's the Greek name for Swine's Snout?

III

Whew! We'll have our platter burnished,
  Laid with care on our own shelf!
With a fire-new spoon we're furnished,

---

[1] Diseased oak shoots, used in tanning.

20   And a goblet for ourself,
             Rinsed like something sacrificial
                Ere 'tis fit to touch our chaps°—   *lips*
             Marked with L. for our initial!
                (He-he! There his lily snaps!)

IV

25   *Saint,* forsooth! While brown Dolores
             Squats outside the Covent bank
             With Sanchicha, telling stories,
               Steeping tresses in the tank,
             Blue-black, lustrous, thick like horsehairs,
30   —Can't I see his dead eye glow,
             Bright as 'twere a Barbary corsair's?°   *pirate's*
                (That is, if he'd let it show!)

V

             When he finishes refection,°   *refreshment*
               Knife and fork he never lays
35   Cross-wise, to my recollection,
               As do I, in Jesu's praise.
             I the Trinity illustrate,
               Drinking watered orange-pulp—
             In three sips the Arian[2] frustrate;
40   While he drains his at one gulp.

VI

             Oh, those melons? If he's able
               We're to have a feast! so nice!
             One goes to the Abbot's table,
               All of us get each a slice.
45   How go on your flowers? None double?
               Not one fruit-sort can you spy?
             Strange!—And I, too, at such trouble,
               Keep them close-nipped on the sly!

VII

             There's a great text in Galatians,[3]
50   Once you trip on it, entails
             Twenty-nine distinct damnations,
             One sure, if another fails:
             If I trip him just a-dying,
               Sure of heaven as sure can be,
55   Spin him round and send him flying
               Off to hell, a Manichee?[4]

---

[2] The Arian heresy (after Arius, 256–336 A.D.) was to deny the doctrine of the Trinity.
[3] See the Bible, Galatians 5:15–23.
[4] A follower of Manes, a third-century Persian philosopher who held that the world was governed by contending principles of light and darkness.

VIII

Or, my scrofulous° French novel   *degenerate*
  On grey paper with blunt type!
Simply glance at it, you grovel
60   Hand and foot in Belial's gripe:°   *the Devil's grip*
If I double down its pages
  At the woeful sixteenth print,
When he gathers his greengages,°   *plums*
  Ope a sieve and slip it in't?

IX

65 Or, there's Satan!—one might venture
  Pledge one's soul to him, yet leave
Such a flaw in the indenture
  As he'd miss till, past retrieve,
Blasted lay that rose-acacia
70   We're so proud of! *Hy, Zy, Hine* . . .
'St, there's Vespers!° *Plena gratiâ*   *evening prayers*
  Ave, Virgo![5] Gr-r-r—you swine!

[1842]

Walt Whitman   *1819–1892*

BEAT! BEAT! DRUMS!

Beat! beat! drums—blow! bugles, blow!
Through the windows—through doors—burst like a ruthless force,
Into the solemn church, and scatter the congregation,
Into the school where the scholar is studying;
5 Leave not the bridegroom quiet—no happiness must he have now with
  his bride,
Nor the peaceful farmer any peace, ploughing his field or gathering his
  grain,
So fierce you whirr and pound you drums—so shrill you bugles blow.

Beat! beat! drums—blow! bugles! blow!
Over the traffic of cities—over the rumble of wheels in the streets;
10 Are beds prepared for sleepers at night in the houses? no sleepers must
  sleep in those beds,
No bargainers' bargains by day—no brokers or speculators—would they
  continue?
Would the talkers be talking? would the singer attempt to sing?
Would the lawyer rise in the court to state his case before the judge?
Then rattle quicker, heavier drums—you bugles wilder blow.

15 Beat! beat! drums!—blow! bugles! blow!
Make no parley—stop for no expostulation,

[5] Hail, Virgin, full of grace.

Mind not the timid—mind not the weeper or prayer,
Mind not the old man beseeching the young man,
Let not the child's voice be heard, nor the mother's entreaties,
20 Make even the trestles to shake the dead where they lie awaiting the
   hearses,
So strong you thump O terrible drums—so loud you bugles blow.

[1867]

WHEN I HEARD THE LEARNED ASTRONOMER

When I heard the learned astronomer,
When the proofs, the figures, were ranged in columns before me,
When I was shown the charts and diagrams, to add, divide,
   and measure them,
When I sitting heard the astronomer where he lectured with much
   applause in the lecture-room,
5 How soon unaccountable I became tired and sick,
Till rising and gliding out I wandered off by myself,
In the mystical moist night-air, and from time to time,
Looked up in perfect silence at the stars.

[1865]

A NOISELESS PATIENT SPIDER

A noiseless patient spider,
I marked where on a little promontory it stood isolated,
Marked how to explore the vacant vast surrounding,
It launched forth filament, filament, filament, out of itself,
5 Ever unreeling them, ever tirelessly speeding them.

And you O my soul where you stand,
Surrounded, detached, in measureless oceans of space,
Ceaselessly musing, venturing, throwing, seeking the spheres to connect
   them,
Till the bridge you will need be formed, till the ductile anchor hold,
10 Till the gossamer thread you fling catch somewhere, O my soul.

[1871]

CAVALRY CROSSING A FORD

A line in long array where they wind betwixt green islands,
They take a serpentine course, their arms flash in the sun—hark to the
   musical clank,
Behold the silvery river; in it the splashing horses loitering stop to drink,
Behold the brown-faced men, each group, each person a picture, the
   negligent rest on the saddles,
5 Some emerge on the opposite bank, others are just entering the ford—
   while,

Scarlet and blue and snowy white,
The guidon flags flutter gayly in the wind.

[1865]

THE DALLIANCE OF THE EAGLES

Skirting the river road, (my forenoon walk, my rest,)
Skyward in air a sudden muffled sound, the dalliance of the eagles,
The rushing amorous contact high in space together,
The clinching interlocking claws, a living, fierce, gyrating wheel,
5   Four beating wings, two beaks, a swirling mass tight grappling,
In tumbling turning clustering loops, straight downward falling,
Till o'er the river pois'd, the twain yet one, a moment's lull,
A motionless still balance in the air, then parting, talons loosing,
Upward again on slow-firm pinions slanting, their separate diverse
      flight,
10 She hers, he his, pursuing.

[1880]

TO A LOCOMOTIVE IN WINTER

Thee for my recitative,
Thee in the driving storm even as now, the snow, the
      winter-day declining,
Thee in thy panoply, thy measur'd dual throbbing and thy
      beat convulsive,
Thy black cylindric body, golden brass and silvery steel,
5   Thy ponderous side-bars, parallel and connecting rods,
      gyrating, shuttling at thy sides,
Thy metrical, now swelling pant and roar, now tapering in
      the distance,
Thy great protruding head-light fix'd in front,
Thy long, pale, floating vapor-pennants, tinged with
      delicate purple,
The dense and murky clouds out-belching from thy
      smoke-stack,
10 Thy knitted frame, thy springs and valves, the tremulous
      twinkle of thy wheels,
Thy train of cars, behind, obedient, merrily following,
Through gale or calm, now swift, now slack, yet steadily
      careering;
Type of the modern—emblem of motion and power—pulse
      of the continent,
For once come serve the Muse and merge in verse, even as
      here I see thee,
15 With storm and buffeting gusts of wind and falling snow,
By day thy warning ringing bell to sound its notes,
By night thy silent signal lamps to swing.

Fierce-throated beauty!
Roll through my chant with all thy lawless music, thy
    swinging lamps at night,
20   Thy madly-whistled laughter, echoing, rumbling like an
    earthquake, rousing all,
Law of thyself complete, thine own track firmly holding,
(No sweetness debonair of tearful harp or glib piano thine,)
Thy trills of shrieks by rocks and hills return'd,
Launch'd o'er the prairies wide, across the lakes,
25   To the free skies unpent° and glad and strong.   *unlimited*

[1876]

Matthew Arnold   *1822–1888*

DOVER BEACH

The sea is calm to-night.
The tide is full, the moon lies fair
Upon the straits;—on the French coast the light
Gleams and is gone; the cliffs of England stand,
5   Glimmering and vast, out in the tranquil bay.
Come to the window, sweet is the night-air!
Only, from the long line of spray
Where the sea meets the moon-blanched sand,
Listen! you hear the grating roar
10   Of pebbles which the waves draw back, and fling,
At their return, up the high strand,°   *shore*
Begin, and cease, and then again begin,
With tremulous cadence slow, and bring
The eternal note of sadness in.

15   Sophocles long ago
Heard it on the Aegæan, and it brought
Into his mind the turbid ebb and flow
Of human misery; we
Find also in the sound a thought,
20   Hearing it by this distant northern sea.

The sea of faith
Was once, too, at the full, and round earth's shore
Lay like the folds of a bright girdle furled.
But now I only hear
25   Its melancholy, long, withdrawing roar,
Retreating, to the breath
Of the night-wind, down the vast edges drear
And naked shingles° of the world.   *gravelly beaches*

Ah, love, let us be true
30   To one another! for the world, which seems

To lie before us like a land of dreams,
So various, so beautiful, so new,
Hath really neither joy, nor love, nor light,
Nor certitude, nor peace, nor help for pain;
35   And we are here as on a darkling° plain   *darkening*
Swept with confused alarms of struggle and flight,
Where ignorant armies clash by night.

[1867]

George Meredith   *1828–1909*

FROM MODERN LOVE[1]

II

It ended, and the morrow brought the task.
Her eyes were guilty gates, that let him in
By shutting all too zealous for their sin:
Each sucked a secret, and each wore a mask.
5   But, oh, the bitter taste her beauty had!
He sickened as at breath of poison-flowers:
A languid humor stole among the hours,
And if their smiles encountered, he went mad,
And raged deep inward, till the light was brown
10   Before his vision, and the world, forgot,
Looked wicked as some old dull murder-spot.
A star with lurid beams, she seemed to crown
The pit of infamy: and then again
He fainted on his vengefulness, and strove
15   To ape the magnanimity of love,
And smote himself, a shuddering heap of pain.

XVI

In our old shipwrecked days there was an hour,
When in the firelight steadily aglow,
Joined slackly, we beheld the red chasm grow
Among the clicking coals. Our library-bower
5   That eve was left to us: and hushed we sat
As lovers to whom Time is whispering.
From sudden-opened doors we heard them sing:
The nodding elders mixed good wine with chat.
Well knew we that Life's greatest treasure lay
10   With us, and of it was our talk. "Ah, yes!
Love dies!" I said: I never thought it less.

[1] This series of fifty sonnet-like poems provides a fictionalized account of the disintegration of Meredith's own marriage. In 1858 his wife, the daughter of the English poet and novelist, Thomas Love Peacock, left him to live with a painter. The first poem in the series (p. 58) describes the poet's initial realization of a problem in his marriage. The four poems given here recount his suffering from this knowledge on the following day (II), his memories of the happier period when their love was young (XVI), his reflections by the sea on the death of love (XLIII), and his final analysis of the flaws in his marriage (L).

She yearned to me that sentence to unsay.
Then when the fire domed blackening, I found
Her cheek was salt against my kiss, and swift
15 Up the sharp scale of sobs her breast did lift:—
Now am I haunted by that taste! that sound!

XLIII

Mark where the pressing wind shoots javelin-like
Its skeleton shadow on broad-backed wave!
Here is a fitting spot to dig Love's grave;
Here where the ponderous breakers plunge and strike,
5 And dart their hissing tongues high up the sand:
In hearing of the ocean, and in sight
Of those ribbed wind-streaks running into white.
If I the death of Love had deeply planned,
I never could have made it half so sure,
10 As by the unblest kisses which upbraid
The full-waked sense; or failing that, degrade!
'Tis morning: but no morning can restore
What we have forfeited. I see no sin:
The wrong is mixed. In tragic life, God wot,
15 No villain need be! Passions spin the plot:
We are betrayed by what is false within.

L

Thus piteously Love closed what he begat:
The union of this ever-diverse pair!
These two were rapid falcons in a snare,
Condemned to do the flitting of the bat.
5 Lovers beneath the singing sky of May,
They wandered once; clear as the dew on flowers:
But they fed not on the advancing hours:
Their hearts held cravings for the buried day.
Then each applied to each that fatal knife,
10 Deep questioning, which probes to endless dole.
Ah, what a dusty answer gets the soul
When hot for certainties in this our life!—
In tragic hints here see what evermore
Moves dark as yonder midnight ocean's force,
15 Thundering like ramping hosts of warrior horse,
To throw that faint thin line upon the shore!

[1862]

Emily Dickinson *1830–1886*

"SUCCESS IS COUNTED SWEETEST"

Success is counted sweetest
By those who ne'er succeed.

To comprehend a nectar
Requires sorest need.

5 Not one of all the purple Host
Who took the Flag today
Can tell the definition
So clear of Victory

As he defeated—dying—
10 On whose forbidden ear
The distant strains of triumph
Burst agonized and clear!
[1878]

"THE SOUL SELECTS HER OWN SOCIETY"

The Soul selects her own Society—
Then—shuts the Door—
To her divine Majority—
Present no more—

5 Unmoved—she notes the Chariots—pausing—
At her low Gate—
Unmoved—an Emperor be kneeling
Upon her Mat—

I've known her—from an ample nation—
10 Choose One—
Then—close the Valves of her attention—
Like Stone—

[posthumous, 1890]

"A BIRD CAME DOWN THE WALK"

A Bird came down the Walk—
He did not know I saw—
He bit an Angleworm in halves
And ate the fellow, raw,

5 And then he drank a Dew
From a convenient Grass—
And then hopped sidewise to the Wall
To let a Beetle pass—

He glanced with rapid eyes
10 That hurried all around—
They looked like frightened Beads, I thought—
He stirred his Velvet Head

Like one in danger, Cautious,
I offered him a Crumb
And he unrolled his feathers
And rowed him softer home—

Than Oars divide the Ocean,
Too silver for a seam—
Or Butterflies, off Banks of Noon
Leap, plashless as they swim.
[posthumous, 1891]

"AFTER GREAT PAIN, A FORMAL FEELING COMES"

After great pain, a formal feeling comes—
The Nerves sit ceremonious, like Tombs—
The stiff Heart questions was it He, that bore,
And Yesterday, or Centuries before?

The Feet, mechanical, go round—
Of Ground, or Air, or Ought—
A Wooden way
Regardless grown,
A Quartz contentment, like a stone—

This is the Hour of Lead—
Remembered, if outlived,
As Freezing persons, recollect the Snow—
First—Chill—then Stupor—then the letting go—
[posthumous, 1929]

"I HEARD A FLY BUZZ—WHEN I DIED"

I heard a Fly buzz—when I died—
The Stillness in the Room
Was like the Stillness in the Air—
Between the Heaves of Storm—

The Eyes around—had wrung them dry—
And Breaths were gathering firm
For that last Onset—when the King
Be witnessed—in the Room—

I willed my Keepsakes—Signed away
What portion of me be
Assignable—and then it was
There interposed a Fly—

With Blue—uncertain stumbling Buzz—
Between the light—and me—

15 And then the Windows failed—and then
I could not see to see—
[posthumous, 1896]

"I LIKE TO SEE IT LAP THE MILES"

I like to see it lap the Miles—
And lick the Valleys up—
And stop to feed itself at Tanks—
And then—prodigious step

5 Around a Pile of Mountains—
And supercilious peer
In Shanties—by the sides of Roads—
And then a Quarry pare

To fit its Ribs
10 And crawl between
Complaining all the while
In horrid—hooting stanza—
Then chase itself down Hill—

And neigh like Boanerges[1]—
15 Then—punctual as a Star
Stop—docile and omnipotent
At its own stable door—
[posthumous, 1891]

"BECAUSE I COULD NOT STOP FOR DEATH"

Because I could not stop for Death—
He kindly stopped for me—
The Carriage held but just Ourselves—
And Immortality.

5 We slowly drove—He knew no haste
And I had put away
My labor and my leisure too,
For His Civility—

We passed the School, where Children strove
10 At Recess—in the Ring—
We passed the Fields of Gazing Grain—
We passed the Setting Sun—

[1] A loud preacher or orator, from two Hebrew words meaning "sons of thunder."

Or rather—He passed Us—
The Dews drew quivering and chill—
15   For only Gossamer, my Gown—
My Tippet° —only Tulle° —   *shawl / silk gauze*

We paused before a House that seemed
A Swelling of the Ground—
The Roof was scarcely visible—
20   The Cornice—in the Ground—

Since then—'tis Centuries—and yet
Feels shorter than the Day
I first surmised the Horses' Heads
Were toward Eternity—

               [posthumous, 1890]

"A NARROW FELLOW IN THE GRASS"

A narrow Fellow in the Grass
Occasionally rides—
You may have met Him—did you not
His notice sudden is—

5   The Grass divides as with a Comb—
A spotted shaft is seen—
And then it closes at your feet
And opens further on—

He likes a Boggy Acre
10   A Floor too cool for Corn—
Yet when a Boy, a Barefoot—
I more than once at Noon

Have passed, I thought, a Whip lash
Unbraiding in the Sun
15   When stooping to secure it
It wrinkled, and was gone—

Several of Nature's People
I know, and they know me—
I feel for them a transport
20   Of cordiality—

But never met this Fellow
Attended, or alone
Without a tighter breathing
And Zero at the Bone—

              [1866]

Christina Rossetti   *1830–1894*

IN AN ARTIST'S STUDIO

One face looks out from all his canvases,
   One selfsame figure sits or walks or leans:
   We found her hidden just behind those screens,
That mirror gave back all her loveliness.
5 A queen in opal or in ruby dress,
   A nameless girl in freshest summer-greens,
   A saint, an angel—every canvas means
The same one meaning, neither more nor less.
He feeds upon her face by day and night,
10 And she with true kind eyes looks back on him,
Fair as the moon and joyful as the light:
   Not wan with waiting, not with sorrow dim;
Not as she is, but was when hope shone bright;
   Not as she is, but as she fills his dream.

                                         [1861]

A BIRTHDAY

My heart is like a singing bird
   Whose nest is in a watered shoot:
My heart is like an apple-tree
   Whose boughs are bent with thickset fruit;
5 My heart is like a rainbow shell
   That paddles in a halcyon° sea;   *calm*
My heart is gladder than all these
   Because my love is come to me.

Raise me a dais° of silk and down;   *throne*
10 Hang it with vair° and purple dyes;   *fur*
Carve it in doves and pomegranates,
   And peacocks with a hundred eyes;
Work it in gold and silver grapes,
   In leaves and silver fleurs-de-lys;°   *lily-shaped emblems*
15 Because the birthday of my life
   Is come, my love is come to me.

                                   [1862]

Algernon Charles Swinburne   *1837–1909*

THE ROUNDEL

A roundel is wrought as a ring or a starbright sphere,
With craft of delight and with cunning of sound unsought,

That the heart of the hearer may smile if to pleasure his ear
    A roundel is wrought.

5   Its jewel of music is carven of all or of aught,—
Love, laughter, or mourning,—remembrance of rapture or fear,—
That fancy may fashion to hang in the ear of thought.

As a bird's quick song runs round, and the hearts in us hear
Pause answer to pause, and again the same strain caught,—
10   So moves the device whence, round as a pearl or tear,
    A roundel is wrought.

                        [1883]

THE SUNBOWS[1]

Spray of song that springs in April, light of love that laughs through
   May,
Live and die and live for ever: nought of all things far less fair
Keeps a surer life than these that seem to pass like fire away.
In the souls they live which are but all the brighter that they were;
5   In the hearts that kindle, thinking what delight of old was there.
Wind that shapes and lifts and shifts them bids perpetual memory play
Over dreams, and in and out of deeds and thoughts, which seem to wear
Light that leaps and runs and revels through the springing flames of
   spray.

Dawn is wild upon the waters where we drink of dawn today:
10 Wide, from wave to wave rekindling in rebound through radiant air,
Flash the fires unwoven, and woven again, of wind that works in play,—
Working wonders more than heart may note, or sight may wellnigh dare,
Wefts[2] of rarer light than colors rain from heaven, though this be rare.
Arch on arch unbuilt in building, reared and ruined ray by ray,
15 Breaks and brightens, laughs and lessens,—even till eyes may hardly bear
Light that leaps and runs and revels through the springing flames of
   spray.

Year on year sheds light and music, rolled and flashed from bay to bay
Round the summer capes of time and winter headlands keen and bare,
Whence the soul keeps watch, and bids her vassal memory watch and
   pray,
20 If perchance the dawn may quicken,[3] or perchance the midnight spare.
Silence quells not music, darkness takes not sunlight in her snare:
Shall not joys endure that perish? Yea, saith dawn, though night say nay:
Life on life goes out; but very life enkindles everywhere
Light that leaps and runs and revels through the springing flames of
   spray.

---

[1] Rainbows from sea spray.   [2] Woven substances.   [3] Come to life.

25 Friend, were life no more than this is, well would yet the living fare.
    All aflower and all afire and all flung heavenward, who shall say
    Such a flash of life were worthless? This is worth a world of care,—
    Light that leaps and runs and revels through the springing flames of
      spray.

[1884]

❧ MODERN POETRY ❧

Thomas Hardy   *1840–1928*

HAP

If but some vengeful god would call to me
From up the sky, and laugh: "Thou suffering thing,
Know that thy sorrow is my ecstasy,
That thy love's loss is my hate's profiting!"

5 Then would I bear it, clench myself, and die,
Steeled by the sense of ire unmerited;
Half-eased in that a Powerfuller than I
Had willed and meted me the tears I shed.

But not so. How arrives it joy lies slain,
10 And why unblooms the best hope ever sown?
—Crass Casualty obstructs the sun and rain,
And dicing Time for gladness casts a moan. . . .
These purblind Doomsters had as readily strown
Blisses about my pilgrimage as pain.

[1898]

NEUTRAL TONES

We stood by a pond that winter day,
And the sun was white, as though chidden of God,
And a few leaves lay on the starving sod;
    —They had fallen from an ash, and were gray.

5 Your eyes on me were as eyes that rove
Over tedious riddles of years ago;
And some words played between us to and fro
    On which lost the more by our love.

The smile on your mouth was the deadest thing
10 Alive enough to have strength to die;
And a grin of bitterness swept thereby
    Like an ominous bird a-wing. . . .

Since then, keen lessons that love deceives,
And wrings with wrong, have shaped to me
15 Your face, and the God-curst sun, and a tree,
    And a pond edged with grayish leaves.

[1898]

THE DARKLING[1] THRUSH

I leant upon a coppice gate[2]
    When Frost was spectre-gray,
And Winter's dregs made desolate
    The weakening eye of day.
The tangled bine-stems[3] scored the sky
    Like strings of broken lyres,
And all mankind that haunted nigh
    Had sought their household fires.

The land's sharp features seemed to be
    The Century's corpse[4] outleant,
His crypt the cloudy canopy,
    The wind his death-lament.
The ancient pulse of germ and birth
    Was shrunken hard and dry,
And every spirit upon earth
    Seemed fervorless as I.

At once a voice arose among
    The bleak twigs overhead
In a full-hearted evensong
    Of joy illimited;
An aged thrush, frail, gaunt, and small,
    In blast-beruffled plume,
Had chosen thus to fling his soul
    Upon the growing gloom.

So little cause for carolings
    Of such ecstatic sound
Was written on terrestrial things
    Afar or nigh around,
That I could think there trembled through
    His happy good-night air
Some blessed Hope, whereof he knew
    And I was unaware.

[1902]

THE CONVERGENCE OF THE TWAIN

(*Lines on the loss of the 'Titanic'*[1])

I

In a solitude of the sea
Deep from human vanity,
And the Pride of Life that planned her, stilly couches she.

---

[1] In the dark.   [2] The gate to a small thicket.   [3] Twining stems of shrubbery.
[4] The poem was composed on December 31, 1900.
[1] The "unsinkable" luxury liner that sank with enormous loss of life after striking an iceberg on
  April 15, 1912.

II

5 Steel chambers, late the pyres
Of her salamandrine[2] fires,
Cold currents thrid,° and turn to rhythmic tidal lyres.   *thread*

III

Over the mirrors meant
To glass the opulent
The sea-worm crawls—grotesque, slimed, dumb, indifferent.

IV

10 Jewels in joy designed
To ravish the sensuous mind
Lie lightless, all their sparkles bleared and black and blind.

V

Dim moon-eyed fishes near
Gaze at the gilded gear
15 And query: "What does this vaingloriousness down here?" . . .

VI

Well: while was fashioning
This creature of cleaving wing,
The Immanent Will that stirs and urges everything

VII

Prepared a sinister mate
20 For her—so gaily great—
A Shape of Ice, for the time far and dissociate.

VIII

And as the smart ship grew
In stature, grace, and hue,
In shadowy silent distance grew the Iceberg too.

IX

25 Alien they seemed to be:
No mortal eye could see
The intimate welding of their later history,

X

Or sign that they were bent
By paths coincident
30 On being anon twin halves of one august event,

---

[2] An allusion to mythological reptiles supposed to be able to live in fire or, possibly, an allusion to the elemental spirit living in fire in the natural philosophy of Paracelsus (c. 1493–1541).

XI

Till the Spinner of the Years
Said "Now!" And each one hears,
And consummation comes, and jars two hemispheres.

[1912]

CHANNEL FIRING[1]

That night your great guns, unawares,
Shook all our coffins as we lay,
And broke the chancel[2] window-squares,
We thought it was the Judgment-day

5   And sat upright. While drearisome
Arose the howl of wakened hounds:
The mouse let fall the altar-crumb,
The worms drew back into the mounds,

The glebe cow[3] drooled. Till God called, "No;
10   It's gunnery practice out at sea
Just as before you went below;
The world is as it used to be:

"All nations striving strong to make
Red war yet redder. Mad as hatters
15   They do no more for Christès sake
Than you who are helpless in such matters.

"That this is not the judgment-hour
For some of them's a blessed thing,
For if it were they'd have to scour
20   Hell's floor for so much threatening. . . .

"Ha, ha. It will be warmer when
I blow the trumpet (if indeed
I ever do; for you are men,
And rest eternal sorely need)."

25   So down we lay again. "I wonder,
Will the world ever saner be,"
Said one, "than when He sent us under
In our indifferent century!"

And many a skeleton shook his head.
30   "Instead of preaching forty year,"
My neighbour Parson Thirdly said,
"I wish I had stuck to pipes and beer."

[1] The title refers to gunnery practice in the English Channel shortly before the commencement
of World War I.
[2] The part of a church around the altar.   [3] The cow of the parsonage.

Again the guns disturbed the hour,
Roaring their readiness to avenge,
35   As far inland as Stourton Tower,[4]
And Camelot, and starlit Stonehenge.

[1914]

Gerard Manley Hopkins   *1844–1889*

GOD'S GRANDEUR

The world is charged with the grandeur of God.
  It will flame out, like shining from shook foil;°   *gold foil*
  It gathers to a greatness, like the ooze of oil
Crushed. Why do men then now not reck° his rod?   *take heed of*
5   Generations have trod, have trod, have trod;
  And all is seared with trade; bleared, smeared with toil;
  And wears man's smudge and shares man's smell: the soil
Is bare now, nor can foot feel, being shod.

And for all this, nature is never spent;
10   There lives the dearest freshness deep down things;
And though the last lights off the black West went
  Oh, morning, at the brown brink eastward, springs—
Because the Holy Ghost over the bent
  World broods with warm breast and with ah! bright
    wings.

[posthumous, 1918]

HEAVEN—HAVEN

A Nun Takes the Veil

I have desired to go
  Where springs not fail,
To fields where flies no sharp and sided hail
  And a few lilies blow.

5   And I have asked to be
  Where no storms come,
Where the green swell is in the havens dumb,
  And out of the swing of the sea.

[posthumous, 1918]

---

[4] Stourton Tower commemorates King Alfred's victory over the invading Danes in 879. Camelot was the location of King Arthur's court (supposedly in the sixth century A.D.). The massive stones at Stonehenge were used in the mysterious Druidic rites of prehistoric England.

PIED BEAUTY

Glory be to God for dappled things—
   For skies of couple-color as a brinded° cow;   *spotted*
      For rose-moles all in stipple° upon trout that swim;   *dots*
Fresh-firecoal chestnut-falls; finches' wings;
5   Landscape plotted and pieced—fold, fallow, and plough;
      And áll trádes, their gear and tackle and trim.°   *equipment*

All things counter, original, spare, strange;
   Whatever is fickle, freckled (who knows how?)
     With swift, slow; sweet, sour; adazzle, dim;
10 He fathers-forth whose beauty is past change:
                      Praise him.
                   [posthumous, 1918]

THE WINDHOVER:[1]

To Christ our Lord

I caught this morning morning's minion,° kingdom of   *favorite*
   daylight's dauphin,° dapple° -dawn-drawn Falcon, in   *heir / mottled*
     his riding
Of the rolling level underneath him steady air, and
     striding
High there, how he rung° upon the rein of a wimpling° *circled / rippling*
     wing
5 In his ecstasy! then off, off forth on swing,
   As a skate's heel sweeps smooth on a bow-bend: the
     hurl and gliding
   Rebuffed the big wind. My heart in hiding
Stirred for a bird,—the achieve of, the mastery of the
     thing!

Brute beauty and valor and act, oh, air, pride, plume, here
10   Buckle! AND the fire that breaks from thee then, a billion
Times told lovelier, more dangerous, O my chevalier!

No wonder of it: shéer plód makes plough down sillion[2]
Shine, and blue-bleak embers, ah my dear,
   Fall, gall° themselves, and gash gold-vermilion.   *chafe*
                  [posthumous, 1918]

---

[1] The sparrowhawk, which seems to hover in a headwind.
[2] An archaic word meaning "a ridge between furrows."

SPRING AND FALL:

To a Young Child

Márgarét, áre you gríeving
Over Goldengrove unleaving?
Leáves, líke the things of man, you
With your fresh thoughts care for, can you?
5   Áh! ás the heart grows older
It will come to such sights colder
By and by, nor spare a sigh
Though worlds of wanwood leafmeal[1] lie;
And yet you *will* weep and know why.
10   Now no matter, child, the name:
Sórrow's spríngs áre the same.
Nor mouth had, no nor mind, expressed
What heart heard of, ghost° guessed: *spirit*
It ís the blight man was born for,
15   It is Margaret you mourn for.
[posthumous, 1918]

A. E. Housman   *1859–1936*

"WHEN I WAS ONE-AND-TWENTY"

When I was one-and-twenty
  I heard a wise man say,
"Give crowns and pounds and guineas
  But not your heart away;
5   Give pearls away and rubies
  But keep your fancy free."
But I was one-and-twenty,
  No use to talk to me.

When I was one-and-twenty
10   I heard him say again,
"The heart out of the bosom
  Was never given in vain;
'Tis paid with sighs a plenty
  And sold for endless rue."
15   And I am two-and-twenty,
  And oh, 'tis true, 'tis true.

[1896]

---

[1] Hopkins has created the words *wanwood* and *leafmeal*. *Leafmeal* is probably a noun meaning "a mulch of leaves." *Wanwood* would then be an adjective meaning "dark-woods."

"WITH RUE MY HEART IS LADEN"

With rue my heart is laden
   For golden friends I had,
For many a rose-lipt maiden
   And many a lightfoot lad.

5   By brooks too broad for leaping
   The lightfoot boys are laid;
The rose-lipt girls are sleeping
   In fields where roses fade.

                    [1896]

TO AN ATHLETE DYING YOUNG

The time you won your town the race
We chaired you through the market-place;
Man and boy stood cheering by,
And home we brought you shoulder-high.

5   Today, the road all runners come,
Shoulder-high we bring you home,
And set you at your threshold down,
Townsman of a stiller town.

Smart lad, to slip betimes away
10   From fields where glory does not stay
And early though the laurel grows
It withers quicker than the rose.

Eyes the shady night has shut
Cannot see the record cut,
15   And silence sounds no worse than cheers
After earth has stopped the ears:

Now you will not swell the rout
Of lads that wore their honors out,
Runners whom renown outran
20   And the name died before the man.

So set, before its echoes fade,
The fleet foot on the sill of shade,
And hold to the low lintel up
The still-defended challenge-cup.

25   And round that early-laurelled head
Will flock to gaze the strengthless dead,
And find unwithered on its curls
The garland briefer than a girl's.

                    [1896]

"TERENCE, THIS IS STUPID STUFF"

"Terence, this[1] is stupid stuff:
You eat your victuals fast enough;
There can't be much amiss, 'tis clear,
To see the rate you drink your beer.
5   But oh, good Lord, the verse you make,
It gives a chap the belly-ache.
The cow, the old cow, she is dead;
It sleeps well, the hornèd head:
We poor lads, 'tis our turn now
10   To hear such tunes as killed the cow.
Pretty friendship 'tis to rhyme
Your friends to death before their time
Moping melancholy mad:
Come, pipe a tune to dance to, lad."

15   Why, if 'tis dancing you would be,
There's brisker pipes than poetry.
Say, for what were hop-yards meant,
Or why was Burton built on Trent?[2]
Oh many a peer of England brews
20   Livelier liquor than the Muse,
And malt does more than Milton can
To justify God's ways to man.[3]
Ale, man, ale's the stuff to drink
For fellows whom it hurts to think:
25   Look into the pewter pot
To see the world as the world's not.
And faith, 'tis pleasant till 'tis past:
The mischief is that 'twill not last.
Oh I have been to Ludlow[4] fair
30   And left my necktie God knows where,
And carried halfway home, or near,
Pints and quarts of Ludlow beer:
Then the world seemed none so bad,
And I myself a sterling lad;
35   And down in lovely muck I've lain,
Happy till I woke again.
Then I saw the morning sky:
Heigho, the tale was all a lie;
The world, it was the old world yet,
40   I was I, my things were wet,
And nothing now remained to do
But begin the game anew.

---

[1] This poetry.   [2] Burton-on-Trent is an English city famous for its breweries.
[3] An allusion to the opening of Milton's *Paradise Lost* (1667).
[4] A town in Shropshire.

Therefore, since the world has still
Much good, but much less good than ill,
And while the sun and moon endure
Luck's a chance, but trouble's sure,
I'd face it as a wise man would,
And train for ill and not for good.
'Tis true, the stuff I bring for sale
Is not so brisk a brew as ale:
Out of a stem that scored[5] the hand
I wrung it in a weary land.
But take it: if the smack is sour,
The better for the embittered hour;
It should do good to heart and head
When your soul is in my soul's stead;
And I will friend you, if I may,
In the dark and cloudy day.

There was a king reigned in the East:
There, when kings will sit to feast,
They get their fill before they think
With poisoned meat and poisoned drink.
He gathered all that springs to birth
From the many-venomed earth;
First a little, thence to more,
He sampled all her killing store;
And easy, smiling, seasoned sound,
Sate the king when healths went round.
They put arsenic in his meat
And stared aghast to watch him eat;
They poured strychnine in his cup
And shook to see him drink it up:
They shook, they stared as white's their shirt:
Them it was their poison hurt.
—I tell the tale that I heard told.
Mithridates,[6] he died old.

[1896]

"ON WENLOCK EDGE"

On Wenlock Edge[1] the wood's in trouble;
His forest fleece the Wrekin[2] heaves;
The gale, it plies the saplings double,
And thick on Severn[3] snow the leaves.

---

[5] Cut.
[6] In his *Natural History* the Roman writer Pliny (23–79 A.D.) tells this story of Mithridates VI,
King of Pontus (ca. 133 B.C.–63 B.C.).
[1] Ridge.   [2] Wrekin Hill.   [3] The Severn River.

5 'Twould blow like this through holt and hanger[4]
   When Uricon[5] the city stood:
'Tis the old wind in the old anger,
   But then it threshed another wood.

Then, 'twas before my time, the Roman
10   At yonder heaving hill would stare:
The blood that warms an English yeoman,
   The thoughts that hurt him, they were there.

There, like the wind through woods in riot,
   Through him the gale of life blew high;
15 The tree of man was never quiet:
   Then 'twas the Roman, now 'tis I.

The gale, it plies the saplings double,
   It blows so hard, 'twill soon be gone:
Today the Roman and his trouble
20   Are ashes under Uricon.

                                          [1896]

"LOVELIEST OF TREES"

Loveliest of trees, the cherry now
Is hung with bloom along the bough,
And stands about the woodland ride
Wearing white for Eastertide.

5 Now, of my threescore years and ten,
Twenty will not come again,
And take from seventy springs a score,
It only leaves me fifty more.

And since to look at things in bloom
10 Fifty springs are little room,
About the woodlands I will go
To see the cherry hung with snow.
                                          [1896]

EIGHT O'CLOCK

He stood, and heard the steeple
   Sprinkle the quarters on the morning town.
One, two, three, four, to market-place and people
   It tossed them down.

---

[4] Woods and shed.   [5] A Roman city once located near Shrewsbury, England.

5   Strapped, noosed, nighing his hour,
         He stood and counted them and cursed his luck;
     And then the clock collected in the tower
         Its strength, and struck.

                                                      [1922]

Rudyard Kipling   *1865–1936*

MANDALAY[1]

By the old Moulmein Pagoda, lookin' lazy at the sea,
There's a Burma girl a-settin', and I know she thinks o' me;
For the wind is in the palm-trees, and the temple-bells they
    say:
"Come you back, you British soldier; come you back to
    Mandalay!"
5   Come you back to Mandalay,
             Where the old Flotilla lay:
             Can't you 'ear their paddles chunkin' from Rangoon[2] to
                 Mandalay?
             On the road to Mandalay,
             Where the flyin'-fishes play,
10   An' the dawn comes up like thunder outer China
                 'crost the Bay!

'Er petticoat was yaller an' 'er little cap was green,
An' 'er name was Supi-yaw-lat—jes' the same as Theebaw's[3]
    Queen,
An' I seed her first a-smokin' of a whackin' white cheroot,°   *cigar*
An' a-wastin' Christian kisses on an 'eathen idol's foot:
15   Bloomin' idol made o' mud—
             Wot they called the Great Gawd Budd—
             Plucky lot she cared for idols when I kissed 'er
                 where she stud!
             On the road to Mandalay . . .

When the mist was on the rice-fields an' the sun was
    droppin' slow,
20   She'd git 'er little banjo an' she'd sing *"Kulla-lo-lo!"*
With 'er arm upon my shoulder an' 'er cheek again my cheek
We useter watch the steamers an' the *hathis*° pilin' teak.   *elephants*
             Elephints a-pilin' teak
             In the sludgy, squdgy creek,
25   Where the silence 'ung that 'eavy you was 'arf afraid to
                 speak!
             On the road to Mandalay . . .

[1] A city in Burma.   [2] The capital of Burma.
[3] Theebaw was king of Upper Burma from 1878 to 1885.

But that's all shove be'ind me—long ago an' fur away,
An' there ain't no 'buses runnin' from the Bank to Mandalay;
An' I'm learnin' 'ere in London what the ten-year soldier
  tells:

30 "If you've 'eard the East a-callin', you won't never 'eed
  naught else."
          No! you won't 'eed nothin' else
          But them spicy garlic smells,
          An' the sunshine an' the palm-trees an' the tinkly
            temple-bells;
          On the road to Mandalay . . .

35 I am sick o' wastin' leather on these gritty pavin'-stones,
An' the blasted English drizzle wakes the fever in my bones;
Tho' I walks with fifty 'ousemaids outer Chelsea to the
  Strand,
An' they talks a lot o' lovin', but wot do they understand?
          Beefy face an' grubby 'and—
40   Law! wot do they understand?
          I've a neater, sweeter maiden in a cleaner, greener
            land!
          On the road to Mandalay . . .

Ship me somewheres east of Suez, where the best is like the
            worst,
Where there aren't no Ten Commandments an' a man can
  raise a thirst;
45 For the temple-bells are callin', an' it's there that I would
  be—
By the old Moulmein Pagoda, looking lazy at the sea;
          On the road to Mandalay,
          Where the old Flotilla lay,
          With our sick beneath the awnings when we went to
            Mandalay!
50   O the road to Mandalay,
          Where the flyin'-fishes play,
          An' the dawn comes up like thunder outer China
            'crost the Bay!

                                        [1890]

William Butler Yeats   *1865–1939*

THE LAKE ISLE OF INNISFREE

I will arise and go now, and go to Innisfree,
And a small cabin build there, of clay and wattles° made: *woven limbs*
Nine bean-rows will I have there, a hive for the honeybee,
And live alone in the bee-loud glade.

5 And I shall have some peace there, for peace comes
        dropping slow,
    Dropping from the veils of the morning to where the cricket
        sings;
    There midnight's all a glimmer, and noon a purple glow,
    And evening full of the linnet's° wings.   *a songbird*

    I will arise and go now, for always night and day
10 I hear lake water lapping with low sounds by the shore;
    While I stand on the roadway, or on the pavements grey,
    I hear it in the deep heart's core.

                                                           [1892]

THE WILD SWANS AT COOLE[1]

    The trees are in their autumn beauty,
    The woodland paths are dry,
    Under the October twilight the water
    Mirrors a still sky;
5   Upon the brimming water among the stones
    Are nine-and-fifty swans.

    The nineteenth autumn has come upon me
    Since I first made my count;
    I saw, before I had well finished,
10 All suddenly mount
    And scatter wheeling in great broken rings
    Upon their clamorous wings.

    I have looked upon those brilliant creatures,
    And now my heart is sore.
15 All's changed since I, hearing at twilight,
    The first time on this shore,
    The bell-beat of their wings above my head,
    Trod with a lighter tread.

    Unwearied still, lover by lover,
20 They paddle in the cold
    Companionable streams or climb the air;
    Their hearts have not grown old;
    Passion or conquest, wander where they will,
    Attend upon them still.

    But now they drift on the still water,
25 Mysterious, beautiful;
    Among what rushes will they build,

---

[1] Between 1897 and 1916 (when this poem was written), Yeats had often been a guest at Coole Park, his friend Lady Gregory's country estate.

By what lake's edge or pool
Delight men's eyes when I awake some day
30   To find they have flown away?

[1917]

THE SECOND COMING[1]

Turning and turning in the widening gyre[2]
The falcon cannot hear the falconer;
Things fall apart; the center cannot hold;
Mere anarchy is loosed upon the world,
5   The blood-dimmed tide is loosed, and everywhere
The ceremony of innocence is drowned;
The best lack all conviction, while the worst
Are full of passionate intensity.

Surely some revelation is at hand;
10   Surely the Second Coming is at hand.
The Second Coming! Hardly are those words out
When a vast image out of *Spiritus Mundi*[3]
Troubles my sight: somewhere in sands of the desert
A shape with lion body and the head of a man,[4]
15   A gaze blank and pitiless as the sun,
Is moving its slow thighs, while all about it
Reel shadows of the indignant desert birds.
The darkness drops again; but now I know
That twenty centuries of stony sleep
20   Were vexed to nightmare by a rocking cradle,[5]
And what rough beast, its hour come round at last,
Slouches toward Bethlehem to be born?

[1921]

LEDA AND THE SWAN[1]

A sudden blow: the great wings beating still
Above the staggering girl, her thighs caressed
By the dark webs, her nape caught in his bill,
He holds her helpless breast upon his breast.

[1] The title alludes to the Second Coming of Christ predicted in Matthew 24, but also symbolizes
the end of one age and the commencement of another.
[2] The widening spiral flown by the falcon takes it so far out that it no longer hears its master.
Yeats uses the gyre or spiral as a symbol of extension and dissolution in the cycle of our civilization.
[3] The spirit of the world, a form of universal subconscious serving as a storehouse of images.
[4] A Sphinx-like creature.
[5] Yeats's idea is, perhaps, that the rocking of Christ's cradle produced, after twenty centuries, the
awakening Sphinx.
[1] In Greek mythology Leda was raped by Zeus in the form of a swan; she subsequently gave
birth to Helen, who caused the destruction of Troy, and Clytemnestra, who murdered her husband
Agamemnon upon his return from Troy.

5 How can those terrified vague fingers push
The feathered glory from her loosening thighs?
And how can body, laid in that white rush,
But feel the strange heart beating where it lies?

A shudder in the loins engenders there
10 The broken wall, the burning roof and tower
And Agamemnon dead.
                                Being so caught up,
So mastered by the brute blood of the air,
Did she put on his knowledge with his power
Before the indifferent beak could let her drop?

[1924]

SAILING TO BYZANTIUM

I

That is no country for old men. The young
In one another's arms, birds in the trees
—Those dying generations—at their song,
The salmon-falls, the mackerel-crowded seas,
5 Fish, flesh, or fowl, commend all summer long
Whatever is begotten, born, and dies.
Caught in that sensual music all neglect
Monuments of unageing intellect.

II

An aged man is but a paltry thing,
10 A tattered coat upon a stick, unless
Soul clap its hands and sing, and louder sing
For every tatter in its mortal dress,
Nor is there singing school but studying
Monuments of its own magnificence;
15 And therefore I have sailed the seas and come
To the holy city of Byzantium.[1]

III

O sages standing in God's holy fire
As in the gold mosaic of a wall,
Come from the holy fire, perne in a gyre,[2]
20 And be the singing-masters of my soul.

[1] Yeats contrasts the sensuality and mortality of the modern world with the permanence and artifice found in medieval Byzantium (the site of modern Istanbul, Turkey). In *A Vision* (1937) he wrote: "I think that in early Byzantium, maybe never before or since in recorded history, religious, aesthetic and practical life were one, that architect and artificer . . . spoke to the multitude and the few alike. The painter, the mosaic worker, the worker in gold and silver, the illuminator of sacred books, were almost impersonal, almost perhaps without the consciousness of individual design, absorbed in their subject-matter and that the vision of a whole people."
[2] Spiral down.

Consume my heart away; sick with desire
And fastened to a dying animal
It knows not what it is; and gather me
Into the artifice of eternity.

IV

25 Once out of nature I shall never take
My bodily form from any natural thing,
But such a form as Grecian goldsmiths make
Of hammered gold and gold enamelling
To keep a drowsy Emperor awake;
30 Or set upon a golden bough to sing
To lords and ladies of Byzantium
Of what is past, or passing, or to come.

[1927]

Ernest Dowson   *1867–1900*

VITAE SUMMA BREVIS SPEM NOS VETAT INCOHARE LONGAM[1]

They are not long, the weeping and the laughter,
    Love and desire and hate:
I think they have no portion in us after
    We pass the gate.

5 They are not long, the days of wine and roses:
    Out of a misty dream
Our path emerges for a while, then closes
    Within a dream.

[1896]

NON SUM QUALIS ERAM BONAE SUB REGNO CYNARAE[2]

Last night, ah, yesternight, betwixt her lips and mine
There fell thy shadow, Cynara! thy breath was shed
Upon my soul between the kisses and the wine;
And I was desolate and sick of an old passion,
5   Yea, I was desolate and bowed my head:
I have been faithful to thee, Cynara! in my fashion.

---

[1] A line by the Roman poet Horace (65–8 B.C.) meaning, "The brevity of life prevents us from entertaining far-reaching expectations."
[2] A line by the Roman poet Horace (65–8 B.C.) meaning, "I am not as I was under the reign of kind Cynara."

All night upon mine heart I felt her warm heart beat,
Night-long within mine arms in love and sleep she lay;
Surely the kisses of her bought red mouth were sweet;
10   But I was desolate and sick of an old passion,
    When I awoke and found the dawn was gray:
I have been faithful to thee, Cynara! in my fashion.

I have forgot much, Cynara! gone with the wind,
Flung roses, roses riotously with the throng,
15   Dancing, to put thy pale, lost lilies out of mind;
But I was desolate and sick of an old passion,
    Yea, all the time, because the dance was long:
I have been faithful to thee, Cynara! in my fashion.

I cried for madder music and for stronger wine,
20   But when the feast is finished and the lamps expire,
Then falls thy shadow, Cynara! the night is thine;
And I am desolate and sick of an old passion,
    Yea hungry for the lips of my desire:
I have been faithful to thee, Cynara! in my fashion.

[1896]

Edwin Arlington Robinson   *1869–1935*

REUBEN BRIGHT

Because he was a butcher and thereby
Did earn an honest living (and did right),
I would not have you think that Reuben Bright
Was any more a brute than you or I;
5   For when they told him that his wife must die,
He stared at them, and shook with grief and fright,
And cried like a great baby half that night,
And made the women cry to see him cry.

And after she was dead, and he had paid
10   The singers and the sexton and the rest,
He packed a lot of things that she had made
Most mournfully away in an old chest
Of hers, and put some chopped-up cedar boughs
In with them, and tore down the slaughter-house.

[1897]

MR. FLOOD'S PARTY

Old Eben Flood, climbing alone one night
Over the hill between the town below
And the forsaken upland hermitage

That held as much as he should ever know
On earth again of home, paused warily.
The road was his with not a native near;
And Eben, having leisure, said aloud,
For no man else in Tillbury Town to hear:

"Well, Mr. Flood, we have the harvest moon
Again, and we may not have many more;
The bird is on the wing, the poet says,[1]
And you and I have said it here before.
Drink to the bird." He raised up to the light
The jug that he had gone so far to fill,
And answered huskily: "Well, Mr. Flood,
Since you propose it, I believe I will."

Alone, as if enduring to the end
A valiant armor of scarred hopes outworn,
He stood there in the middle of the road
Like Roland's ghost winding a silent horn.[2]
Below him, in the town among the trees,
Where friends of other days had honored him,
A phantom salutation of the dead
Rang thinly till old Eben's eyes were dim.

Then, as a mother lays her sleeping child
Down tenderly, fearing it may awake,
He set the jug down slowly at his feet
With trembling care, knowing that most things break;
And only when assured that on firm earth
It stood, as the uncertain lives of men
Assuredly did not, he paced away,
And with his hand extended paused again:

"Well, Mr. Flood, we have not met like this
In a long time; and many a change has come
To both of us, I fear, since last it was
We had a drop together. Welcome home!"
Convivially returning with himself,
Again he raised the jug up to the light;
And with an acquiescent quaver said:
"Well, Mr. Flood, if you insist, I might.

"Only a very little, Mr. Flood—
For auld lang syne. No more, sir; that will do."
So, for the time, apparently it did,

---

[1] The poet is Edward FitzGerald (1809–1883) in his "The Rubáiyát of Omar Khayyám" (1859).
See p. 268.
[2] Roland is the hero of the twelfth-century French romance *The Song of Roland,* who fought valiantly
against the Saracens (Spanish Moslems), at Roncesvalles (778) and, overwhelmed at last, sounded
his horn to summon help from Charlemagne, and died.

45 And Eben evidently thought so too;
For soon amid the silver loneliness
Of night he lifted up his voice and sang,
Secure, with only two moons listening,
Until the whole harmonious landscape rang—

"For auld lang syne." The weary throat gave out,
50 The last word wavered, and the song was done.
He raised again the jug regretfully
And shook his head, and was again alone.
There was not much that was ahead of him,
And there was nothing in the town below—
55 Where strangers would have shut the many doors
That many friends had opened long ago.

[1920]

NEW ENGLAND

Here where the wind is always north-north-east
And children learn to walk on frozen toes,
Wonder begets an envy of all those
Who boil elsewhere with such a lyric yeast
5 Of love that you will hear them at a feast
Where demons would appeal for some repose,
Still clamoring where the chalice overflows
And crying wildest who have drunk the least.

Passion is here a soilure of the wits,
10 We're told, and Love a cross for them to bear;
Joy shivers in the corner where she knits
And Conscience always has the rocking-chair,
Cheerful as when she tortured into fits
The first cat that was ever killed by Care.

[1923]

Paul Laurence Dunbar   *1872–1906*

SYMPATHY

I know what the caged bird feels, alas!
When the sun is bright on the upland slopes;
When the wind stirs soft through the springing grass,
And the river flows like a stream of glass;
5 When the first bird sings and the first bud opes,
And the faint perfume from its chalice steals—
I know what the caged bird feels!

I know why the caged bird beats his wing
   Till its blood is red on the cruel bars;
10   For he must fly back to his perch and cling
When he fain would be on the bough a-swing;
   And a pain still throbs in the old, old scars
And they pulse again with a keener sting—
I know why he beats his wing!

15   I know why the caged bird sings, ah me,
   When his wing is bruised and his bosom sore,—
When he beats his bars and he would be free;
It is not a carol of joy or glee,
   But a prayer that he sends from his heart's deep core,
20   But a plea, that upward to Heaven he flings—
I know why the caged bird sings!

[1899]

Amy Lowell *1874–1925*

PATTERNS

I walk down the garden paths,
And all the daffodils
Are blowing, and the bright blue squills.
I walk down the patterned garden-paths
5   In my stiff, brocaded gown.
With my powdered hair and jewelled fan,
I too am a rare
Pattern. As I wander down
The garden paths.

10   My dress is richly figured,
And the train
Makes a pink and silver stain
On the gravel, and the thrift
Of the borders.
15   Just a plate of current fashion,
Tripping by in high-heeled, ribboned shoes.
Not a softness anywhere about me,
Only whalebone and brocade.
And I sink on a seat in the shade
20   Of a lime tree. For my passion
Wars against the stiff brocade.
The daffodils and squills
Flutter in the breeze
As they please.
25   And I weep;
For the lime-tree is in blossom
And one small flower has dropped upon my bosom.

And the plashing of waterdrops
In the marble fountain
30 Comes down the garden-paths.
The dripping never stops.
Underneath my stiffened gown
Is the softness of a woman bathing in a marble basin,
A basin in the midst of hedges grown
35 So thick, she cannot see her lover hiding,
But she guesses he is near,
And the sliding of the water
Seems the stroking of a dear
Hand upon her.
40 What is Summer in a fine brocaded gown!
I should like to see it lying in a heap upon the ground.
All the pink and silver crumpled up on the ground.

I would be the pink and silver as I ran along the paths,
And he would stumble after,
45 Bewildered by my laughter.
I should see the sun flashing from his sword-hilt and the buckles
    on his shoes.
I would choose
To lead him in a maze along the patterned paths,
A bright and laughing maze for my heavy-booted lover.
50 Till he caught me in the shade,
And the buttons of his waistcoat bruised my body as he clasped me,
Aching, melting, unafraid.
With the shadows of the leaves and the sundrops
And the plopping of the waterdrops,
55 All about us in the open afternoon—
I am very like to swoon
With the weight of this brocade,
For the sun sifts through the shade.

Underneath the fallen blossom
60 In my bosom,
Is a letter I have hid.
It was brought to me this morning by a rider from the Duke.
"Madam, we regret to inform you that Lord Hartwell
Died in action Thursday se'nnight."[1]
65 As I read it in the white, morning sunlight,
The letters squirmed like snakes.
"Any answer, Madam?" said my footman.
"No," I told him.
"See that the messenger takes some refreshment.
70 No, no answer."
And I walked into the garden,
Up and down the patterned paths,
In my stiff, correct brocade.

[1] Seven days and nights, a week.

The blue and yellow flowers stood up proudly in the sun,
75 Each one.
I stood upright too,
Held rigid to the pattern
By the stiffness of my gown.
Up and down I walked,
80 Up and down.

In a month he would have been my husband.
In a month, here, underneath this lime,
We would have broken the pattern;
He for me, and I for him,
85 He as Colonel, I as Lady,
On this shady seat.
He had a whim
That sunlight carried blessing.
And I answered, "It shall be as you have said."
90 Now he is dead.

In Summer and in Winter I shall walk
Up and down
The patterned garden-paths
In my stiff, brocaded gown.
95 The squills and daffodils
Will give place to pillared roses, and to asters, and to snow.
I shall go
Up and down,
In my gown.
100 Gorgeously arrayed,
Boned and stayed.
And the softness of my body will be guarded from embrace
By each button, hook, and lace.
For the man who should loose me is dead,
105 Fighting with the Duke in Flanders,
In a pattern called a war.
Christ! What are patterns *for?*

[1915]

Robert Frost   *1874–1963*

BIRCHES

When I see birches bend to left and right
Across the lines of straighter darker trees,
I like to think some boy's been swinging them.
But swinging doesn't bend them down to stay
5 As ice-storms do. Often you must have seen them
Loaded with ice a sunny winter morning

After a rain. They click upon themselves
As the breeze rises, and turn many-colored
As the stir cracks and crazes their enamel.
10 Soon the sun's warmth makes them shed crystal shells
Shattering and avalanching on the snow-crust—
Such heaps of broken glass to sweep away
You'd think the inner dome of heaven had fallen.
They are dragged to the withered bracken° by the load,   *coarse ferns*
15 And they seem not to break; though once they are bowed
So low for long, they never right themselves:
You may see their trunks arching in the woods
Years afterwards, trailing their leaves on the ground
Like girls on hands and knees that throw their hair
20 Before them over their heads to dry in the sun.
But I was going to say when Truth broke in
With all her matter-of-fact about the ice-storm
I should prefer to have some boy bend them
As he went out and in to fetch the cows—
25 Some boy too far from town to learn baseball,
Whose only play was what he found himself,
Summer or winter, and could play alone.
One by one he subdued his father's trees
By riding them down over and over again
30 Until he took the stiffness out of them,
And not one but hung limp, not one was left
For him to conquer. He learned all there was
To learn about not launching out too soon
And so not carrying the tree away
35 Clear to the ground. He always kept his poise
To the top branches, climbing carefully
With the same pains you use to fill a cup
Up to the brim, and even above the brim.
Then he flung outward, feet first, with a swish,
40 Kicking his way down through the air to the ground.
So was I once myself a swinger of birches.
And so I dream of going back to be.
It's when I'm weary of considerations,
And life is too much like a pathless wood
45 Where your face burns and tickles with the cobwebs
Broken across it, and one eye is weeping
From a twig's having lashed across it open.
I'd like to get away from earth awhile
And then come back to it and begin over.
50 May no fate willfully misunderstand me
And half grant what I wish and snatch me away
Not to return. Earth's the right place for love:
I don't know where it's likely to go better.
I'd like to go by climbing a birch tree,
55 And climb black branches up a snow-white trunk
Toward heaven, till the tree could bear no more,
But dipped its top and set me down again.

That would be good both going and coming back.
One could do worse than be a swinger of birches.

[1916]

THE OVEN BIRD[1]

There is a singer everyone has heard,
Loud, a mid-summer and a mid-wood bird,
Who makes the solid tree trunks sound again.
He says that leaves are old and that for flowers
Mid-summer is to spring as one to ten.
He says the early petal-fall is past
When pear and cherry bloom went down in showers
On sunny days a moment overcast;
And comes that other fall we name the fall.
He says the highway dust is over all.
The bird would cease and be as other birds
But that he knows in singing not to sing.
The question that he frames in all but words
Is what to make of a diminished thing.

[1916]

DUST OF SNOW

The way a crow
Shook down on me
The dust of snow
From a hemlock tree

Has given my heart
A change of mood
And saved some part
Of a day I had rued.

[1923]

FIRE AND ICE

Some say the world will end in fire,
Some say in ice.
From what I've tasted of desire
I hold with those who favor fire.
But if it had to perish twice,
I think I know enough of hate
To say that for destruction ice

---

[1] An American warbler noted for its shrill call and for the dome-shaped oven-like nests which it builds on the ground.

Is also great
And would suffice.

[1923]

NOTHING GOLD CAN STAY

Nature's first green is gold,
Her hardest hue to hold.
Her early leaf's a flower;
But only so an hour.

5   Then leaf subsides to leaf.
So Eden sank to grief,
So dawn goes down to day.
Nothing gold can stay.

[1923]

ACQUAINTED WITH THE NIGHT

I have been one acquainted with the night.
I have walked out in rain—and back in rain.
I have outwalked the furthest city light.

I have looked down the saddest city lane.
5   I have passed by the watchman on his beat
And dropped my eyes, unwilling to explain.

I have stood still and stopped the sound of feet
When far away an interrupted cry
Came over houses from another street,

10   But not to call me back or say good-by;
And further still at an unearthly height,
One luminary clock against the sky

Proclaimed the time was neither wrong nor right.
I have been one acquainted with the night.

[1928]

NEITHER OUT FAR NOR IN DEEP

The people along the sand
All turn and look one way.
They turn their back on the land.
They look at the sea all day.

5   As long as it takes to pass
A ship keeps raising its hull;

The wetter ground like glass
Reflects a standing gull.

10 The land may vary more;
But wherever the truth may be—
The water comes ashore,
And the people look at the sea.

They cannot look out far.
They cannot look in deep.
15 But when was that ever a bar
To any watch they keep?

[1936]

DEPARTMENTAL

An ant on the tablecloth
Ran into a dormant moth
Of many times his size.
He showed not the least surprise.
5 His business wasn't with such.
He gave it scarcely a touch,
And was off on his duty run.
Yet if he encountered one
Of the hive's enquiry squad
10 Whose work is to find out God
And the nature of time and space,
He would put him onto the case.
Ants are a curious race;
One crossing with hurried tread
15 The body of one of their dead
Isn't given a moment's arrest—
Seems not even impressed.
But he no doubt reports to any
With whom he crosses antennae,
20 And they no doubt report
To the higher up at court.
Then word goes forth in Formic:[1]
'Death's come to Jerry McCormic,
Our selfless forager Jerry.
25 Will the special Janizary[2]
Whose office it is to bury
The dead of the commissary
Go bring him home to his people.
Lay him in state on a sepal.
30 Wrap him for shroud in a petal.

[1] A type of acid found in ants—here used as a name for the language of ants.
[2] Literally, a soldier in an elite corps of Turkish troops.

Embalm him with ichor[3] of nettle.
This is the word of your Queen.'
And presently on the scene
Appears a solemn mortician;
35   And taking formal position
With feelers calmly atwiddle,
Seizes the dead by the middle,
And heaving him high in air,
Carries him out of there.
40   No one stands round to stare.
It is nobody else's affair.

It couldn't be called ungentle.
But how thoroughly departmental.
                                        [1936]

THE SPAN OF LIFE

The old dog barks backward without getting up
I can remember when he was a pup.
                                        [1936]

THE GIFT OUTRIGHT[1]

The land was ours before we were the land's.
She was our land more than a hundred years
Before we were her people. She was ours
In Massachusetts, in Virginia,
5   But we were England's, still colonials,
Possessing what we still were unpossessed by,
Possessed by what we now no more possessed.
Something we were withholding made us weak
Until we found out that it was ourselves
10   We were withholding from our land of living,
And forthwith found salvation in surrender.
Such as we were we gave ourselves outright
(The deed of gift was many deeds of war)
To the land vaguely realizing westward,
15   But still unstoried, artless, unenhanced,
Such as she was, such as she would become.
                                        [1942]

DIRECTIVE

Back out of all this now too much for us,
Back in a time made simple by the loss

---

[3] The fluid flowing in the veins of the Greek gods.
[1] Frost read this poem at the inauguration of John F. Kennedy in January 1961.

Of detail, burned, dissolved, and broken off
Like graveyard marble sculpture in the weather,
5   There is a house that is no more a house
Upon a farm that is no more a farm
And in a town that is no more a town.
The road there, if you'll let a guide direct you
Who only has at heart your getting lost,
10   May seem as if it should have been a quarry—
Great monolithic knees the former town
Long since gave up pretence of keeping covered.
And there's a story in a book about it:
Besides the wear of iron wagon wheels
15   The ledges show lines ruled southeast northwest,
The chisel work of an enormous Glacier
That braced his feet against the Arctic Pole.
You must not mind a certain coolness from him
Still said to haunt this side of Panther Mountain.
20   Nor need you mind the serial ordeal
Of being watched from forty cellar holes
As if by eye pairs out of forty firkins.[1]
As for the woods' excitement over you
That sends light rustle rushes to their leaves,
25   Charge that to upstart inexperience.
Where were they all not twenty years ago?
They think too much of having shaded out
A few old pecker-fretted apple trees.
Make yourself up a cheering song of how
30   Someone's road home from work this once was,
Who may be just ahead of you on foot
Or creaking with a buggy load of grain.
The height of the adventure is the height
Of country where two village cultures faded
35   Into each other. Both of them are lost.
And if you're lost enough to find yourself
By now, pull in your ladder road behind you
And put a sign up CLOSED to all but me.
Then make yourself at home. The only field
40   Now left's no bigger than a harness gall.[2]
First there's the children's house of make believe,
Some shattered dishes underneath a pine,
The playthings in the playhouse of the children.
Weep for what little things could make them glad.
45   Then for the house that is no more a house,
But only a belilaced cellar hole,
Now slowly closing like a dent in dough.
This was no playhouse but a house in earnest.
Your destination and your destiny's
50   A brook that was the water of the house,

---

[1] Small wooden casks.
[2] An abrasion or sore on a horse caused by the rubbing of the harness.

Cold as a spring as yet so near its source,
Too lofty and original to rage.
(We know the valley streams that when aroused
Will leave their tatters hung on barb and thorn.)
55   I have kept hidden in the instep arch
Of an old cedar at the waterside
A broken drinking goblet like the Grail[3]
Under a spell so the wrong ones can't find it,
So can't get saved, as Saint Mark says they mustn't.[4]
60   (I stole the goblet from the children's playhouse.)
Here are your waters and your watering place.
Drink and be whole again beyond confusion.

[1947]

Carl Sandburg   *1878–1967*

CHICAGO

Hog Butcher for the World,
Tool Maker, Stacker of Wheat,
Player with Railroads and the Nation's Freight Handler;
Stormy, husky, brawling,
5   City of the Big Shoulders:
They tell me you are wicked and I believe them, for I have seen
    your painted women under the gas lamps luring the farm boys.
And they tell me you are crooked and I answer: Yes, it is true I
    have seen the gunman kill and go free to kill again.
And they tell me you are brutal and my reply is: On the faces of
    women and children I have seen the marks of wanton hunger.
And having answered so I turn once more to those who sneer at this
    my city, and I give them back the sneer and say to them:
10   Come and show me another city with lifted head singing so proud
    to be alive and coarse and strong and cunning.
Flinging magnetic curses amid the toil of piling job on job, here is a tall
    bold slugger set vivid against the little soft cities;
Fierce as a dog with tongue lapping for action, cunning as a savage
    pitted against the wilderness,
        Bareheaded,
        Shoveling,
15   Wrecking,
        Planning,
        Building, breaking, rebuilding,
Under the smoke, dust all over his mouth, laughing with white teeth,

---

[3] The cup or chalice which Jesus drank from during the Last Supper, which subsequently became
  the object of many medieval quests in Arthurian romance, including those by "wrong ones"
  who were unworthy of its pursuit.
[4] See Mark 4:11–12.

Under the terrible burden of destiny laughing as a young man
   laughs,
20 Laughing even as an ignorant fighter laughs who has never lost a
   battle,
Bragging and laughing that under his wrist is the pulse, and under his
   ribs the heart of the people,
     Laughing!
Laughing the stormy, husky, brawling laughter of Youth, half-naked,
   sweating, proud to be Hog Butcher, Tool Maker, Stacker of
   Wheat, Player with railroads and Freight Handler to the Nation.
[1916]

Wallace Stevens   *1879–1955*

DISILLUSIONMENT OF TEN O'CLOCK

The houses are haunted
By white night-gowns.
None are green,
Or purple with green rings,
5 Or green with yellow rings,
Or yellow with blue rings.
None of them are strange,
With socks of lace
And beaded ceintures.°   *sashes or belts*
10 People are not going
To dream of baboons and periwinkles.°   *edible snails*
Only, here and there, an old sailor,
Drunk and asleep in his boots,
Catches tigers
15 In red weather.
[1915]

PETER QUINCE AT THE CLAVIER[1]

I

Just as my fingers on these keys
Make music, so the selfsame sounds
On my spirit make a music, too.

Music is feeling, then, not sound;
5 And thus it is that what I feel,
Here in this room, desiring you,

---

[1] A keyboard; presumably the keyboard of a harmonium or reed organ. *Harmonium* (1923) was
the title of Stevens' first volume of collected poems.

Thinking of your blue-shadowed silk,
Is music. It is like the strain
Waked in the elders by Susanna.[2]

10

Of a green evening, clear and warm,
She bathed in her still garden, while
The red-eyed elders watching, felt

The basses of their beings throb
In witching chords, and their thin blood
15   Pulse pizzicati[3] of Hosanna.[4]

II

In the green water, clear and warm,
Susanna lay.
She searched
The touch of springs,
20   And found
Concealed imaginings.
She sighed,
For so much melody.

Upon the bank, she stood
25   In the cool
Of spent emotions.
She felt, among the leaves,
The dew
Of old devotions.

30   She walked upon the grass,
Still quavering.
The winds were like her maids,
On timid feet,
Fetching her woven scarves,
35   Yet wavering.

A breath upon her hand
Muted the night,
She turned—
A cymbal crashed,
40   And roaring horns.

III

Soon, with a noise like tambourines,
Came her attendant Byzantines.[5]

[2] The virtuous wife in "The History of Susanna" in the Old Testament Apocrypha, falsely accused of adultery by two Hebrew elders whose advances she had rejected. Their charge was exposed by Daniel who had the two men put to death.
[3] Musical notes produced by plucking a stringed instrument.
[4] An exclamation of praise or adoration to God.
[5] Natives of the Greek city of Byzantium, now Istanbul in Turkey.

They wondered why Susanna cried
Against the elders by her side;

45 And as they whispered, the refrain
Was like a willow swept by rain.

Anon, their lamps' uplifted flame
Revealed Susanna and her shame.

And then, the simpering Byzantines
50 Fled, with a noise like tambourines.

IV

Beauty is momentary in the mind—
The fitful tracing of a portal;
But in the flesh it is immortal.

The body dies; the body's beauty lives.
55 So evenings die, in their green going,
A wave, interminably flowing.
So gardens die, their meek breath scenting
The cowl of winter, done repenting.
So maidens die, to the auroral°   *dawn*
60 Celebration of a maiden's choral.

Susanna's music touched the bawdy strings
Of those white elders; but, escaping,
Left only Death's ironic scraping.
Now, in its immortality, it plays
65 On the clear viol of her memory,
And makes a constant sacrament of praise.

[1923]

ANECDOTE OF THE JAR

I placed a jar in Tennessee,
And round it was, upon a hill.
It made the slovenly wilderness
Surround that hill.

5 The wilderness rose up to it,
And sprawled around, no longer wild.
The jar was round upon the ground
And tall and of a port in air.

It took dominion everywhere.
10 The jar was gray and bare.
It did not give of bird or bush,
Like nothing else in Tennessee.

[1923]

THE EMPEROR OF ICE-CREAM

Call the roller of big cigars,
The muscular one, and bid him whip
In kitchen cups concupiscent curds.
Let the wenches dawdle in such dress
5   As they are used to wear, and let the boys
Bring flowers in last month's newspapers.
Let be be finale of seem.
The only emperor is the emperor of ice-cream.

Take from the dresser of deal,°   *pine*
10   Lacking the three glass knobs, that sheet
On which she embroidered fantails once
And spread it so as to cover her face.
If her horny feet protrude, they come
To show how cold she is, and dumb.
15   Let the lamp affix its beam.
The only emperor is the emperor of ice-cream.

                                [1923]

William Carlos Williams   *1883–1963*

QUEEN-ANN'S-LACE

Her body is not so white as
anemone petals nor so smooth—nor
so remote a thing. It is a field
of the wild carrot[1] taking
5   the field by force; the grass
does not raise above it.
Here is no question of whiteness,
white as can be, with a purple mole
at the center of each flower.
10   Each flower is a hand's span
of her whiteness. Wherever
his hand has lain there is
a tiny purple blemish. Each part
is a blossom under his touch
15   to which the fibres of her being
stem one by one, each to its end,
until the whole field is a
white desire, empty, a single stem,
a cluster, flower by flower,
20   a pious wish to whiteness gone over—
or nothing.

                                  [1921]

---

[1] Queen Anne's Lace, or wild carrot, is a plant with numerous tiny white blossoms clustered around a single purple one, or mole.

THIS IS JUST TO SAY

I have eaten
the plums
that were in
the icebox

5   and which
you were probably
saving
for breakfast

Forgive me
10   they were delicious
so sweet
and so cold

[1934]

THE DANCE

In Breughel's great picture, The Kermess,[1]
the dancers go round, they go round and
around, the squeal and the blare and the
tweedle of bagpipes, a bugle and fiddles
5   tipping their bellies (round as the thick-
sided glasses whose wash they impound)
their hips and their bellies off balance
to turn them. Kicking and rolling about
the Fair Grounds, swinging their butts, those
10   shanks must be sound to bear up under such
rollicking measures, prance as they dance
in Breughel's great picture, The Kermess.

[1944]

LANDSCAPE WITH THE FALL OF ICARUS[2]

According to Brueghel
when Icarus fell
it was spring

a farmer was ploughing
5   his field
the whole pageantry

[1] The picture by Flemish painter Peter Breughel (c. 1525–1569) depicts the annual outdoor festival or fair (the kermess) celebrated in the Low Countries (the Netherlands, Belgium, and Luxembourg).

[2] The title of a painting by Peter Breughel (ca. 1525–1569). It depicts the myth of Icarus, a young Greek, who, in escaping with his father from the island of Crete by means of wings held together by wax, flew too near the sun; the wax melted and Icarus fell to his death in the sea.

of the year was
awake tingling
near

10   the edge of the sea
concerned
with itself

sweating in the sun
that melted
15   the wings' wax

unsignificantly
off the coast
there was

a splash quite unnoticed
20   this was
Icarus drowning
[1960]

Sara Teasdale   *1884–1933*

BARTER

Life has loveliness to sell—
    All beautiful and splendid things,
Blue waves whitened on a cliff,
    Climbing fire that sways and sings,
5   And children's faces looking up
Holding wonder like a cup.

Life has loveliness to sell—
    Music like a curve of gold,
Scent of pine trees in the rain,
10   Eyes that love you, arms that hold,
And for your spirit's still delight,
Holy thoughts that star the night.

Spend all you have for loveliness,
    Buy it and never count the cost,
15 For one white singing hour of peace
    Count many a year of strife well lost,
And for a breath of ecstasy
Give all you have been or could be.
[1917]

Ezra Pound   *1885–1972*

IN A STATION OF THE METRO°   *The Paris subway*

The apparition of these faces in the crowd;
Petals on a wet, black bough.

[1916]

ANCIENT MUSIC[1]

Winter is icumen in,
Lhude sing Goddamm,
Raineth drop and staineth slop,
And how the wind doth ramm!
5   Sing: Goddamm.
Skiddeth bus and sloppeth us,
An ague hath my ham.
Freezeth river, turneth liver,
        Damn you, sing: Goddamm.
10 Goddamm, Goddamm, 'tis why I am, Goddamm,
        So 'gainst the winter's balm.
Sing goddamm, damm, sing Goddamm,
Sing goddamm, sing goddamm, DAMM.

[1926]

Robinson Jeffers   *1887–1962*

HURT HAWKS

I

The broken pillar of the wing jags from the clotted shoulder,
The wing trails like a banner in defeat,
No more to use the sky forever but live with famine
And pain a few days: cat nor coyote
5 Will shorten the week of waiting for death, there is game without
   talons.
He stands under the oak-bush and waits
The lame feet of salvation; at night he remembers freedom
And flies in a dream, the dawns ruin it.
He is strong and pain is worse to the strong, incapacity is worse.
10 The curs of the day come and torment him
At distance, no one but death the redeemer will humble that head,
The intrepid readiness, the terrible eyes.

---

[1] Compare Pound's poem with the medieval lyric he is parodying, "Sumer Is Icumen In," p. 151.

The wild God of the world is sometimes merciful to those
That ask mercy, not often to the arrogant.
15 You do not know him, you communal people, or you have forgotten
      him;
Intemperate and savage, the hawk remembers him;
Beautiful and wild, the hawks, and men that are dying, remember
      him.

                                    II
I'd sooner, except the penalties, kill a man than a hawk; but the
      great redtail
Had nothing left but unable misery
20 From the bone too shattered for mending, the wing that trailed
      under his talons when he moved.
We had fed him six weeks, I gave him freedom,
He wandered over the foreland hill and returned in the evening,
      asking for death,
Not like a beggar, still eyed with the old
Implacable arrogance. I gave him the lead gift in the twilight. What fell
      was relaxed,
25 Owl-downy, soft feminine feathers; but what
Soared: the fierce rush: the night-herons by the flooded river cried
      fear at its rising
Before it was quite unsheathed from reality.

                                                            [1928]

Marianne Moore   *1887–1972*

POETRY

      I, too, dislike it: there are things that are important beyond
            all this fiddle.
         Reading it, however, with a perfect contempt for it, one
            discovers in
5   it after all, a place for the genuine.
               Hands that can grasp, eyes
            that can dilate, hair that can rise
               if it must, these things are important not because a

         high-sounding interpretation can be put upon them but be-
10   cause they are
            useful. When they become so derivative as to become
               unintelligible,
            the same thing may be said for all of us, that we
               do not admire what
15   we cannot understand: the bat
               holding on upside down or in quest of something to

eat, elephants pushing, a wild horse taking a roll, a tireless
      wolf under
a tree, the immovable critic twitching his skin like a horse
20   that feels a flea, the base-
ball fan, the statistician—
      nor is it valid
      to discriminate against "business documents and

school-books"; all these phenomena are important. One
25   must make a distinction
however: when dragged into prominence by half poets,
      the result is not poetry,
nor till the poets among us can be
      "literalists of
30   the imagination"—above
      insolence and triviality and can present

for inspection, "imaginary gardens with real toads in them,"
      shall we have
it. In the meantime, if you demand on the one hand,
35   the raw material of poetry in
      all its rawness and
that which is on the other hand
      genuine, you are interested in poetry.

               [1921]

T. S. Eliot   *1888–1965*

THE LOVE SONG OF J. ALFRED PRUFROCK

S'io credesse che mia risposta fosse
A persona che mai tornasse al mondo,
Questa fiamma staria senza piu scosse.
Ma perciocche giammai di questo fondo
Non torno vivo alcun, s'i'odo il vero,
Senza tema d'infamia ti rispondo.[1]

Let us go then, you and I,
When the evening is spread out against the sky
Like a patient etherised upon a table;
Let us go, through certain half-deserted streets,
5 The muttering retreats
Of restless nights in one-night cheap hotels
And sawdust restaurants with oyster-shells:

[1] The statement introducing the confession of the poet Guido da Montefeltro in Dante's *Inferno* (1321), canto xxvii, 61–66: "If I thought that I was speaking/ to someone who would go back to the world,/ this flame would shake no more. / But since nobody has ever gone back alive from this place, if what I hear is true,/ I answer you without fear of infamy."

Streets that follow like a tedious argument
Of insidious intent
10 To lead you to an overwhelming question. . .
Oh, do not ask, "What is it?"
Let us go and make our visit.

In the room the women come and go
Talking of Michelangelo.[2]

15 The yellow fog that rubs its back upon the window-panes,
The yellow smoke that rubs its muzzle on the window-panes
Licked its tongue into the corners of the evening,
Lingered upon the pools that stand in drains,
Let fall upon its back the soot that falls from chimneys,
20 Slipped by the terrace, made a sudden leap,
And seeing that it was a soft October night,
Curled once about the house, and fell asleep.

And indeed there will be time
For the yellow smoke that slides along the street,
25 Rubbing its back upon the window-panes;
There will be time, there will be time
To prepare a face to meet the faces that you meet;
There will be time to murder and create,
And time for all the works and days[3] of hands
30 That lift and drop a question on your plate;
Time for you and time for me,
And time yet for a hundred indecisions,
And for a hundred visions and revisions,
Before the taking of a toast and tea.

35 In the room the women come and go
Talking of Michelangelo.

And indeed there will be time
To wonder, "Do I dare?" and, "Do I dare?"
Time to turn back and descend the stair,
40 With a bald spot in the middle of my hair—
[They will say: "How his hair is growing thin!"]
My morning coat, my collar mounting firmly to the chin,
My necktie rich and modest, but asserted by a simple pin—
[They will say: "But how his arms and legs are thin!"]
45 Do I dare
Disturb the universe?
In a minute there is time
For decisions and revisions which a minute will reverse.

---

[2] Michelangelo (1474–1564), the most famous artist of the Italian Renaissance.
[3] Possibly an allusion to *Works and Days,* a poem giving practical advice on farming by the Greek poet Hesiod (8th century B.C.).

For I have known them all already, known them all:—
50 Have known the evenings, mornings, afternoons,
I have measured out my life with coffee spoons;
I know the voices dying with a dying fall[4]
Beneath the music from a farther room.
So how should I presume?

55 And I have known the eyes already, known them all—
The eyes that fix you in a formulated phrase,
And when I am formulated, sprawling on a pin,
When I am pinned and wriggling on the wall,
Then how should I begin
60 To spit out all the butt-ends of my days and ways?
And how should I presume?

And I have known the arms already, known them all—
Arms that are braceleted and white and bare
[But in the lamplight, downed with light brown hair!]
65 Is it perfume from a dress
That makes me so digress?
Arms that lie along a table, or wrap about a shawl.
And should I then presume?
And how should I begin?
. . . . .

70 Shall I say, I have gone at dusk through narrow streets
And watched the smoke that rises from the pipes
Of lonely men in shirt-sleeves, leaning out of windows? . . .

I should have been a pair of ragged claws
Scuttling across the floors of silent seas.
. . . . .

75 And the afternoon, the evening, sleeps so peacefully!
Smoothed by long fingers,
Asleep . . . tired . . . or it malingers,
Stretched on the floor, here beside you and me.
Should I, after tea and cakes and ices,
80 Have the strength to force the moment to its crisis?
But though I have wept and fasted, wept and prayed,
Though I have seen my head [grown slightly bald] brought in
    upon a platter,[5]
I am no prophet—and here's no great matter;
I have seen the moment of my greatness flicker,
85 And I have seen the eternal Footman hold my coat, and snicker,
And in short, I was afraid.

And would it have been worth it, after all,
After the cups, the marmalade, the tea,

---

[4] See Shakespeare's *Twelfth Night* (1623), Act 1, Scene 1, 1–4.
[5] An allusion to John the Baptist, the New Testament prophet, whose head was presented to Queen Herodias on a charger. Matthew 14:3–11.

Among the porcelain, among some talk of you and me,
90   Would it have been worth while,
To have bitten off the matter with a smile,
To have squeezed the universe into a ball[6]
To roll it toward some overwhelming question,
To say: "I am Lazarus,[7] come from the dead,
95   Come back to tell you all, I shall tell you all"—
If one, settling a pillow by her head,
    Should say: "That is not what I meant at all.
    That is not it, at all."

    And would it have been worth it, after all,
100   Would it have been worth while,
After the sunsets and the dooryards and the sprinkled streets,
After the novels, after the teacups, after the skirts that trail along
    the floor—
And this, and so much more?—
It is impossible to say just what I mean!
105   But as if a magic lantern threw the nerves in patterns on a
    screen:
Would it have been worth while
If one, settling a pillow or throwing off a shawl,
And turning toward the window, should say:
    "That is not it at all,
110   That is not what I meant, at all."
          . . . . .

No! I am not Prince Hamlet,[8] nor was meant to be;
Am an attendant lord, one that will do
To swell a progress,[9] start a scene or two,
Advise the prince; no doubt, an easy tool,
115   Deferential, glad to be of use,
Politic, cautious, and meticulous;
Full of high sentence[10] but a bit obtuse;
At times, indeed, almost ridiculous—
Almost, at times, the Fool.

120   I grow old . . . I grow old . . .
I shall wear the bottoms of my trousers rolled.

    Shall I part my hair behind? Do I dare to eat a peach?
I shall wear white flannel trousers, and walk upon the beach.
I have heard the mermaids singing, each to each.

125   I do not think that they will sing to me.

---

[6] See Andrew Marvell's "To His Coy Mistress" (1681), lines 41–42, p. 208.
[7] The man raised by Jesus from the dead, John 11:1–44.
[8] The hero of Shakespeare's tragedy (1603); the "attendant lord" may refer to Polonius, the sententious courtier in the same play.
[9] A formal state journey by a king through his realm.   [10] Sententiousness.

I have seen them riding seaward on the waves
Combing the white hair of the waves blown back
When the wind blows the water white and black.

We have lingered in the chambers of the sea
130 By sea-girls wreathed with seaweed red and brown
Till human voices wake us, and we drown.

[1917]

JOURNEY OF THE MAGI[1]

"A cold coming we had of it,
Just the worst time of the year
For a journey, and such a long journey:
The ways deep and the weather sharp,
5 The very dead of winter."
And the camels galled,[2] sore-footed, refractory,
Lying down in the melting snow.
There were times we regretted
The summer palaces on slopes, the terraces,
10 And the silken girls bringing sherbet.
Then the camel men cursing and grumbling
And running away, and wanting their liquor and women,
And the night-fires going out, and the lack of shelters,
And the cities hostile and the towns unfriendly
15 And the villages dirty and charging high prices:
A hard time we had of it.
At the end we preferred to travel all night,
Sleeping in snatches,
With the voices singing in our ears, saying
20 That this was all folly.

Then at dawn we came down to a temperate valley,
Wet, below the snow line, smelling of vegetation;
With a running stream and a water-mill beating the darkness,
And three trees on the low sky,
25 And an old white horse galloped away in the meadow.
Then we came to a tavern with vine-leaves over the lintel,
Six hands at an open door dicing for pieces of silver,
And feet kicking the empty wine-skins.
But there was no information, and so we continued
30 And arrived at evening, not a moment too soon
Finding the place; it was (you may say) satisfactory.

All this was a long time ago, I remember,
And I would do it again, but set down

---

[1] The wise men from the East who journeyed to Bethlehem to pay homage to the baby Jesus (Matthew 2:1–12).
[2] Sores caused by the friction of a saddle.

This set down
35   This: were we led all that way for
Birth or Death? There was a Birth, certainly,
We had evidence and no doubt. I had seen birth and death,
But had thought they were different; this Birth was
Hard and bitter agony for us, like Death, our death.
40   We returned to our places, these Kingdoms,
But no longer at ease here, in the old dispensation,
With an alien people clutching their gods.
I should be glad of another death.

[1927]

John Crowe Ransom   *1888–1974*

BELLS FOR JOHN WHITESIDE'S DAUGHTER

There was such speed in her little body,
And such lightness in her footfall,
It is no wonder her brown study
Astonishes us all.

5   Her wars were bruited in our high window.
We looked among orchard trees and beyond
Where she took arms against her shadow,
Or harried unto the pond

The lazy geese, like a snow cloud
10   Dripping their snow on the green grass,
Tricking and stopping, sleepy and proud,
Who cried in goose, Alas,

For the tireless heart within the little
Lady with rod that made them rise
15   From their noon apple-dreams and scuttle
Goose-fashion under the skies!

But now go the bells, and we are ready,
In one house we are sternly stopped
To say we are vexed at her brown study,
20   Lying so primly propped.

[1924]

PIAZZA PIECE

—I am a gentleman in a dustcoat trying
To make you hear. Your ears are soft and small
And listen to an old man not at all,

They want the young men's whispering and sighing.
5 But see the roses on your trellis dying
And hear the spectral singing of the moon;
For I must have my lovely lady soon,
I am a gentleman in a dustcoat trying.

—I am a lady young in beauty waiting
10 Until my truelove comes, and then we kiss.
But what grey man among the vines is this
Whose words are dry and faint as in a dream?
Back from my trellis, Sir, before I scream!
I am a lady young in beauty waiting.

[1927]

Claude McKay   *1890–1948*

THE HARLEM DANCER

Applauding youths laughed with young prostitutes
And watched her perfect, half-clothed body sway;
Her voice was like the sound of blended flutes
Blown by black players upon a picnic day.
5 She sang and danced on gracefully and calm,
The light gauze hanging loose about her form;
To me she seemed a proudly-swaying palm
Grown lovelier for passing through a storm.
Upon her swarthy neck black shiny curls
10 Luxuriant fell; and tossing coins in praise,
The wine-flushed, bold-eyed boys, and even the girls,
Devoured her shape with eager, passionate gaze;
But looking at her falsely-smiling face,
I knew her self was not in that strange place.

[1922]

Archibald MacLeish   *1892–1982*

YOU, ANDREW MARVELL[1]

And here face down beneath the sun
And here upon earth's noonward height
To feel the always coming on
The always rising of the night:

---

[1] The allusion is to English seventeenth-century poet Andrew Marvell (1621–1678), and specifically to lines 21–22 of his "To His Coy Mistress" (1681); see p. 208.

5   To feel creep up the curving east
    The earthly chill of dusk and slow
    Upon those under lands the vast
    And ever climbing shadow grow

    And strange at Ecbatan[2] the trees
10 Take leaf by leaf the evening strange
    The flooding dark about their knees
    The mountains over Persia change

    And now at Kermanshah the gate
    Dark empty and the withered grass
15 And through the twilight now the late
    Few travelers in the westward pass

    And Baghdad darken and the bridge
    Across the silent river gone
    And through Arabia the edge
20 Of evening widen and steal on

    And deepen on Palmyra's street
    The wheel rut in the ruined stone
    And Lebanon fade out and Crete
    High through the clouds and overblown

25 And over Sicily the air
    Still flashing with the landward gulls
    And loom and slowly disappear
    The sails above the shadowy hulls

    And Spain go under and the shore
30 Of Africa the gilded sand
    And evening vanish and no more
    The low pale light across that land

    Nor now the long light on the sea:
    And here face downward in the sun
35 To feel how swiftly how secretly
    The shadow of the night comes on . . .

                                            [1930]

Dorothy Parker   *1893–1967*

RÉSUMÉ

Razors pain you;
Rivers are damp;

---

[2] A city in ancient Persia; the cities that follow, Kermanshah in Iran, Baghdad in Iraq, and Palmyra in Syria, are all associated with ancient civilizations.

Acids stain you;
And drugs cause cramp.
Guns aren't lawful;
Nooses give;
Gas smells awful;
You might as well live.
[1926]

Morris Bishop   *1893–1973*

$E = mc^2$

What was our trust, we trust not,
  What was our faith, we doubt;
Whether we must or must not
  We may debate about.
The soul perhaps is a gust of gas
  And wrong is a form of right—
But we know that Energy equals Mass
  By the Square of the Speed of Light.

What we have known, we know not,
  What we have proved, abjure.
Life is a tangled bow-knot,
  But one thing still is sure.
Come, little lad; come, little lass,
  Your docile creed recite:
"We know that Energy equals Mass
  By the Square of the Speed of light."
[1954]

e. e. cummings   *1894–1962*

"BUFFALO BILL'S"

Buffalo Bill's[1]
defunct
    who used to
    ride a watersmooth-silver
                    stallion
and break onetwothreefourfive pigeonsjustlikethat
                                        Jesus

---

[1] The nickname of William F. Cody (1846–1917), a famous American Indian fighter and frontier scout and an impresario of the wild west show.

he was a handsome man
                    and what i want to know is
10   how do you like your blueeyed boy
        Mister Death

                                              [1923]

"IN JUST-"

        in Just-
        spring   when the world is mud-
        luscious the little
        lame balloonman

5   whistles   far   and wee

        and eddieandbill come
        running from marbles and
        piracies and it's
        spring

10   when the world is puddle-wonderful

        the queer
        old balloonman whistles
        far   and   wee
        and bettyandisbel come dancing

15   from hop-scotch and jump-rope and

        it's
        spring
        and
            the

20   goat-footed

        balloonMan   whistles
        far
        and
        wee

                                    [1923]

"NOBODY LOSES ALL THE TIME"

nobody loses all the time

i had an uncle named
Sol who was a born failure and

nearly everybody said he should have gone
5   into vaudeville perhaps because my Uncle Sol could
sing McCann He Was A Diver on Xmas Eve like Hell Itself which
may or may not account for the fact that my Uncle

Sol indulged in that possibly most inexcusable
of all to use a highfalootin phrase
10 luxuries that is or to
wit farming and be
it needlessly
added

my Uncle Sol's farm
15 failed because the chickens
ate the vegetables so
my Uncle Sol had a
chicken farm till the
skunks ate the chickens when

20 my Uncle Sol
had a skunk farm but
the skunks caught cold and
died and so
my Uncle Sol imitated the
25 skunks in a subtle manner

or by drowning himself in the watertank
but somebody who'd given my Uncle Sol a Victor
Victrola and records while he lived presented to
him upon the auspicious occasion of his decease a
30 scrumptious not to mention splendiferous funeral with
tall boys in black gloves and flowers and everything and

i remember we all cried like the Missouri
when my Uncle Sol's coffin lurched because
somebody pressed a button
35 (and down went
my Uncle
Sol

and started a worm farm)

[1923]

"NEXT TO OF COURSE GOD AMERICA I"

"next to of course god america i
love you land of the pilgrims' and so forth oh
say can you see by the dawn's early my
country 'tis of centuries come and go

5   and are no more what of it we should worry
    in every language even deafanddumb
    thy sons acclaim your glorious name by gorry
    by jingo by gee by gosh by gum
    why talk of beauty what could be more beaut-
10 iful than these heroic happy dead
    who rushed like lions to the roaring slaughter
    they did not stop to think they died instead
    then shall the voice of liberty be mute?"

    He spoke. And drank rapidly a glass of water
                                              [1926]

"MY SWEET OLD ETCETERA"

      my sweet old etcetera
      aunt lucy during the recent

      war could and what
      is more did tell you just
5   what everybody was fighting

      for,
      my sister
      isabel created hundreds
      (and
10   hundreds)of socks not to
      mention shirts fleaproof earwarmers

      etcetera wristers etcetera, my
      mother hoped that

      i would die etcetera
15   bravely of course my father used
      to become hoarse talking about how it was
      a privilege and if only he
      could meanwhile my

      self etcetera lay quietly
20   in the deep mud et

      cetera
      (dreaming,
      et
        cetera, of
25   Your smile
      eyes knees and of your Etcetera)
                                              [1926]

"ANYONE LIVED IN A PRETTY HOW TOWN"

anyone lived in a pretty how town
(with up so floating many bells down)
spring summer autumn winter
he sang his didn't he danced his did.

Women and men (both little and small)
cared for anyone not at all
they sowed their isn't they reaped their same
sun moon stars rain

children guessed (but only a few
and down they forgot as up they grew
autumn winter spring summer)
that noone loved him more by more

when by now and tree by leaf
she laughed his joy she cried his grief
bird by snow and stir by still
anyone's any was all to her

someone married their everyones
laughed their cryings and did their dance
(sleep wake hope and then) they
said their nevers they slept their dream

stars rain sun moon
(and only the snow can begin to explain
how children are apt to forget to remember
with up so floating many bells down)

one day anyone died i guess
(and noone stooped to kiss his face)
busy folk buried them side by side
little by little and was by was

all by all and deep by deep
and more by more they dream their sleep
noone and anyone earth by april
wish by spirit and if by yes.

Women and men (both dong and ding)
summer autumn winter spring
reaped their sowing and went their came
sun moon stars rain

[1940]

"PITY THIS BUSY MONSTER,MANUNKIND,"

pity this busy monster,manunkind,

not. Progress is a comfortable disease:
your victim(death and life safely beyond)

plays with the bigness of his littleness
5   —electrons deify one razorblade
into a mountainrange;lenses extend

unwish through curving wherewhen till unwish
returns on its unself.
                    A world of made
10   is not a world of born—pity poor flesh

and trees,poor stars and stones,but never this
fine specimen of hypermagical

ultraomnipotence. We doctors know

a hopeless case if—listen:there's a hell
15   of a good universe next door;let's go

                                    [1943]

Hart Crane *1899–1932*

BLACK TAMBOURINE

The interests of a black man in a cellar
Mark tardy judgment on the world's closed door.
Gnats toss in the shadow of a bottle,
And a roach spans a crevice in the floor.

5   Aesop,[1] driven to pondering, found
Heaven with the tortoise and the hare;
Fox brush and sow ear top his grave
And mingling incantations on the air.

The black man, forlorn in the cellar,
10   Wanders in some mid-kingdom, dark, that lies,
Between his tambourine, stuck on the wall,
And, in Africa, a carcass quick with flies.

                                    [1926]

---

[1] The sixth-century B.C. slave to whom is attributed the famous collection of beast fables.

Langston Hughes   *1902–1967*

THE NEGRO SPEAKS OF RIVERS

I've known rivers:
I've known rivers ancient as the world and older than the
    flow of human blood in human veins.

My soul has grown deep like the rivers.

5   I bathed in the Euphrates[1] when dawns were young.
I built my hut near the Congo and it lulled me to sleep.
I looked upon the Nile and raised the pyramids above it.
I heard the singing of the Mississippi when Abe Lincoln
    went down to New Orleans, and I've seen its muddy
10   bosom turn all golden in the sunset.

I've known rivers:
Ancient, dusky rivers.

My soul has grown deep like the rivers.

                       [1926]

HARLEM[2]

What happens to a dream deferred?
    Does it dry up
    like a raisin in the sun?
    Or fester like a sore—
5   And then run?

    Does it stink like rotten meat?
    Or crust and sugar over—
    like a syrupy sweet?

    Maybe it just sags
10   like a heavy load.

    Or does it explode?

                  [1951]

---

[1] The Euphrates, flowing from Turkey into Syria and Iraq, and the Nile, flowing through Egypt, helped to nurture the ancient Babylonian and Egyptian civilizations. The Congo flows through central Africa to the Atlantic, while the Mississippi cuts through the heartland of the United States on its way to New Orleans and the Gulf of Mexico.

[2] Traditionally Black section of New York City.

THEME FOR ENGLISH B

The instructor said,

>*Go home and write*
>*a page tonight.*
>*And let that page come out of you—*
5 >*Then, it will be true.*

I wonder if it's that simple?
I am twenty-two, colored, born in Winston-Salem.
I went to school there, then Durham,[1] then here
to this college[2] on the hill above Harlem.
10 I am the only colored student in my class.

The steps from the hill lead down into Harlem,
through a park, then I cross St. Nicholas,[3]
Eighth Avenue, Seventh, and I come to the Y,
the Harlem Branch Y, where I take the elevator
15 up to my room, sit down, and write this page:

It's not easy to know what is true for you or me
at twenty-two, my age. But I guess I'm what
I feel and see and hear, Harlem, I hear you:
hear you, hear me—we two—you, me, talk on this page,
20 (I hear New York, too.) Me—who?

Well, I like to eat, sleep, drink, and be in love.
I like to work, read, learn, and understand life.
I like a pipe for a Christmas present,
or records—Bessie,[4] bop, or Bach.[5]
25 I guess being colored doesn't make me *not* like
the same things other folks like who are other races.
So will my page be colored that I write?

Being me, it will not be white.
But it will be
30 a part of you, instructor.
You are white—
yet a part of me, as I am a part of you.
That's American.
Sometimes perhaps you don't want to be a part of me.
35 Nor do I often want to be a part of you.
But we are, that's true!
As I learn from you,

---

[1] Cities in North Carolina.
[2] Columbia University.
[3] Avenue in Harlem.
[4] Bessie Smith (1898?–1937), the famous American blues singer.
[5] Johann Sebastian Bach (1685–1750), the German composer.

I guess you learn from me—
although you're older—and white—
40 and somewhat more free.

This is my page for English B.

[1951]

ADVICE

Folks, I'm telling you,
birthing is hard
and dying is mean—
so get yourself
5 a little loving
in between.

[1946]

Ogden Nash   *1902–1971*

VERY LIKE A WHALE

One thing that literature would be greatly the better for
Would be a more restricted employment by authors of simile and
metaphor.
Authors of all races, be they Greeks, Romans, Teutons or Celts,
Can't seem just to say that anything is the thing it is but have to go out
of their way to say that it is like something else.
5 What does it mean when we are told
That the Assyrian came down like a wolf on the fold?[1]
In the first place, George Gordon Byron had had enough experience
To know that it probably wasn't just one Assyrian, it was a lot of
Assyrians.
However, as too many arguments are apt to induce apoplexy and thus
hinder longevity,
10 We'll let it pass as one Assyrian for the sake of brevity.
Now then, this particular Assyrian, the one whose cohorts were gleaming
in purple and gold,
Just what does the poet mean when he says he came down like a wolf on
the fold?
In heaven and earth more than is dreamed of in our philosophy there
are a great many things.
But I don't imagine that among them there is a wolf with purple and
gold cohorts or purple and gold anythings.
15 No, no, Lord Byron, before I'll believe that this Assyrian was actually like
a wolf I must have some kind of proof;

[1] The first line of "The Destruction of Sennacherib" (1815) by Lord Byron (1788–1824); see p.
850. (Assyria was an ancient culture of the Near East.)

Did he run on all fours and did he have a hairy tail and a big red mouth
    and big white teeth and did he say Woof woof?
Frankly I think it very unlikely, and all you were entitled to say, at the
    very most,
Was that the Assyrian cohorts came down like a lot of Assyrian cohorts
    about to destroy the Hebrew host.
But that wasn't fancy enough for Lord Byron, oh dear me no, he had to
    invent a lot of figures of speech and then interpolate them.
20 With the result that whenever you mention Old Testament soldiers to
    people they say Oh yes, they're the ones that a lot of wolves dressed
    up in gold and purple ate them.
That's the kind of thing that's being done all the time by poets, from
    Homer to Tennyson;
They're always comparing ladies to lilies and veal to venison.
And they always say things like that the snow is a white blanket after a
    winter storm.
Oh it is, is it, all right then, you sleep under a six-inch blanket of snow
    and I'll sleep under a half-inch blanket of unpoetical blanket material
    and we'll see which one keeps warm.
25 And after that maybe you'll begin to comprehend dimly
What I mean by too much metaphor and simile.

                                        [1935]

Stevie Smith   *1902–1971*

WAS HE MARRIED?

Was he married, did he try
To support as he grew less fond of them
Wife and family?

No,
5 He never suffered such a blow.

Did he feel pointless, feeble and distrait,
Unwanted by everyone and in the way?

From his cradle he was purposeful,
His bent strong and his mind full.

10 Did he love people very much
Yet find them die one day?

He did not love in the human way.

Did he ask how long it would go on,
Wonder if Death could be counted on for an end?

15 He did not feel like this,
He had a future of bliss.

Did he never feel strong
Pain for being wrong?

He was not wrong, he was right,
20   He suffered from others', not his own, spite.

But there *is* no suffering like having made a mistake
Because of being of an inferior make.

He was not inferior,
He was superior.

25   He knew then that power corrupts but some must govern?

His thoughts were different.

Did he lack friends? Worse,
Think it was for his fault, not theirs?

He did not lack friends,
30   He had disciples he moulded to his ends.

Did he feel over-handicapped sometimes, yet must draw even?

How could he feel like this? He was the King of Heaven.

. . . find a sudden brightness one day in everything
Because a mood had been conquered, or a sin?

35   I tell you, he did not sin.

Do only human beings suffer from the irritation
I have mentioned? learn too that being comical
Does not ameliorate the desperation?

Only human beings feel this,
40   It is because they are so mixed.

All human beings should have a medal,
A god cannot carry it, he is not able.

A god is Man's doll, you ass,
He makes him up like this on purpose.

45   He might have made him up worse.

He often has, in the past.

To choose a god of love, as he did and does,
Is a little move then?

Yes, it is.

50 A larger one will be when men
Love love and hate hate but do not deify them?

It will be a larger one.

[1962]

Countee Cullen   *1903–1946*

FOR A LADY I KNOW

She even thinks that up in heaven
  Her class lies late and snores,
While poor black cherubs rise at seven
  To do celestial chores.

[1924]

INCIDENT

(For Eric Walrond)

Once riding in old Baltimore,
  Heart-filled, head-filled with glee,
I saw a Baltimorean
  Keep looking straight at me.

5 Now I was eight and very small,
  And he was no whit bigger,
And so I smiled, but he poked out
  His tongue, and called me, "Nigger."

I saw the whole of Baltimore
10   From May until December;
Of all the things that happened there
  That's all that I remember.

[1925]

Richard Eberhart   *1904–*

THE GROUNDHOG

In June, amid the golden fields,
I saw a groundhog lying dead.
Dead lay he; my senses shook,
And mind outshot our naked frailty.
5 There lowly in the vigorous summer

His form began its senseless change,
And made my senses waver dim
Seeing nature ferocious in him.
Inspecting close his maggots' might
10 And seething cauldron of his being,
Half with loathing, half with a strange love,
I poked him with an angry stick.
The fever arose, became a flame
And Vigour circumscribed the skies,
15 Immense energy in the sun,
And through my frame a sunless trembling.
My stick had done nor good nor harm.
Then stood I silent in the day
Watching the object, as before;
20 And kept my reverence for knowledge
Trying for control, to be still,
To quell the passion of the blood;
Until I had bent down on my knees
Praying for joy in the sight of decay.
25 And so I left; and I returned
In Autumn strict of eye, to see
The sap gone out of the groundhog,
But the bony sodden hulk remained.
But the year had lost its meaning,
30 And in intellectual chains
I lost both love and loathing,
Mured° up in the wall of wisdom.   *walled*
Another summer took the fields again
Massive and burning, full of life,
35 But when I chanced upon the spot
There was only a little hair left,
And bones bleaching in the sunlight
Beautiful as architecture;
I watched them like a geometer,[1]
40 And cut a walking stick from a birch.
It has been three years, now.
There is no sign of the groundhog.
I stood there in the whirling summer,
My hand capped a withered heart,
45 And thought of China and of Greece,
Of Alexander in his tent;[2]
Of Montaigne in his tower,[3]
Of Saint Theresa in her wild lament.[4]

[1936]

---

[1] A specialist in geometry.
[2] Alexander the Great (356–323 B.C.), the King of Macedonia and the conqueror of much of the civilized world.
[3] Michel de Montaigne (1533–1592), a French essayist who maintained his study in a tower.
[4] Saint Theresa of Avila (1515–1582), a Spanish nun who became famous for her visions and mysticism.

Phyllis McGinley   *1905–1978*

PORTRAIT OF GIRL
WITH COMIC BOOK

Thirteen's no age at all. Thirteen is nothing.
It is not wit, or powder on the face,
Or Wednesday matinees, or misses' clothing,
Or intellect, or grace.
5   Twelve has its tribal customs. But thirteen
Is neither boys in battered cars nor dolls,
Not *Sara Crewe,* or movie magazine,
Or pennants on the walls.

Thirteen keeps diaries and tropical fish
10   (A month, at most); scorns jumpropes in the spring;
Could not, would fortune grant it, name its wish;
Wants nothing, everything;
Has secrets from itself, friends it despises;
Admits none to the terrors that it feels;
15   Owns half a hundred masks but no disguises;
And walks upon its heels.

Thirteen's anomalous—not that, not this:
Not folded bud, or wave that laps a shore,
Or moth proverbial from the chrysalis.
20   Is the one age defeats the metaphor.
Is not a town, like childhood, strongly walled
But easily surrounded; is no city.
Nor, quitted once, can it be quite recalled—
Not even with pity.

[1952]

W. H. Auden   *1907–1973*

MUSÉE DES BEAUX ARTS[1]

About suffering they were never wrong,
The Old Masters: how well they understood
Its human position; how it takes place
While someone else is eating or opening a window or just walking
                                   dully along;
5   How, when the aged are reverently, passionately waiting
For the miraculous birth, there always must be
Children who did not specially want it to happen, skating

[1] Museum of Fine Arts

On a pond at the edge of the wood:
They never forgot
10   That even the dreadful martyrdom must run its course
Anyhow in a corner, some untidy spot
Where the dogs go on with their doggy life and the torturer's horse
Scratches its innocent behind on a tree.

In Brueghel's *Icarus*,[2] for instance: how everything turns away
15   Quite leisurely from the disaster; the ploughman may
Have heard the splash, the forsaken cry,
But for him it was not an important failure; the sun shone
As it had to on the white legs disappearing into the green
Water; and the expensive delicate ship that must have seen
20   Something amazing, a boy falling out of the sky,
Had somewhere to get to and sailed calmly on.

[1940]

THE UNKNOWN CITIZEN

(To JS/07/M/378
This Marble Monument
Is Erected by the State)

He was found by the Bureau of Statistics to be
One against whom there was no official complaint,
And all the reports on his conduct agree
That, in the modern sense of an old-fashioned word, he was a saint,
5   For in everything he did he served the Greater Community.
Except for the War till the day he retired
He worked in a factory and never got fired,
But satisfied his employers, Fudge Motors Inc.
Yet he wasn't a scab or odd in his views,
10   For his Union reports that he paid his dues,
(Our report on his Union shows it was sound)
And our Social Psychology workers found
That he was popular with his mates and liked a drink.
The Press are convinced that he bought a paper every day
15   And that his reactions to advertisements were normal in every way.
Policies taken out in his name prove that he was fully insured,
And his Health-card shows he was once in hospital but left it cured.
Both Producers Research and High-Grade Living declare
He was fully sensible to the advantages of the Instalment Plan
20   And had everything necessary to the Modern Man,
A phonograph, a radio, a car and a frigidaire.
Our researchers into Public Opinion are content
That he held the proper opinions for the time of year;

---

[2] *Icarus* by the Flemish painter Pieter Brueghel (c. 1520–1569) depicts the fall of Icarus, who, in Greek mythology, had flown too close to the sun on man-made wings of feathers and wax.

When there was peace, he was for peace; when there was war, he
    went.
25 He was married and added five children to the population,
Which our Eugenist says was the right number for a parent of his
    generation,
And our teachers report that he never interfered with their education.
Was he free? Was he happy? The question is absurd:
Had anything been wrong, we should certainly have heard.

                                               [1939]

Theodore Roethke   *1908–1963*

DOLOR

I have known the inexorable sadness of pencils,
Neat in their boxes, dolor of pad and paper-weight,
All the misery of manilla folders and mucilage,
Desolation in immaculate public places,
5 Lonely reception room, lavatory, switchboard,
The unalterable pathos of basin and pitcher,
Ritual of multigraph, paper-clip, comma,
Endless duplication of lives and objects.
And I have seen dust from the walls of institutions,
10 Finer than flour, alive, more dangerous than silica,
Sift, almost invisible, through long afternoons of tedium,
Dropping a fine film on nails and delicate eyebrows,
Glazing the pale hair, the duplicate grey standard faces.

                                               [1948]

ELEGY FOR JANE

My Student, Thrown by a Horse

I remember the neckcurls, limp and damp as tendrils;
And her quick look, a sidelong pickerel smile;
And how, once startled into talk, the light syllables leaped for her,
And she balanced in the delight of her thought,
5 A wren, happy, tail into the wind,
Her song trembling the twigs and small branches.
The shade sang with her;
The leaves, their whispers turned to kissing;
And the mold sang in the bleached valleys under the rose.

10 Oh, when she was sad, she cast herself down into such a pure depth,
Even a father could not find her:

Scraping her cheek against straw;
Stirring the clearest water.

My sparrow, you are not here,
15 Waiting like a fern, making a spiny shadow.
The sides of wet stones cannot console me,
Nor the moss, wound with the last light.

If only I could nudge you from this sleep,
My maimed darling, my skittery pigeon.
20 Over this damp grave I speak the words of my love:
I, with no rights in this matter,
Neither father nor lover.

[1953]

I KNEW A WOMAN

I knew a woman, lovely in her bones,
When small birds sighed, she would sigh back at them;
Ah, when she moved, she moved more ways than one:
The shapes a bright container can contain!
5 Of her choice virtues only gods should speak,
Or English poets who grew up on Greek
(I'd have them sing in chorus, cheek to cheek).

How well her wishes went! She stroked my chin,
She taught me Turn, and Counter-turn, and Stand;
10 She taught me Touch, that undulant white skin;
I nibbled meekly from her proffered hand;
She was the sickle; I, poor I, the rake,
Coming behind her for her pretty sake
(But what prodigious mowing we did make).

15 Love likes a gander, and adores a goose:
Her full lips pursed, the errant note to seize;
She played it quick, she played it light and loose;
My eyes, they dazzled at her flowing knees;
Her several parts could keep a pure repose,
20 Or one hip quiver with a mobile nose
(She moved in circles, and those circles moved).

Let seed be grass, and grass turn into hay:
I'm martyr to a motion not my own;
What's freedom for? To know eternity.
25 I swear she cast a shadow white as stone.
But who would count eternity in days?
These old bones live to learn her wanton ways:
(I measure time by how a body sways).

[1958]

ROOT CELLAR

Nothing would sleep in that cellar, dank as a ditch,
Bulbs broke out of boxes hunting for chinks in the dark,
Shoots dangled and drooped,
Lolling obscenely from mildewed crates,
5   Hung down long yellow evil necks, like tropical snakes.
And what a congress of stinks!—
Roots ripe as old bait,
Pulpy stems, rank, silo-rich,
Leaf-mold, manure, lime, piled against slippery planks.
10   Nothing would give up life:
Even the dirt kept breathing a small breath.

[1948]

Elizabeth Bishop *1911–1979*

AT THE FISHHOUSES

Although it is a cold evening,
down by one of the fishhouses
an old man sits netting,
his net, in the gloaming[1] almost invisible
5   a dark purple-brown,
and his shuttle[2] worn and polished.
The air smells so strong of codfish
it makes one's nose run and one's eyes water.
The five fishhouses have steeply peaked roofs
10   and narrow, cleated gangplanks slant up
to storerooms in the gables
for the wheelbarrows to be pushed up and down on.
All is silver: the heavy surface of the sea,
swelling slowly as if considering spilling over,
15   is opaque, but the silver of the benches,
the lobster pots, and masts, scattered
among the wild jagged rocks,
is of an apparent translucence
like the small old buildings with an emerald moss
20   growing on their shoreward walls.
The big fish tubs are completely lined
with layers of beautiful herring scales
and the wheelbarrows are similarly plastered
with creamy iridescent coats of mail,
25   with small iridescent flies crawling on them.
Up on the little slope behind the houses,
set in the sparse bright sprinkle of grass,

_____
[1] Dusk or twilight.   [2] A device used for weaving.

is an ancient wooden capstan,[3]
cracked, with two long bleached handles
30 and some melancholy stains, like dried blood,
where the ironwork has rusted.
The old man accepts a Lucky Strike.[4]
He was a friend of my grandfather.
We talk of the decline in the population
35 and of codfish and herring
while he waits for a herring boat to come in.
There are sequins on his vest and on his thumb.
He has scraped the scales, the principal beauty,
from unnumbered fish with that black old knife,
40 the blade of which is almost worn away.

Down at the water's edge, at the place
where they haul up the boats, up the long ramp
descending into the water, thin silver
tree trunks are laid horizontally
45 across the gray stones, down and down
at intervals of four or five feet.

Cold dark deep and absolutely clear,
element bearable to no mortal,
to fish and to seals . . . One seal particularly
50 I have seen here evening after evening.
He was curious about me. He was interested in music;
like me a believer in total immersion,[5]
so I used to sing him Baptist hymns.
I also sang "A Mighty Fortress Is Our God."
55 He stood up in the water and regarded me
steadily, moving his head a little.
Then he would disappear, then suddenly emerge
almost in the same spot, with a sort of shrug
as if it were against his better judgment.
60 Cold dark deep and absolutely clear,
the clear gray icy water . . . Back, behind us,
the dignified tall firs begin.
Bluish, associated with their shadows,
a million Christmas trees stand
65 waiting for Christmas. The water seems suspended
above the rounded gray and blue-gray stones.
I have seen it over and over, the same sea, the same,
slightly, indifferently swinging above the stones,
icily free above the stones,
70 above the stones and then the world.
If you should dip your hand in,
your wrist would ache immediately,

---

[3] A vertical drum used in hauling, around which rope or cable is wound.
[4] A brand of cigarettes.
[5] A form of baptism practiced by the Baptist Church.

your bones would begin to ache and your hand would burn
as if the water were a transmutation of fire
75   that feeds on stones and burns with a dark gray flame.
If you tasted it, it would first taste bitter,
then briny, then surely burn your tongue.
It is like what we imagine knowledge to be:
dark, salt, clear, moving, utterly free,
80   drawn from the cold hard mouth
of the world, derived from the rocky breasts
forever, flowing and drawn, and since
our knowledge is historical, flowing, and flown.

[1955]

THE ARMADILLO

For Robert Lowell

This is the time of year
When almost every night
the frail, illegal fire balloons appear.
Climbing the mountain height,

5   rising toward a saint
still honored in these parts,
the paper chambers flush and fill with light
that comes and goes, like hearts.

Once up against the sky it's hard
10   to tell them from the stars—
planets, that is—the tinted ones:
Venus going down, or Mars,

or the pale green one. With a wind,
they flare and falter, wobble and toss;
15   but if it's still they steer between
the kite sticks of the Southern Cross,

receding, dwindling, solemnly
and steadily forsaking us,
or, in the downdraft from a peak,
20   suddenly turning dangerous.

Last night another big one fell.
It splattered like an egg of fire
against the cliff behind the house.
The flame ran down. We saw the pair

25   of owls who nest there flying up
and up, their whirling black-and-white

stained bright pink underneath, until
they shrieked up out of sight.

30 The ancient owls' nest must have burned.
Hastily, all alone,
a glistening armadillo left the scene,
rose-flecked, head down, tail down,

and then a baby rabbit jumped out,
short-eared, to our surprise.
35 So soft!—a handful of intangible ash
with fixed, ignited eyes.

Too pretty, dreamlike mimicry!
O falling fire and piercing cry
and panic, and a weak mailed fist
40 *clenched ignorant against the sky!*

[1965]

Josephine Miles *1911–1985*

REASON

Said, Pull her up a bit will you, Mac, I want to unload there.
Said, Pull her up my rear end, first come first serve.
Said, Give her the gun, Bud, he needs a taste of his own bumper.
Then the usher came out and got into the act:
5 Said, Pull her up, pull her up a bit, we need this space, sir.
Said, For God's sake, is this still a free country or what?
'You go back and take care of Gary Cooper's horse
And leave me handle my own car.

Saw them unloading the lame old lady,
10 Ducked out under the wheel and gave her an elbow,
Said, All you needed to do was just explain;
Reason, Reason is my middle name.

[1955]

Robert Hayden *1913–1980*

THOSE WINTER SUNDAYS

Sundays too my father got up early
and put his clothes on in the blueblack cold,
then with cracked hands that ached

from labor in the weekday weather made
banked fires blaze. No one ever thanked him.

I'd wake and hear the cold splintering, breaking.
When the rooms were warm, he'd call,
and slowly I would rise and dress,
fearing the chronic angers of that house,

Speaking indifferently to him,
who had driven out the cold
and polished my good shoes as well.
What did I know, what did I know
of love's austere and lonely offices?

[1962]

Karl Shapiro   *1913–*

DRUG STORE

I do remember an apothecary,
And hereabouts 'a dwells[1]

It baffles the foreigner like an idiom,
And he is right to adopt it as a form
Less serious than the living-room or bar;
    For it disestablishes the cafe,
Is a collective, and on basic country.

Not that it praises hygiene and corrupts
The ice-cream parlor and the tobacconist's
Is it a center; but that the attractive symbols
    Watch over puberty and leer
Like rubber bottles waiting for sick-use.

Youth comes to jingle nickels and crack wise;
The baseball scores are his, the magazines
Devoted to lust, the jazz, the Coca-Cola,
    The lending-library of love's latest.
He is the customer; he is heroized.

And every nook and cranny of the flesh
Is spoken to by packages with wiles.
"Buy me, buy me," they whimper and cajole;
    The hectic range of lipsticks pouts,
Revealing the wicked and the simple mouth.

[1] The quotation is from William Shakespeare's *Romeo and Juliet* (1597), Act 5, Scene 1.

With scarcely any evasion in their eye
They smoke, undress their girls, exact a stance;
But only for a moment. The clock goes round;
       Crude fellowships are made and lost;
25   They slump on booths like rags, not even drunk.

                      [1942]

AUTO WRECK

Its quick soft silver bell beating, beating,
And down the dark one ruby flare
Pulsing out red light like an artery,
The ambulance at top speed floating down
5   Past beacons and illuminated clocks
Wings in a heavy curve, dips down,
And brakes speed, entering the crowd.
The doors leap open, emptying light;
Stretchers are laid out, the mangled lifted
10 And stowed into the little hospital.
Then the bell, breaking the hush, tolls once,
And the ambulance with its terrible cargo
Rocking, slightly rocking, moves away,
As the doors, an afterthought, are closed.

15 We are deranged, walking among the cops
Who sweep glass and are large and composed.
One is still making notes under the light.
One with a bucket douches ponds of blood
Into the street and gutter.
20 One hangs lanterns on the wrecks that cling,
Empty husks of locusts, to iron poles.

Our throats were tight as tourniquets,
Our feet were bound with splints, but now,
Like convalescents intimate and gauche,
25 We speak through sickly smiles and warn
With the stubborn saw of common sense,
The grim joke and the banal resolution.
The traffic moves around with care,
But we remain, touching a wound
30 That opens to our richest horror.
Already old, the question Who shall die?
Becomes unspoken Who is innocent?
For death in war is done by hands;
Suicide has cause and stillbirth, logic;
35 And cancer, simple as a flower, blooms.
But this invites the occult mind,
Cancels our physics with a sneer,

And spatters all we knew of denouement
Across the expedient and wicked stones.

[1942]

Dylan Thomas   *1914–1953*

THE FORCE THAT THROUGH THE GREEN FUSE DRIVES THE FLOWER

The force that through the green fuse drives the flower
Drives my green age; that blasts the roots of trees
Is my destroyer.
And I am dumb to tell the crooked rose
5   My youth is bent by the same wintry fever.

The force that drives the water through the rocks
Drives my red blood; that dries the mouthing streams
Turns mine to wax.
And I am dumb to mouth unto my veins
10 How at the mountain spring the same mouth sucks.

The hand that whirls the water in the pool
Stirs the quicksand; that ropes the blowing wind
Hauls my shroud sail.
And I am dumb to tell the hanging man
15 How of my clay is made the hangman's lime.

The lips of time leech to the fountain head;
Love drips and gathers, but the fallen blood
Shall calm her sores.
And I am dumb to tell a weather's wind
20 How time has ticked a heaven round the stars.

And I am dumb to tell the lover's tomb
How at my sheet goes the same crooked worm.

[1934]

FERN HILL[1]

Now as I was young and easy under the apple boughs
About the lilting house and happy as the grass was green,
   The night above the dingle° starry,   *wooded dale*
      Time let me hail and climb

---

[1] A farm owned by Thomas's aunt.

5   Golden in the heydays of his eyes,
    And honoured among wagons I was prince of the apple
            towns
    And once below a time I lordly had the trees and leaves
            Trail with daisies and barley
            Down the rivers of the windfall light.

10   And as I was green and carefree, famous among the barns
    About the happy yard and singing as the farm was home,
            In the sun that is young once only,
                Time let me play and be
            Golden in the mercy of his means,
15   And green and golden I was huntsman and herdsman, the
            calves
    Sang to my horn, the foxes on the hills barked clear and
            cold,
            And the sabbath rang slowly
            In the pebbles of the holy streams.

    All the sun long it was running, it was lovely, the hay
20   Fields high as the house, the tunes from the chimneys,
            it was air
            And playing, lovely and watery
                And fire green as grass.
            And nightly under the simple stars
    As I rode to sleep the owls were bearing the farm away,
25   All the moon long I heard, blessed among stables, the
            night-jars°   *nighthawks*
            Flying with the ricks,° and the horses   *haystacks*
                Flashing into the dark.

    And then to awake, and the farm, like a wanderer white
    With the dew, come back, the cock on his shoulder: it was
            all
30   Shining, it was Adam and maiden,
                The sky gathered again
            And the sun grew round that very day.
    So it must have been after the birth of the simple light
    In the first, spinning place, the spellbound horses walking
            warm
35   Out of the whinnying green stable
                On to the fields of praise.

    And honoured among foxes and pheasants by the gay house
    Under the new made clouds and happy as the heart was
            long,
            In the sun born over and over,
40   I ran my heedless ways,
            My wishes raced through the house high hay
    And nothing I cared, at my sky blue trades, that time allows
    In all his tuneful turning so few and such morning songs

Before the children green and golden
45   Follow him out of grace.

Nothing I cared, in the lamb white days, that time would
       take me
Up to the swallow thronged loft by the shadow of my hand,
              In the moon that is always rising,
                     Nor that riding to sleep
50   I should hear him fly with the high fields
And wake to the farm forever fled from the childless land.
Oh as I was young and easy in the mercy of his means,
                Time held me green and dying
           Though I sang in my chains like the sea.

                                                         [1946]

IN MY CRAFT OR SULLEN ART

              In my craft or sullen art
              Exercised in the still night
              When only the moon rages
              And the lovers lie abed
5   With all their griefs in their arms,
              I labour by singing light
              Not for ambition or bread
              Or the strut and trade of charms
              On the ivory stages
10   But for the common wages
              Of their most secret heart.

              Not for the proud man apart
              From the raging moon I write
              On these spindrift° pages
15   Nor for the towering dead   *spray from surf*
              With their nightingales and psalms
              But for the lovers, their arms
              Round the griefs of the ages,
              Who pay no praise or wages
20   Nor heed my craft or art.
                                          [1946]

DO NOT GO GENTLE INTO THAT GOOD NIGHT

       Do not go gentle into that good night,
       Old age should burn and rave at close of day;
       Rage, rage against the dying of the light.

       Though wise men at their end know dark is right,
5   Because their words had forked no lightning they
       Do not go gentle into that good night.

Good men, the last wave by, crying how bright
Their frail deeds might have danced in a green bay,
Rage, rage against the dying of the light.

10 Wild men who caught and sang the sun in flight,
And learn, too late, they grieved it on its way,
Do not go gentle into that good night.

Grave men, near death, who see with blinding sight
Blind eyes could blaze like meteors and be gay,
15 Rage, rage against the dying of the light.

And you, my father, there on the sad height,
Curse, bless, me now with your fierce tears, I pray.
Do not go gentle into that good night.
Rage, rage against the dying of the light.

[1952]

Randall Jarrell   *1914–1965*

THE DEATH OF THE BALL TURRET GUNNER[1]

From my mother's sleep I fell into the State,
And I hunched in its belly till my wet fur froze.
Six miles from earth, loosed from its dream of life,
I woke to black flak and the nightmare fighters.
5 When I died they washed me out of the turret with a hose.

[1945]

EIGHTH AIR FORCE

If, in an odd angle of the hutment,°   *encampment*
A puppy laps the water from a can
Of flowers, and the drunk sergeant shaving
Whistles *O Paradiso!*[2]—shall I say that man
5 Is not as men have said: a wolf to man?

The other murderers troop in yawning;
Three of them play Pitch,° one sleeps, and one   *a card game*
Lies counting missions, lies there sweating
Till even his heart beats: One; One; One.
10 *O murderers!* . . . Still, this is how it's done:

This is a war. . . . But since these play, before they die,
Like puppies with their puppy; since, a man,

---

[1] "A ball turret was a plexiglass sphere set into the belly of a B-17 or B-24, and inhabited by two
.50 caliber machine guns and one man, a short small man." (Jarrell's note)
[2] Aria from Giacomo Meyerbeer's opera *L'Africaine* (1865).

I did as these have done, but did not die—
I will content the people as I can
15   And give up these to them: Behold the man![3]

I have suffered, in a dream, because of him,
Many things;[4] for this last savior, man,
I have lied as I lie now. But what is lying?
Men wash their hands, in blood, as best they can:
20   I find no fault in this just man.

                                                                              [1948]

William Stafford *1914–*

FOR THE GRAVE OF DANIEL BOONE[1]

The farther he went the farther home grew.
Kentucky became another room;
the mansion arched over the Mississippi;
flowers were spread all over the floor.
5   He traced ahead a deepening home,
and better, with goldenrod:

Leaving the snakeskin of place after place,
going on—after the trees
the grass, a bird flying after a song.
10   Rifle so level, sighting so well
his picture freezes down to now,
a story-picture for children.

They go over the velvet falls
into the tapestry of his time,
15   heirs to the landscape, feeling no jar:
it is like evening; they are the quail
surrounding his fire, coming in for the kill;
their little feet move sacred sand.

Children, we live in a barbwire time
20   but like to follow the old hands back—
the ring in the light, the knuckle, the palm,
all the way to Daniel Boone,

---

[3] See John 19:4–5.   [4] See Matthew 27:19.
[1] Daniel Boone (1734–1820), the American pathfinder whose early explorations led to the settlement
of Kentucky. In 1775, it was Boone, at the head of a party of woodsmen, who blazed the famous
Wilderness Road through the Appalachians, which opened up the American West. In 1799, at
the age of 65, Boone again moved westward, "over the Mississippi" into Missouri, because,
according to legend, "I want more elbow-room." Boone died in Missouri at the age of 86; in
1845 his remains and those of his wife were moved to Frankfort, Kentucky.

hunting our own kind of deepening home.
From the land that was his I heft this rock.

25   Here on his grave I put it down.

                                    [1957]

AT THE BOMB TESTING SITE

At noon in the desert a panting lizard
waited for history, its elbows tense,
watching the curve of a particular road
as if something might happen.

5   It was looking at something farther off
than people could see, an important scene
acted in stone for little selves
at the flute end of consequences.

There was just a continent without much on it
10   under a sky that never cared less.
Ready for a change, the elbows waited.
The hands gripped hard on the desert.

                                    [1966]

TRAVELING THROUGH THE DARK

Traveling through the dark I found a deer
dead on the edge of the Wilson River road.
It is usually best to roll them into the canyon:
that road is narrow; to swerve might make more dead.

5   By glow of the tail-light I stumbled back of the car
and stood by the heap, a doe, a recent killing;
she had stiffened already, almost cold.
I dragged her off; she was large in the belly.

My fingers touching her side brought me the reason—
10   her side was warm; her fawn lay there waiting,
alive, still, never to be born.
Beside that mountain road I hesitated.

The car aimed ahead its lowered parking lights;
under the hood purred the steady engine.
15   I stood in the glare of the warm exhaust turning red;
around our group I could hear the wilderness listen.

I thought hard for us all—my only swerving—
then pushed her over the edge into the river.

                                    [1962]

Robert Lowell   *1917–1977*

FOR THE UNION DEAD

"Relinquunt omnia servare rem publicam." [1]

The old South Boston Aquarium stands
in a Sahara of snow now. Its broken windows are boarded.
The bronze weathervane cod has lost half its scales.
The airy tanks are dry.

5 Once my nose crawled like a snail on the glass;
my hand tingled
to burst the bubbles
drifting from the noses of the cowed, compliant fish.

My hand draws back. I often sigh still
10 for the dark downward and vegetating kingdom
of the fish and reptile. One morning last March,
I pressed against the new barbed and galvanized

fence on the Boston Common. Behind their cage,
yellow dinosaur steamshovels were grunting
15 as they cropped up tons of mush and grass
to gouge their underworld garage.

Parking spaces luxuriate like civic
sandpiles in the heart of Boston.
A girdle of orange, Puritan-pumpkin colored girders
20 braces the tingling Statehouse,

shaking over the excavations, as it faces Colonel Shaw
and his bell-cheeked Negro infantry
on St. Gaudens' shaking Civil War relief,
propped by a plank splint against the garage's earthquake.

25 Two months after marching through Boston,
half the regiment was dead;
at the dedication,
William James[2] could almost hear the bronze Negroes breathe.

---

[1] *Latin:* "They give up everything to serve the Republic." The headnote is a slightly altered version of the inscription on the monument to Robert Gould Shaw (1837–1863), commander of the first black Northern regiment during the Civil War, who was killed during the attack on Fort Wagner in South Carolina. The monument, erected on the Boston Common (a public park) opposite the Massachusetts State House, is a bronze relief by the sculptor Augustus Saint-Gaudens (1848–1907); it was dedicated in 1897.

[2] William James (1842–1910), the Harvard psychologist and philosopher; brother of American novelist Henry James.

Their monument sticks like a fishbone
30   in the city's throat.
Its Colonel is as lean
as a compass-needle.

He has an angry wrenlike vigilance,
a greyhound's gentle tautness;
35   he seems to wince at pleasure,
and suffocate for privacy.

He is out of bounds now. He rejoices in man's lovely,
peculiar power to choose life and die—
when he leads his black soldiers to death,
40   he cannot bend his back.

On a thousand small town New England greens,
the old white churches hold their air
of sparse, sincere rebellion; frayed flags
quilt the graveyards of the Grand Army of the Republic.

45   The stone statues of the abstract Union Soldier
grow slimmer and younger each year—
wasp-waisted, they doze over muskets
and muse through their sideburns . . .

Shaw's father wanted no monument
50   except the ditch,
where his son's body was thrown[3]
and lost with his "niggers."

The ditch is nearer.
There are no statues for the last war[4] here;
55   on Boylston Street,[5] a commercial photograph
shows Hiroshima boiling

over a Mosler Safe, the "Rock of Ages"
that survived the blast. Space is nearer.
When I crouch to my television set,
60   the drained faces of Negro school-children rise like balloons.

Colonel Shaw
is riding on his bubble,
he waits
for the blessèd break.

65   The Aquarium is gone. Everywhere,
giant finned cars nose forward like fish;
a savage servility
slides by on grease.

[1959]

---

[3] By Confederate soldiers.   [4] World War II.   [5] A street in Boston.

SKUNK HOUR

(For Elizabeth Bishop)[1]

Nautilus Island's[2] hermit
heiress still lives through winter in her Spartan cottage;
her sheep still graze above the sea.
Her son's a bishop. Her farmer
5 is first selectman[3] in our village;
she's in her dotage.

Thirsting for
the hierarchic privacy
of Queen Victoria's century,[4]
10 she buys up all
the eyesores facing her shore,
and lets them fall.

The season's ill—
we've lost our summer millionaire,
15 who seemed to leap from an L. L. Bean[5]
catalogue. His nine-knot yawl[6]
was auctioned off to lobstermen.
A red fox stain covers Blue Hill.[7]

And now our fairy
20 decorator brightens his shop for fall;
his fishnet's filled with orange cork,
orange, his cobbler's bench and awl;
there is no money in his work,
he'd rather marry.

25 One dark night,
my Tudor Ford[8] climbed the hill's skull;
I watched for love-cars. Lights turned down,
they lay together, hull to hull,
where the graveyard shelves on the town. . . .
30 My mind's not right.

---

[1] Elizabeth Bishop (1911–1979), the American poet. Lowell has indicated in one of his essays that his poem is modeled on her poem "The Armadillo": both poems "use short line stanzas, start with drifting description and end with a single animal."

[2] The poem is set in the vicinity of Castine, Maine, on Penobscot Bay, where Lowell had a summer home.

[3] An elected New England town official.

[4] Queen Victoria ruled Great Britain from 1837 to 1901.

[5] The famous mail-order house in Freeport, Maine, specializing in sporting goods and camping equipment.

[6] A sailboat capable of doing nine nautical miles an hour.

[7] According to Lowell: "the rusty reddish color of autumn on Blue Hill near [Bangor, Maine] where we were living."

[8] The name given by the Ford Motor Company to its two-door model.

A car radio bleats,
"Love, O careless Love. . . ."[9] I hear
my ill-spirit sob in each blood cell,
as if my hand were at its throat. . . .
35 I myself am hell;[10]
nobody's here—

only skunks, that search
in the moonlight for a bite to eat.
They march on their soles up Main Street:
40 white stripes, moonstruck eyes' red fire
under the chalk-dry and spar spire
of the Trinitarian Church.[11]

I stand on top
of our back steps and breathe the rich air—
45 a mother skunk with her column of kittens swills the garbage pail.
She jabs her wedge-head in a cup
of sour cream, drops her ostrich tail,
and will not scare.

[1959]

THE MOUTH OF THE HUDSON[1]

(For Esther Brooks)

A single man stands like a bird-watcher,
and scuffles the pepper and salt snow
from a discarded, gray
Westinghouse Electric cable drum.
5 He cannot discover America by counting
the chains of condemned freight-trains
from thirty states. They jolt and jar
and junk in the siding below him.
He has trouble with his balance.
10 His eyes drop,
and he drifts with the wild ice
ticking seaward down the Hudson,
like the blank sides of a jig-saw puzzle.

The ice ticks seaward like a clock.
15 A Negro toasts
wheat-seeds over the coke-fumes

---

[9] Words from a well-known folksong.
[10] An allusion to Milton's *Paradise Lost*, IV, 75, where Satan says: "Which way I fly is hell; myself am hell."
[11] A church which subscribes to a belief in the doctrine of the Trinity, the theological union of Father, Son, and Holy Ghost, in one godhead.
[1] The Hudson River flows into New York Bay.

of a punctured barrel.
Chemical air
sweeps in from New Jersey,
20   and smells of coffee.

Across the river,
ledges of suburban factories tan
in the sulphur-yellow sun
of the unforgivable landscape.

[1964]

Gwendolyn Brooks   *1917–*

SADIE AND MAUD

Maud went to college.
Sadie stayed at home.
Sadie scraped life
With a fine-tooth comb.

5   She didn't leave a tangle in.
Her comb found every strand.
Sadie was one of the livingest chits[1]
In all the land.

Sadie bore two babies
10   Under her maiden name.
Maud and Ma and Papa
Nearly died of shame.
Every one but Sadie
Nearly died of shame.

15   When Sadie said her last so-long
Her girls struck out from home.
(Sadie had left as heritage
Her fine-tooth comb.)

Maud, who went to college,
20   Is a thin brown mouse.
She is living all alone
In this old house.

[1945]

[1] Pert young women.

THE CHICAGO *DEFENDER*[1] SENDS
A MAN TO LITTLE ROCK

Fall, 1957[2]

In Little Rock the people bear
Babes, and comb and part their hair
And watch the want ads, put repair
To roof and latch. While wheat toast burns
5   A woman waters multiferns.

Time upholds or overturns
The many, tight, and small concerns.

In Little Rock the people sing
Sunday hymns like anything,
10   Through Sunday pomp and polishing.

And after testament and tunes,
Some soften Sunday afternoons
With lemon tea and Lorna Doones.[3]

   I forcast
15   And I believe
Come Christmas Little Rock will cleave
To Christmas tree and trifle, weave,
From laugh and tinsel, texture fast.

In Little Rock is baseball; Barcarolle.[4]
20   That hotness in July . . . the uniformed figures raw and implacable
And not intellectual,
Battling the hotness or clawing the suffering dust.
The Open Air Concert, on the special twilight green . . .
When Beethoven is brutal or whispers to lady-like air.
25   Blanket-sitters are solemn, as Johann troubles to lean
To tell them what to mean. . . .

There is love, too, in Little Rock. Soft women softly
Opening themselves in kindness,
Or, pitying one's blindness,
30   Awaiting one's pleasure
In azure
Glory with anguished rose at the root. . . .
To wash away old semi-discomfitures.
They re-teach purple and unsullen blue.

---

[1] A Chicago newspaper.
[2] Little Rock, Arkansas, the scene of racial disturbances in 1957 when the governor of the state tried to prevent court-ordered integration of a city high school.
[3] A brand of cookies.   [4] A Venetial gondolier's song.

35   The wispy soils go. And uncertain
     Half-havings have they clarified to sures.

     In Little Rock they know
     Not answering the telephone is a way of rejecting life,
     That it is our business to be bothered, is our business
40   To cherish bores or boredom, be polite
     To lies and love and many-faceted fuzziness.

     I scratch my head, massage the hate-I-had.
     I blink across my prim and pencilled pad.
     The saga I was sent for is not down.
45   Because there is a puzzle in this town.
     The biggest News I do not dare
     Telegraph to the Editor's chair:
     "They are like people everywhere."

     The angry Editor would reply
50   In hundred harryings of Why.

     And true, they are hurling spittle, rock,
     Garbage and fruit in Little Rock.
     And I saw coiling storm a-writhe
     On bright madonnas. And a scythe
55   Of men harassing brownish girls.
     (The bows and barrettes in the curls
     And braids declined away from joy.)

     I saw a bleeding brownish boy. . . .

     The lariat lynch-wish I deplored.

60   The loveliest lynchee was our Lord.

                                        [1960]

THE BEAN EATERS

     They eat beans mostly, this old yellow pair.
     Dinner is a casual affair.   ·
     Plain chipware on a plain and creaking wood,
     Tin flatware.

5   Two who are Mostly Good.
     Two who have lived their day,
     But keep on putting on their clothes
     And putting things away.

     And remembering . . .
10   Remembering, with twinklings and twinges,

As they lean over the beans in their rented back room
    that is full of beads and receipts and dolls and cloths,
    tobacco crumbs, vases and fringes.

                [1959]

Lawrence Ferlinghetti *1919–*

CONSTANTLY RISKING ABSURDITY

Constantly risking absurdity
             and death
    whenever he performs
          above the heads
              of his audience
5   the poet like an acrobat
        climbs on rime
           to a high wire of his own making
   and balancing on eyebeams
          above a sea of faces
10   paces his way
        to the other side of day
   performing entrechats
        and sleight-of-foot tricks
15   and other high theatrics
        and all without mistaking
      any thing
        for what it may not be

    For he's the super realist
20   who must perforce perceive
     taut truth
       before the taking of each stance or step
  in his supposed advance
        toward that still higher perch
25   where Beauty stands and waits
       with gravity
         to start her death-defying leap

    And he
      a little charleychaplin man
30   who may or may not catch
      her fair eternal form
         spreadeagled in the empty air
    of existence
                [1958]

May Swenson 1919–

WOMEN

Women
  should be
    pedestals
     moving
5   pedestals
     moving
    to the
    motions
   of men

Or they
  should be
   little horses
    those wooden
    sweet
     oldfashioned
    painted
   rocking
    horses

10   the gladdest things in the toyroom

    The
   pegs
  of their
  ears
15 so familiar
 and dear
  to the trusting
fists
To be chafed

    feelingly
   and then
   unfeelingly
  To be
  joyfully
 ridden
 rockingly
ridden until
the restored

20 egos dismount and the legs stride away

Immobile
  sweetlipped
  sturdy
   and smiling
25   women
    should always
    be waiting

  willing
  to be set
   into motion
   Women
    should be
    pedestals
    to men

Howard Nemerov 1920–

THE GOOSE FISH[1]

On the long shore, lit by the moon
To show them properly alone,

---

[1] The goosefish, or "monkfish," is common to the waters of the North Atlantic.

Two lovers suddenly embraced
So that their shadows were as one.
The ordinary night was graced
For them by the swift tide of blood
That silently they took at flood,
And for a little time they prized
   Themselves emparadised.

Then, as if shaken by stage-fright
Beneath the hard moon's bony light,
They stood together on the sand
Embarrassed in each other's sight
But still conspiring hand in hand,
Until they saw, there underfoot,
As though the world had found them out,
The goose fish turning up, though dead,
   His hugely grinning head.

There in the china light he lay,
Most ancient and corrupt and grey
They hesitated at his smile,
Wondering what it seemed to say
To lovers who a little while
Before had thought to understand,
By violence upon the sand,
The only way that could be known
   To make a world their own.

It was a wide and moony grin
Together peaceful and obscene;
They know not what he would express,
So finished a comedian
He might mean failure or success,
But took it for an emblem of
Their sudden, new and guilty love
To be observed by, when they kissed,
   That rigid optimist.

So he became their patriarch,
Dreadfully mild in the half-dark.
His throat that the sand seemed to choke,
His picket teeth, these left their mark
But never did explain the joke
That so amused him, lying there
While the moon went down to disappear
Along the still and tilted track
   That bears the zodiac.

                           [1955]

Richard Wilbur   *1921–*

A SIMILE FOR HER SMILE

Your smiling, or the hope, the thought of it,
Makes in my mind such pause and abrupt ease
As when the highway bridgegates fall,
Balking the hasty traffic, which must sit
On each side massed and staring, while
Deliberately the drawbridge starts to rise:

Then horns are hushed, the oilsmoke rarifies,
Above the idling motors one can tell
The packet's smooth approach, the slip,
Slip of the silken river past the sides,
The ringing of clear bells, the dip
And slow cascading of the paddle wheel.

                                                  [1950]

MUSEUM PIECE

The good gray guardians of art
Patrol the halls on spongy shoes,
Impartially protective, though
Perhaps suspicious of Toulouse.[1]

Here dozes one against the wall,
Disposed upon a funeral chair.
A Degas dancer pirouettes[2]
Upon the parting of his hair.

See how she spins! The grace is there,
But strain as well is plain to see.
Degas loved the two together:
Beauty joined to energy.

Edgar Degas purchased once
A fine El Greco,[3] which he kept
Against the wall beside his bed
To hang his pants on while he slept.

                                                  [1950]

[1] Henri de Toulouse-Lautrec (1864–1901), a French painter and lithographer.
[2] Edgar Degas (1834–1917), a French painter noted for his pictures of ballet dancers.
[3] El Greco (1548?–1614?), a Spanish painter.

SLEEPLESS AT CROWN POINT

All night, this headland
Lunges into the rumpling
Capework of the wind
[1976]

THE STAR SYSTEM

While you're a white-hot youth, emit the rays
Which, now unmarked, shall dazzle future days.
Burn for the joy of it, and waste no juice
On hopes of prompt discovery. Produce!
5   Then, white with years, live wisely and survive.
Thus you may be on hand when you arrive,
And, like Antares, rosily dilate,
And for a time be gaseous and great.

Philip Larkin   *1922–1985*

CHURCH GOING

Once I am sure there's nothing going on
I step inside, letting the door thud shut.
Another church: matting, seats, and stone,
And little books; sprawlings of flowers, cut
5   For Sunday, brownish now; some brass and stuff
Up at the holy end; the small neat organ;
And a tense, musty, unignorable silence,
Brewed God knows how long. Hatless, I take off
My cycle-clips in awkward reverence,

10   Move forward, run my hand around the font.
From where I stand, the roof looks almost new—
Cleaned, or restored? Someone would know: I don't.
Mounting the lectern, I peruse a few
Hectoring large-scale verses, and pronounce
15   "Here endeth" much more loudly than I'd meant.
The echoes snigger briefly. Back at the door
I sign the book, donate an Irish sixpence,
Reflect the place was not worth stopping for.

Yet stop I did: in fact I often do,
20   And always end much at a loss like this,
Wondering what to look for; wondering, too,
When churches fall completely out of use
What we shall turn them into, if we shall keep

A few cathedrals chronically on show,
25   Their parchment, plate and pyx[1] in locked cases,
And let the rest rent-free to rain and sheep.
Shall we avoid them as unlucky places?

Or, after dark, will dubious women come
To make their children touch a particular stone;
30   Pick simples[2] for a cancer; or on some
Advised night see walking a dead one?
Power of some sort or other will go on
In games, in riddles, seemingly at random;
But superstition, like belief, must die,
35   And what remains when disbelief has gone?
Grass, weedy pavement, brambles, buttress,[3] sky,

A shape less recognisable each week,
A purpose more obscure. I wonder who
Will be the last, the very last, to seek
40   This place for what it was; one of the crew
That tap and jot and know what rood-lofts[4] were?
Some ruin-bibber,[5] randy[6] for antique,
Or Christmas-addict, counting on a whiff
Of gown-and-bands and organ-pipes and myrrh?[7]
45   Or will he be my representative,

Bored, uninformed, knowing the ghostly silt
Dispersed, yet tending to this cross of ground
Through suburb scrub because it held unspilt
So long and equably what since is found
50   Only in separation—marriage, and birth,
And death, and thoughts of these—for whom was built
This special shell? For, though I've no idea
What this accoutred frowsty[8] barn is worth,
It pleases me to stand in silence here;

55   A serious house on serious earth it is,
In whose blent air all our compulsions meet,
Are recognized, and robed as destinies.
And that much never can be obsolete,
Since someone will forever be surprising
60   A hunger in himself to be more serious,
And gravitating with it to this ground,
Which, he once heard, was proper to grow wise in,
If only that so many dead lie round.

[1955]

[1] A container in which the Communion wafers are kept.
[2] Plants or herbs with real or reputed medicinal powers.
[3] A structure, often of stone, lending support to a wall.
[4] Lofts or galleries within a church.   [5] An habitué of ruins.   [6] Literally, lecherous.
[7] Incense.   [8] Must.

SUNNY PRESTATYN[1]

Come to Sunny Prestatyn
Laughed the girl on the poster,
Kneeling up on the sand
In tautened white satin.
Behind her, a hunk of coast, a
Hotel with palms
Seemed to expand from her thighs and
Spread breast-lifting arms.

She was slapped up one day in March.
A couple of weeks, and her face
Was snaggle-toothed and boss-eyed;
Huge tits and a fissured crotch
Were scored well in, and the space
Between her legs held scrawls
That set her fairly astride
A tuberous cock and balls

Autographed *Titch Thomas,* while
Someone had used a knife
Or something to stab right through
The moustached lips of her smile.
She was too good for this life.
Very soon, a great transverse tear
Left only a hand and some blue.
Now *Fight Cancer* is there.

[1964]

Anthony Hecht   *1923–*

"MORE LIGHT! MORE LIGHT!"[1]

For Heinrich Blücher and Hannah Arendt[2]

Composed in the Tower before his execution
These moving verses, and being brought at that time
Painfully to the stake, submitted, declaring thus:
"I implore my God to witness that I have made no crime."

---

[1] A seaside resort in northern Wales.

[1] Supposedly the final words of Johann Wolfgang von Goethe (1749–1832), a German whose accomplishments as a poet, novelist, playwright, scientist, and philosopher made him one of the intellectual giants of his age.

[2] Hannah Arendt (1906–1975), the author of the classic *Origins of Totalitarianism* (1951), who came to the United States from Germany in 1941 with her husband Heinrich Blücher, a professor of philosophy.

5 Nor was he forsaken of courage, but the death was horrible,
   The sack of gunpowder failing to ignite.
   His legs were blistered sticks on which the black sap
   Bubbled and burst as he howled for the Kindly Light.

   And that was but one, and by no means one of the worst;
10 Permitted at least his pitiful dignity;
   And such as were by made prayers in the name of Christ,
   That shall judge all men, for his soul's tranquility.

   We move now to outside a German wood
   Three men are there commanded to dig a hole
15 In which the two Jews are ordered to lie down
   And be buried alive by the third, who is a Pole.

   Not light from the shrine at Weimar[3] beyond the hill
   Nor light from heaven appeared. But he did refuse.
   A Lüger[4] settled back deeply in its glove.
20 He was ordered to change places with the Jews.

   Much casual death had drained away their souls.
   The thick dirt mounted toward the quivering chin.
   When only the head was exposed the order came
   To dig him out again and to get back in.

25 No light, no light in the blue Polish eye.
   When he finished a riding boot packed down the earth.
   The Lüger hovered lightly in its glove.
   He was shot in the belly and in three hours bled to death.

   No prayers or incense rose up in those hours
30 Which grew to be years, and every day came mute
   Ghosts from the ovens, sifting through crisp air,
   And settled upon his eyes in a black soot.

                                                    [1967]

THE DOVER BITCH

A Criticism of Life

So there stood Matthew Arnold and this girl
With the cliffs of England crumbling away behind them,
And he said to her, "Try to be true to me,

---

[3] A city in Germany, once the home of Goethe; nearby stood Buchenwald, the infamous Nazi concentration camp.
[4] A German make of pistol.

And I'll do the same for you, for things are bad
5   All over, etc., etc."
Well now, I knew this girl. It's true she had read
Sophocles in a fairly good translation
And caught that bitter allusion to the sea,
But all the time he was talking she had in mind
10   The notion of what his whiskers would feel like
On the back of her neck. She told me later on
That after a while she got to looking out
At the lights across the channel, and really felt sad,
Thinking of all the wine and enormous beds
15   And blandishments in French and the perfumes.
And then she got really angry. To have been brought
All the way down from London, and then be addressed
As sort of a mournful cosmic last resort
Is really tough on a girl, and she was pretty.
20   Anyway, she watched him pace the room
And finger his watch-chain and seem to sweat a bit,
And then she said one or two unprintable things.
But you mustn't judge her by that. What I mean to say is,
She's really all right. I still see her once in a while
25   And she always treats me right. We have a drink
And I give her a good time, and perhaps it's a year
Before I see her again, but there she is,
Running to fat, but dependable as they come,
And sometimes I bring her a bottle of *Nuit d'Amour.*

[1968]

Denise Levertov   *1923–*

AT THE EDGE

How much I should like to begin
a poem with And—presupposing
the hardest said—
the moss cleared off the stone,
5   the letters plain.
How the round moon
would shine into all the corners
of such a poem and show
the words! Moths and dazzled
10   awakened birds
would freeze in its light!
The lines would be
an outbreak of bells
and I swinging on the rope!

15 Yet, not desiring apocrypha[1]
but true revelation,
what use to pretend the stone discovered,
anything visible?
That poem indeed
20 may not be carved there, may lie
—the quick of mystery—
in animal eyes gazing
from the thicket,
a creature of unknown size,
25 fierce, terrified, having teeth or
no defense, but whom
no And may approach suddenly.

[1959]

Louis Simpson   1923–

SUMMER STORM

In that so sudden summer storm they tried
Each bed, couch, closet, carpet, car-seat, table,
Both river banks, five fields, a mountain side,
Covering as much ground as they were able.

5 A lady, coming on them in the dark
In a white fixture, wrote to the newspapers
Complaining of the statues in the park.
By Cupid, but they cut some pretty capers!

The envious oxen in still rings would stand
10 Ruminating. Their sweet incessant plows
I think had changed the contours of the land
And made two modest conies° move their house.   *rabbits*

God rest them well, and firmly shut the door.
Now they are married Nature breathes once more.

[1949]

Lisel Mueller   1924–

FIRST SNOW IN LAKE COUNTY

All night it fell around us
as if the sky had been sheared,

[1] Books of the Bible that are of questionable authority or authenticity as opposed to those which have the sanction of "true revelation."

its fleece dropping forever
past our windows, until our room
was as chaste and sheltered
as Ursula's, where she lay
and dreamed herself in heaven:
and in the morning we saw
that the vision had held, looked out
on such a sight as we wish for
all our lives:
a thing, place, time
untouched and uncorrupted,
the world before we were here.

Even the wind held its peace.

And already, as our eyes
hung on, hung on, we longed
to make that patience bear
our tracks, already our daughter
put on her boots and screamed,
and the dog jumped with the joy
of splashing the white with yellow
and digging through the snow
to the scents and sounds below.

[1965]

Maxine Kumin   *1925–*

TOGETHER

The water closing
over us and the
going down is all.
Gills are given.
We convert in a
town of broken hulls
and green doubloons.
O you dead pirates
hear us! There is
no salvage. All
you know is the color
of warm caramel. All
is salt. See how
our eyes have migrated
to the uphill side?
Now we are new round

mouths and no spines
letting the water cover.
It happens over
20 and over, me in
your body and you
in mine.

[1970]

WOODCHUCKS

Gassing the woodchucks didn't turn out right.
The knockout bomb from the Feed and Grain Exchange
was featured as merciful, quick at the bone
and the case we had against them was airtight
5 both exits shoehorned shut with puddingstone,°   *cement*
but they had a sub-sub-basement out of range.

Next morning they turned up again, no worse
for the cyanide than we for our cigarettes
and state-store Scotch, all of us up to scratch.
10 They brought down the marigolds as a matter of course
and then took over the vegetable patch
nipping the broccoli shoots, beheading the carrots.

The food from our mouths, I said, righteously thrilling
to the feel of the .22, the bullets' neat noses.
15 I, a lapsed pacifist fallen from grace
puffed with Darwinian pieties for killing,
now drew a bead on the littlest woodchuck's face.
He died down in the everbearing roses.

Ten minutes later I dropped the mother. She
20 flipflopped in the air and fell, her needle teeth
still hooked in a leaf of early Swiss chard.
Another baby next. O one-two-three
the murderer inside me rose up hard,
the hawkeye killer came on stage forthwith.

25 There's one chuck left. Old wily fellow, he keeps
me cocked and ready day after day after day.
All night I hunt his humped-up form. I dream
I sight along the barrel in my sleep.
If only they'd all consented to die unseen
30 gassed underground the quiet Nazi way.

[1972]

A. R. Ammons *1926–*

THE CITY LIMITS

When you consider the radiance, that it does not withhold
itself but pours its abundance without selection into every
nook and cranny not overhung or hidden; when you consider

that birds' bones make no awful noise against the light but
lie low in the light as in a high testimony; when you consider
the radiance, that it will look into the guiltiest

swervings of the weaving heart and bear itself upon them,
not flinching into disguise or darkening; when you consider
the abundance of such resource as illuminates the glow-blue

bodies and gold-skeined wings of flies swarming the dumped
guts of a natural slaughter or the coil of shit and in no
way winces from its storms of generosity; when you consider

that air or vacuum, snow or shale, squid or wolf, rose or lichen,
each is accepted into as much light as it will take, then
the heart moves roomier, the man stands and looks about, the

leaf does not increase itself above the grass, and the dark
work of the deepest cells is of a tune with May bushes
and fear lit by the breadth of such calmly turns to praise.

[1971]

Robert Creeley *1926–*

I KNOW A MAN

As I sd to my
friend, because I am
always talking,—John, I

sd, which was not his
name, the darkness sur-
rounds us, what

can we do against
it, or else, shall we &
why not, buy a goddamn big car,

drive, he sd, for
       christ's sake, look
       out where yr going.

                              [1962]

Allen Ginsberg   *1926–*

FIRST PARTY AT KEN KESEY'S[1]
WITH HELL'S ANGELS

Cool black night thru the redwoods
cars parked outside in shade
behind the gate, stars dim above
the ravine, a fire burning by the side
porch and a few tired souls hunched over
in black leather jackets. In the huge
wooden house, a yellow chandelier
at 3AM the blast of loudspeakers
hi-fi Rolling Stones Ray Charles Beatles
Jumping Joe Jackson and twenty youths
dancing to the vibration thru the floor,
a little weed in the bathroom, girls in scarlet
tights, one muscular smooth skinned man
sweating dancing for hours, beer cans
bent littering the yard, a hanged man
sculpture dangling from a high creek branch,
children sleeping softly in their bedroom bunks.
And 4 police cars parked outside the painted
gate, red lights revolving in the leaves.

                              [1974]

W. D. Snodgrass   *1926–*

APRIL INVENTORY

The green catalpa tree has turned
All white; the cherry blooms once more.
In one whole year I haven't learned
A blessed thing they pay you for.

---

[1] Ken Kesey (1935–   ) is the author of *One Flew Over the Cuckoo's Nest* and *Sometimes a Great Notion* (1964). The incidents described in this poem actually took place and are more fully related in Tom Wolfe's book about Kesey entitled *The Electric Kool-Aid Acid Test.*

5 The blossoms snow down in my hair;
The trees and I will soon be bare.

The trees have more than I to spare.
The sleek, expensive girls I teach,
Younger and pinker every year,
10 Bloom gradually out of reach.
The pear tree lets its petals drop
Like dandruff on a tabletop.

The girls have grown so girlish now
I have to nudge myself to stare.
15 This year they smile and mind me how
My teeth are falling with my hair.
In thirty years I may not get
Younger, shrewder, or out of debt.

The tenth time, just a year ago,
20 I made myself a little list
Of all the things I'd ought to know,
Then told my parents, analyst,
And everyone who's trusted me
I'd be substantial, presently.

25 I haven't read one book about
A book or memorized one plot.
Or found a mind I did not doubt.
I learned one date. And then forgot.
And one by one the solid scholars
30 Get the degrees, the jobs, the dollars.

And smile above their starchy collars.
I taught my classes Whitehead's[1] notions;
One lovely girl, a song of Mahler's.[2]
Lacking a source book and promotions,
35 I taught one child the colors of
A luna moth and how to love.

I taught myself to name my name,
To bark back, loosen love and crying;
To ease my woman so she came,
40 To ease an old man who was dying.
I have not learned how often I
Can win, can love, but choose to die.

---

[1] Alfred North Whitehead (1861–1947), an English philosopher and mathematician.
[2] Gustav Mahler (1860–1911), an Austrian composer and conductor.

I have not learned there is a lie
Love shall be blonder, slimmer, younger;
45 That my equivocating eye
Loves only by my body's hunger;
That I have forces, true to feel,
Or that the lovely world is real.

While scholars speak authority
50 And wear their ulcers on their sleeves,
My eyes in spectacles shall see
These trees procure and spend their leaves.
There is a value underneath
The gold and silver in my teeth.

55 Though trees turn bare and girls turn wives,
We shall afford our costly seasons;
There is a gentleness survives
That will outspeak and has its reasons.
There is a loveliness exists,
60 Preserves us; not for specialists.

[1959]

David Wagoner   *1926–*

MEETING A BEAR

If you haven't made noise enough to warn him, singing, shouting,
Or thumping sticks against trees as you walk in the woods,
Giving him time to vanish
(As he wants to) quietly sideways through the nearest thicket,
5 You may wind up standing face to face with a bear.
Your near future,
Even your distant future, may depend on how he feels
Looking at you, on what he makes of you
And your upright posture   •
10 Which, in his world, like a down-swayed head and humped shoulders,
Is a standing offer to fight for territory
And a mate to go with it.
Gaping and staring directly are as risky as running:
To try for dominance or moral authority
15 Is an empty gesture,
And taking to your heels is an invitation to a dance
Which, from your point of view, will be no circus.
He won't enjoy your smell
Or anything else about you, including your ancestors
20 Or the shape of your snout. If the feeling's mutual,

It's still out of balance:
He doesn't *care* what you think or calculate; your disapproval
Leaves him as cold as the opinions of salmon.
He may feel free
25 To act out all his own displeasures with a vengeance:
You would do well to try your meekest behavior,
Standing still
As long as you're not mauled or hugged, your eyes downcast.
But if you must make a stir, do everything sidelong,
30 Gently and naturally,
Vaguely oblique. Withdraw without turning and start saying
Softly, monotonously, whatever comes to mind
Without special pleading:
Nothing hurt or reproachful to appeal to his better feelings.
35 He has none, only a harder life than yours.
There's no use singing
National anthems or battle hymns or alma maters[1]
Or any other charming or beastly music.
Use only the dullest,
40 Blandest, most colorless, undemonstrative speech you can think of,
Bears, for good reason, find it embarrassing
Or at least disarming
And will forget their claws and cover their eyeteeth as an answer.
Meanwhile, move off, yielding the forest floor
45 As carefully as your honor.

[1975]

WALKING IN A SWAMP

When you first feel the ground under your feet
Going soft and uncertain,
It's best to start running as fast as you can slog
Even though falling
5 Forward on your knees and lunging like a cripple.
You may escape completely
Being bogged down in those few scampering seconds.
But if you're caught standing
In deep mud, unable to walk or stagger,
10 It's time to reconsider
Your favorite postures, textures, and means of moving,
Coming to even terms
With the kind of dirt that won't take no for an answer.
You must lie down now,
15 Like it or not: if you're in it up to your thighs,
Be seated gently,
Lie back, open your arms, and dream of floating

---

[1] School or college songs.

In a sweet backwater.
Slowly your sunken feet will rise together,
20 And you may slither
Spread-ottered casually backwards out of trouble.
If you stay vertical
And, worse, imagine you're in a fearful struggle,
Trying to swivel
25 One stuck leg at a time, keeping your body
Above it all,
Immaculate, you'll sink in even deeper,
Becoming an object lesson
For those who wallow after you through the mire,
30 In which case you should know
For near-future reference: muck is one part water,
One part what-have-you,
Including yourself, now in it over your head,
As upright as ever.

[1975]

James Wright   *1927–1980*

A BLESSING

Just off the highway to Rochester, Minnesota,
Twilight bounds softly forth on the grass.
And the eyes of those two Indian ponies
Darken with kindness.
5 They have come gladly out of the willows
To welcome my friend and me.
We step over the barbed wire into the pasture
Where they have been grazing all day, alone.
They ripple tensely, they can hardly contain their happiness
10 That we have come.
They bow shyly as wet swans. They love each other.
There is no loneliness like theirs.
At home once more,
They begin munching the young tufts of spring in the darkness.
15 I would like to hold the slenderer one in my arms,
For she has walked over to me
And nuzzled my left hand.
She is black and white.
Her mane falls wild on her forehead,
20 And the light breeze moves me to caress her long ear
That is delicate as the skin over a girl's wrist.
Suddenly I realize

That if I stepped out of my body I would break
Into blossom.

[1963]

AUTUMN BEGINS IN MARTINS FERRY, OHIO[1]

In the Shreve High football stadium,
I think of Polacks nursing long beers in Tiltonsville,
And gray faces of Negroes in the blast furnace at Benwood,
And the ruptured night watchman of Wheeling Steel,
5   Dreaming of heroes.

All the proud fathers are ashamed to go home.
Their women cluck like starved pullets,
Dying for love.

Therefore,
10   Their sons grow suicidally beautiful
At the beginning of October,
And gallop terribly against each other's bodies.

[1963]

LYING IN A HAMMOCK AT WILLIAM DUFFY'S FARM IN PINE ISLAND, MINNESOTA

Over my head, I see the bronze butterfly,
Asleep on the black trunk,
Blowing like a leaf in green shadow.
Down the ravine behind the empty house,
5   The cowbells follow one another
Into the distances of the afternoon.
To my right,
In a field of sunlight between two pines,
The droppings of last year's horses
10   Blaze up into golden stones.
I lean back, as the evening darkens and comes on.
A chicken hawk floats over, looking for home.
I have wasted my life.

[1961]

---

[1] Martins Ferry and Tiltonsville, Ohio, and Benwood and Wheeling, West Virginia, are all steel towns lying along the banks of the Ohio River that serves as the border between the two states.

Galway Kinnell   *1927–*

BLACKBERRY EATING

I love to go out in late September
among the fat, overripe, icy, black blackberries
to eat blackberries for breakfast,
the stalks very prickly, a penalty
5   they earn for knowing the black art
of blackberry-making; and as I stand among them
lifting the stalks to my mouth, the ripest berries
fall almost unbidden to my tongue,
as words sometimes do, certain peculiar words
10   like *strengths* or *squinched,*
many-lettered, one-syllabled lumps,
which I squeeze, squinch open, and splurge well
in the silent, startled, icy, black language
of blackberry-eating in late September.

[1980]

W. S. Merwin   *1927–*

LEVIATHAN[1]

This is the black sea-brute bulling through wave-wrack,
Ancient as ocean's shifting hills, who in sea-toils
Travelling, who furrowing the salt acres
Heavily, his wake hoary behind him,[2]
5   Shoulder spouting, the fist of his forehead
Over wastes gray-green crashing, among horses unbroken
From bellowing fields, past bone-wreck of vessels,
Tide-ruin, wash of lost bodies bobbing
No longer sought for, and islands of ice gleaming,
10   Who ravening the rank flood, wave-marshalling,
Overmastering the dark sea-marches, finds home
And harvest. Frightening to foolhardiest
Mariners, his size were difficult to describe:
The hulk of him is like hills heaving,
15   Dark, yet as crags of drift-ice, crowns cracking in thunder,
Like land's self by night black-looming, surf churning and trailing
Along his shores' rushing, shoal-water boding
About the dark of his jaws; and who should moor at his edge
And fare on afoot would find gates of no gardens,
20   But the hill of dark underfoot diving,

[1] Literally, any large creature; usually associated with the whale.
[2] See Job 41:32.

Closing overhead, the cold deep, and drowning.
He is called Leviathan, and named for rolling,
First created he was of all creatures,[3]
He has held Jonah[4] three days and nights,
25   He is that curling serpent that in ocean is,[5]
Sea-fright he is, and the shadow under the earth.
Days there are, nonetheless, when he lies
Like an angel, although a lost angel
On the waste's unease, no eye of man moving,
30   Bird hovering, fish flashing, creature whatever
Who after him came to herit earth's emptiness.
Froth at flanks seething soothes to stillness,
Waits; with one eye he watches
Dark of night sinking last, with one eye dayrise
35   As at first over foaming pastures. He makes no cry
Though that light is a breath. The sea curling,
Star-climbed, wind-combed, cumbered with itself still
As at first it was, is the hand not yet contented
Of the Creator. And he waits for the world to begin.

[1956]

THE DRUNK IN THE FURNACE

For a good decade
The furnace stood in the naked gully, fireless
And vacant as any hat. Then when it was
No more to them than a hulking black fossil
5   To erode unnoticed with the rest of the junk-hill
By the poisonous creek, and rapidly to be added
To their ignorance,

They were afterwards astonished
To confirm, one morning, a twist of smoke like a pale
10   Resurrection, staggering out of its chewed hole,
And to remark then other tokens that someone,
Cosily bolted behind the eye-holed iron
Door of the drafty burner, had there established
His bad castle.

15   Where he gets his spirits
It's a mystery. But the stuff keeps him musical:
Hammer-and-anvilling with poker and bottle
To his jugged bellowings, till the last groaning clang
As he collapses onto the rioting
20   Springs of a litter of car-seats ranged on the grates,
To sleep like an iron pig.

---

[3] See Genesis 1:21.
[4] The Old Testament prophet who was swallowed by a "great fish." See the Book of Jonah.
[5] See Isaiah 27:1.

In their tar-paper church
On a text about stoke-holes that are sated never
Their Reverend lingers. They nod and hate trespassers.
25   When the furnace wakes, though, all afternoon
Their witless offspring flock like piped rats to its siren
Crescendo, and agape on the crumbling ridge
Stand in a row and learn.

[1960]

Anne Sexton   *1928–1974*

LULLABY

It is a summer evening.
The yellow moths sag
against the locked screens
and the faded curtains
5   suck over the window sills
and from another building
a goat calls in his dreams.
This is the TV parlour
in the best ward at Bedlam[1]
10   The night nurse is passing
out the evening pills.
She walks on two erasers,
padding by us one by one.

My sleeping pill is white.
15   It is a splendid pearl;
it floats me out of myself,
my stung skin as alien
as a loose bolt of cloth.
I will ignore the bed.
20   I am linen on a shelf.
Let the others moan in secret;
let each lost butterfly
go home. Old woollen head,
take me like a yellow moth
25   while the goat calls hush-
a-bye.

[1960]

HER KIND

I have gone out, a possessed witch,
haunting the black air, braver at night;

---

[1] A lunatic asylum or madhouse; originally the popular name for the Hospital of St. Mary of
Bethlehem in London, an early asylum for the insane.

dreaming evil, I have done my hitch
over the plain houses, light by light:
lonely thing, twelve-fingered, out of mind.
A woman like that is not a woman, quite.
I have been her kind.

I have found the warm caves in the woods,
filled them with skillets, carvings, shelves,
closets, silks, innumerable goods;
fixed the suppers for the worms and the elves:
whining, rearranging the disaligned.
A woman like that is misunderstood.
I have been her kind.

I have ridden in your cart, driver,
waved my nude arms at villages going by,
learning the last bright routes, survivor
where your flames still bite my thigh
and my ribs crack where your wheels wind.
A woman like that is not ashamed to die.
I have been her kind.

[1960]

THE TRUTH THE DEAD KNOW

*For My Mother, Born March 1902, Died March 1959
and My Father, Born February 1900, Died June 1959*

Gone, I say and walk from church,
refusing the stiff procession to the grave,
letting the dead ride alone in the hearse.
It is June. I am tired of being brave.

We drive to the Cape.[1] I cultivate
myself where the sun gutters from the sky,
where the sea swings in like an iron gate
and we touch. In another country people die.

My darling, the wind falls in like stones
from the whitehearted water and when we touch
we enter touch entirely. No one's alone.
Men kill for this, or for as much.

And what of the dead? They lie without shoes
in their stone boats. They are more like stone
than the sea would be if it stopped. They refuse
to be blessed, throat, eye and knucklebone.

[1962]

---

[1] Cape Cod, Massachusetts.

Donald Finkel   *1929–*

HUNTING SONG

The fox he came lolloping, lolloping,
Lolloping. His eyes were bright,
His ears were high.
He was like death at the end of a string
5   When he came to the hollow
Log. He ran in one side
And out of the other. O
He was sly.

The hounds they came tumbling, tumbling,
10   Tumbling. Their heads were low,
Their eyes were red.
The sound of their breath was louder than death
When they came to the hollow
Log. They boiled at one end
15   But a bitch found the scent. O
They were mad.

The hunter came galloping, galloping,
Galloping. All damp was his mare
From her hooves to her mane.
20   His coat and his mouth were redder than death
When he came to the hollow
Log. He took in the rein
And over he went. O
He was fine.

25   The log he just lay there, alone in
The clearing. No fox nor hound
Nor mounted man
Saw his black round eyes in their perfect disguise
(As the ends of a hollow
30   Log). He watched death go through him,
Around him and over him. O
He was wise.

                         [1987]

Thom Gunn   *1929–*

BLACK JACKETS

In the silence that prolongs the span
Rawly of music when the record ends,

The red-haired boy who drove a van
In weekday overalls but, like his friends,

5
   Wore cycle boots and jacket here
To suit the Sunday hangout he was in,
   Heard, as he stretched back from his beer,
Leather creak softly round his neck and chin.

   Before him, on a coal-black sleeve
10
Remote exertion had lined, scratched, and burned
   Insignia that could not revive
The heroic fall or climb where they were earned.

   On the other drinkers bent together,
Concocting selves for their impervious kit,
15
   He saw it as no more than leather
Which, taut across the shoulders grown to it,

   Sent through the dimness of a bar
As sudden and anonymous hints of light
   As those that shipping give, that are
20
Now flickers in the Bay, now lost in night.

   He stretched out like a cat, and rolled
The bitterish taste of beer upon his tongue,
   And listened to a joke being told:
The present was the things he stayed among.

25
   If it was only loss he wore,
He wore it to assert, with fierce devotion,
   Complicity and nothing more.
He recollected his initiation,

   And one especially of the rites.
30
For on his shoulders they had put tattoos:
   The group's name on the left, The Knights,
And on the right the slogan Born To Lose.

                           [1973]

X. J. Kennedy   *1929–*

CROSS TIES

Out walking ties left over from a track
Where nothing travels now but rust and grass,
I could take stock in something that would pass
Bearing down Hell-bent from behind my back:
5
A thing to sidestep or go down before,

Far-off, indifferent as that curfew's wail
The evening wind flings like a sack of mail
Or close up as the moon whose headbeam stirs
A flock of cloud to make tracks. Down to strafe
10 The bristled grass a hawk falls—there's a screech
Like steel wrenched taut till severed. Out of reach
Or else beneath desiring, I go safe,
Walk on, tensed for a leap, unreconciled
To a dark void all kindness.
                                        When I spill
15 The salt I throw the Devil some and, still,
I let them sprinkle water on my child.

                                                        [1969]

SPACE

for Martin Green

I

Who could have thought, but for eight days in space,
The heart might learn to thrive on weightlessness,
As though with no flesh holding it in place,
Yearning by choice, not made to by distress,
5 Turning in free fall on reprieve from earth
We tug-of-war with daily for the sakes
Of those we long for, those we help bring forth.
How will it be when all the strength it takes
To rip moons loose from planet boughs, or send
10 Engines of slag careening from their track
Into the unending dark, end over slow end,
Is in the twist that opens a door a crack?
Who will need long to savor his desire
When wishes no more blunt them against bulk,
15 But pierce straight through; when acts, once dreamt, transpire?
Man may imagine man's own mother's milk.

II

Heads bowed in fetal crouch, the Gemini[1]
Float in their pear-shaped comfort. Data grows
By little clicks, as pine cones, drying free
20 And dropping, pile up. Enter, through a hose,
Essence of roast beef. Signs that flash ABORT
Bespeak a tube's break. If all hold, instead,
The moon's thin skin shall cringe under their boots—
Just as we always thought, the thing's stone dead.

---

[1] The Gemini space program from March 23, 1965, through November 15, 1966, consisted of twelve two-man flights in preparation for the Apollo program, which was to land men on the moon.

III

25 Hope to be disembodied reconciles
Our drifted hearts to that exacting beat.
We clerks-without-church look on while slide-rules
Render our lusts and madnesses concrete.
It may well be that when I rev my car
30 And let it overtake and pass my thinking,
It's space I crave; when my electric bar
Sets up a moonshot, lemon-oiled and clinking,
And gulp by gulp, I shrug the world's dull weight,
Out after what I had long thought I'd hate.

[1969]

Adrienne Rich *1929–*

STORM WARNINGS

The glass° has been falling all the afternoon,   *barometer*
And knowing better than the instrument
What winds are walking overhead, what zone
Of gray unrest is moving across the land,
5 I leave the book upon a pillowed chair
And walk from window to closed window, watching
Boughs strain against the sky

And think again, as often when the air
Moves inward toward a silent core of waiting,
10 How with a single purpose time has traveled
By secret currents of the undiscerned
Into this polar realm. Weather abroad
And weather in the heart alike come on
Regardless of prediction.

15 Between foreseeing and averting change
Lies all the mastery of elements
Which clocks and weatherglasses cannot alter.
Time in the hand is not control of time,
Nor shattered fragments of an instrument
20 A proof against the wind; the wind will rise,
We can only close the shutters.

I draw the curtains as the sky goes black
And set a match to candles sheathed in glass
Against the keyhole draught, the insistent whine
25 Of weather through the unsealed aperture.
This is our sole defense against the season;

These are the things that we have learned to do
Who live in troubled regions.

[1951]

THE KNIGHT

A knight rides into the noon,
and his helmet points to the sun,
and a thousand splintered suns
are the gaiety of his mail.
5 The soles of his feet glitter
and his palms flash in reply,
and under his crackling banner
he rides like a ship in sail.

A knight rides into the noon,
10 and only his eye is living,
a lump of bitter jelly
set in a metal mask,
betraying rags and tatters
that cling to the flesh beneath
15 and wear his nerves to ribbons
under the radiant casque.

Who will unhorse this rider
and free him from between
the walls of iron, the emblems
20 crushing his chest with their weight?
Will they defeat him gently,
or leave him hurled on the green,
his rags and wounds still hidden
under the great breastplate?

[1957]

Ted Hughes   *1930–*

PIKE

Pike, three inches long, perfect
Pike in all parts, green tigering the gold.
Killers from the egg: the malevolent aged grin.
They dance on the surface among the flies.

5 Or move, stunned by their own grandeur,
Over a bed of emerald, silhouette

Of submarine delicacy and horror.
A hundred feet long in their world.

10

In ponds, under the heat-struck lily pads—
Gloom of their stillness:
Logged on last year's black leaves, watching upwards.
Or hung in an amber cavern of weeds

15

The jaw's hooked clamp and fangs
Not to be changed at this date;
A life subdued to its instrument;
The gills kneading quietly, and the pectorals.

20

Three we kept behind glass,
Jungled in weed: three inches, four,
And four and a half: fed fry to them—
Suddenly there were two. Finally one

With a sag belly and the grin it was born with.
And indeed they spare nobody.
Two, six pounds each, over two feet long,
High and dry and dead in the willow-herb—

25

One jammed past its gills down the other's gullet:
The outside eye stared: as a vice locks—
The same iron in this eye
Though its film shrank in death.

30

A pond I fished, fifty yards across,
Whose lilies and muscular tench[1]
Had outlasted every visible stone
Of the monastery that planted them—

35

Stilled legendary depth:
It was as deep as England. It held
Pike too immense to stir, so immense and old
That past nightfall I dared not cast

40

But silently cast and fished
With the hair frozen on my head
For what might move, for what eye might move.
The still splashes on the dark pond,

Owls hushing the floating woods
Frail on my ear against the dream
Darkness beneath night's darkness had freed,
That rose slowly towards me, watching.

[1959]

---

[1] Fish similar to carp.

George Starbuck   *1931–*

MARGARET ARE YOU DRUG[1]

Cool it Mag.
Sure it's a drag
With all that green flaked out.
Next thing you know they'll be changing the color of bread.

5 But look, Chick,
Why panic?
Sevennyeighty years, we'll *all* be dead.

Roll with it, Kid,
I did.
10 Give it the old benefit of the doubt.

I mean leaves
Schmeaves.
You sure you aint just feeling sorry for yourself?

              [1966]

Sylvia Plath   *1932–1963*

METAPHORS

I'm a riddle in nine syllables,
An elephant, a ponderous house,
A melon strolling on two tendrils.
O red fruit, ivory, fine timbers!
5 This loaf's big with its yeasty rising.
Money's new-minted in this fat purse.
I'm a means, a stage, a cow in calf.
I've eaten a bag of green apples,
Boarded the train there's no getting off.

            [1960]

MEDALLION

By the gate with star and moon
Worked into the peeled orange wood
The bronze snake lay in the sun

---

[1] This is one of Starbuck's "Translations from the English." Compare it with its source poem, Gerard Manley Hopkins's "Spring and Fall" (p. 903).

Inert as a shoelace; dead
But pliable still, his jaw
Unhinged and his grin crooked,

Tongue a rose-colored arrow.
Over my hand I hung him.
His little vermilion eye

Ignited with a glassed flame
As I turned him in the light;
When I split a rock one time

The garnet bits burned like that.
Dust dulled his back to ochre
The way sun ruins a trout.

Yet his belly kept its fire
Going under the chainmail,
The old jewels smoldering there

In each opaque belly-scale:
Sunset looked at through milk glass.
And I saw white maggots coil

Thin as pins in the dark bruise
Where his innards bulged as if
He were digesting a mouse.

Knifelike, he was chaste enough,
Pure death's metal. The yardman's
Flung brick perfected his laugh.

[1962]

Peter Meinke   *1932–*

ADVICE TO MY SON

The trick is, to live your days
as if each one may be your last
(for they go fast, and young men lose their lives
in strange and unimaginable ways)
but at the same time, plan long range
(for they go slow: if you survive
the shattered windshield and the bursting shell
you will arrive
at our approximation here below
of heaven or hell).

To be specific, between the peony and the rose
plant squash and spinach, turnips and tomatoes;
beauty is nectar
and nectar, in a desert, saves—
15 but the stomach craves stronger sustenance
than the honied vine.

Therefore, marry a pretty girl
after seeing her mother;
speak truth to one man,
20 work with another;
and always serve bread with your wine.

But, son
always serve wine.

[1965]

Linda Pastan   *1932–*

JUMP CABLING

When our cars	touched
When you lifted the hood	of mine
To see the intimate workings	underneath,
When we were bound	together
By a pulse of pure	energy,
When my car like the	princess
In the tale woke with a	start,

5

I thought why not ride the rest of the way together?

[1984]

John Updike   *1932–*

SLEEPLESS IN SCARSDALE[1]

Prosperity has stolen stupor from me.
The terraced lawn beneath my window
has drained off fatigue; the alertness
of the happy seizes me like rage.

---

[1] Scarsdale, New York, an upper middle-class bedroom community located some eight miles north of New York City, is often associated with affluent suburban living.

Downstairs, the furniture matches.
The husband and wife are in love.
One son at Yale, another in law,
a third bowls them over in high school.

I rejoice. The bed is narrow.
I long for squalor's relaxation,
fantasizing a dirty scene
and mopping the sheet with a hanky.

There is a tension here. The books
look arranged. The bathroom
has towels of too many sizes.
I weigh myself on the scales.

Somewhere, a step. Muffled.
The stairs are carpeted.
A burglar has found us. A son
is drunk. The wife desires me.

But nothing happens, not even
oblivion. Life can be too clean.
Success like a screeching of brakes
pollutes the tunnel of silence.

Mock-Tudor, the houses are dark.
Even these decent trees sleep.
I await the hours guiltily,
hoping for one with whom I can make a deal.

[1977]

Mark Strand   *1934–*

KEEPING THINGS WHOLE

In a field
I am the absence
of field.
This is
always the case.
Wherever I am
I am what is missing.

When I walk
I part the air
and always
the air moves in

to fill the spaces
where my body's been.

15 We all have reasons
for moving.
I move
to keep things whole.

[1968]

Amy Jo Schoonover   1937–

RONDEAU:[1] AN UN-LOVE SONG

Among the other things that do not matter
I hear you boasting your unending love.
That trap, at least, I know to rise above
As quicksand lie or envy's brittle patter.

5 While dreams decay and lifetime idols shatter
What in the world can you be thinking of?
Among the other things that do not matter
I hear you boasting your unending love.

10 I watch the rosy petals fall and scatter
And listen for the melancholy dove:
He does not mourn his poor rejected love!
You mimic now the squirrel's antic chatter
Among the other things that do not matter.

[1978]

Margaret Atwood   1939–

YOU FIT INTO ME

you fit into me
like a hook into an eye

a fish hook
an open eye

[1971]

---

[1] In a letter to the editors, Miss Schoonover has pointed out that this is "a Rondeau in the style of Charles d'Orleans." A brief definition of a rondeau may be found in the glossary at the back of this book.

Pattiann Rogers   *1940–*

PORTRAIT

This is a picture of you
Reading this poem. Concentrate
On the finite movement
Of your eyes as they travel
At this moment across
The page, your fingers
Maintaining the stability
Of the sheet. Focus on the particular
Fall of your hair, the scent
Of your hands, the placement of your
Feet now as they acknowledge
Their name.

Simultaneously with these words, be aware
Of your tongue against
Your teeth, the aura
Of heat at your neckline
And wrists, the sense
Of your breath inside its own hollows.

Imagine yourself
Ten feet away and look back
At your body positioned
Here with this book. Picture
The perspective, the attitude
Of your shoulders and hips,
The bend of your head as you
Read of yourself.

Watch how you turn back as you
Remember the sounds surrounding you now,
As you recall the odors
Of wood fibers in this place
Or the lack of them.

And take note of this part
Of your portrait—the actual
Mechanism by which you are perceiving
The picture, the fixed
Expression on your face as you
Arrange these words at this moment
Into their proper circles, as you
Straighten out the aspects
Of the page, the linguistics of the sight
And color of light on the paper.

This is the printed
Form of you watching
Yourself now as you consider
45 Your person. This portrait is
Finished when you raise
Your eyes.

[1978]

Alice Walker *1944–*

WOMEN

They were women then
My mama's generation
Husky of voice—Stout of
Step
5 With fists as well as
Hands
How they battered down
Doors
And ironed
10 Starched white
Shirts
How they led
Armies
Headragged Generals
15 Across mined
Fields
Booby-trapped
Ditches
To discover books
20 Desks
A place for us
How they knew what we
Must know
Without knowing a page
25 Of it
Themselves.

[1973]

Jack Butler *1944–*

ATTACK OF THE ZOMBI POETS

One morning they were everywhere: the lawn,
the cafeterias, the swimming pools.

They chatted at the parties, went on and on.
They taught the little children poetry-in-the-schools.

5
"What's the strangest thing you can think of?" they said.
"Let's listen to the silence, loosen the knots
that hold the night together, pretend we're dead."
They reviewed each other's books by carload lots:

"It is not indefensible to declare
10
so-and-so is conceivably among
(though this last book's a falling-off) the four
or five dozen of our most promising young . . ."

They spoke of subtleties and of nuance,
twelve shades of gray to sketch a loss of nerve,
15
as if their rigor were the only dance,
and hardballs at a hundred didn't curve.

All masters of the verbal knowing nod,
the merest ghosts in their own works, and proud
they'd done away with bad old ego (God
20
help those who said what they meant or laughed out loud),

they still were their own only subject—could
not praise without considering that praise
was suspect in our century. What good
devising (sure, they *could*) some elegant phrase,

25
when Angel de Pilotes, a close friend,
lay prisoned down in South America,
a victim of the junta, and the end
(not unexpected, because of the bitter flaw

in Love itself) of another relationship
30
began to announce itself in studious *frissons?*
Their fathers died off at a remarkable clip:
Oh, remorse—but my true father is Villon.

Their favorite pronoun was *we,* their second *you:*
as in, "We understand that poetry
35
has as its subject, poetry: the new
poetry can never . . . ," but not as in "We

all went out to Big Bend last week and Pappy
cooked beef stew Provençale and the wind blew
a tent down and ate my hat and I was happy";
40
as in, "You ask the phone for a date. You/

laugh when it/ says *Yes.* You/ whisper, *Sorry,*
wrong/number. You/laugh, laugh, thinking/how, soon,
your/mysterious caller will/die," but not as in, "Carry
the garbage out right now you dead-ass goon."

45   Their favorite verbal clearly was the gerund,
      mostly for use in titles: *Burning the Ladder,*
      Letting the Birds Grow Feathers, Saving Air, and
      Tearing the Shirt, to name a few that matter.

      Their cadence was the musical phrase, the breath,
50   a natural measure, and breathlessly they each
      broke free of iambic five, succeeding forthwith
      in somehow manufacturing a speech

      so spitless, airless, and dispirited
      that stones would sigh, and computers weep to hear.
55   They got back to nature, but when they did,
      nature was never there: oh it was clear

      the wind blew emptily under the empty sky,
      propelling them jerkily into drink and sex . . .
      One morning they were everywhere, but why?
60   What mycological cycle had hit apex?

      They ate Cleveland, and then they ate L.A.
      They had it all, at last, and it all made
      good subject matter: "The aftertaste of clay. . . ."
      And when one put a pistol to his head

65   to ratify his impact on the scene,
      or walked out to the middle of a bridge and fell
      (though the bridge stood), the others would stir and keen
      the disappointment of the particle,

      the distances and horror of the word.
70   —No doubt about it, the situation stank,
      in fact was hopeless: No poetry occurred
      thenceforward thereafter, and the screen went blank.

      So much for the matinee. Now day and smoke,
      traffic, the vacant lot's wild sassafras
75   cracking the sidewalk up with a green joke,
      the sun-stunned onions in the silly grass.

                                                          [1984]

Michael Blumenthal   *1949–*

BACK FROM THE WORD PROCESSING COURSE,
I SAY TO MY OLD TYPEWRITER

          Old friend, you
          who were once in the avant-garde,

you of the thick cord
and the battered plug,
the slow and deliberate characters
proportionally spaced, shall we
go on together as before?
Shall we remain married
out of the cold dittos of conviction
and habit? Or should we move on
to some new technology of ease
and embellishment—Should I run off
with her, so much like you when
you were young, my aged Puella
of the battered keys, so lovely
in that bleached light of the first morning?

Old horse,
what will it be like
when the next young filly
comes along? How will I love you,
crate of my practised strokes,
when she cries out: *new new*
and asks me to dance again?
Oh plow for now, old boat,
through these familiar waters,
make the tides come in
once more! Concubined love,
take me again into your easy arms,
make this page wild once more
like a lustful sheet! Be wet,
sweet toy, with your old ink:
vibrate those aging hips again
beneath these trembling hands.

[1984]

Edward Hirsch   *1950–*

FAST BREAK

(*In Memory of Dennis Turner, 1946–1984*)

A hook shot kisses the rim and
hangs there, helplessly, but doesn't drop,

and for once our gangly starting center
boxes out his man and times his jump

perfectly, gathering the orange leather
from the air like a cherished possession

and spinning around to throw a strike
to the outlet who is already shovelling

an underhand pass toward the other guard
scissoring past a flat-footed defender

who looks stunned and nailed to the floor
in the wrong direction, trying to catch sight

of a high, gliding dribble and a man
letting the play develop in front of him

in slow-motion, almost exactly
like a coach's drawing on the blackboard,

both forwards racing down the court
the way that forwards should, fanning out

and filling the lanes in tandem, moving
together as brothers passing the ball

between them without a dribble, without
a single bounce hitting the hardwood

until the guard finally lunges out
and commits to the wrong man

while the power-forward explodes past them
in a fury, taking the ball into the air

by himself now and laying it gently
against the glass for a lay-up,

but losing his balance in the process,
inexplicably falling, hitting the floor

with a wild, headlong motion
for the game he loved like a country

and swivelling back to see an orange blur
floating perfectly through the net.

[1986]

Bert Leston Taylor ("B.L.T.")   *1866–1921*

UPON JULIA'S ARCTICS

Whenas galoshed my Julia goes,
Unbuckled all from top to toes,
How swift the poem becometh prose!
And when I cast mine eyes and see
Those arctics flopping each way free,
Oh, how that flopping floppeth me!

❧ CONTEMPORARY SONGS AND BALLADS ❧

Tom Jones *1927–*

TRY TO REMEMBER

Try to remember the kind of September
When life was slow and, oh, so mellow.
Try to remember the kind of September
When grass was green and grain was yellow.
Try to remember the kind of September
When you were a tender and callow fellow.
Try to remember and if you remember,
Then follow. *(Echo)* Follow, follow, follow.

Try to remember when life was so tender
That no one wept except the willow.
Try to remember when life was so tender
That dreams were kept beside your pillow.
Try to remember when life was so tender
That love was an ember about to billow.
Try to remember and if you remember,
Then follow. *(Echo)* Follow, follow, follow.

Deep in December it's nice to remember
Although you know the snow will follow.
Deep in December it's nice to remember
Without a hurt the heart is hollow.
Deep in December, it's nice to remember
The fire of September that made us mellow.
Deep in December our hearts should remember,
And follow. *(Echo)* Follow, follow, follow.

[1960]

Stephen Sondheim *1930–*

SEND IN THE CLOWNS

Isn't it rich?
Are we a pair?

414

Me here at last on the ground,
You in mid-air . . .
Send in the clowns.

Isn't it bliss?
Don't you approve?
One who keeps tearing around,
One who can't move . . .
Where are the clowns?
Send in the clowns.

Just when I'd stopped
Opening doors,
Finally knowing the one that I wanted was yours,
Making my entrance again with my usual flair,
Sure of my lines,
No one is there.

Don't you love farce?
My fault, I fear.
I thought that you'd want what I want,
Sorry, my dear.
But where are the clowns?
Quick send in the clowns.
Don't bother, they're here.

Isn't it rich?
Isn't it queer,
Losing my timing this late
In my career?
And where are the clowns?
There ought to be clowns.
Well, maybe next year . . .

[1973]

Leonard Cohen   *1934–*

SUZANNE

Suzanne takes you down
to her place near the river,
you can hear the boats go by
you can stay the night beside her.
And you know that she's half crazy
but that's why you want to be there
and she feeds you tea and oranges
that come all the way from China.

Just when you mean to tell her
that you have no gifts to give her,
she gets you on her wave-length
and she lets the river answer
that you've always been her lover.
    And you want to travel with her,
    you want to travel blind
    and you know that she can trust you
    because you've touched her perfect body
    with your mind.

Jesus was a sailor
when he walked upon the water[1]
and he spent a long time watching
from a lonely wooden tower
and when he knew for certain
only drowning men could see him
he said All men will be sailors then
until the sea shall free them,
but he himself was broken
long before the sky would open,
forsaken, almost human,
he sank beneath your wisdom like a stone.
    And you want to travel with him,
    you want to travel blind
    and you think maybe you'll trust him
    because he touched your perfect body
    with his mind.

Now Suzanne takes your hand
and she leads you to the river,
she is wearing rags and feathers
from Salvation Army counters,
and the sun pours down like honey
on our lady of the harbour,
and she shows you where to look
among the garbage and the flowers.
There are heroes in the seaweed,
there are children in the morning,
they are leaning out for love
and they will lean that way forever
while Suzanne holds the mirror.
    And you want to travel with her,
    and you want to travel blind
    and you know that you can trust her
    because she's touched your perfect body
    with her mind.

                   [1966]

[1] See Matthew 14:25–31.

Kris Kristofferson   *1936–*

ME AND BOBBY McGEE

Busted flat in Baton Rouge;
Headin' for the trains,
Feelin' nearly faded as my jeans,
Bobby thumbed a diesel down
5 Just before it rained;
Took us all the way to New Orleans,
I took my harpoon° out of my dirty red bandanna   *harmonica*
And was blowin' sad, while Bobby sang the blues;
With them windshield wipers slappin' time and Bobby clappin' hands
10 We fin'ly sang up every song that driver knew;

Freedom's just another word for nothin' left to lose,
And nothin' ain't worth nothin' but it's free;
Feeling good was easy, Lord, when Bobby sang the blues;
And, Buddy, that was good enough for me;
15 Good enough for me and Bobby McGee.

From the coal mines of Kentucky to the
California sun,
Bobby shared the secret of my soul;
Standin' right beside me, Lord, through
20 Everything I done,
And every night she kept me from the cold;
Then somewhere near Salinas, Lord, I let her slip away
Lookin' for the home I hope she'll find;
And I'd trade all of my tomorrows for a
25 Single yesterday, holdin' Bobby's body next to mine;

Freedom's just another word for nothin' left to lose,
And nothin' is all she left for me;
Feelin' good was easy, Lord, when Bobby sang the blues;
And, Buddy, that was good enough for me;
30 Good enough for me and Bobby McGee.

[1971]

Gordon Lightfoot   *1939–*

THE WRECK OF THE *EDMUND FITZGERALD*

The legend lives on from the Chippewa on down
Of the big lake they called Gitche Gumee;
The lake it is said never gives up her dead
When the skies of November turn gloomy.

With a load of iron ore 26,000 tons more
Than the *Edmund Fitzgerald* weighed empty
That good ship and true was a bone to be chewed
When the gales of November came early.

The ship was the pride of the American side
Comin' back from some mill in Wisconsin;
As the big freighters go it was bigger than most
With a crew and good captain well seasoned.

Concluding some terms with a couple of steel firms
When they left fully loaded for Cleveland;
And later that night when the ship's bell rang:
Could it be the north wind they'd been feelin'?

The wind in the wires made a tattletale sound
And a wave broke over the railing;
And every man knew as the captain did too
'Twas the witch of November come stealin'.

The dawn came late and the breakfast had to wait
When the gales of November came slashin'
When afternoon came it was freezin' rain
In the face of a hurricane west wind.

When suppertime came the old cook came on deck
Sayin', "Fellas, it's too rough to feed ya."
At seven P.M. a main hatchway caved in,
He said, "Fellas, it's been good to know ya."

The captain wired in he had water comin' in
And the good ship and crew was in peril,
And later that night 'is lights went out of sight,
Came the wreck of the *Edmund Fitzgerald.*

Does anyone know where the love of God goes
When the waves turn the minutes to hours?
The searchers all say they'd have made Whitefish Bay
If they'd put fifteen more miles behind 'er.

They might have split up or they might have capsized,
They may have broke deep and took water,
And all that remains is the faces and the names
Of the wives and the sons and the daughters.

In a musty old hall in Detroit they prayed
In the maritime sailors' cathedral.
The church bell chimed 'til it rang twenty-nine times
For each man on the *Edmund Fitzgerald.*

45 The legend lives on from the Chippewa on down
Of the big lake they called Gitche Gumee;
Superior they said never gives up her dead
When the gales of November come early.

Lake Huron rolls, Superior sings,
50 In the rooms of her ice water mansion;
Old Michigan steams like a young man's dreams;
The islands and bays are for sportsmen;

And further below Lake Ontario
Takes in what Lake Erie can send her,
55 And the iron boats do as the mariners all know
With the gales of November remembered.

[1976]

Grace Slick *1939–*

WHITE RABBIT

One pill makes you larger
And one pill makes you small.
And the ones that mother gives you
Don't do anything at all.
5 Go ask Alice
When she's ten feet tall.

And if you go chasing rabbits
And you know you're going to fall,
Tell 'em a hookah[1] smoking caterpillar
10 Has given you the call.
Call Alice
When she was just small.

When men on the chessboard
Get up and tell you where to go.
15 And you've just had some kind of mushroom,
And your mind is moving low.
Go ask Alice
I think she'll know.

When logic and proportion
20 Have fallen sloppy dead,
And the White Knight is talking backwards
And the Red Queen's lost her head.

[1] A large water-pipe.

Remember what the dormouse said:
"Feed your head.
25   Feed your head.
Feed your head."

[1967]

John Lennon   *1940–1980*

IMAGINE

Imagine there's no heaven
It's easy if you try
No hell below us
Above us only sky
5   Imagine all the people
Living for today . . .

Imagine there's no countries
It isn't hard to do
Nothing to kill or die for
10   And no religion too
Imagine all the people
Living life in peace . . .

Imagine no possessions
I wonder if you can
15   No need for greed or hunger a
Brotherhood of man
Imagine all the people
Sharing all the earth . . .

You may say I'm a dreamer
20   But I'm not the only one
I hope some day you'll join us
And the world will be as one

[1971]

Bob Dylan   *1941–*

ALL ALONG THE WATCHTOWER

"There must be some way out of here," said the joker to the thief,
"There's too much confusion, I can't get no relief.
Businessmen, they drink my wine, plowmen dig my earth,
None of them along the line know what any of it is worth."

5   "No reason to get excited," the thief, he kindly spoke,
     "There are many here among us who feel that life is but a joke.
     But you and I, we've been through that, and this is not our fate,
     So let us not talk falsely now, the hour is getting late."

     All along the watchtower, princes kept the view
10   While all the women came and went, barefoot servants too.

     Outside in the distance a wildcat did growl,
     Two riders were approaching, the wind began to howl.

                                                    [1968]

Jimmy Buffett   *1947–*

WASTIN' AWAY AGAIN IN MARGARITAVILLE

          Nibblin' on sponge cake
          Watchin' the sun bake
          All of those tourists
          Covered with oil

5   Strummin' my six string
          On the front porch swing
          Smell those shrimp they're beginning to boil

          Wastin' away again in Margaritaville
          Searchin' for my lost shaker of salt
10   Some people claim that there's a woman to blame
          But I know it's nobody's fault

          I don't know the reason I stayed here all season
          With nothing to show but this brand new tatoo
          But it's a real beauty a Mexican cutie
15   How it got here I haven't a clue

          Wastin' away again in Margaritaville
          Searchin' for my lost shaker of salt
          Some people claim that there's a woman to blame
          Now I think, hell, it could be my fault

20   I blew out my flip flop stepped on a pop top
          Cut my heel had to cruise on back home
          But there's booze in the blender and soon it will render
          That frozen concoction that helps me hang on

          Wastin' away again in Margaritaville
25   Searchin' for my lost shaker of salt
          Some people claim that there's a woman to blame
          But I know that it's my own damn fault

Yes sir some people claim that there's a woman to blame
And I know it's my own damn fault

[1977]

Bruce Springsteen *1949–*

GLORY DAYS

I had a friend was a big baseball player back in high school
He could throw that speedball by you
Make you look like a fool boy.
Saw him the other night at this roadside bar I was walking
    in and he was walking out.
5 We went back inside sat down, had a few drinks but all he
    kept talking about was

Chorus
Glory days well they'll pass you by
10 Glory days in the wink of a young girl's eye
Glory days, glory days.

There's a girl that lives up the block back in school she
    could turn all the boys' heads
10 Sometimes on a Friday I'll stop by and have a few drinks
    after she puts her kids to bed.
Her and her husband Bobby well they split up
I guess it's two years gone by now
We just sit around talking about the old times, she says
    when she feels like crying, she starts laughing thinking
    about

Chorus
Think I'm going down to the well tonight and I'm gonna drink
    till I get my fill
15 And I hope when I get old I don't sit around thinking about
    it but I probably will
Yeah, just sitting back trying to recapture little of the
    glory of, but time slips away and leaves you with nothing,
    mister but boring stories of

Chorus

[1984]

A Poetry Handbook

ABBREVIATIONS: Common abbreviations encountered in literary study include the following.

anon. anonymous
app. appendix
art., arts. article(s)
b. born
biblio. bibliography, bibliographer
bk., bks. book(s)
bull. bulletin
ca. (or *c.*) "about," used to indicate an approximate date; for example, ca. 1776
ch., chs. chapter(s)
col., cols. column(s)
coll. college
comp. compiler, compiled by
d. died
dept. department
diss. Ph.D dissertation
doc., docs. document(s)
ed., eds. editor(s), edited by
e.g. (*exempli gratia*) "for example"—set off by commas
esp. especially
et al. (*et alii*) "and others"
etc. (*et cetera*) "and so forth"
ex., exs. example(s)
f., ff. page or pages following a specific reference; for example, p. 12 ff.
fig., figs. figure(s)

front. frontispiece

ibid. (*ibidem*) "in the same place"; that is, the title cited in the immediately preceding note

i.e. (*id est*) "that is," preceded and followed by a comma

illus. illustrator, illustrated by, illustration(s)

intro., introd. introduction, introduced by

jour. journal

l., ll. line(s)

loc. cit. (*loco citato*) "in the place (or passage) cited"

mag., mags. magazine(s)

ms, mss manuscript, capitalized and followed by a period when referring to a specific manuscript.

n., nn. note(s)

n.d. no date; for example, on the title page of a book

no., nos. number(s)

n.p. no place of publication cited

p. pp. page(s)

par., pars. paragraph(s)

passim "here and there throughout the work"; for example, p. 23 et passim

pref. preface

pseud. pseudonym

pt., pts. part(s)

pub., pubs. published by, publication(s)

rev. revised or revised by; reviewed or reviewed by

rpt. reprint, reprinted

sc. scene

sec., secs. section(s)

sic "thus"; Placed in square brackets [sic] to indicate that there is an error in the quoted passage and that the passage in question has been quoted accurately.

st., sts. stanza(s)

tr., trans. translator, translated by

univ. university

v., vs. verse(s)

vol., vols. volume(s)

ABSTRACT: The opposite of *concrete;* used to describe a word or group of words representing attitudes, generalities, ideas, or qualities that cannot be perceived directly through the senses. Language is best seen as forming a continuous ladder ranging from earthly concrete at its base to airily abstract at its top. On this ladder the word *insect* is relatively abstract while *spittle bug* is quite concrete.

ACCENT (PP. 93–95): Used in English poetry to describe the stress or emphasis accorded to certain syllables. When a pronounced syllable receives no stress or emphasis, it is, by contrast, referred to as unaccented. In English poetry, *meter* depends on the pattern of accented and unaccented syllables. For example, in the following couplet from Byron's "Don Juan" (1819), the meter is iambic pentameter and the stresses fall on the even numbered syllables:

> There's NOT a SEA the PASSenGER e'er PUKES in,
> Turns UP more DANG'rous BREAKers THAN the EUXine.

ACROSTIC (P. 143): A poem in which certain letters (ordinarily the first in each line) spell out a word or words.

ACTION: The events or incidents that take place within a literary work which, taken together, provide the *plot*. See *plot*. When we speak of the "action" of a poem, we are referring to the narrative events the poem relates.

ADAGE: A wise saying or proverb familiar to most people. For example, "Honey catches more flies than vinegar."

AESTHETIC DISTANCE: See *psychic distance*.

AESTHETICS: The study of the beautiful. A branch of philosophy which attempts to define the nature of art and the criteria by which it may be judged.

AFFECTIVE FALLACY: A term employed in modern criticism to describe the supposed error of judging a literary work by its effect—usually its emotional effect—upon the reader.

ALEXANDRINE (P. 138): A line of poetry of twelve syllables, consisting of six iambic feet (iambic hexameter). Example:

> A needless Alexandrine ends the song,
> That, like a wounded snake, drags its slow length along.
> (Alexander Pope, from *An Essay on Criticism*, 1711)

ALLEGORY (PP. 77–78): A type of narrative that attempts to reinforce its thesis by making its characters (and sometimes its events and setting, as well) represent specific abstract ideas or qualities; see *fable, parable,* and *symbol*.

ALLITERATION (PP. 125–127): The repetition in two or more nearby words of initial consonant sounds. See also *assonance* and *consonance*. Alliteration is what gives punch to Abraham Lincoln's contention that "the ballot is stronger than the bullet."

ALLITERATIVE VERSE (PP. 112–114): A metrical system in which each line contains a fixed number of accented syllables and a variable number of unaccented ones.

ALLUSION (PP. 31–34): A reference, generally brief, to a person, place, thing, or event with which the reader is presumably familiar. Allusion is a device that allows a writer to compress a great deal of meaning into a very few words. Allusions "work" to the extent they are recognized and understood; when they are not they tend to confuse.

AMBIGUITY (PP. 38–40): The use of a word or phrase in such a way as to give it two or more competing meanings. Example: "Nowadays we are all so hard up that the only pleasant things to pay are compliments. They're the only things we can pay" (Oscar Wilde, from *Lady Windemere's Fan*, 1892).

AMBIVALENCE: The existence of two mutually opposed or contradictory feelings about a given issue, idea, person, or object. You feel ambivalent, for example, when you want to celebrate St. Patrick's Day with plenty of green beer, but you also want to pass your accounting test the next morning.

ANACHRONISM: A person or thing that is chronologically out of place.

ANAGRAM: A word, name, or phrase made by rearranging the letters of another. For example, *eat* is an anagram of *tea*.

ANALOGY: A comparison, usually imaginative, of two essentially unlike things which nonetheless share one or more common features. Writers use analogies as a method of exploring familiar subjects in new and fresh ways or as a method of exploring difficult ideas by comparing them to things known and familiar.

ANALYSIS (PP. 9–13): An attempt to study one element or part of a literary work. See *criticism*.

ANAPEST (ANAPESTIC) (PP. 108–110): A foot of two unaccented syllables followed by an accented one. Example: "It was MANy and MANy a YEAR aGO" (Edgar Allan Poe, "Annabelle Lee," 1850).

ANECDOTE: A brief, unadorned narrative about a particular person or incident. Short stories differ from anecdotes by virtue of their greater length and the deliberate artistic arrangement of their elements.

ANIMISM (PP. 71–72): A poetic figure of speech in which an idea or inanimate object is described as though it were living, without attributing human traits to it; see also *personification*. Example: "The fog comes on little cat feet" (Carl Sandburg, "Fog," 1916).

ANNOTATED BIBLIOGRAPHY: A bibliography that includes a brief summary or description of each title included.

ANNOTATION: The explanatory note (or notes) that an author or editor supplies for a given text.

ANTAGONIST: The rival or opponent against whom the major character (the *protagonist* or *hero*) is contending.

ANTECEDENT EVENTS: Events that have taken place before the plot begins, but which are somehow important to that plot.

ANTHOLOGY: A collection of essays, short stories, poems, and/or plays written by a number of different authors. This text is an anthology.

ANTICLIMAX: A sudden transition from the important (or serious) to the trivial (or ludicrous). We speak of something being anticlimactic when it occurs after the *crisis* (or *climax*) of the plot has been reached. In most cases the Republican and Democratic National Conventions are anticlimactic because the candidates and the major planks of the platform have been decided well in advance.

APHORISM: A short, pithy saying, usually by a known author. Example: "Fortune favors the brave" (Virgil, *The Aeneid,* X).

APOLOGY: In literature a term meaning a justification or a defense.

APOSTROPHE (P. 71): A figure of speech in which a person (usually not present) or a personified quality or object is addressed as if present. Example: "Judge of nations, spare us yet,/ Lest we forget—lest we forget" (Rudyard Kipling, "Recessional," 1897).

ARCHAISM: Obsolete words, phrases, syntax, or spelling. Example:

> Winter is icumen in,
> Lhude sing Goddamm,
> Raineth drop and staineth slop,
> And how the wind doth ramm!
>   (Ezra Pound,
>   from "Ancient Music," 1926)

ARCHETYPE (P. 77): Used in literary analysis to describe certain basic and recurrent patterns of plot, character, or theme; see also *symbol*.

ARGUMENT: A summary statement of the content or thesis of a literary work.

ASSONANCE (PP. 125–127): The repetition in two or more nearby words of similar vowel sounds; see also *consonance* and *alliteration*. Example: ". . . the chalk wall falls" (W. H. Auden, "Look Stranger," 1936).

ATMOSPHERE: The mood or feeling pervading a literary work. Example: The gloomy melancholy in Edgar Allan Poe's "The Raven" (1845).

BALLAD (PP. 135–137): A narrative poem consisting of a series of four-line stanzas, originally sung or recited as part of the oral traditions of an unsophisticated rural folk society. Ballads that are the genuine products of a folk society are sometimes referred to as "popular," "folk," or "traditional" ballads as opposed to "literary" ballads deliberately composed by educated poets in imitation of the form and spirit of those originals. See also *broadside ballad* and *Child ballad*.

BARD: Originally an ancient order of Celtic minstrel-poets who composed and sang (usually accompanied on a harp) verses celebrating the deeds of their warriors and chiefs; now chiefly used as a synonym for poet.

BATHOS: A ludicrous appearance of the trivial or mundane within a context of supposed sublimity. Example of bathos from "The Ode to Stephen Dowling Bots, De'd" in Mark Twain's *Adventures of Huckleberry Finn* (1885):

> Despised love struck not with woe
>   That head of curly knots
> Nor stomach troubles laid him low,
>   Young Stephen Dowling Bots.
>
> O no. Then list with tearful eye,
>   Whilst I his fate do tell.
> His soul did from this cold world fly,
>   By falling down a well.

BIBLIOGRAPHY: A list of books, articles, and other references on a particular subject.

BLANK VERSE (P. 133): Lines of unrhymed iambic pentameter, as, for example, in Shakespeare's *Othello* (1604) or Milton's *Paradise Lost* (1667).

BOMBAST: Language that is inflated, extravagant, verbose, and insincere.

BROADSIDE BALLAD: A ballad printed on a single sheet and hawked in the streets. See *ballad*.

BURLESQUE: A form of humor that ridicules persons, attitudes, actions, or things by means of distortion and exaggeration. Burlesque of a particular literary work or style is referred to as *parody*. *Caricature*, on the other hand, creates humor by distorting or exaggerating an individual's prominent physical features; see also *satire*.

CACOPHONY: See *euphony and cacophony*.

CADENCE: The rhythmical "tune" established in verse or prose by patterns of stressed and unstressed syllables, or the inflection of a speaker's voice. Great speeches like Lincoln's "Gettysburg Address" are said to have cadence, as, of course, does great poetry.

CAESURA (PP. 98–99): A pause or break occurring near the middle of a line of poetry, customarily marked by a double slash in scansion. Example:

> Treason doth never prosper;//what's the reason?
> For if it prosper,//none dare call it treason.
> (Sir John Harington, "Of Treason," 1612)

CANTO: A section or division of a long poem.

CARPE DIEM: A Latin phrase meaning "seize the day," generally applied to lyric poems that urge the celebration of the fleeting present. Robert Herrick's "To the Virgins, to Make Much of Time" (1648) is a good example of a carpe diem poem.

CAVALIER POETS: A group of poets—including Carew, Herrick, Lovelace, and Suckling—associated with the court of Charles I of England (1625–1649), whose supporters were known as Cavaliers. The Cavalier poets were known for their light and amorous verse.

CHARACTER: An individual within a literary work. Characters may be complex and well developed (*round characters*) or undifferentiated and one-dimensional (*flat characters*); they may change in the course of the plot (*dynamic characters*) or remain essentially the same (*static characters*).

CHARACTERIZATION: The process by which an author creates, develops, and presents a character.

CHAUCERIAN STANZA: See *rhyme royal.*

CHILD BALLAD: The name given to one of the 305 ballads brought together and published by Francis J. Child in his five-volume collection *English and Scottish Popular Ballads* (1882–1898). These ballads are frequently cited by the number assigned them by Child.

CHRONOLOGICAL: A pattern of organization or presentation that introduces events or things in their normal time sequence.

CINQUAIN: A five-line stanza, particularly as popularized by Adelaide Crapsey (1878–1914). Example:

> These be
> Three silent things
> The falling snow . . . the hour
> Before the dawn . . . the mouth of one
> Just dead.
> ("Cinquain, Triad," 1915)

CLASSIC: A piece of literature which by common agreement of readers and critics has come to be regarded as a major work.

CLICHÉ: A trite, worn-out expression that has lost its original vitality and freshness. Examples: "sharp as a tack," "dumb as a doorknob," "boring as a bump on a log." As Alexander Pope explains in "An Essay on Criticism" (1711), a writer indulges in predictable clichés at his or her peril:

> Where'er you find "the cooling western breeze,"
> In the next line, it "whispers through the trees";
> If crystal streams "with pleasing murmers creep,"
> The reader's threatened (not in vain) with "sleep."

CLOSED COUPLET (P. 133): See *couplet.*

COHERENCE: A principle that insists that the various parts of a literary work be related to one another in a clear and logical manner.

CONCEIT: Usually refers to a startling, ingenious, perhaps even farfetched, metaphor establishing an analogy or comparison between two apparently incongruous things. Examples: John Donne's "The Flea" (1633), George Herbert's "The Pulley" (1633), Andrew Marvell's "The Definition of Love" (1681).

CONCORDANCE: An alphabetical index of the words used in a given text or in the work of a given author.

CONCRETE: Opposite of *abstract.* Language referring directly to what we see, hear, touch, taste, or smell is concrete. Most literature uses concrete language and expresses even abstract concepts concretely through images and metaphors.

CONNOTATION (PP. 27–28): The ideas associated with or suggested by a given word or phrase, as opposed to its literal meaning. A word's connotations are the product of its common usage and emotional overtones, not of its simple definition. Thus, owning a Porsche carries connotations of wealth, flashiness, and conspicuous consumption that are quite different from the connotation of stodgy aristocracy associated with owning an equally expensive Rolls Royce or Bentley. See *denotation.*

CONSISTENCY: The internal coherence of the various parts and the tone of a literary work.

CONSONANCE (PP. 125–127): The repetition in two or more nearby words of similar consonant sounds preceded by different accented vowels, e.g., "pl*uck*" and "kn*ock*." When it occurs at the end of lines, consonance often serves as a substitute for *end rhyme;* see *alliteration.*

CONTROLLING IMAGE: The image or metaphor that runs throughout a literary work and determines its structure or nature. For example, the white spider in Robert Frost's poem "Design" (1936).

CONVENTION: Any literary device, technique, style, or form, or any aspect of subject matter, characterization, or theme that has become recognized and accepted by authors and audiences through repeated use.

COUPLET (PP. 133–134): A single pair of rhymed lines. When they form a complete thought or statement, they are referred to as a *closed couplet.* Example of a closed couplet:

> What's Fame? a fanc'd life in others' breath,
> A thing beyond us, ev'n before our death.

CRITIC: An individual who evaluates and passes judgment on the quality and worth of a literary work. The critic who writes about contemporary works is also known as a reviewer and tends to be much maligned by authors. In this context Richard Le Gallienne has said that "a critic is a man created to praise greater men than himself, but he is never able to find them."

CRITICISM: The description, analysis, interpretation, or evaluation of a literary work of art; see also *deconstruction, historical criticism, new criticism, psychological/ psychoanalytic criticism, reader response criticism, structuralism, textual criticism,* and *theoretical criticism* and *practical criticism*. Perhaps Pope's comment in his *Essay on Criticism* (1711) is still as relevant as ever:

> Some are bewilder'd in the maze of schools,
> And some made coxcombs nature meant but fools.

CRITIQUE: A critical examination of a work of art.

DACTYL (PP. 106–108): A foot of one accented syllable followed by two unaccented syllables. Example: DIFFicult.

DECONSTRUCTION: A contemporary critical movement greatly indebted to French theorist Jacques Derrida that holds that there is an inherently unstable relationship between words and meaning. A deconstructionist critic objectively examines each element of the literary text for its internal signification in order to demonstrate that every text finally generates innumerable, contradictory, and ultimately indeterminate meanings. Major texts include Derrida's *Of Grammatology* (tr. 1976) and *Writing and Difference* (tr. 1978); Paul De Man's *Allegories of Reading* (1979) and *Blindness and Insight* (1981); and Jonathan Culler's *On Deconstruction* (1982).

DEDUCTION: A method of reasoning which moves from the general to the specific.

DENOTATION (PP. 25–27): The literal, dictionary meaning of a given word or phrase. See *connotation*.

DIALOGUE: The conversation that goes on between or among characters in a literary work.

DICTION: The author's choice or selection of words (vocabulary). The artistic arrangement of those words constitutes *style*.

DIDACTIC: Literature designed more to teach a lesson or instruct the reader or audience than to present an experience objectively. In a didactic work *theme* is generally the most important element. Alexander Pope's *Essay on Criticism* (1711) and Edmund Spenser's *The Faerie Queene* (1590) are good examples of didactic poetry.

DIGRESSION: The insertion into a work of material that is not closely related to its main subject.

DIMETER: A line of poetry consisting of two metrical feet; see *foot*. See, for example, Robert Frost's "Dust of Snow" (1923).

DISSONANCE: See *euphony and cacophony*.

DISTANCE: The degree of detachment achieved by the reader and audience from the people and events of a literary work.

DOGGEREL: A deprecatory term for inferior poetry.

DOUBLE ENTENDRE (PP. 43–44): A form of pun in which one of the two meanings is risqué or sexually suggestive.

DOUBLE RHYME: See *masculine and feminine rhyme*.

DRAMATIC IRONY: See *irony*.

DRAMATIC MONOLOGUE (P. 132): A type of poem in which a character, at some specific critical moment, addresses an identifiable but silent audience, thereby unintentionally revealing his or her essential temperament and personality. Classic examples are Robert Browning's "Porphyria's Lover" (1836), "My Last Duchess" (1842), and "Soliloquy of the Spanish Cloister" (1842).

DYNAMIC AND STATIC CHARACTERS: See *character.*

EFFECT: The total impression or impact of a work upon the reader or audience.

ELEGY: In its more modern usage, a poem that laments or solemnly meditates on death, loss, or the passing of things of value. See, for example, Theodore Roethke's "Elegy for Jane: My Student, Thrown by a Horse" (1953).

EMPHASIS: The weight or stress that an author gives to one or more of the elements of the work.

END RHYME: Rhyme that occurs at the end of lines of poetry; also called terminal rhyme; see *masculine and feminine rhyme.*

END-STOPPED LINE (PP. 98–99): A line of poetry that concludes with a pause. For example:

> A little learning is a dangerous thing;
> Drink deep, or taste not the Pierian spring:
> (from "An Essay on Criticism,"
> Alexander Pope, 1711)

ENGLISH SONNET: See *sonnet.*

ENJAMBMENT (PP. 98–99): A line of poetry that carries its idea or thought over to the next line without a grammatical pause; also called a *run-on line.*

EPIC: A long narrative poem, elevated and dignified in theme, tone, and style, celebrating heroic deeds and historically (at times cosmically) important events; usually focuses on the adventures of a hero who has qualities that are superhuman or divine and on whose very fate very often depends the destiny of a tribe, a nation, or even the whole of the human race. *The Iliad, The Odyssey,* and *The Aeneid* are the most important epics in western world literature.

EPIGRAM (P. 134): A short, pointed, and witty statement, either constituting an entire poem (often in the form of a two-line couplet) or "buried" within a larger one. Here, for example, is a short, savage epigram by John Wilmot, Earl of Rochester, entitled "On King Charles":

> We have a pretty witty king
> And whose word no man relys on:
> He never said a foolish thing,
> And never did a wise one.

To which Charles II replied: "This is very true: for my words are my own, and my actions are my ministers'."

EPIGRAPH: A quotation prefacing a literary work, often containing a clue to the writer's intention. Consider, for example, the epigraph from Dante's *Inferno* that precedes T. S. Eliot's "The Love Song of J. Alfred Prufrock" (1917).

EPISODE: A single, unified *incident* within a narrative that may or may not advance the plot. Plots containing a series of episodes, arranged chronologically, are said to be "episodic."

EPITAPH: Verses written to commemorate the dead. Most epitaphs are lauda-
tory, as in Alexander Pope's lines on Sir Isaac Newton:

> Nature and nature's laws lay hid in night:
> God said, "Let Newton be!" and all was light.
> ("Epitaph," 1730)

Some, however, are bitter and intemperate, as in these lines by Byron on
Lord Castlereagh, the British Foreign Secretary who helped reestablish mon-
archies in Europe following the downfall of Napoleon:

> Posterity will ne'er survey
>   A nobler grave than this:
> Here lie the bones of Castlereagh:
>   Stop, traveller—
> ("Epitaph," 1820)

EPITHALAMION/EPITHALAMIUM: A song or poem celebrating a wedding, from
the Greek meaning "poem upon or at the bridal chamber." Edmund Spenser's
Epithalamion (1595) is the most famous example of such poetry.

EPITHET: A word or phrase that characterizes a person or thing. Literary epithets
include phrases like Homer's "rosy-fingered dawn" or Shakespeare's "honest
Iago." Vulgar insults are also known as epithets, as in Earle Birney's alliterative
poem, "Anglosaxon Street" (1942):

> Here is a ghetto   gotten for goyim
> O with care denuded   of nigger and kike

EUPHONY AND CACOPHONY (PP. 125–126): *Euphony* describes language that is
harmonious, smooth, and pleasing to the ear. Harsh, nonharmonious, and
discordant language is *cacophony*; cacophony is also referred to as *dissonance*.
For an example of the effective use of euphony and cacophony examine
Robert Herrick's quatrain "Upon Julia's Voice" (1648). Note particularly
the hard, cacophonous consonants describing the damned in line 2 and
the euphonious *m* and *l* sounds in the final image of Julia's voice:

> So smooth, so sweet, so silvery is thy voice,
> As, could they hear, the Damned would make no noise,
> But listen to thee (walking in thy chamber)
> Melting melodious words to Lutes of Amber.

EVALUATION: A judgment about the particular merits or success of a given
work.

EVIDENCE: The facts, examples, or arguments given in support of a writer's
assertion or thesis. Literary analysis invariably requires the amassing of evidence from the work itself.

END RHYME: See *visual rhyme*.

EXPLICATION (PP. 5–9): A detailed word-by-word and line-by-line attempt to
explain the entire meaning of a literary work. From a Latin word meaning
"unfolding."

FALSE RHYME (P. 123): Rhyme pairing the sounds of accented and unaccented
syllables, e.g., "tennis" and "remiss."

FEMININE RHYME: See *masculine and feminine rhyme.*

FEMINIST CRITICISM: Literary criticism written from the perspective of women, reflecting female attitudes, concerns, and values. Feminist criticism is concerned both with how the meaning of a literary work is affected when read from a woman's perspective and how female characters and women in general are treated within the work. This literary movement grows out of (and is part of) the feminist movement which since the late 1960s has attempted to improve equal rights and equal opportunities for women by identifying and removing the political, social, and psychological obstacles that prevent them from achieving their full possibilities as human beings. Major texts include Elaine Showalter, *A Literature of Their Own* (1977) and *The New Feminist Criticism* (1985); Judith Fetterley, *The Resistant Reader* (1978); and Sandra M. Gilbert and Susan Gubar, *The Madwoman in the Attic* (1979).

FICTION: A prose narrative that is the product of the imagination.

FIGURATIVE LANGUAGE (PP. 62–81): Language used imaginatively and non-literally. Figurative language is composed of such figures of speech (or tropes) as *metaphor, simile, personification, metonymy, synecdoche, apostrophe, hyperbole, symbol, irony,* and *paradox.*

FIRST DRAFT: A writer's first unrevised and unedited version of a complete work. Also called the *rough draft.* When the manuscript is in the author's handwriting it is called a *holograph.*

FOLK BALLAD: See *ballad.*

FOOT (PP. 93–99): The basic metrical or rhythmical unit within a line of poetry. A foot of poetry generally consists of an accented syllable and one or more unaccented syllables arranged in a variety of patterns; see *scansion.*

FORM: A term used either as a synonym for literary *genre* or type, or to describe the essential organizational structure of a work of art.

FORMAT: The physical makeup of a book, journal, or other type of publication, including its page size, typeface, margins, paper, binding, and cover.

FOURTEENERS: Lines of poetry with fourteen syllables (seven iambic) feet.

FRAME NARRATIVE/FRAME STORY: A narrative (or story) that encloses one or more other narratives (or stories) to produce a "story within a story." Chaucer's *Canterbury Tales* (ca. 1390) is a familiar example.

FREE VERSE (PP. 117–119): A type of poetry that deliberately seeks to free itself from the restrictions imposed by traditionally fixed conventions of meter, rhyme, and stanza. Free verse is now often called poetry in open forms. T. S. Eliot's "The Love Song of J. Alfred Prufrock" (1917) and the various poems from Walt Whitman's *Leaves of Grass* (1855) are good examples of free verse.

GENRE: A *form,* class, or type of literary work—e.g., the short story, novel, poem, play, or essay; often used to denote such literary subclassifications as the detective story, the gothic novel, the pastoral elegy, or the revenge tragedy.

GLOSS: An explanation of a difficult word or passage, often by means of a footnote.

GLOSSARY: A list of words followed by definitions or explanations—usually at the rear of a book.

HAIKU (P. 140): A Japanese form of poetry; three lines of five, seven, and five syllables, respectively, present a single concentrated image or emotion. Here, for example, is a haiku by the Japanese poet Issa (1763–1827):

> only one guy and
> only one fly trying to
> make the guest room do
> (translated by Cid Corman)

HEPTAMETER: A line of poetry consisting of seven metrical feet; see *foot*.

HERMENEUTICS: A synonym for the theory or art of criticism.

HERO/HEROINE: The central character in a literary work; also often referred to as the *protagonist*.

HEROIC COUPLET: A pair of rhymed iambic pentameter lines; a stanza composed of two heroic couplets is called a *heroic quatrain*. Example:

> Men must be taught as if you taught them not,
> And things unknown proposed as things forgot.
> (Alexander Pope,
> from *An Essay on Criticism,* 1711)

HEROIC LINE: The term given to iambic pentameter because it is so often associated with epic or heroic poetry.

HEXAMETER: A line of poetry consisting of six metrical feet; see *foot*. See, for example, Ernest Dowson's "Non Sum Qualis Eram Bonae Sub Regno Cynarae" (1896), which begins

> Last night, ah, yesternight, betwixt her lips and mine
> There fell thy shadow, Cynara! thy breath was shed
> Upon my soul between the kisses and the wine;

HIGH STYLE AND LOW STYLE: *High style* is a formal and elevated literary style rich in poetic devices. Percy Bysshe Shelley's "Ode to the West Wind" (1820) is a good example of a poem written in the high style. *Low style* is casual and conversational. "Nobody Loses All the Time" (1923) by e. e. cummings is written in the low style.

HISTORICAL CRITICISM: Seeks to understand and explain a literary work in terms of the author's life and the historical context and circumstances in which it was written.

HYPERBOLE (P. 51): A figure of speech that achieves emphasis and heightened effect (either serious or comic) through deliberate exaggeration. Consider, for example, Byron's hyperbolic claim that

> Man, being reasonable, must get drunk;
> The best of life is but intoxication:
> Glory, the grape, love, gold, in these are sunk
> The hopes of all men, and of every nation;
> (from *Don Juan,* 1819, Canto 2, CLXXIX)

IAMB (IAMBIC) (PP. 95–99): A foot composed of an unaccented syllable followed by an accented one, as in the word "em*bark*."

IDENTICAL RHYME: Rhyme achieved through the repetition of the same word or two words that have the same sound but are spelled differently and have different meanings; e.g., "right" and "night."

ILLUSTRATION: The use of examples to develop a generalization.

IMAGERY (PP. 55–61): Most commonly refers to visual pictures produced verbally through literal or figurative language, although it is often defined more broadly to include sensory experience other than the visual.

IMITATION: A concept, originating in classical criticism with Aristotle's *Poetics,* that all art is a form of imitation.

INCONGRUITY (P. 46): A word, phrase, or idea that is out of keeping, inconsistent, or inappropriate in its context.

INDUCTION: The method of reasoning which moves from the consideration of specifics or particulars to a conclusion about them.

INTENTIONAL FALLACY: A term employed in modern criticism to describe the error of interpreting the meaning of a literary work as if the stated purpose or intention of its author resolves all doubts about its meaning. See *new criticism.*

INTERNAL RHYME (P. 122): Rhyme within a line of poetry; also called *middle rhyme;* e.g., "For the moon never *beams* without bringing me *dreams*/Of the beautiful Annabel Lee" (from "Annabel Lee," 1850 by Edgar Allan Poe).

INVECTIVE: Insulting or abusive language. Here, for example, is a nice example of invective from James Stephen's poem, "A Glass of Beer" (1918):

> May the devil grip the whey-faced slut by the hair,
> And beat bad manners out of her skin for a year.

INVOCATION: An appeal to a deity for help or support usually occurring at the beginning of a long poem or play. See, for example, the opening lines of John Milton's *Paradise Lost* (1667).

IRONY (PP. 49–54): Refers to some contrast or discrepancy between appearance and reality. Irony takes a number of special forms: in *verbal irony* there is a contrast between what is literally said and what is actually meant; in *dramatic irony* the state of affairs known to the reader (or audience) is the reverse of what its participants suppose it to be; in *situational irony* a set of circumstances turns out to be the reverse of what is expected or is appropriate.

ITALIAN SONNET: See *sonnet.*

JUXTAPOSITION (PP. 65–67): A form of implied comparison or contrast created by placing two items side by side. In John Crowe Ransom's "Piazza Piece" (1927), for example, the words of the "gentleman in a dustcoat" and the "lady young in beauty" are juxtaposed to create a dramatic and ironic contrast.

LAMENT: A song of complaint, often expressing grief.

LEITMOTIF: A word, phrase, or *theme* that recurs in a literary work.

LETTERS: The name sometimes given to literature.

LIGHT VERSE: Poems, usually short, that are humorous and witty. The following lines by Bert Leston Taylor are light verse:

> Whenas galoshed my Julia goes,
> Unbuckled all from top to toes,
> How swift the poem becometh prose!
>   (from "Upon Julia's Arctics")

LIMERICK (P. 140): A light, humorous (and often scurrilous and pornographic) verse form composed of five anapestic lines, rhyming AABBA; lines one, two, and five contain three feet (trimeter), lines three and four contain two (dimeter). Most limericks are anonymous. The following poem by Morris Bishop (1893–1973) is a limerick about limericks:

> The limerick is furtive and mean;
> You must keep her in close quarantine,
>   Or she sneaks to the slums
>   And promptly becomes
> Disorderly, drunk and obscene.

LITERAL: Accurate, exact, and concrete language, i.e., nonfigurative language; see *figurative language.*

LITERARY BALLAD: See *ballad.*

LITERARY RESEARCH, GUIDES TO: The single most complete guide to literary research is Margaret C. Patterson, *Literary Research Guide* (New York: Modern Language Association, 1983). For discussion of the purposes and methods of literary research in English and American literature see Richard D. Altick, *The Art of Liberary Research* (New York: W. W. Norton, 1982).

LONG MEASURE: A stanza that consists of four lines of iambic tetrameter, rhyming either ABCB or ABAB.

LYRIC (P. 132): A short, songlike poem, by a single speaker on a single subject, expressing a personal thought, mood, or feeling.

MASCULINE AND FEMININE RHYME (P. 122): The most common kinds of end rhyme. *Masculine end rhyme,* predominant in English poetry, consists of accented words of one syllable or polysyllabic words where the final syllable is accented; for example, *"fond"* and *"despond." Feminine end rhyme* (or *double rhyme*) consists of rhyming words of two syllables in which the accent falls on the first syllable; e.g., *"wooings"* and *"cooings."* A variation of feminine rhyme, called *triple rhyme,* occurs when there is a correspondence of sound in the final three syllables, an accented syllable followed by two unaccented ones; e.g., *"glorious"* and *"uxorious."* (These examples are taken from three successive stanzas of Byron's *Don Juan* (1821). See Canto 3, stanzas vi–viii.)

MEASURE: A synonym for *meter.*

METAPHOR (PP. 62–65): A figure of speech in which two unlike objects are implicitly compared without the use of *like* or *as;* see also *conceit* and *simile.* Most readers of poetry take delight in discovering fresh metaphors, such as Sylvia Plath's description of a nurse who walks on "two erasers" in "Lullaby" (1960) or Dylan Thomas's reference to his own poems as "spindrift pages" in "In My Craft or Sullen Art" (1946) or Gwendolyn Brooks's description of the "scythe" of angry men who harass black schoolgirls in "The Chicago *Defender* Sends a Man to Little Rock" (1960).

METAPHYSICAL POETRY: A kind of realistic, often ironic and witty, verse combining intellectual ingenuity and psychological insight. Metaphysical poetry was written partly in reaction to the conventions of Elizabethan love poetry by such seventeenth-century poets as John Donne, George Herbert, and Andrew Marvell. One of its hallmarks is the metaphysical *conceit,* a particularly interesting and ingenious type of metaphor.

METER: See *rhythm and meter.*

METONYMY (P. 65): A figure of speech in which one object or idea takes the place of another with which it is closely associated. We sometimes refer, for example, to the White House when we actually mean the president. In the same way we speak of the crown when we mean the reigning monarch.

METRICS: A synonym for *prosody.* See *prosody.*

MILIEU: The environment or surroundings in which an author lives or in which a work is written.

MIMESIS: The Greek word for *imitation.* Because of the influence of Eric Auerbach's seminal study, *Mimesis: The Representation of Reality in Western Literature* (translated by Willard Trask, Princeton University Press, 1953), the word *mimesis* generally means the imitation of reality in literature.

MIXED METAPHOR (P. 86): Two or more metaphors combined together in such a way as to be incongruous, illogical, or even ludicrous. Example: That rat cheats on his honey with every vixen in the neighborhood.

MODERN: A term applied to works written in the twentieth century. In the sense that it connotes *new,* the term *modern* often implies a break with tradition and a rejection of past ideas, values, assumptions, and techniques.

MONODY: An elegy for the dead recited or delivered by a single speaker. See *elegy.*

MONOMETER: A line of poetry consisting of a single metrical foot; see *foot.* In George Herbert's "Easter Wings" (1633), for example, each stanza narrows to two monometer lines at its exact midpoint.

MOOD: See *atmosphere.*

MOTIF: An idea, theme, character, situation, or element that recurs in literature or folklore.

MOTIVE: The cause that moves a character to act.

MS (MSS): The abbreviation for manuscript(s), an author's handwritten or typed copy of a text prepared and submitted for publication.

MUSES: The Greek goddesses presiding over the arts, including history, music, drama, dance, and poetry.

MYTH: Broadly, any idea or belief to which many people subscribe; see *legend.*

NARRATIVE POEM (PP. 131–132): A poem that tells a story.

NARRATIVE SEQUENCE: The order in which events are recounted.

NARRATIVE TECHNIQUE: The author's methods of presenting or telling a story.

NARRATOR: Character or voice telling the story; see *point of view* and *persona.*

NEW CRITICISM: The New Criticism refers to a type or "school" of criticism that seeks to analyze and study a literary work as autonomous, without reference to the author's intention, the impact or effect on the reader, the historical or cultural period in which the work was written (see *historical criticism*), or the validity of the ideas that may be extrapolated from it. Its method is based on the close reading and analysis of the verbal elements of the text, although its leading exponents and practitioners (academic critics such as John Crowe Ransom, I. A. Richards, Cleanth Brooks, Robert Penn Warren,

Allen Tate, R. P. Blackmur, Yvor Winters, and Kenneth Burke) often disagree on just how this analysis is to be undertaken. The term originates from the title of John Crowe Ransom's book *The New Criticism* (1941) and is "new" in the sense that it constituted a deliberate break with the older subjective and impressionistic theories of art that allowed extrinsic rather than solely intrinsic considerations to influence evaluation.

OBJECTIVE: See *subjective.*

OCCASIONAL VERSE: Poetry written to celebrate or commemorate a particular event or occasion. For example, "Alexander's Feast" by John Dryden was commissioned in 1697 for the celebration of St. Cecilia's Day.

OCTAMETER: A line of poetry consisting of eight metrical feet; see *foot.*

OCTAVE: See *sonnet.*

OCTET: A synonym for *octave;* see *sonnet.*

ODE (P. 139): A long lyric poem, serious and dignified in subject, tone, and style, sometimes with an elaborate stanzaic structure, often written to commemorate or celebrate an event or individual. Among the better-known odes in this text are "Alexander's Feast" (1697 by John Dryden), "Ode on a Grecian Urn" (1820) by John Keats, and "Ode to the West Wind" (1820) by Percy Bysshe Shelley.

ONOMATOPOEIA (P. 127): A word (or a group of words) whose sound has the effect of suggesting or reinforcing its denotative meaning. Words like *buzz* and *pop* are said to be onomatopoetic.

ORGANIZATION: The overall plan or design that shapes the work.

OTTAVA RIMA (P. 138): A stanza of Italian origin consisting of eight iambic pentameter lines rhyming ABABABCC. The stanza is most famous in English because of its use in Byron's *Don Juan* (1819–1824).

OXYMORON: A figure of speech, used for rhetorical effect, which brings together and combines antithetical, paradoxical, or contradictory terms, e.g., "living death," "wise fool," "sweet sorrow." Other, more cynical examples might include "military intelligence" and "business ethics."

PARADOX (PP. 44–46): A self-contradictory and absurd statement that turns out to be, in some sense at least, actually true and valid. There is, for example, a startling paradox when John Donne cries out in "Batter My Heart, Three-Personed God" (1633):

> . . . for I,
> Except you enthrall me, never shall be free;
> Nor ever chaste, except you ravish me.

PARAPHRASE (PP. 85–86): A restatement, using different words, of the essential ideas or argument of a piece or passage of writing. To paraphrase a poem is to restate its ideas in prose.

PARODY: See *burlesque.*

PASTORAL: A literary work dealing with, and often celebrating, a rural world and a way of life lived close to nature. Pastoral denotes subject matter rather than form; hence, the terms *pastoral lyric, pastoral ode, pastoral elegy, pastoral drama, pastoral epic,* and *pastoral novel.* A good example of pastoral poetic conventions occurs in Christopher Marlowe's "The Passionate Shepherd to His Love" (1599).

PATHETIC FALLACY: A form of *personification,* which attributes human qualities or feelings to inanimate objects. Although first used disapprovingly by John Ruskin in *Modern Painters* (1856), the phrase no longer necessarily carries with it Ruskin's negative connotation; see *personification.* For example, Coleridge refers in "Christabel" (1816) to

> The one red leaf, the last of its clan,
> That dances as often as dance it can.

PATHOS: The quality in a literary work that evokes a feeling of pity, tenderness, and sympathy from the reader or audience. Overdone or misused pathos becomes mere *sentimentality.*

PENTAMETER: A line of poetry consisting of five metrical feet; see *foot.* Here, for example, is a fine epigram in iambic pentameter by Thomas Bancroft:

> Weapons in peace grow hungry, and will eat
> Themselves with rust; but war allows them meat.

PERFECT AND IMPERFECT RHYME (PP. 120–125): In *perfect rhyme* (also called *full rhyme* or *true rhyme*) the vowel and any succeeding consonant sounds are identical and the preceding consonant sounds different; e.g., "true" and "blue." Some poets, particularly modern ones, deliberately alternate perfect rhyme with *imperfect rhyme,* in which the correspondence of sound is inexact, approximate, and "imperfect." Imperfectly rhymed words generally end with identical vowels or identical consonants, but not both; for example, "blue" and "boot." Imperfect rhyme is also referred to as *approximate rhyme, half-rhyme, near rhyme, oblique rhyme,* or *slant rhyme. Alliteration, assonance,* and *consonance* are types of imperfect rhyme.

PERSONA (P: PERSONAE): The voice or mask the author adopts for the purpose of telling the story or "speaking" the words of a lyric poem. The term *persona* is a way of reminding us that the narrator of the work is not to be confused with the author, and should be regarded as another of the author's creations or fictions.

PERSONIFICATION (PP. 70–71): A figure of speech in which an idea or thing is given human attributes or feelings or is spoken of as if it were alive; see also *pathetic fallacy.* For instance, in the poem "Ex-Basketball Player" (1957), John Updike writes of how the former high school star Flick Webb is reduced to playing pinball at Mae's luncheonette before the "bright applauding tiers/ Of Necco Wafers, Nibs, and Juju Beads."

PICTURE POEM (PP. 142–143): A poem printed in such a way as to create a visual image of the object or idea described. See George Herbert's "Easter Wings" (1633) for an example.

PLAGIARISM: The act of borrowing the words or ideas of someone else without appropriate attribution.

PLOT: The patterned arrangement of the events in a narrative.

POETIC DICTION: Words deliberately chosen because of their poetic quality.

POETIC JUSTICE: The doctrine (now generally discredited in theory and practice) that good should be rewarded and evil punished—that characters in the end should reap their just rewards.

Poetic License: Used to describe (and justify) literary experimentation: a writer's deliberate departure from conventions of form and language—and at times even the departure from logic and fact.

Poetics: A theory or set of theories about the nature of poetry. The most famous example is Aristotle's *Poetics* (ca. 335 B.C.).

Poet Laureate: Originally a court poet, maintained by the royal family to give literary expression to their accomplishments. Since the late seventeenth century the position in England has become a formal title conferred by the monarch and carrying with it national distinction. Recent Poet Laureates have included John Masefield (1930–1967), Cecil Day Lewis (1968–1972), Sir John Betjeman (1973–1984), and Ted Hughes (1984–   ).

Poetry Criticism: The single most important bibliography of poetry criticism is Joseph M. Kuntz and Nancy C. Martinez, eds., *Poetry Explication: A Checklist of Interpretation Since 1925 of British and American Poems Past and Present* (Boston: G. K. Hall, 1980). See also Gloria S. Cline and Jeffrey A. Baker, comps., *Index to Criticisms of British and American Poetry* (Metuchen, N.J.: Scarecrow Press, 1973); Phillis Gershator, ed., *A Bibliographical Guide to the Literature of Contemporary American Poetry, 1970–1975* (Metuchen, N.J.: Scarecrow Press, 1976); George Hendrick and Donna Gerstenberger, eds., *American and British Poetry: A Guide to the Criticism, 1925–1978* (Athens, Ohio: Ohio Univ. Press, 1984).

Poetry Index: See *Granger's Index to Poetry* (New York: Columbia Univ. Press, 1986). Lists by title, first line, author, and subject poems appearing in anthologies. Earlier editions cover earlier anthologies. This standard guide can be supplemented by *Index of American Periodical Verse* (Metuchen, N.J.: Scarecrow Press), published annually.

Point of View: The angle or perspective from which a story is told.

Polemic: A work vigorously setting forth the author's point of view, usually on a controversial subject.

Popular Ballad: See *ballad*.

Post-Modern: A term used to describe contemporary writing (roughly since 1965) that is experimental in nature.

Practical Criticism: See *theoretical criticism and practical criticism*.

Précis: An abstract or concise summary which provides, in the same order as the original, the essential points, statements, or facts of a work.

Preface: The author's or editor's introduction, in which the writer states his or her purposes and assumptions and makes any acknowledgments.

Prelude: A short poem introducing a longer one.

Primary and Secondary Sources: *Primary sources* are the original documents; *secondary sources* are those that comment on or analyze those original documents.

Proofreading: The stage in the process of revision in which the author checks for typographical errors or for basic errors in spelling, grammar, and punctuation.

Prosody: The description and study of the underlying principles of poetry, e.g., its meter, rhyme, and stanzaic form.

Protagonist: The chief character of a literary work. Also commonly referred to as the *hero* or *heroine; see antagonist.*

Pseudonym: A fictitious name assumed by an author; also referred to as a *pen name* or (French) *nom de plume.* The most famous example of a pseudonym in American literature is Samuel L. Clemens's choice of "Mark Twain."

Psychic Distance: The necessary emotional distance or detachment that readers must achieve if they are to regard a literary work objectively. Implicit in achieving psychic distance is the realization that literature is not life. Also called *aesthetic distance.*

Psychological/Psychoanalytic Criticism: The use of a psychological and psychoanalytic theory to interpret a writer's work or to understand the personality of the writer. Interpretations based on the theories of Sigmund Freud (1856–1939) are called Freudian and tend to focus on subconscious conflicts— particularly those involving Freud's hypothesis that children develop through oral, anal, Oedipal, and phallic stages. Freud's interpretation of the Oedipal conflict in *The Interpretation of Dreams* (1900) is particularly famous. The psychoanalytic theories of Freud's disciple Carl Jung (1875–1961) are also popular among critics. Jung postulated that human beings share a "collective unconscious" of common myths and archetypes.

Pun (pp. 43–44): A play on words, involving words with similar or identical sounds but with different meanings. Puns are usually humorous, but not always. In George Herbert's devoutly religious poem, "The Pulley" (1633), much of the significance arises from Herbert's playful punning on the meanings of the "rest" that God denies man while granting so many other blessings. The word here means "remainder," "repose;" and "freedom from troubles."

Purpose: The author's basic reason for writing; the goal or objective which the author sets out to achieve.

Quantitative Meter (pp. 116–117): A metrical system (used in Greek and Latin verse) in which units are measured not by stress but by the length of time it takes to pronounce long and short syllables.

Quatrain (p. 135): A four line stanza employing a variety of rhyme schemes.

Quotations, Source of: The standard dictionaries used for attributing quotations are *The Oxford Dictionary of Quotations* (New York: Oxford University Press, 1979) and *Bartlett's Familiar Quotations* (Boston: Little, Brown, 1968). See also *The Macmillan Book of Proverbs, Maxims, and Famous Phrases* (New York: Macmillan, 1966).

Reader Response Criticism: A critical approach (also referred to as "reception theory," "subjective criticism," or "the phenomenology of reading") that begins by assuming that texts are meant to be read; that a text does not really exist until it is in fact read; and that, to some extent at least, the meaning of a text is created or produced by the reader. Reader response criticism examines those elements and features of the work that arouse and shape the response of a hypothetical or *implied reader* whose presence can be derived or implied from the work itself. Major texts include Norman Holland, *The Dynamics of Literary Response* (1968), Walter J. Slatoff, *With Respect to Readers: The Dimension of Literary Response* (1970); Louise M. Rosenblatt, *The Reader, the Text, the Poem: The Transactional Theory of the Literary Work* (1978); Wolfgang

Iser, *The Act of Reading: A Theory of Aesthetic Response* (tr. 1978); David Bleich, *Subjective Criticism* (1978); Jane Tompkins, ed., *Reader-Response Criticism* (1980); Susan R. Suleiman and Inge Crosman, eds., *The Reader in the Text: Essays on Audience and Interpretation* (1980).

REFRAIN (PP. 36–38): A line, in whole or in part, or a group of lines that recur, sometimes with slight variation, in a poem or song, at the close of a stanza and help establish meter, sustain mood, or add emphasis. In a song the refrain is usually called the chorus and listeners are expected to join in. For an especially effective use of the refrain see Joni Mitchell's popular song "Both Sides Now" (1967).

RESEARCH, GUIDES TO: See *literary research, guides to.*

RESEARCH PAPER: See *style, manuals of.*

REVIEW: A critical appraisal of a play, book, film, or performance published in a periodical.

RHETORICAL QUESTION: A question asked for effect, to which no response or reply is expected.

RHYME (PP. 120–124): The repetition at regular intervals in a line or lines of poetry of similar or identical sounds based on a correspondence between the vowels and succeeding consonants of accented syllables; see also *end rhyme, false rhyme, identical rhyme, internal rhyme, masculine and feminine rhyme, perfect and imperfect rhyme,* and *visual rhyme;* also *alliteration, assonance,* and *consonance.*

RHYME ROYAL (PP. 137–138): A stanza of seven iambic pentameter lines rhyming ABABBCC.

RHYME SCHEME (P. 124): The pattern of end rhymes within a given stanza of poetry.

RHYTHM AND METER (PP. 91–119): Rhythm is the general term given to the measured repetition of accent or beats in units of poetry or prose. In English poetry, rhythm is generally established by manipulating both the pattern of accent and the number of syllables in a given line. Meter refers to the predominant rhythmic pattern within any given line (or lines) of poetry.

RONDEAU, RONDEL, AND ROUNDEL: These terms are sometimes used interchangeably and may refer to a variety of short, fixed-form poems. Characteristic of them all is the use of a limited number of rhymes (usually only two) and of a refrain formed of the beginning words or lines. The repetitions of the refrain "round" the poem to its conclusion and thus give rise to the name used to describe it. See Leigh Hunt's "Rondeau" (p. 243), Algernon Swinburne's "Roundel" (p. 288), and Amy Jo Schoonover's "Rondeau: An Un-Love Song" (p. 406).

ROUND AND FLAT CHARACTERS: See *character.*

RUBAIS (P. 135): An iambic pentameter quatrain in which the first two lines rhyme with the last one, AAXA. The form was popularized by Edward Fitzgerald in his free translation of *The Rubáiyát of Omar Khayyám* (1895). Here is a typical rubais:

> They say the Lion and the Lizard keep
> The Courts where Jamshyd gloried and drank deep:
> 　　And Bahram, the great Hunter—the Wild Ass
> Stamps o'er his Head, but cannot break his Sleep.

Run-on Line: See *enjambment.*

Sarcasm (p. 51): A form of verbal irony delivered in a derisive, caustic, and bitter manner to belittle or ridicule its subject.

Satire (p. 51): A type of writing that holds up persons, ideas, or things to varying degrees of amusement, ridicule, or contempt in order, presumably, to improve, correct, or bring about some desirable change.

Scansion (pp. 93–112): The analysis of a poem's metrical pattern.

Semiotics: The study of signs (including words, sounds, gestures, postures, facial expressions and other communication signals). According to Jonathan Culler, semiotics is "A program . . . which seeks to identify the conventions and operations by which any signifying practice (such as literature) produces its observable effects of meaning."

Sensuous: In literature, sensuous refers to writing that appeals to one or more of the reader's five senses.

Sentimentality: The presence of emotion or feeling that seems excessive or unjustified in terms of the circumstances; see *pathos.*

Septet (pp. 137–138): A seven line stanza employing a variety of rhyme schemes. Adrienne Rich's "Storm Warnings" (1951), Theodore Roethke's "I Knew a Woman" (1958), and Anne Sexton's "Her Kind" (1960) are good examples of poems in septets.

Sestet: A six line stanza. Robert Graves's "The Naked and the Nude" (1957), Henry Reed's "Naming of Parts" (1947), and W. D. Snodgrass's "April Inventory" (1959) are examples of poems in sestets.

Sestina: A fixed verse form (originally French) consisting of six sestets and a tercet. Instead of using rhyme, a sestina uses the final word in each line of the first sestet to conclude a line in each subsequent sestet. In the following scheme, each letter represents the word ending a line; each row of letters represents a stanza:

$$
\begin{array}{cccccc}
a & b & c & d & e & f \\
f & a & e & b & d & c \\
c & f & d & a & b & e \\
e & c & b & f & a & d \\
d & e & a & c & f & b \\
b & d & f & e & c & a \\
  & e & c & a &   &   \\
\end{array}
$$

Often, the final tercet includes all six end-words, with two words used per line.

Setting: The time and place in which the action of a story, poem, or play occurs; physical setting alone is often referred to as the *locale.*

Shakespearean Sonnet: See *sonnet.*

Simile (pp. 62–65): A figure of speech in which two essentially dissimilar objects are expressly compared with one another by the use of *like* or *as;* see *metaphor* and *figurative language.* Gerard Manley Hopkins (1844–1889), for example, uses a simile when he writes that god's grandeur "will shine out, like shining from shook foil."

SITUATION: Either the basic set of circumstances in which a group of characters find themselves at some point during the plot, or the set of circumstances in effect at the beginning of the plot before the action begins.

SITUATIONAL IRONY (IRONY OF SITUATION): See *irony.*

SOLILOQUY: A dramatic convention in which a character, alone on stage (*solus*), speaks aloud and thus shares his or her thoughts with the audience.

SONG: A lyric poem set to music.

SONNET (PP. 141–142): A poem of 14 iambic pentameter lines expressing a single thought or idea and utilizing one of several established rhyme schemes. The sonnet in English generally follows one of two basic patterns: the *Italian sonnet* (or *Petrarchan sonnet* named after the Italian Renaissance poet Petrarch) consists of an eight-line *octave,* rhyming ABBAABBA, followed by a six-line *sestet,* rhyming variously CDECDE, CDCCDC, etc.; and the *English sonnet* (or *Shakespearean sonnet*) consists of three four-line *quatrains* and a concluding *couplet,* rhyming ABAB CDCD EFEF GG. A variant of the English sonnet, the *Spenserian sonnet* (named after English poet Edmund Spenser), links its quatrains by employing the rhyme scheme ABAB BCBC CDCD EE. This text includes numerous sonnets by Shakespeare, as well as others by Spenser, Drayton, Sidney, Donne, Milton, Wordsworth, Shelley, E. B. Browning, and Frost.

SPENSERIAN SONNET: See *sonnet.*

SPENSERIAN STANZA (PP. 138–139): A nine-line stanza consisting of eight lines of iambic pentameter and a concluding line of iambic hexameter, rhyming ABABBCBCC—made famous by the English poet Edmund Spenser in the *Faerie Queene* (1590–1596).

SPONDEE (SPONDAIC) (PP. 110–111): A foot of two accented syllables; e.g., "dew-drop."

STANZA (PP. 133–139): A group of lines forming a structural unit or division of a poem. Stanzas may be units of form established through similarity in the number of lines, by length of lines, meter and rhyme scheme, or stanzas may exist as logical units determined by their thought or content.

STRATEGY: The method an author chooses to achieve his or her purpose or ends.

STRESS: The accent or emphasis given certain syllables in the scansion of verse.

STRUCTURALISM: A critical approach, utilizing methodology of anthropology and linguistics, that attempts to analyze literature in terms of its underlying structural patterns. In critic Jonathan Culler's words "Structuralists take linguistics as a model and attempt to develop grammars . . . that would account for the form and meaning of literary works." Major texts include Culler's *Structuralist Poetics* (1973); Robert Scholes, *Structuralism in Literature: An Introduction* (1974); Terence Hawkes, *Structuralism and Semiotics* (1977); John Sturrock, ed., *Structuralism and Since: From Levi-Strauss to Derrida* (1979).

STRUCTURE: The overall pattern or design of a literary work.

STYLE: The author's characteristic manner of expression; style includes the author's diction, syntax, sentence patterns, punctuation, and spelling, as well as the use made of such devices as sound, rhythm, imagery, and figurative language.

STYLE, MANUALS OF: The most widely used manuals of style or style sheets for information on the most widely accepted conventions for such matters as footnotes, bibliography, punctuation, quotations, abbreviations and the presentation of research include the *MLA Handbook for Writers of Research Papers, Theses, and Dissertations,* Joseph Gibaldi and Walter S. Achtert, eds. (New York: Modern Language Association, 1988); Kate L. Turabian, *Student's Guide for Writing College Papers* (Chicago: University of Chicago Press, 1982); *A Manual of Style: For Authors, Editors, and Copywriters* (Chicago: University of Chicago Press, 1982).

STYLISTICS: The study of the *style* of literary texts.

SUBJECTIVE: In literary criticism, judgments based on personal or emotional beliefs are subjective, as opposed to those based on criteria that are objective and impersonal.

SUMMARY: A brief overview of the ideas and information already developed.

SUPPORT: The evidence or proof that an author marshals to back up his or her argument.

SUSPENSE: The psychological tension or anxiety resulting from the reader's or audience's uncertainty of just how a situation or conflict is likely to end.

SYLLABIC METER (PP. 114–117): A metrical system (common to Japanese and Romance verse but rare in English) in which units are measured by the number of syllables in a line.

SYMBOL (PP. 75–81): Literally, something that stands for something else. In literature, any word, object, action, or character that embodies and evokes a range of additional meaning and significance. See also *allegory*.

SYNECHDOCHE (P. 65): A figure of speech in which a part is used to signify the whole or, less frequently, the whole is used to signify the part; e.g., "greaser" for a youth affecting the tough-guy look of the 1950s.

SYNESTHESIA: From the Greek meaning "perceiving together." The simultaneous experiencing of two or more senses when only one of them is being stimulated, as, for example, when color is attributed to sound ("blue note").

SYNOPSIS: A summary or résumé of a piece of writing.

TALE: A short and simple narrative in prose or verse. Though tale was once used as a synonym for short story, the term short story is now reserved for short fictional narratives that demonstrate a conscious artistry in their design.

TERCET (PP. 134–135): A stanza of three lines. Hardy's "The Convergence of the Twain" (1912) is an interesting example of a poem in tercets.

TERMINAL RHYME: See *end rhyme*.

TERZA RIMA (P. 135): A verse form composed of interlocking three-line stanzas, or *tercets*, rhyming ABA BCB CDC, etc. Shelley's "Ode to the West Wind" (1820) and Frost's "Acquainted with the Night" (1928) are good examples.

TETRAMETER: A line of poetry consisting of four metrical feet. Robert Burns's "Tam O'Shanter" (1791) is a good example of a long poem in tetrameter.

TEXTUAL CRITICISM: The kind of scholarship that attempts to establish through reconstruction the "correct" and authoritative text of a literary work as its author originally wrote it. The standard introduction to the theory and practice of textual criticism is James Thorpe, *Principles of Textual Criticism* (1972).

THEME (PP. 87–88): The controlling idea or meaning of a work of art.

THEORETICAL CRITICISM AND PRACTICAL CRITICISM: Theoretical criticism is concerned with identifying and establishing the general, underlying principles of art; *practical criticism* (or *applied criticism*) concerns itself with the study and analysis of specific individual works.

THESIS: The assertion or proposition that unifies and controls the entire work.

TONE (PP. 86–87): The author's attitude toward the subject or audience.

TOUR DE FORCE: A feat of skill and ingenuity.

TRADITIONAL BALLAD: A synonym for folk ballad; see *ballad*.

TRIMETER: A line of poetry consisting of three metrical feet; see *foot*.

TRIPLE RHYME: See *masculine and feminine rhyme*.

TRIPLET (PP. 134–135): A stanza of three lines rhyming AAA. See *tercet*.

TROCHEE (TROCHAIC) (PP. 104–106): A foot composed of an accented syllable followed by an unaccented one; e.g., "*tur*key."

TROPE: Another name for *figure of speech*.

UNDERSTATEMENT: A figure of speech in which what is literally said falls considerably short (or "under") the magnitude or seriousness of what is being discussed. Understatement thus has the effect of emphasizing the very thing it apparently tries to minimize. For example, the speaker in T. S. Eliot's "Journey of the Magi" (1927) uses understatement when he says of the birth of Christ, "it was (you may say) satisfactory."

UNITY: The quality of a work of art in which every element or part clearly and effectively relates to the accomplishment of a complete and independent whole. Unity in a literary work requires the presence of some central organizing principle to which all the parts are necessarily related, making the work an organic whole.

VERBAL IRONY: See *irony*.

VERSIFICATION: An all-inclusive term for the art and practice of writing poetry.

VILLANELLE: A fixed verse form (originally French) consisting of five three-line stanzas (or *tercets*) followed by a *quatrain,* rhyming ABA ABA ABA ABA ABA BBAA. The first line of the poem is repeated in lines 6, 12, and 18; the third line is repeated in lines 9, 15, and 19. See Dylan Thomas's "Do Not Go Gentle into That Good Night" (p. 362) and Theodore Roethke's "The Waking" (p. 146).

VISUAL RHYME (P. 123): Words that rhyme to the eye but not to the ear; their spelling is similar, but they are pronounced differently: "plow" and "blow."

Index to Authors, Titles, and First Lines